VIZ GRAPHIC NOVEL

STEAM DETECTIVES

VOL. 1

STORY AND ART BY
KIA ASAMIYA

CONTENTS

This volume contains the STEAM DETECTIVES installments from
MANGA VIZION Vol. 3, No. 10 through Vol. 4, No. 5 in their entirety.

STORY AND ART BY
KIA ASAMIYA

ENGLISH ADAPTATION BY
YUJI ONIKI

Touch-Up Art & Lettering/Bill Spicer
Cover Design/Hidemi Sahara
Layout & Graphics/Benjamin Wright
Editor/Annette Roman

Senior Editor/Trish Ledoux
Managing Editor/Hyoe Narita
Editor-in-Chief/Satoru Fujii
Publisher/Seiji Horibuchi

Printed in Canada

Published by Viz Communications, Inc.
P.O. Box 77010 • San Francisco, CA 94107

10 9 8 7 6 5 4 3 2 1
First printing, August 1998

Vizit our web sites at www.viz.com, www.pulp-mag.com, www.animerica-mag.com,
and our Internet magazine at www.j-pop.com!

CASE 1

BIRTH OF THE STEAM DETECTIVES

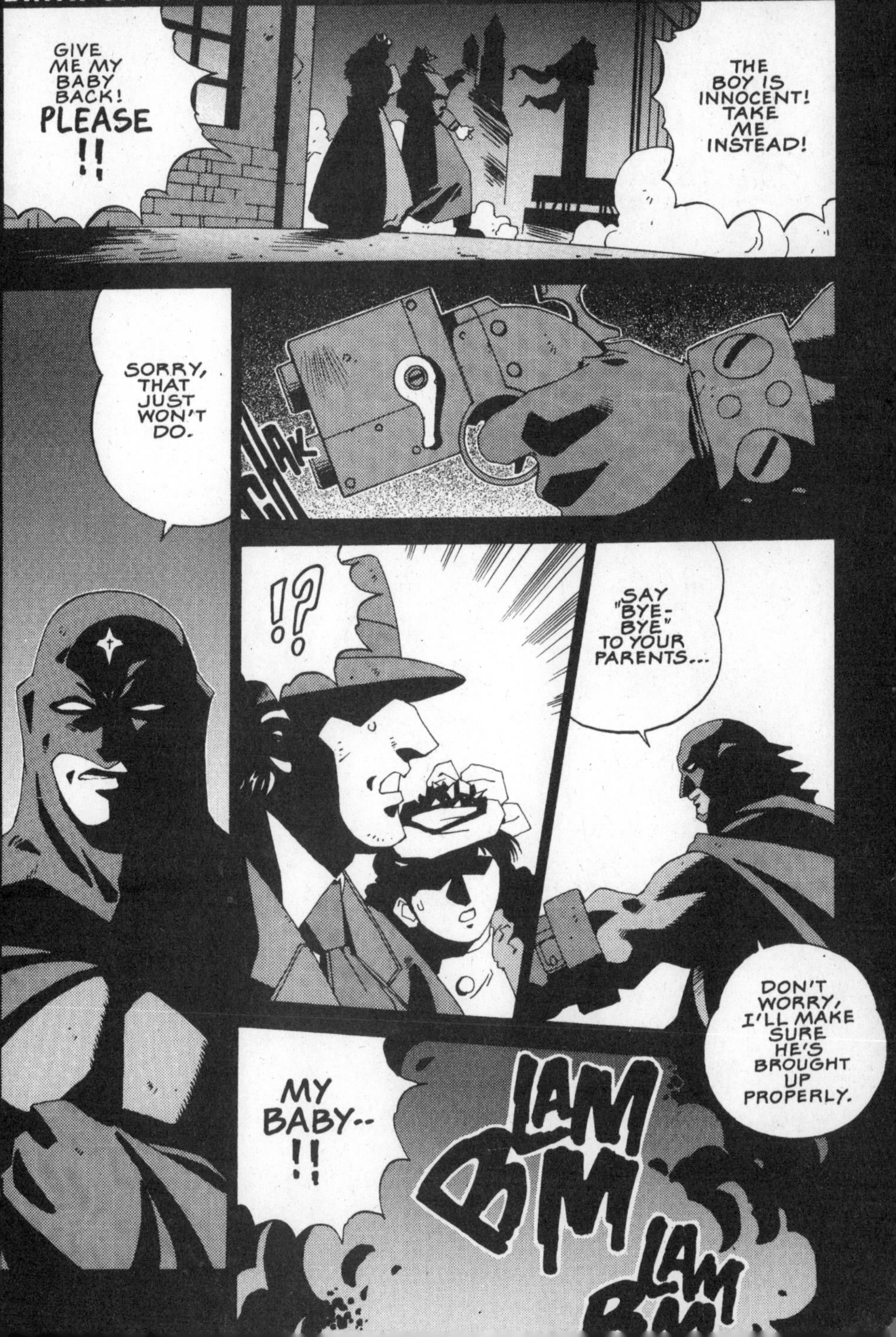
GIVE ME MY BABY BACK! PLEASE !!
THE BOY IS INNOCENT! TAKE ME INSTEAD!
SORRY, THAT JUST WON'T DO.
!?
SAY "BYE-BYE" TO YOUR PARENTS...
DON'T WORRY, I'LL MAKE SURE HE'S BROUGHT UP PROPERLY.
MY BABY-- !!
BLAM

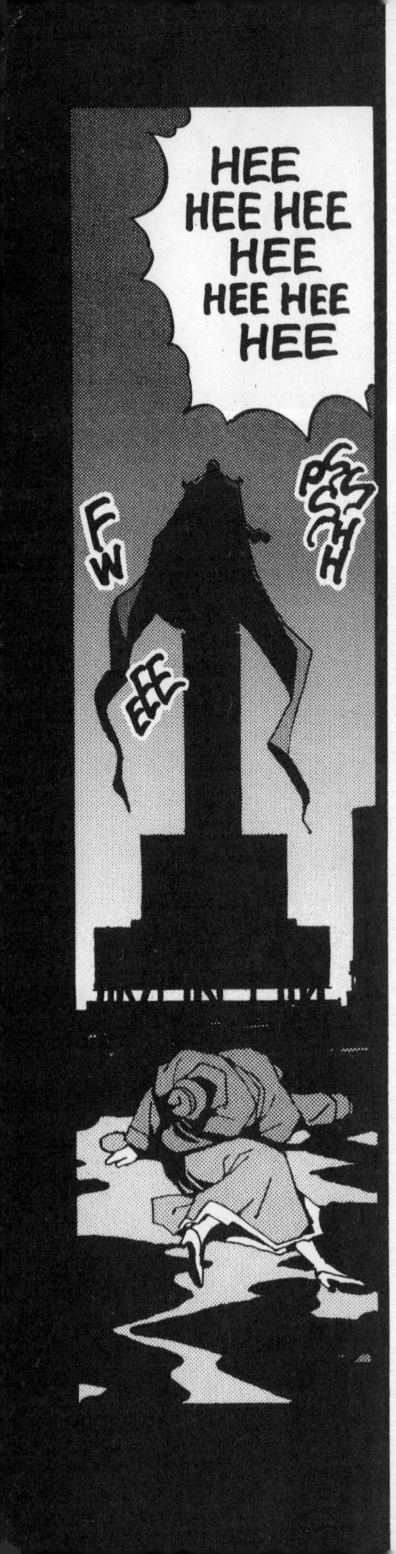
HEE HEE HEE HEE HEE HEE HEE
FW
EEE
PSSSHH
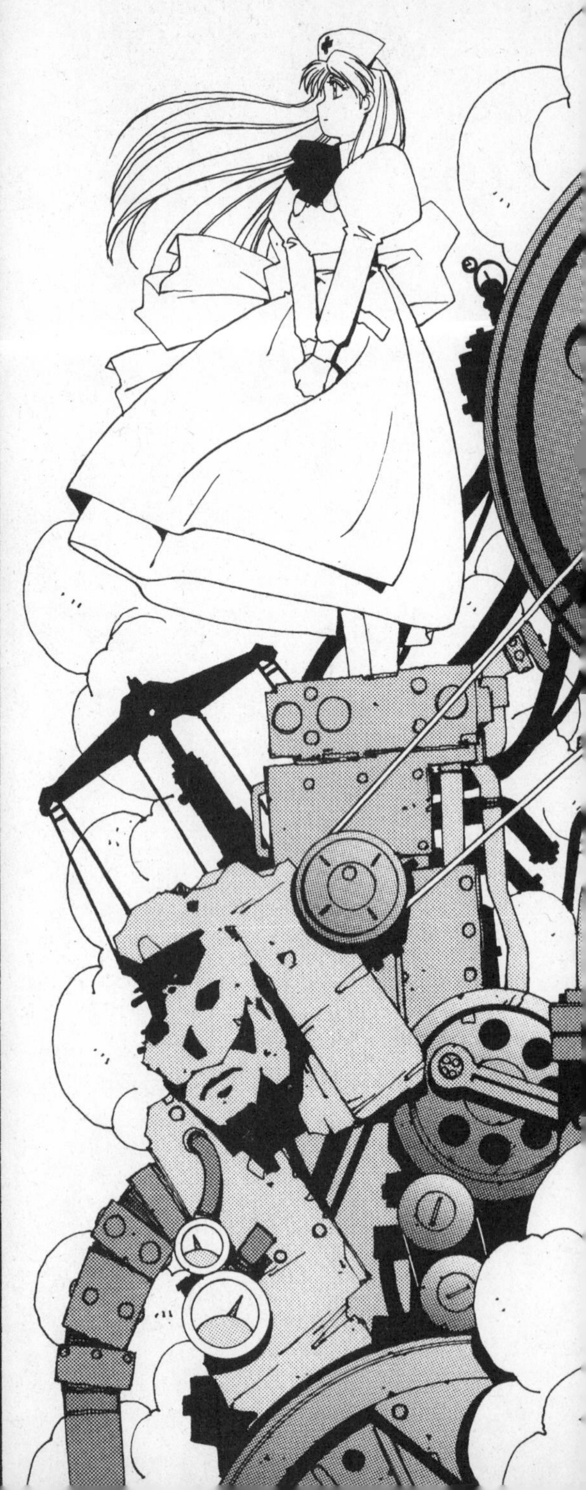

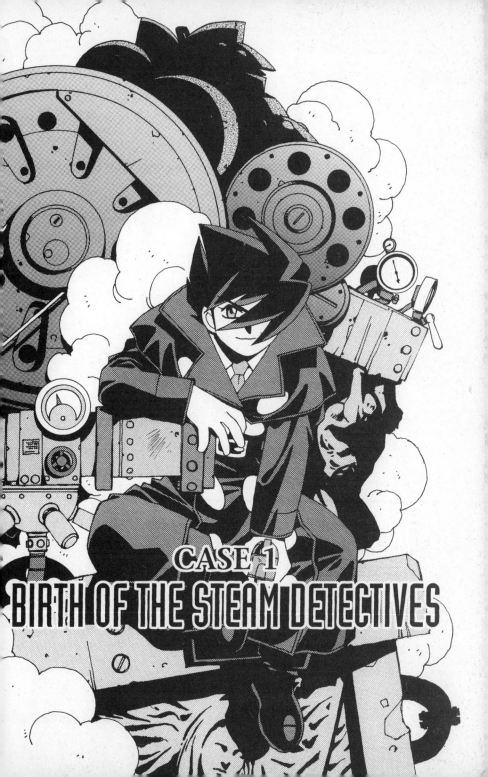

CASE 1
BIRTH OF THE STEAM DETECTIVES

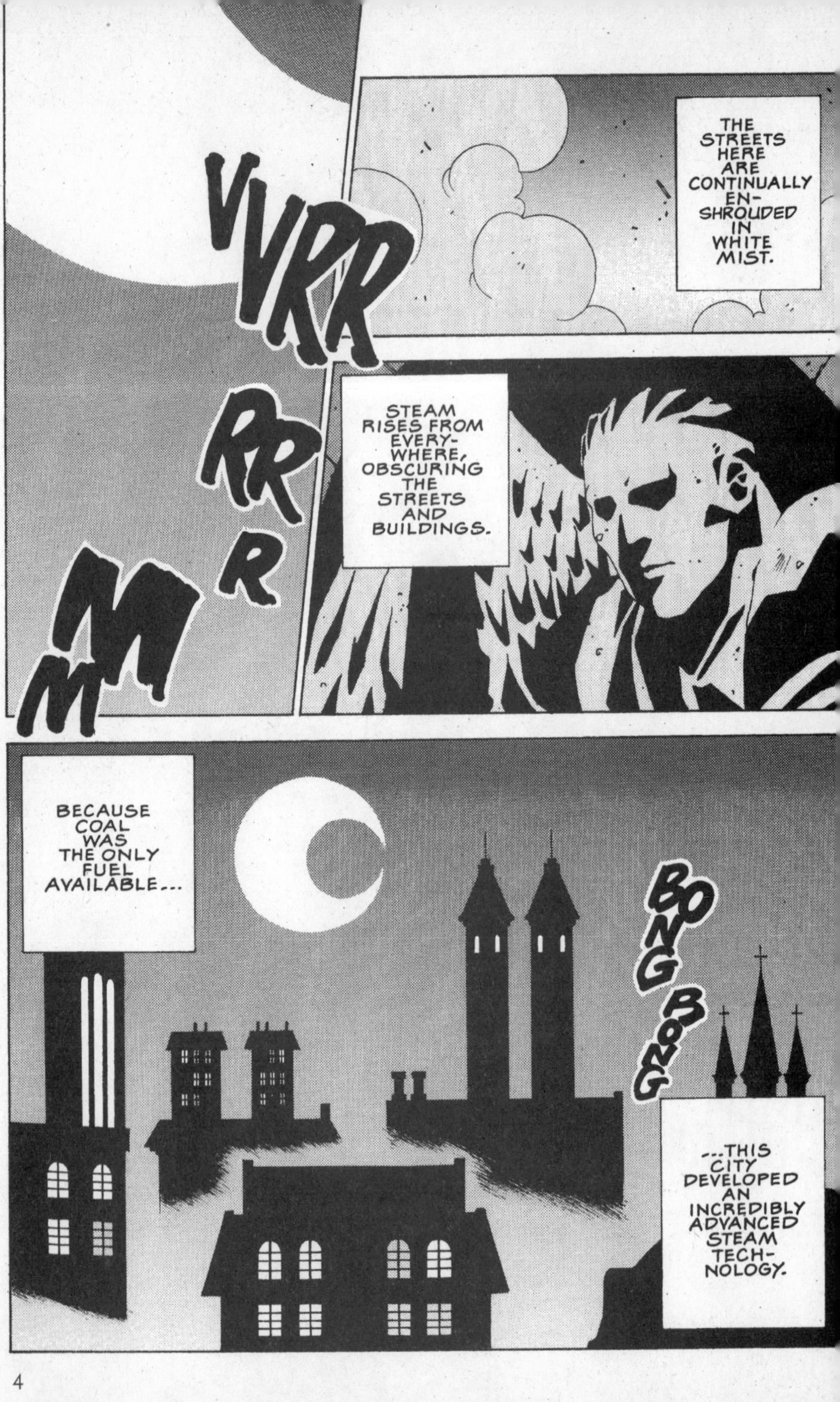
VVRR
RR
R
MMM
THE STREETS HERE ARE CONTINUALLY EN-SHROUDED IN WHITE MIST.
STEAM RISES FROM EVERY-WHERE, OBSCURING THE STREETS AND BUILDINGS.
BECAUSE COAL WAS THE ONLY FUEL AVAILABLE...
BONG BONG
...THIS CITY DEVELOPED AN INCREDIBLY ADVANCED STEAM TECH-NOLOGY.

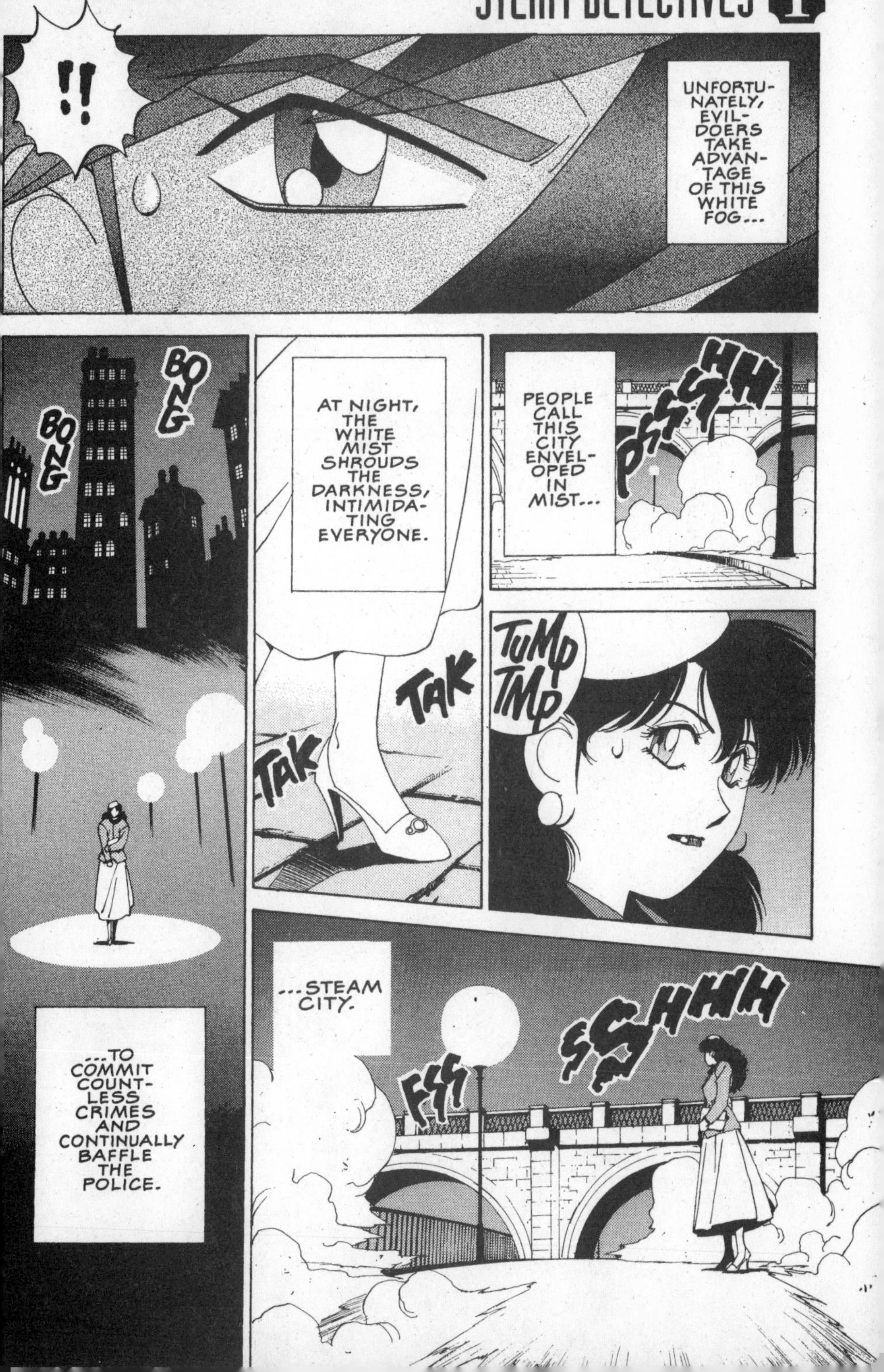
!!
UNFORTU-NATELY, EVIL-DOERS TAKE ADVAN-TAGE OF THIS WHITE FOG...
BONG
BONG
...TO COMMIT COUNT-LESS CRIMES AND CONTINUALLY BAFFLE THE POLICE.
AT NIGHT, THE WHITE MIST SHROUDS THE DARKNESS, INTIMIDA-TING EVERYONE.
TAK
TAK
PEOPLE CALL THIS CITY ENVEL-OPED IN MIST...
PSSSHHH
TUMP TMP
...STEAM CITY.
FSS
SSHHHH

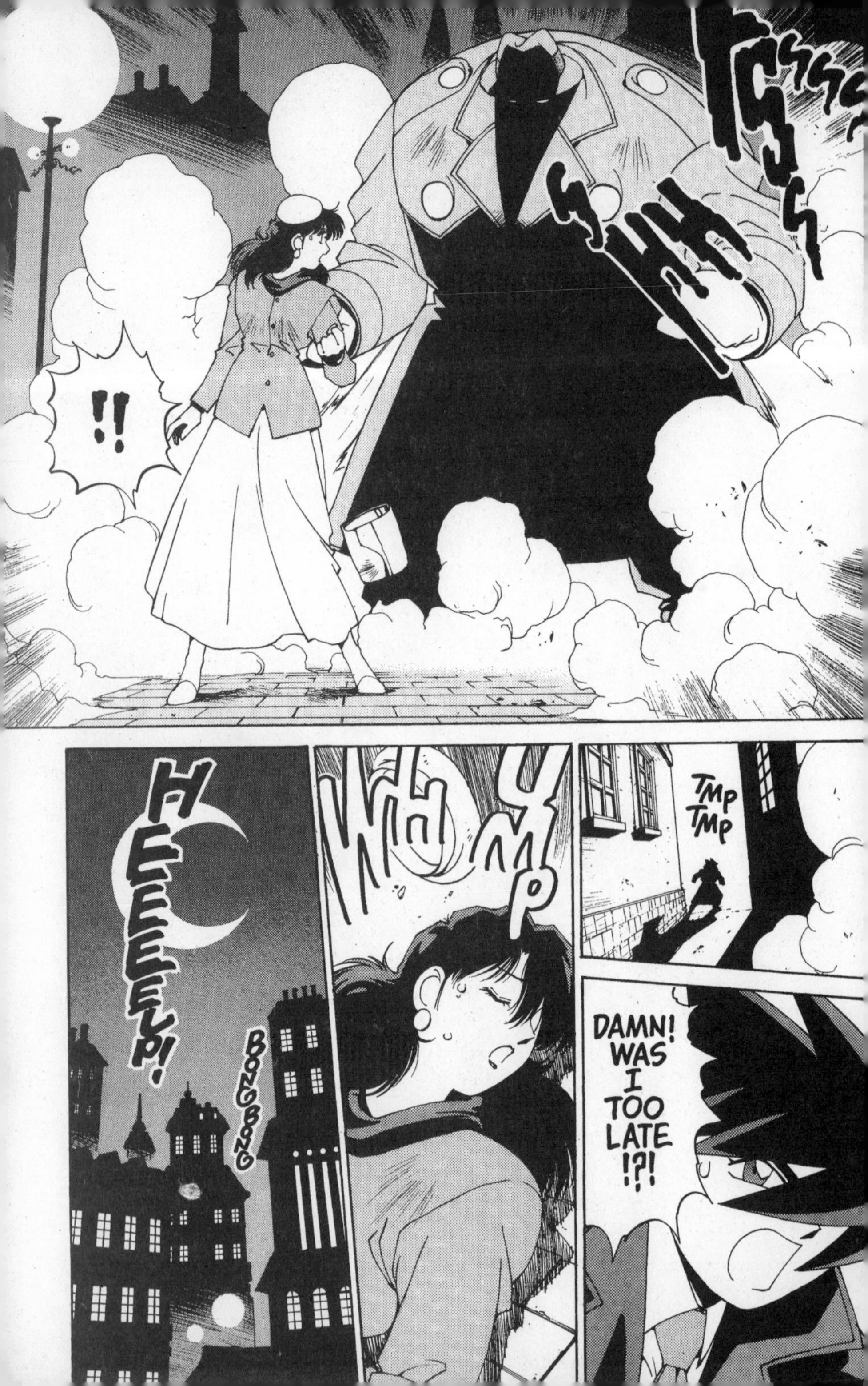
!!
HEEEEELP!
BONGBONG
WHUMP
TMP TMP
DAMN! WAS I TOO LATE!?!

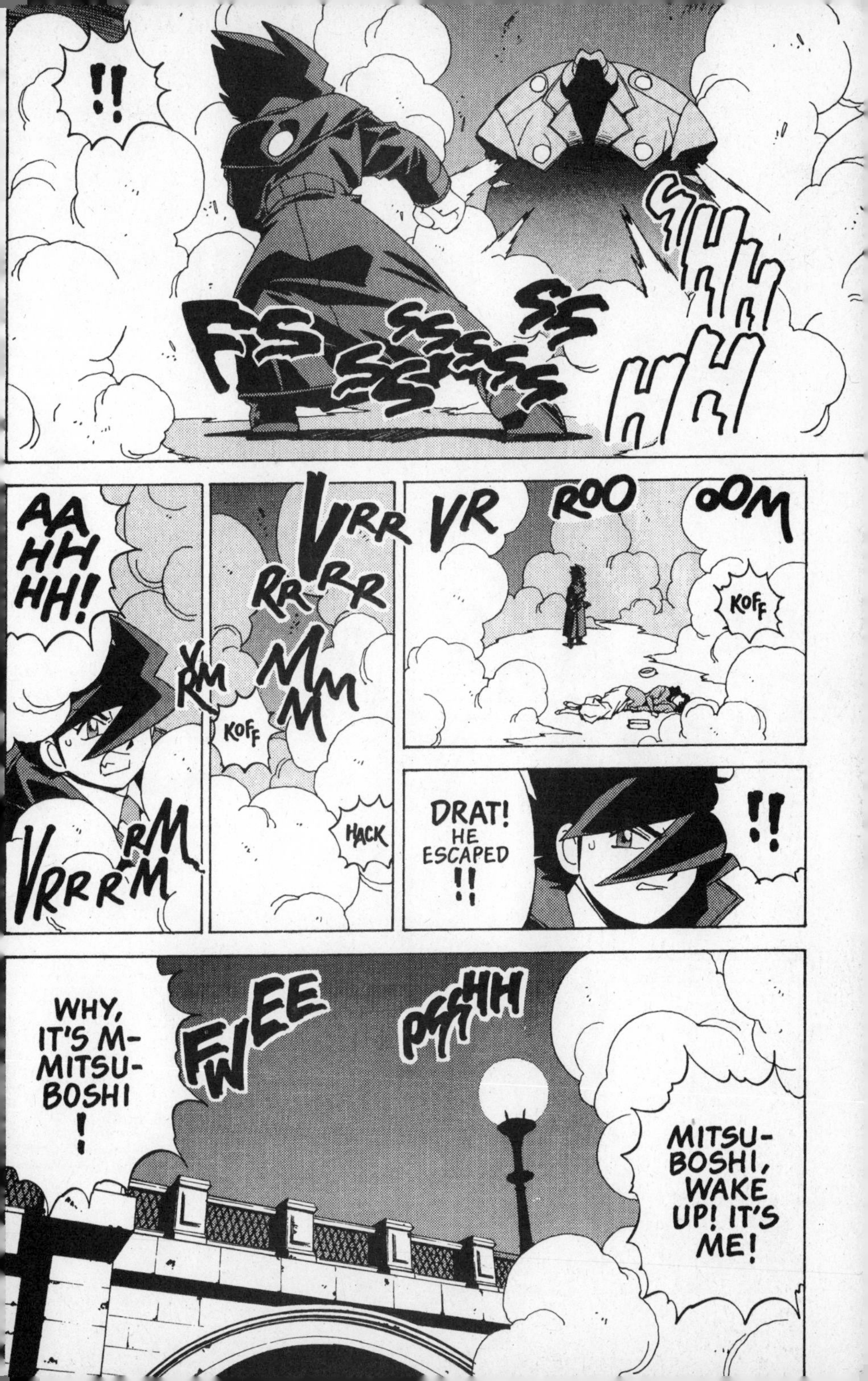
!!
FSSSSSSSSSSSSS
SHHHHH
AAHHHH!
VRM
VRRRRMRM
VRRRVRRRRRMMMM
KOFF
HACK
VR ROO OOM
KOFF
DRAT! HE ESCAPED !!
!!
WHY, IT'S M-MITSU-BOSHI !
FWEE
PSSHHH
MITSU-BOSHI, WAKE UP! IT'S ME!

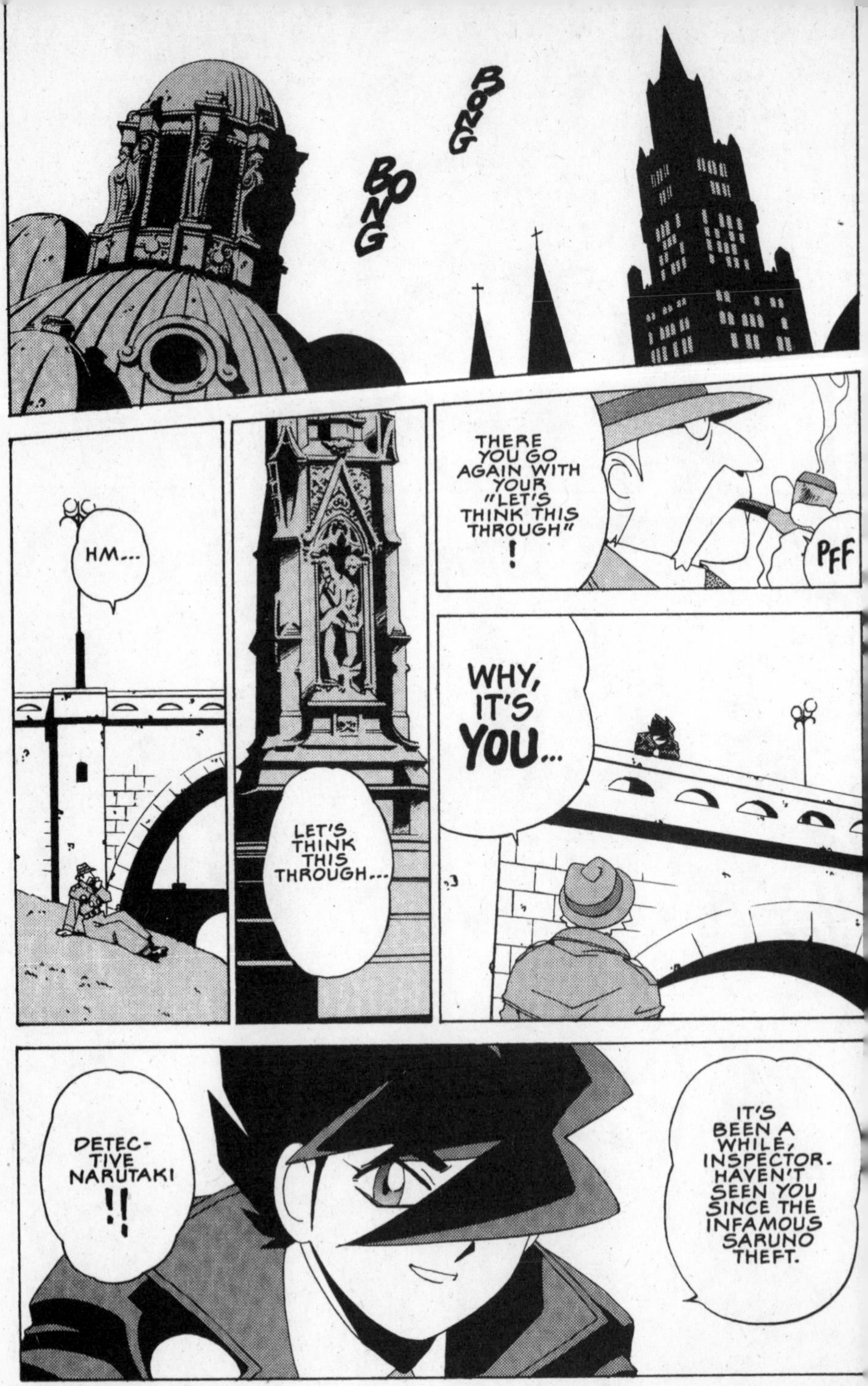
BONG
BONG
HM...
LET'S THINK THIS THROUGH...
THERE YOU GO AGAIN WITH YOUR "LET'S THINK THIS THROUGH"!
PFF
WHY, IT'S YOU...
DETEC-TIVE NARUTAKI!!
IT'S BEEN A WHILE, INSPECTOR. HAVEN'T SEEN YOU SINCE THE INFAMOUS SARUNO THEFT.

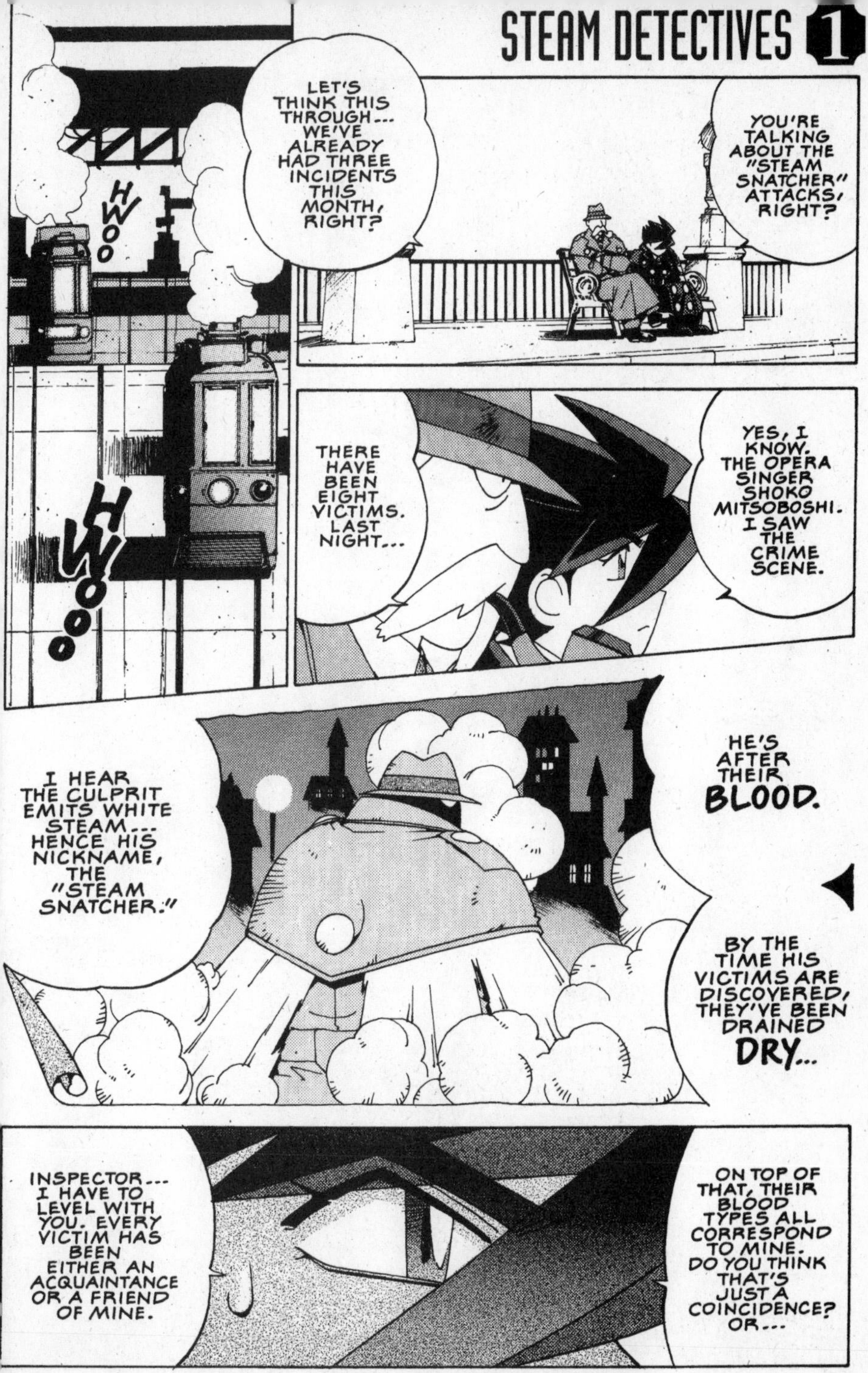
LET'S THINK THIS THROUGH... WE'VE ALREADY HAD THREE INCIDENTS THIS MONTH, RIGHT?
HWOO
HWOOOO
YOU'RE TALKING ABOUT THE "STEAM SNATCHER" ATTACKS, RIGHT?
THERE HAVE BEEN EIGHT VICTIMS. LAST NIGHT...
YES, I KNOW. THE OPERA SINGER SHOKO MITSOBOSHI. I SAW THE CRIME SCENE.
I HEAR THE CULPRIT EMITS WHITE STEAM... HENCE HIS NICKNAME, THE "STEAM SNATCHER."
HE'S AFTER THEIR BLOOD.
BY THE TIME HIS VICTIMS ARE DISCOVERED, THEY'VE BEEN DRAINED DRY...
INSPECTOR... I HAVE TO LEVEL WITH YOU. EVERY VICTIM HAS BEEN EITHER AN ACQUAINTANCE OR A FRIEND OF MINE.
ON TOP OF THAT, THEIR BLOOD TYPES ALL CORRESPOND TO MINE. DO YOU THINK THAT'S JUST A COINCIDENCE? OR...

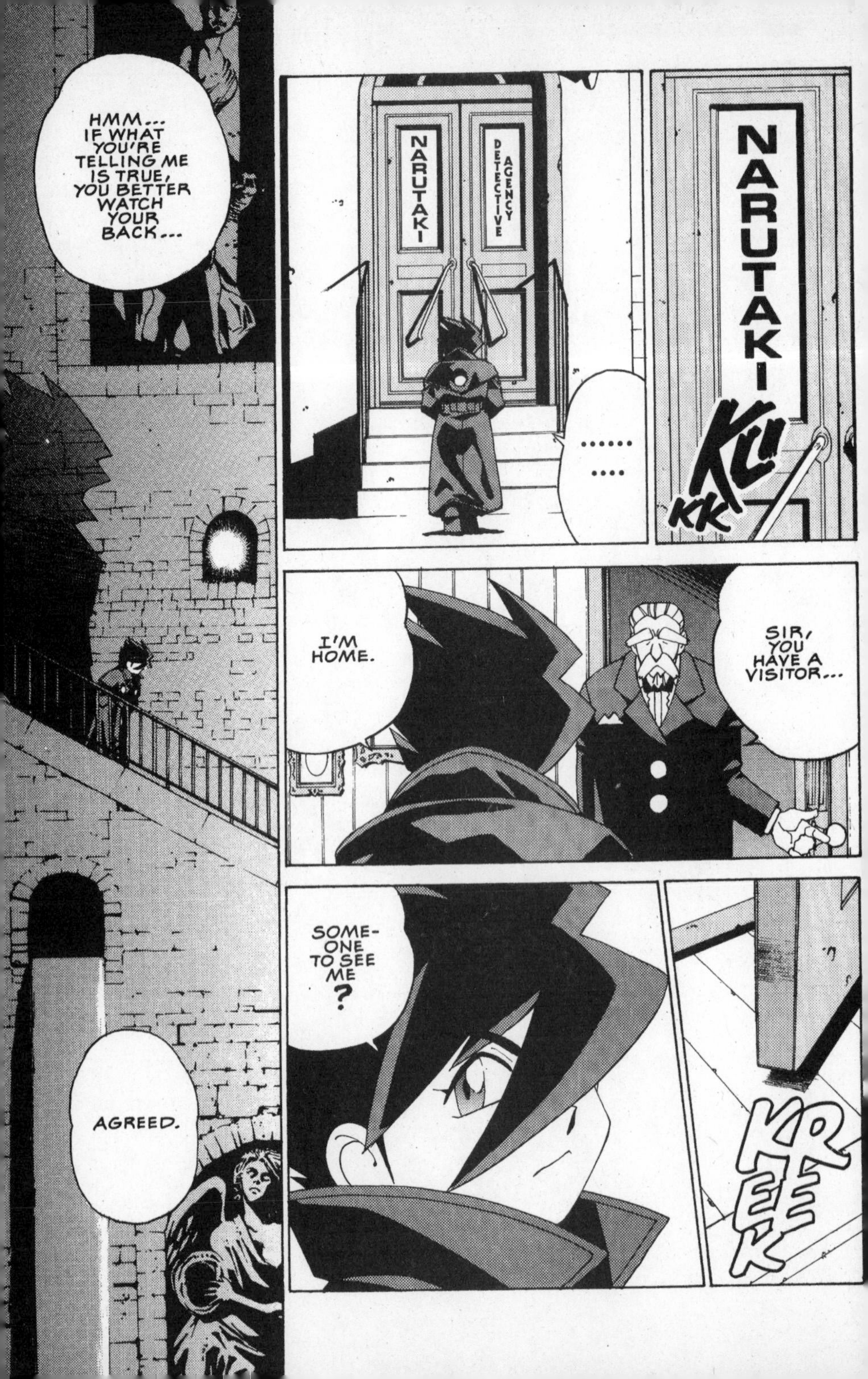
HMM... IF WHAT YOU'RE TELLING ME IS TRUE, YOU BETTER WATCH YOUR BACK...
AGREED.
NARUTAKI
DETECTIVE AGENCY
....
....
NARUTAKI
KLI
KK
I'M HOME.
SIR, YOU HAVE A VISITOR...
SOME-ONE TO SEE ME ?
KREEK

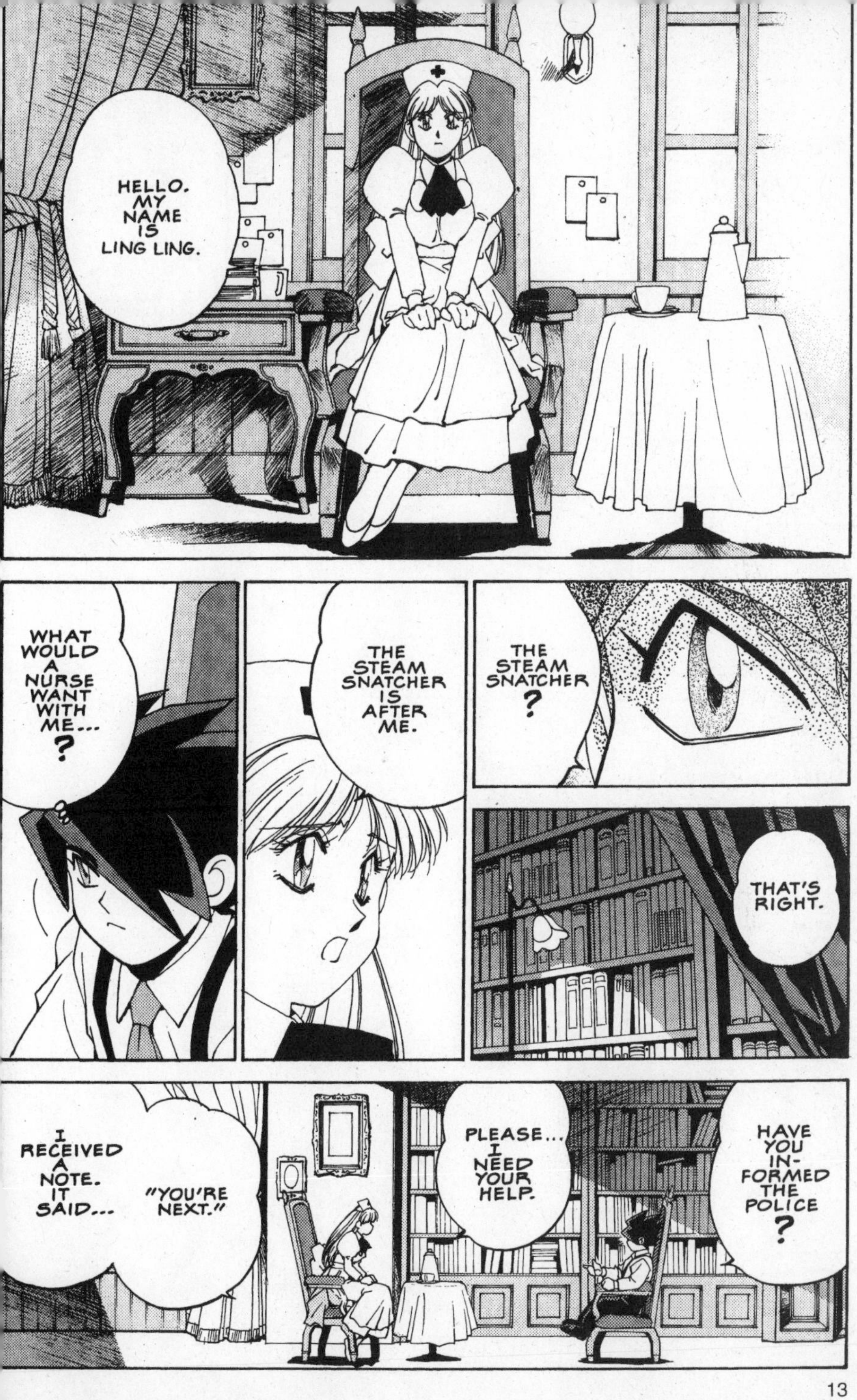
HELLO. MY NAME IS LING LING.
WHAT WOULD A NURSE WANT WITH ME...?
THE STEAM SNATCHER IS AFTER ME.
THE STEAM SNATCHER?
THAT'S RIGHT.
I RECEIVED A NOTE. IT SAID...
"YOU'RE NEXT."
PLEASE... I NEED YOUR HELP.
HAVE YOU INFORMED THE POLICE?

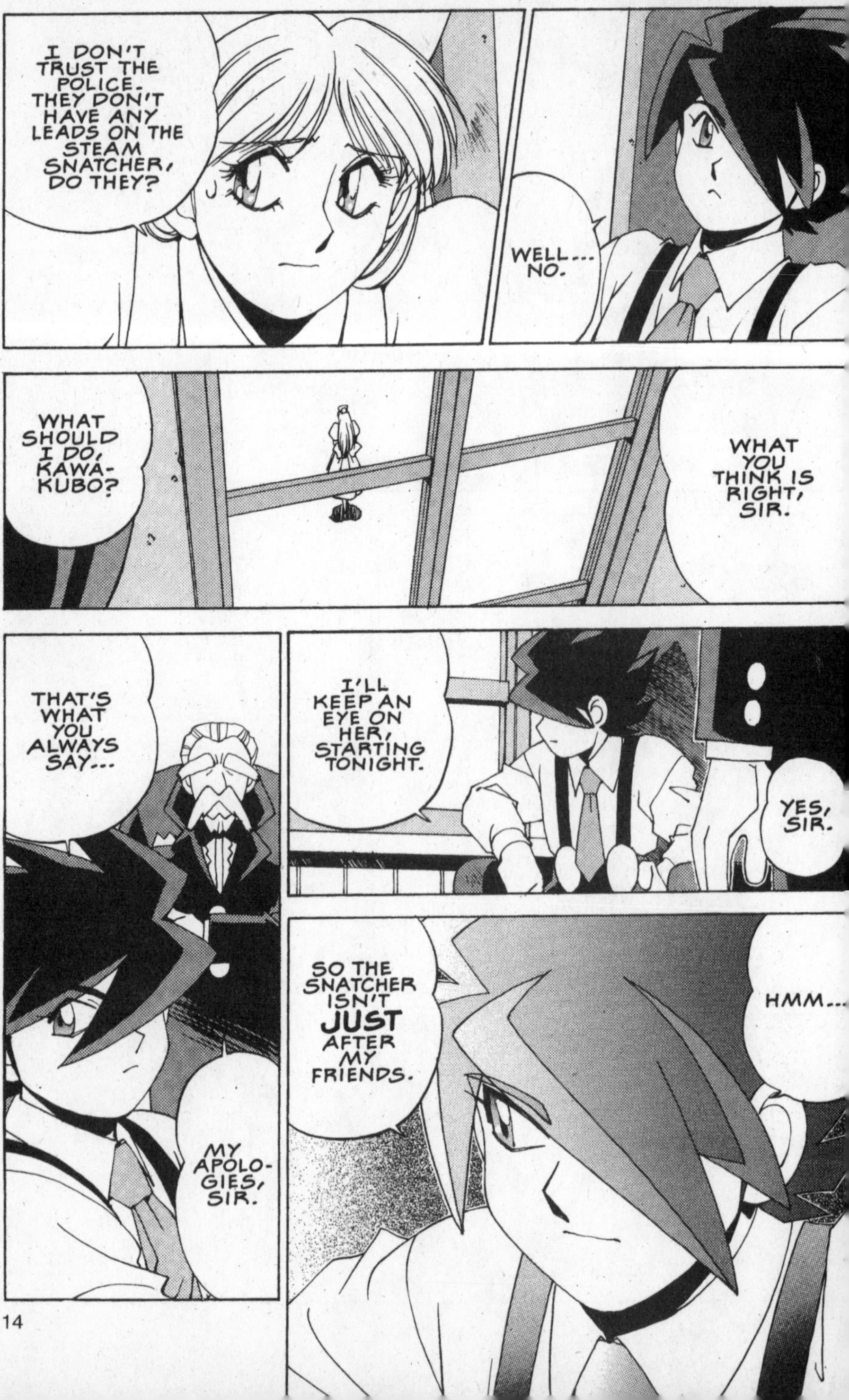
I DON'T TRUST THE POLICE. THEY DON'T HAVE ANY LEADS ON THE STEAM SNATCHER, DO THEY?
WELL... NO.
WHAT SHOULD I DO, KAWA-KUBO?
WHAT YOU THINK IS RIGHT, SIR.
THAT'S WHAT YOU ALWAYS SAY...
MY APOLO-GIES, SIR.
I'LL KEEP AN EYE ON HER, STARTING TONIGHT.
YES, SIR.
SO THE SNATCHER ISN'T **JUST** AFTER MY FRIENDS.
HMM...

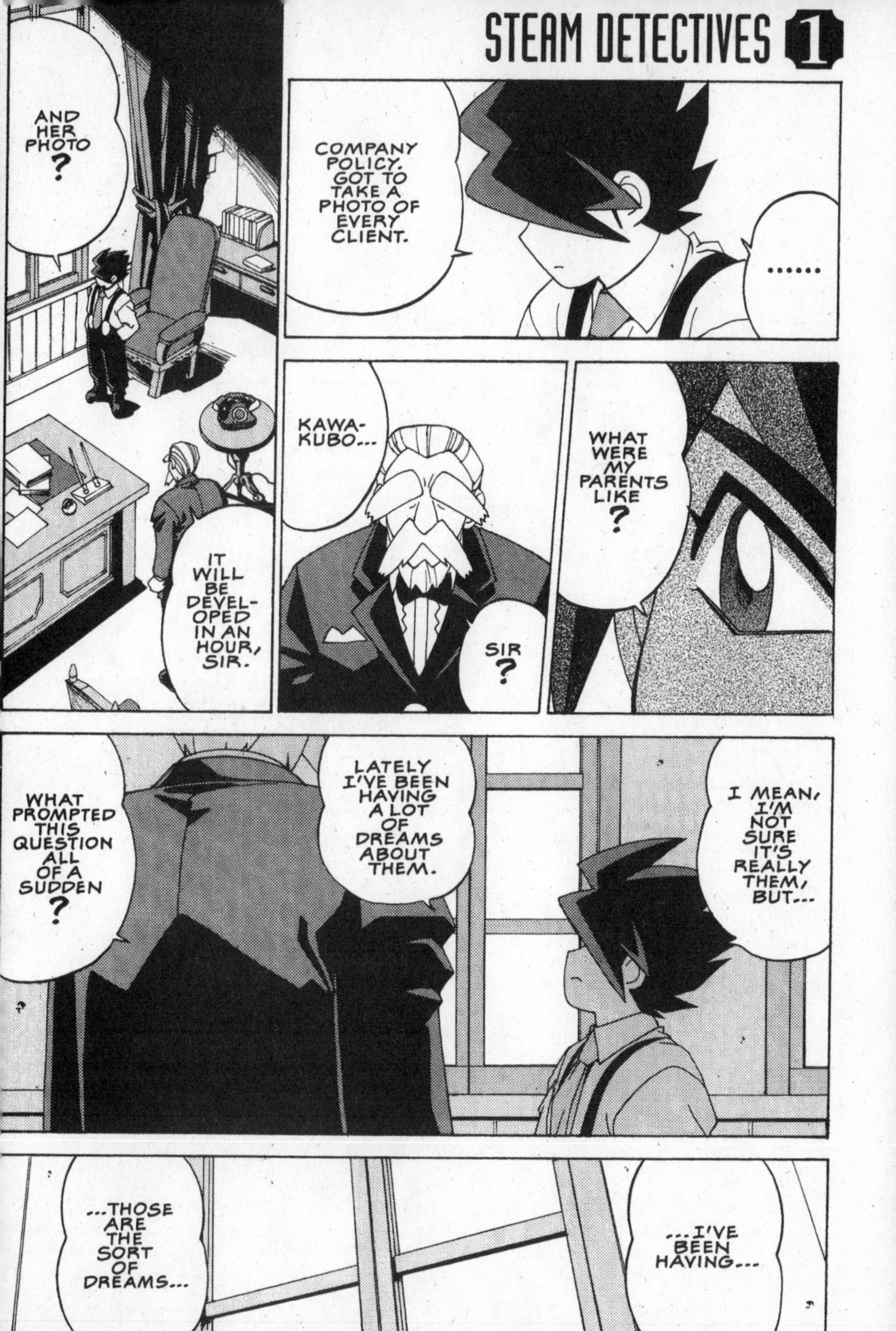
AND HER PHOTO?
IT WILL BE DEVELOPED IN AN HOUR, SIR.
COMPANY POLICY. GOT TO TAKE A PHOTO OF EVERY CLIENT.
......
KAWAKUBO...
SIR?
WHAT WERE MY PARENTS LIKE?
WHAT PROMPTED THIS QUESTION ALL OF A SUDDEN?
LATELY I'VE BEEN HAVING A LOT OF DREAMS ABOUT THEM.
I MEAN, I'M NOT SURE IT'S REALLY THEM, BUT...
...THOSE ARE THE SORT OF DREAMS...
...I'VE BEEN HAVING...

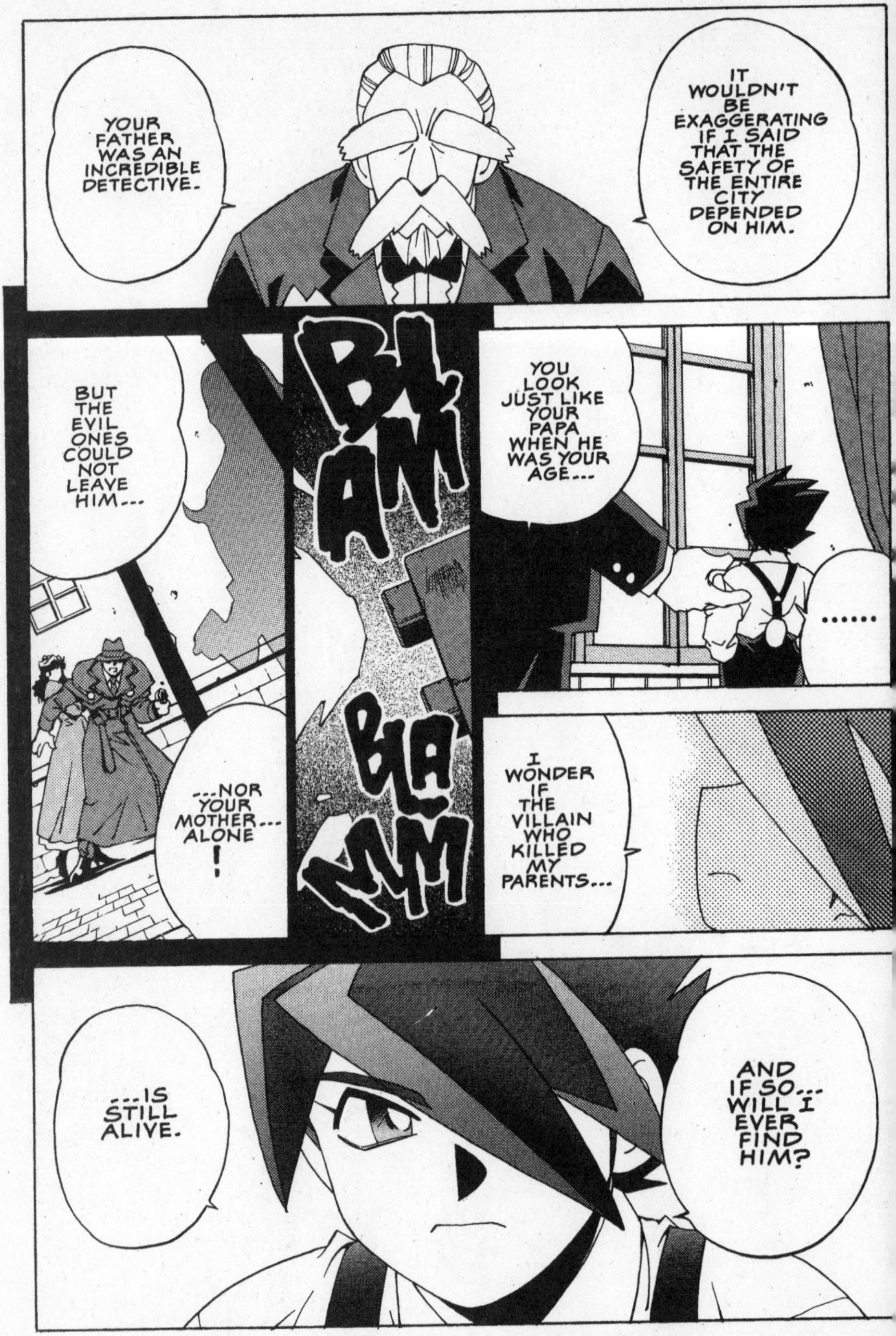
YOUR FATHER WAS AN INCREDIBLE DETECTIVE.
IT WOULDN'T BE EXAGGERATING IF I SAID THAT THE SAFETY OF THE ENTIRE CITY DEPENDED ON HIM.
BUT THE EVIL ONES COULD NOT LEAVE HIM...
...NOR YOUR MOTHER ALONE!
BLAM
BLAMM
YOU LOOK JUST LIKE YOUR PAPA WHEN HE WAS YOUR AGE...
......
I WONDER IF THE VILLAIN WHO KILLED MY PARENTS...
...IS STILL ALIVE.
AND IF SO... WILL I EVER FIND HIM?

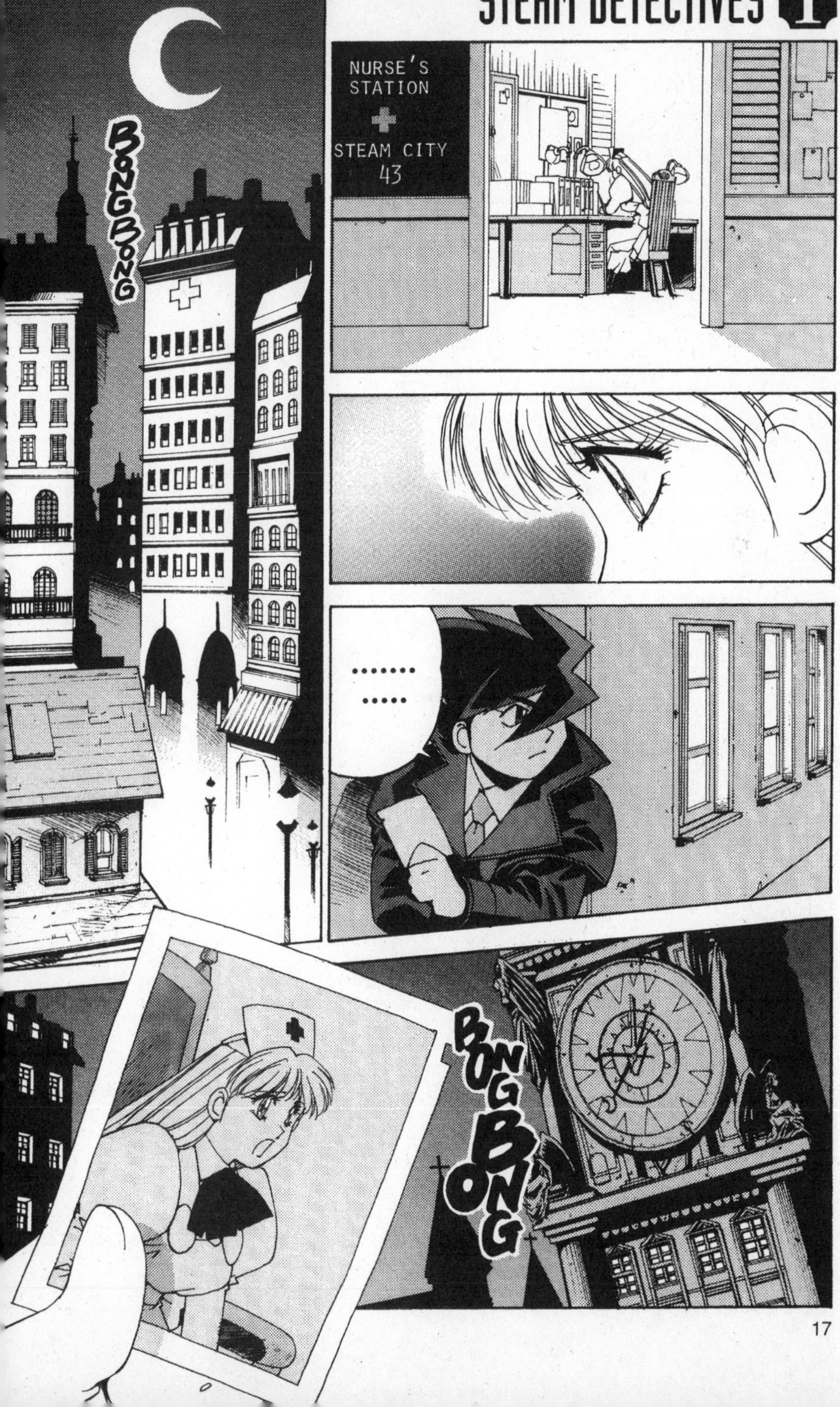
BONG BONG
NURSE'S STATION
STEAM CITY 43
....
.....
BONG BONG BONG BONG

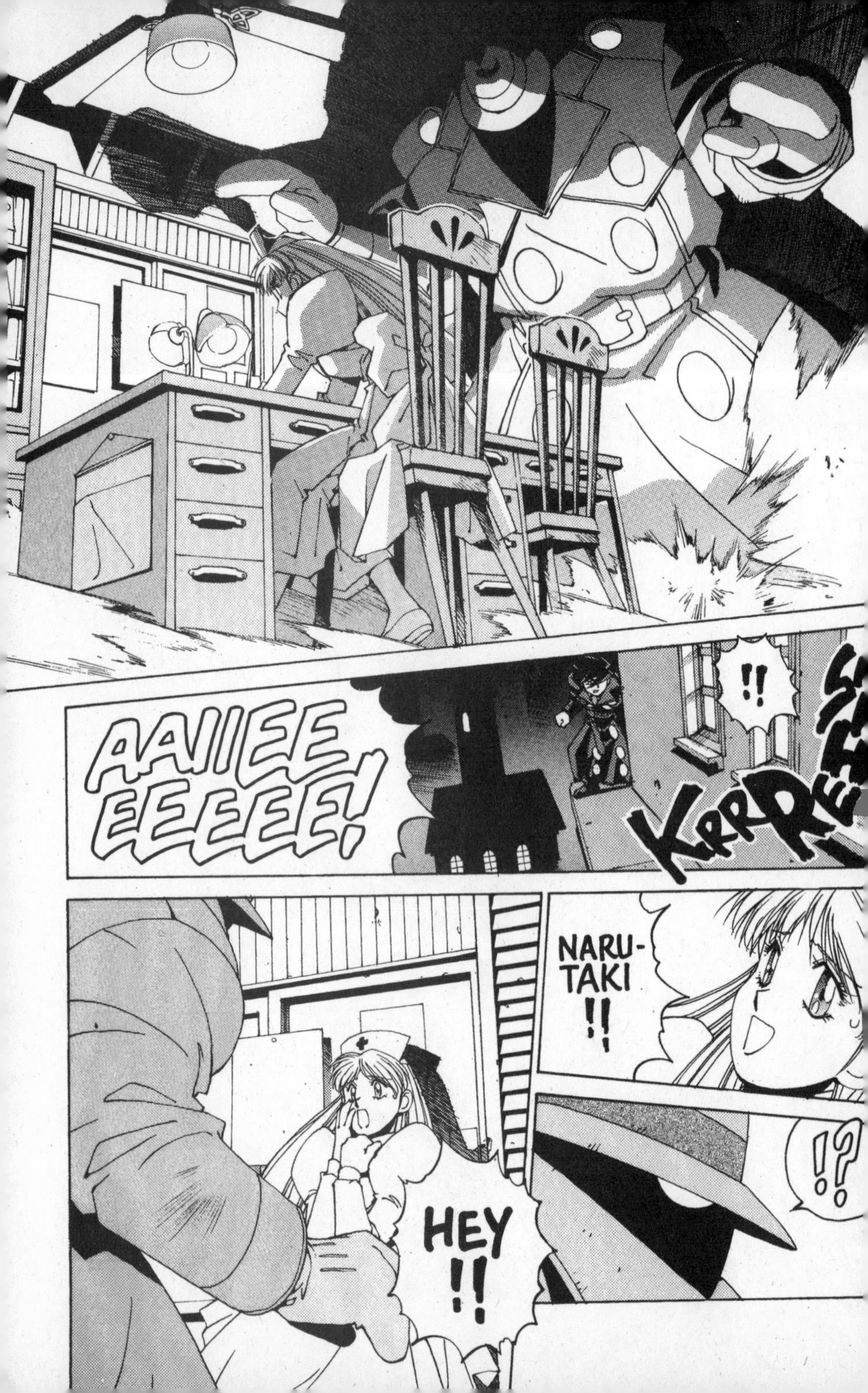
AAIIEE EEEEE!
!!
KRREES
HEY !!
NARU-TAKI !!
!?

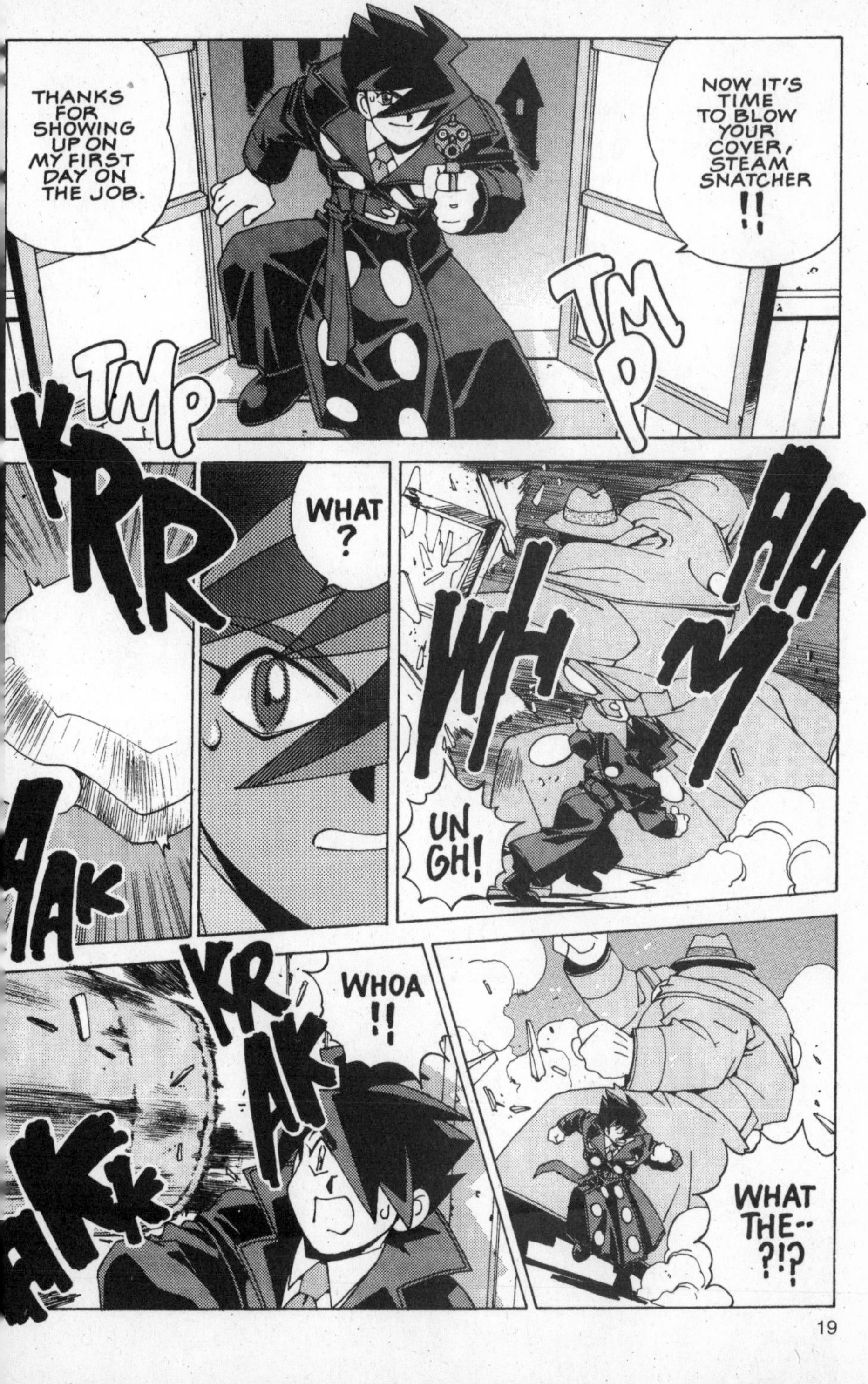

THANKS FOR SHOWING UP ON MY FIRST DAY ON THE JOB.
NOW IT'S TIME TO BLOW YOUR COVER, STEAM SNATCHER !!
TMP
TMP
KRR
AAK
WHAT ?
WHAAAAM
UNGH!
KRAKAK
AKK
WHOA !!
WHAT THE-- ?!?

WHAT'S GOIN' ON HERE--!?!

WHAT'RE YOU DOING ?!

IT'S AS IF HE'S AFTER ME INSTEAD OF YOU!

!?

POIT

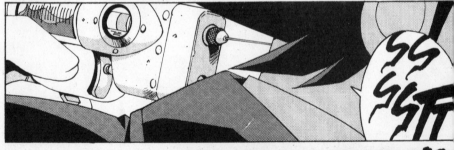

SSSSTT UNK

WHAT ARE... YOU...

TH

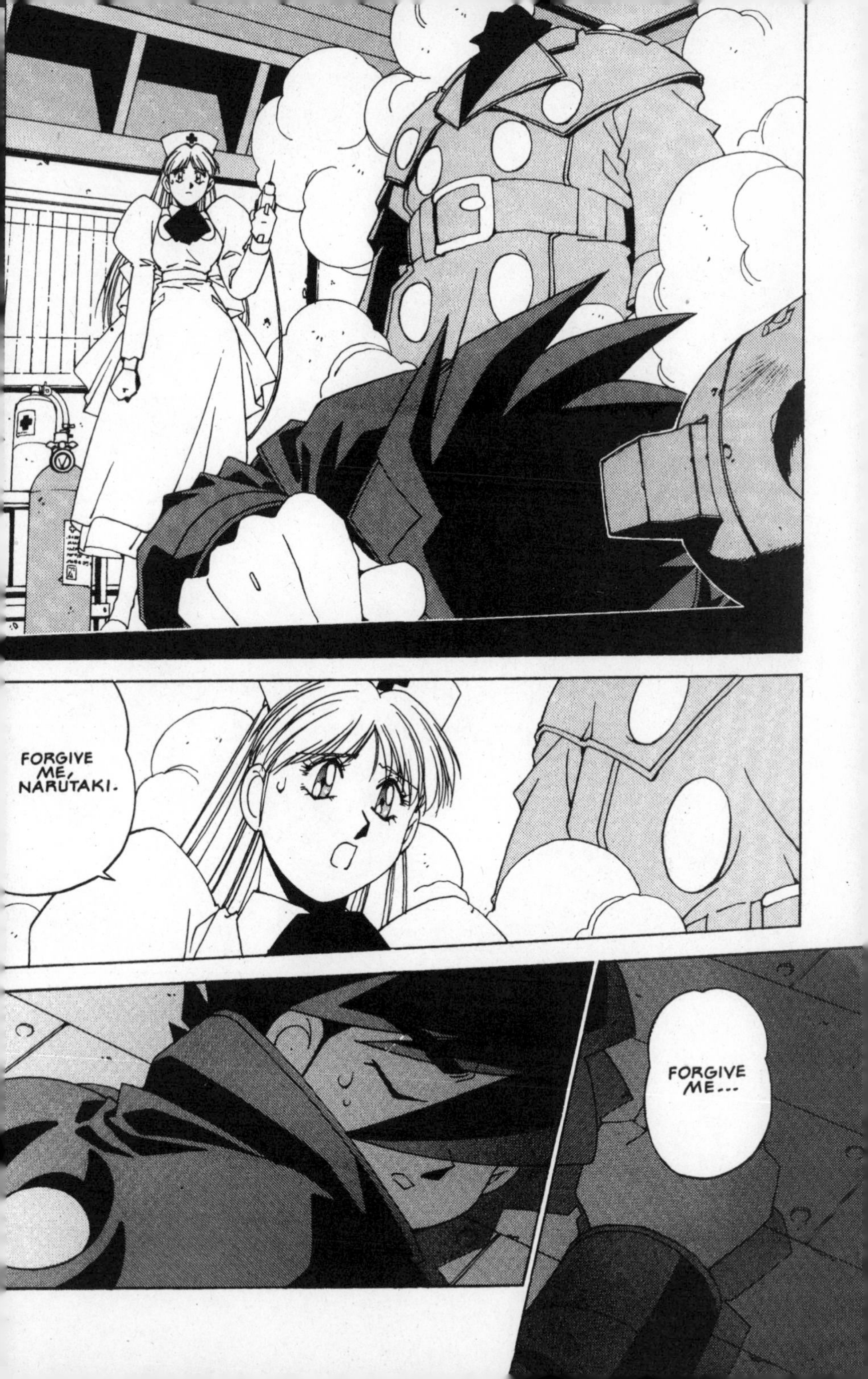
FORGIVE ME, NARUTAKI.
FORGIVE ME...

......
.....

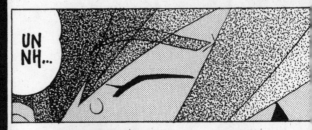

UNNH...

HUH?

SIR...

ARE YOU AWAKE, SIR?

KAWA-KUBO...? WHERE AM I--?

SIR...

YOU'RE IN THE BASE-MENT OF THE AGENCY. I FOUND YOU IN AN UNCONSCIOUS STATE, SO I BROUGHT YOU HERE.

YOU LOST A LOT OF BLOOD, SO I GAVE YOU A BLOOD TRANSFUSION. YOU'VE BEEN ASLEEP FOR THREE DAYS AND THREE NIGHTS.

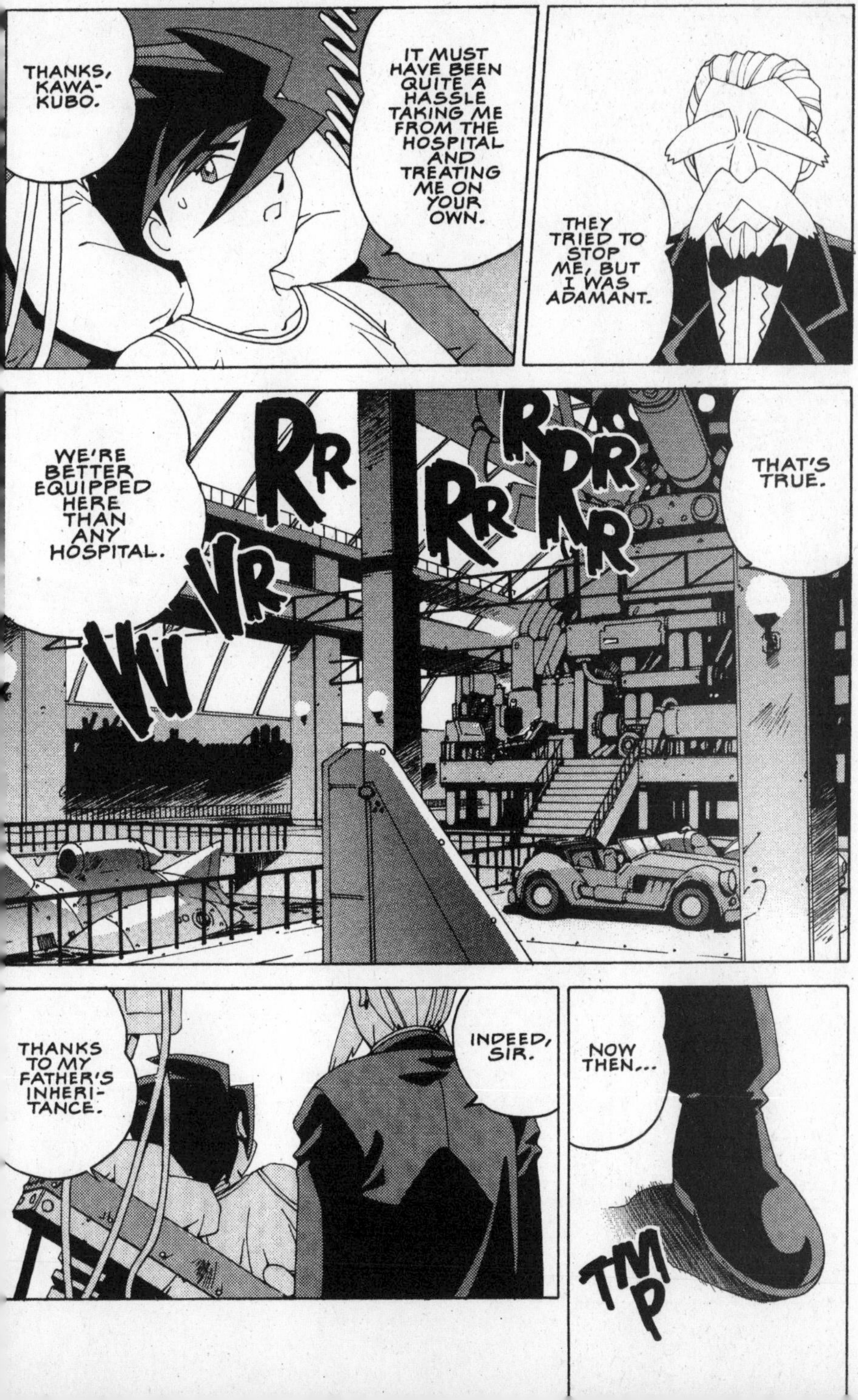
THANKS, KAWA-KUBO.
IT MUST HAVE BEEN QUITE A HASSLE TAKING ME FROM THE HOSPITAL AND TREATING ME ON YOUR OWN.
THEY TRIED TO STOP ME, BUT I WAS ADAMANT.
WE'RE BETTER EQUIPPED HERE THAN ANY HOSPITAL.
VVVR
RR
RR
RRRR
THAT'S TRUE.
THANKS TO MY FATHER'S INHERI-TANCE.
INDEED, SIR.
NOW THEN...
TMP

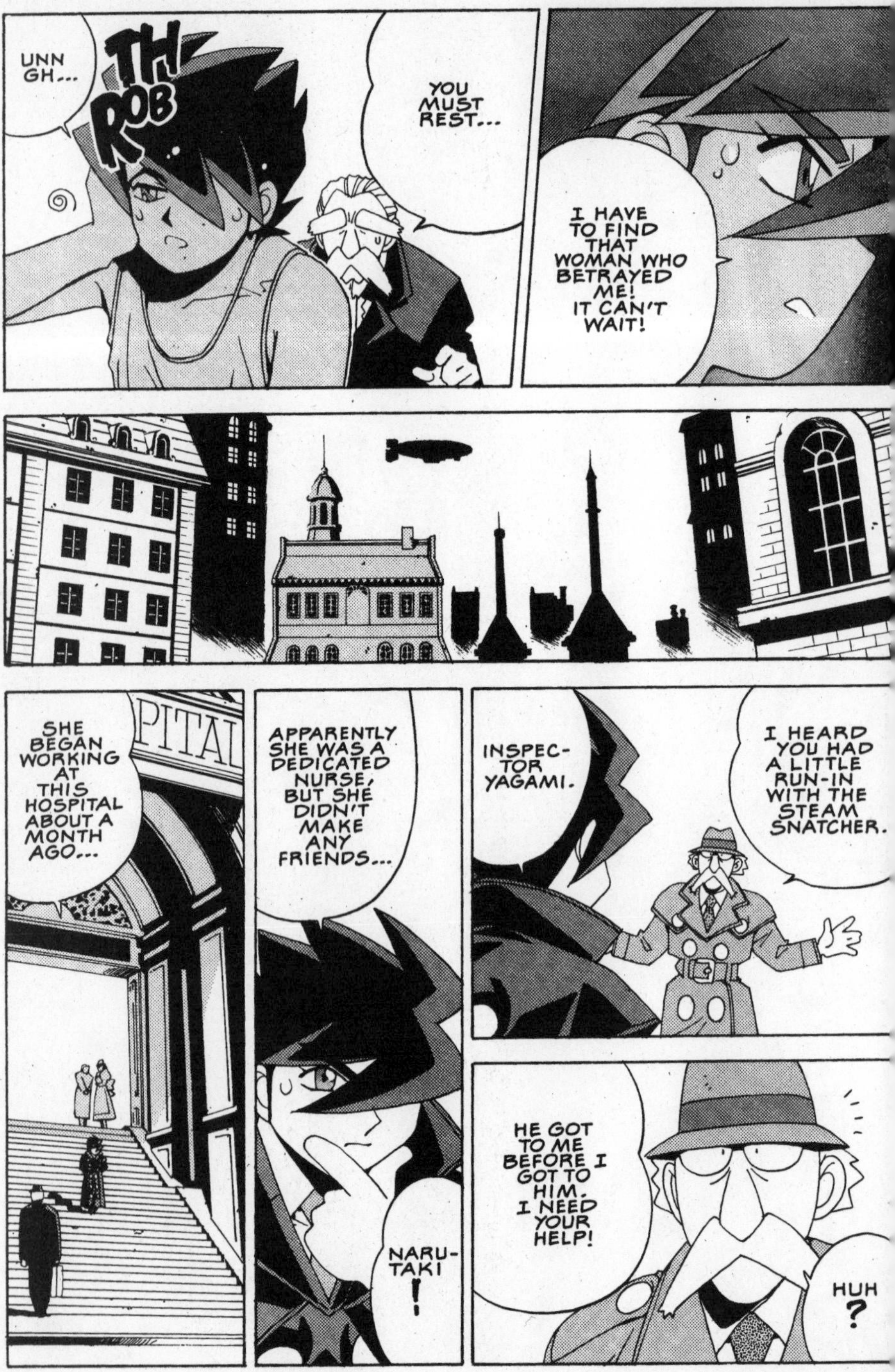
UNN GH...
THROB
YOU MUST REST...
I HAVE TO FIND THAT WOMAN WHO BETRAYED ME! IT CAN'T WAIT!
PITAL
SHE BEGAN WORKING AT THIS HOSPITAL ABOUT A MONTH AGO...
APPARENTLY SHE WAS A DEDICATED NURSE, BUT SHE DIDN'T MAKE ANY FRIENDS...
NARU-TAKI!
INSPEC-TOR YAGAMI.
I HEARD YOU HAD A LITTLE RUN-IN WITH THE STEAM SNATCHER.
HE GOT TO ME BEFORE I GOT TO HIM. I NEED YOUR HELP!
HUH?

I'VE GOT TO LOOK HER UP IN YOUR POLICE FILES.

BUT WOULDN'T SHE HAVE USED A FALSE NAME?

PERHAPS.

HMM...

I'VE FOUND SOMETHING...

REALLY!?

LING LING **IS** HER REAL NAME. SHE GOT HER NURSE'S LICENSE A YEAR AGO, AFTER LOSING HER PARENTS IN A CAR ACCIDENT...

•104402111348114

SHE HAS ONE OLDER SISTER. HER FATHER WAS THE FAMOUS BIO-ENGINEER DOCTOR HSU. HMMM....

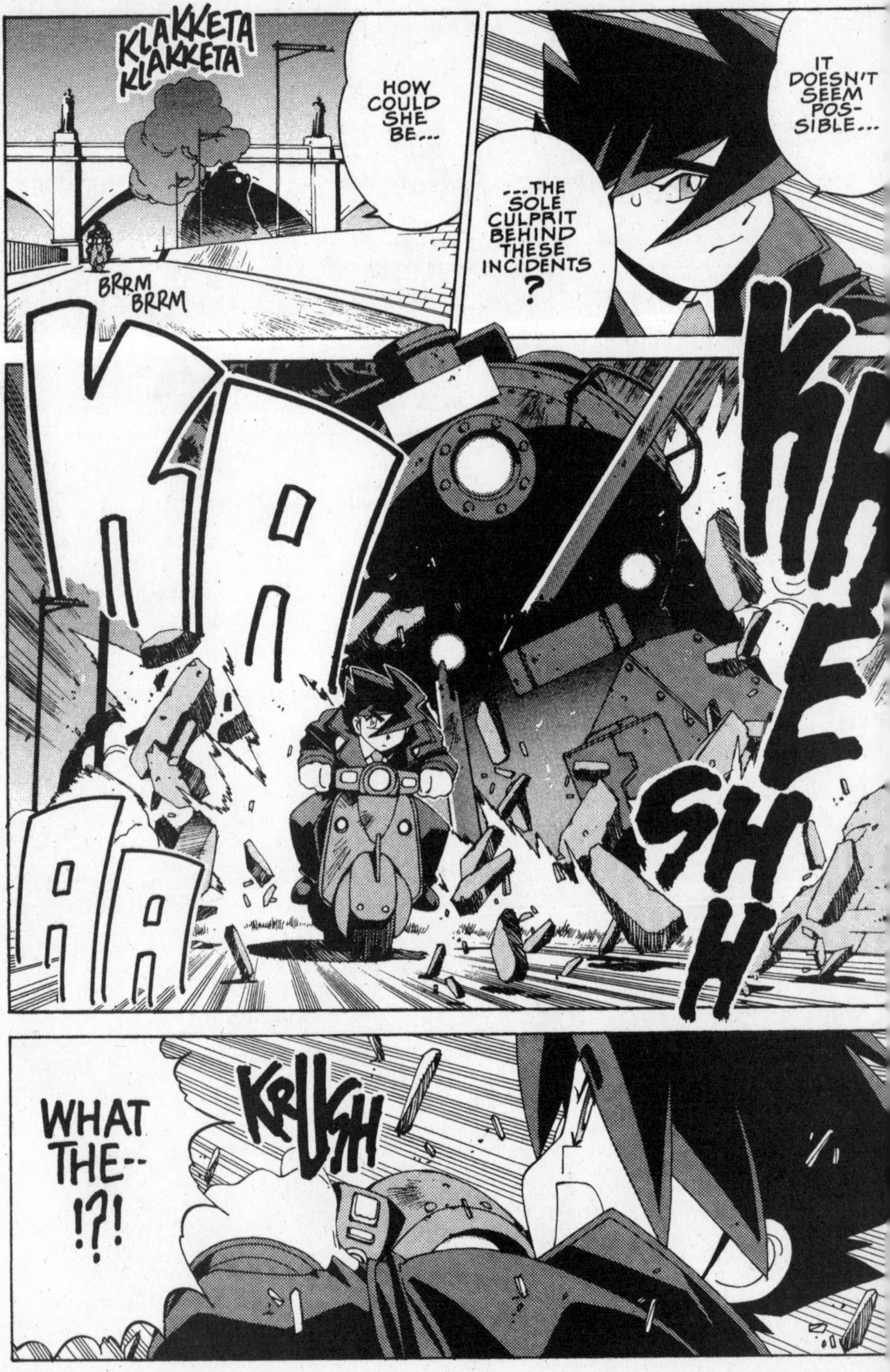
KLAKKETA KLAKKETA
HOW COULD SHE BE...
BRRM BRRM
IT DOESN'T SEEM POS-SIBLE...
...THE SOLE CULPRIT BEHIND THESE INCIDENTS?
WHAT THE--!?!
KRUSH

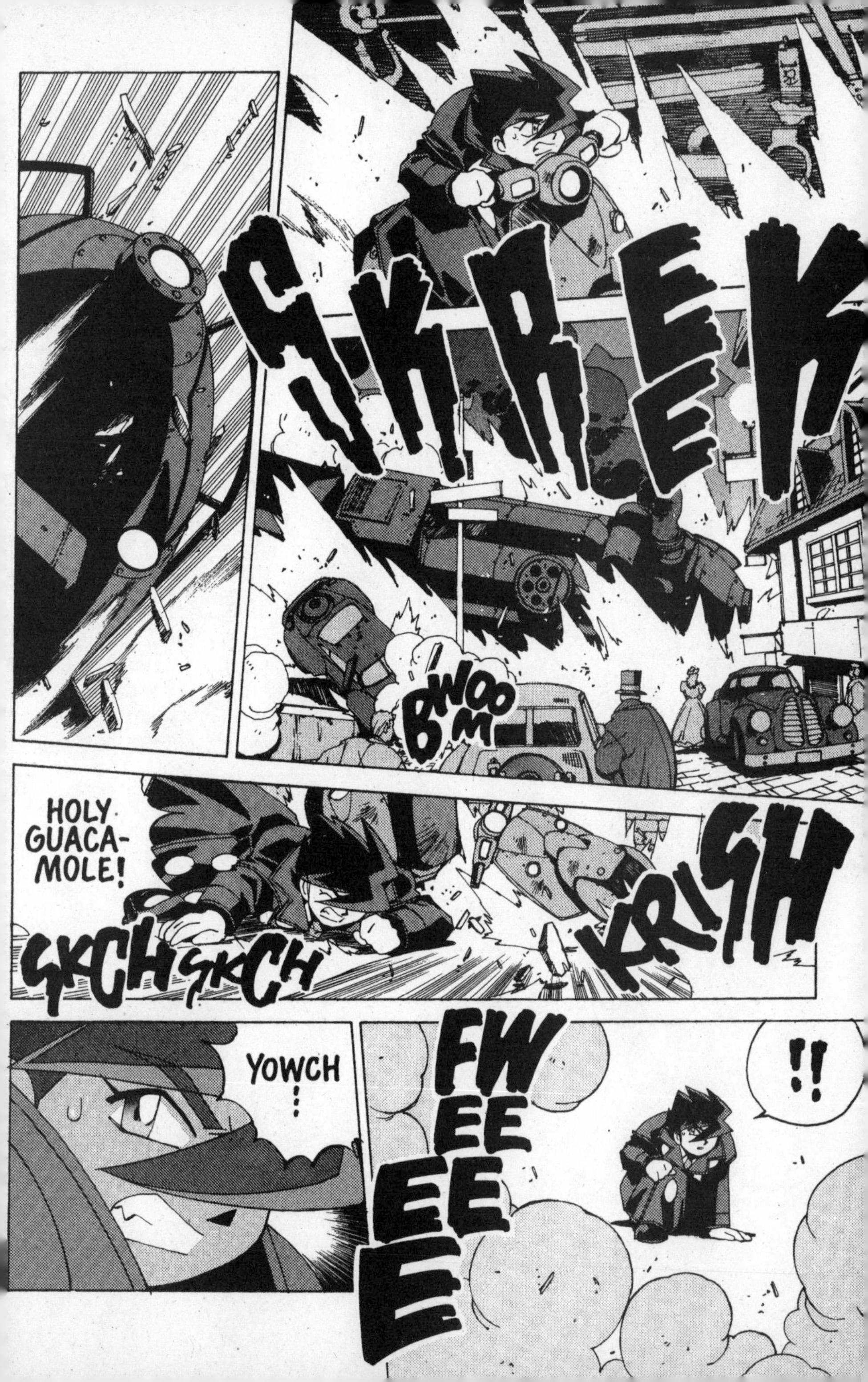
SHKREEK
BWOOM
HOLY GUACAMOLE!
SKCH SKCH
KRISH
YOWCH!
FWEEEEE
!!

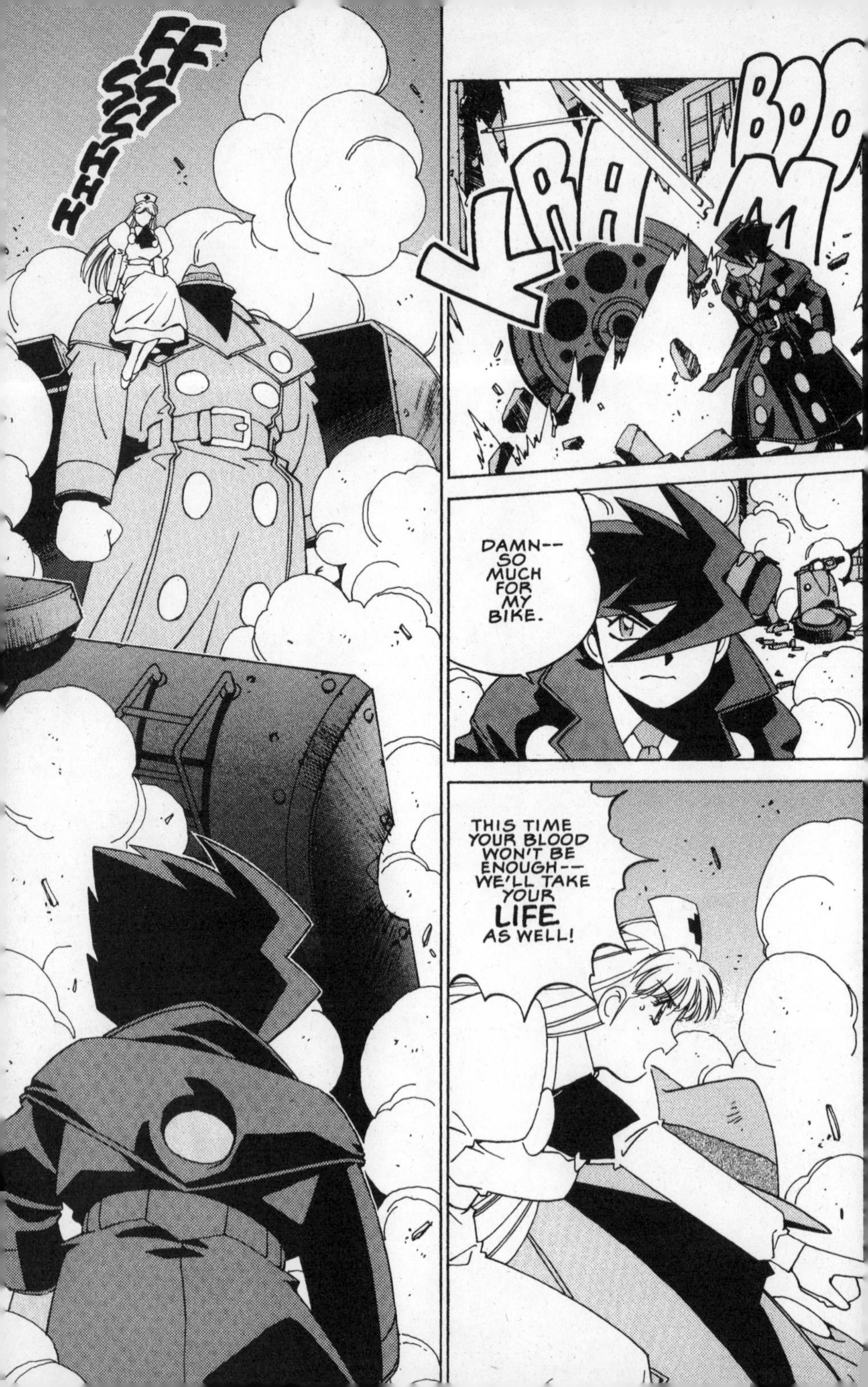
FFSSSSHHHH
KRAA
BOOOM
DAMN-- SO MUCH FOR MY BIKE.
THIS TIME YOUR BLOOD WON'T BE ENOUGH-- WE'LL TAKE YOUR **LIFE** AS WELL!

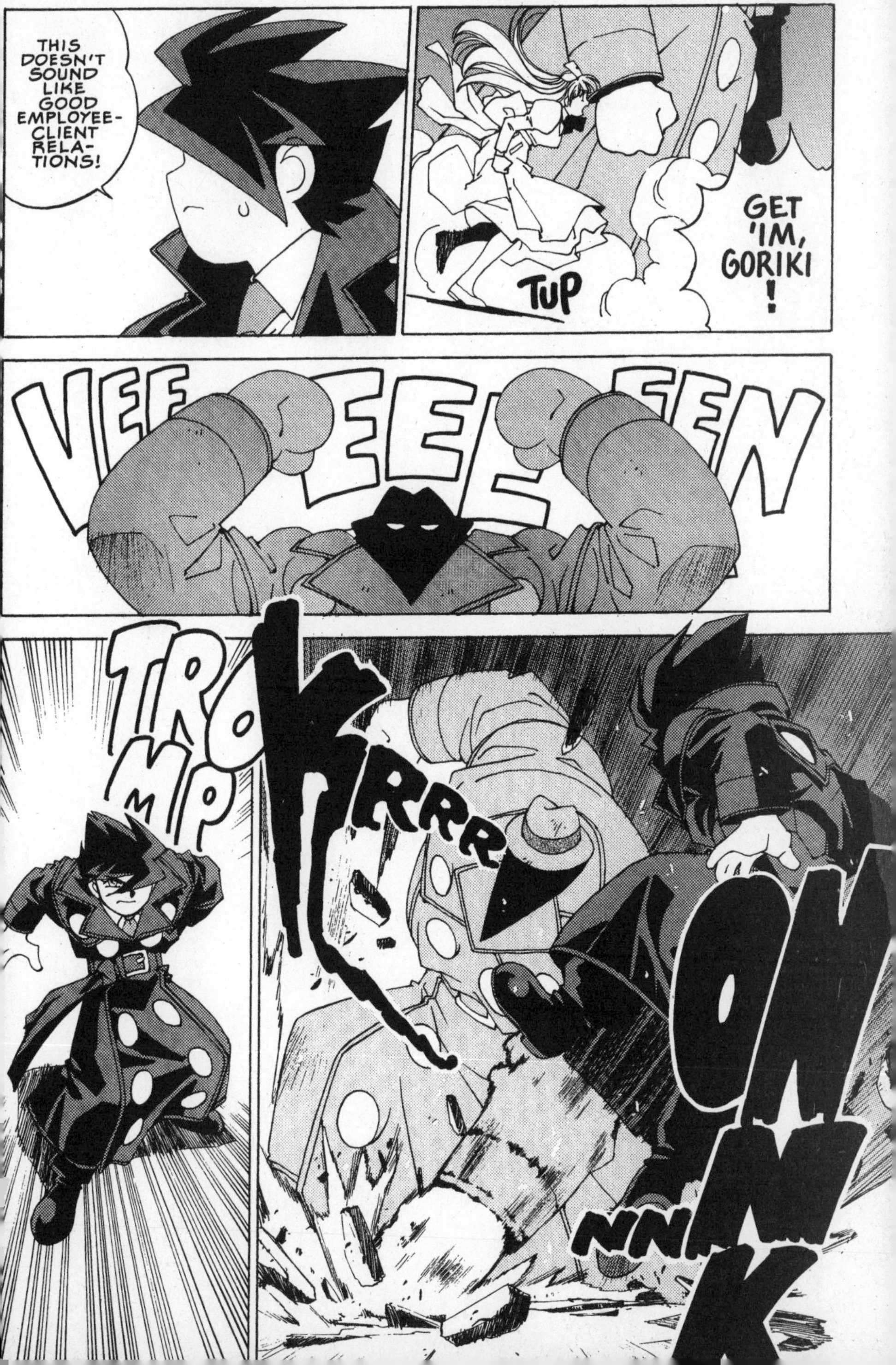
THIS DOESN'T SOUND LIKE GOOD EMPLOYEE-CLIENT RELATIONS!
TUP
GET 'IM, GORIKI!
TROMP
KRRR

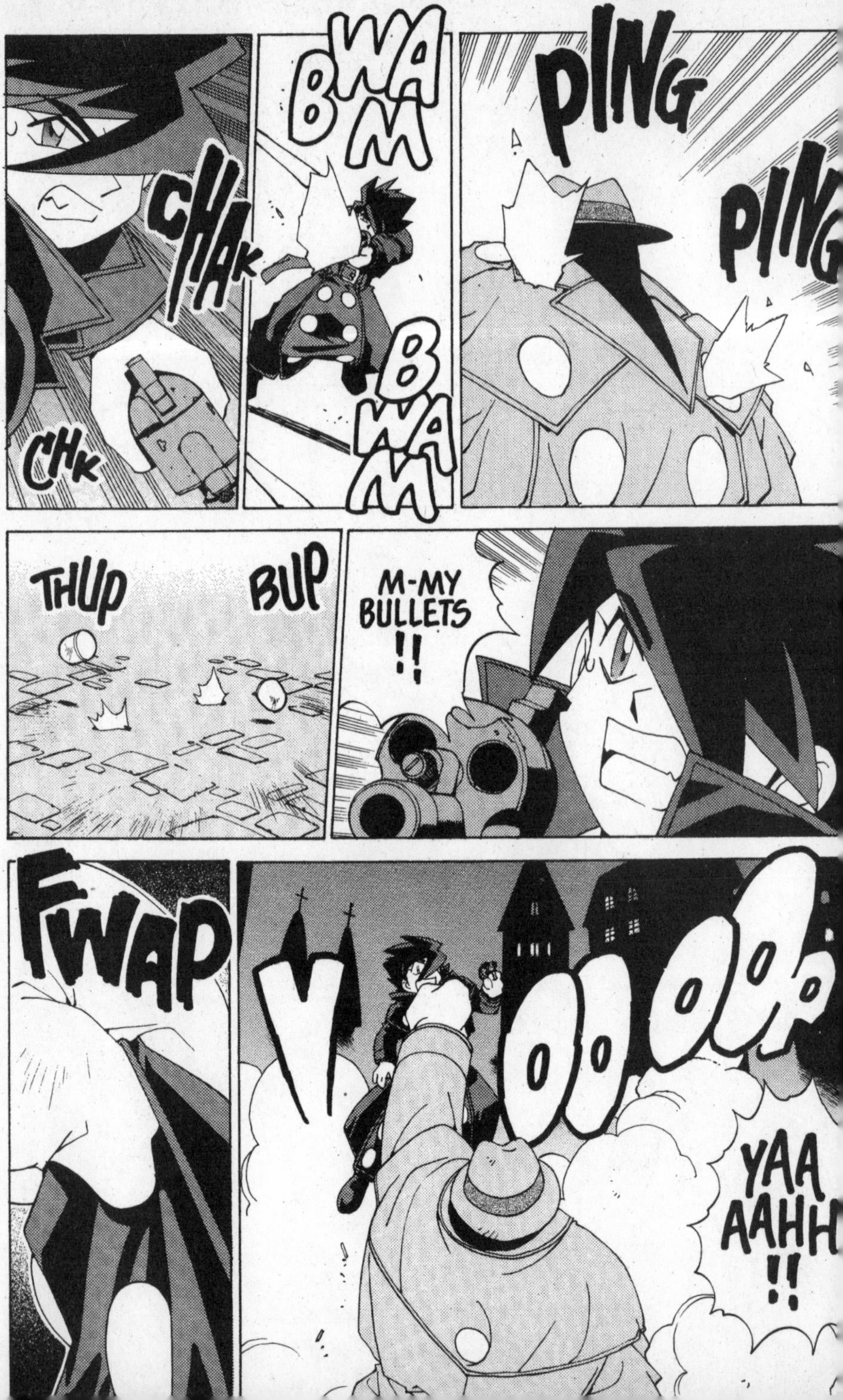
CHAK
CHK
BWAM
BWAM
PING
PING
THUP
BUP
M-MY BULLETS!!
FWAP
WOOOOOP
YAAAAHH!!

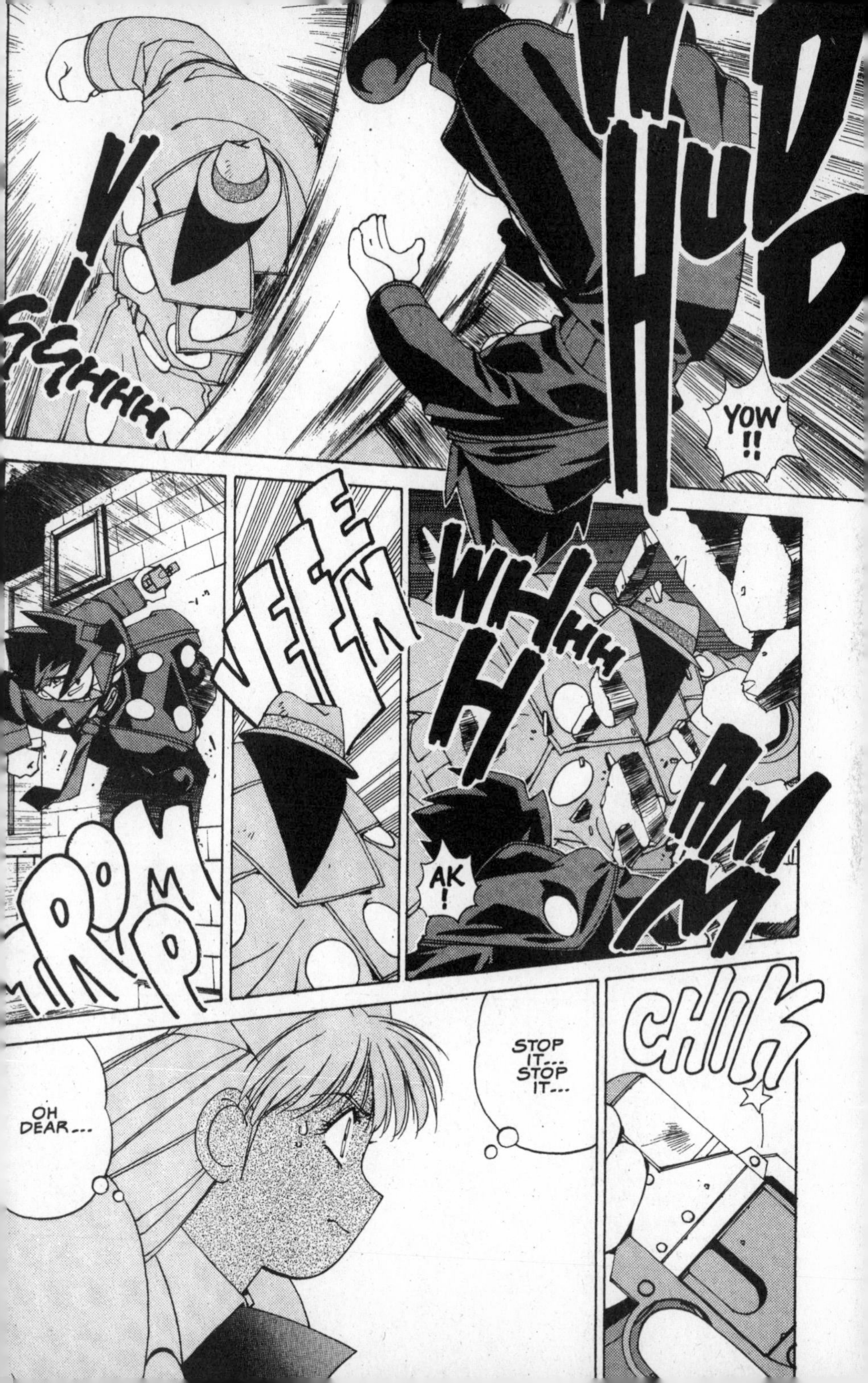
YOW !!
AK !
OH DEAR...
STOP IT... STOP IT...
CHIK

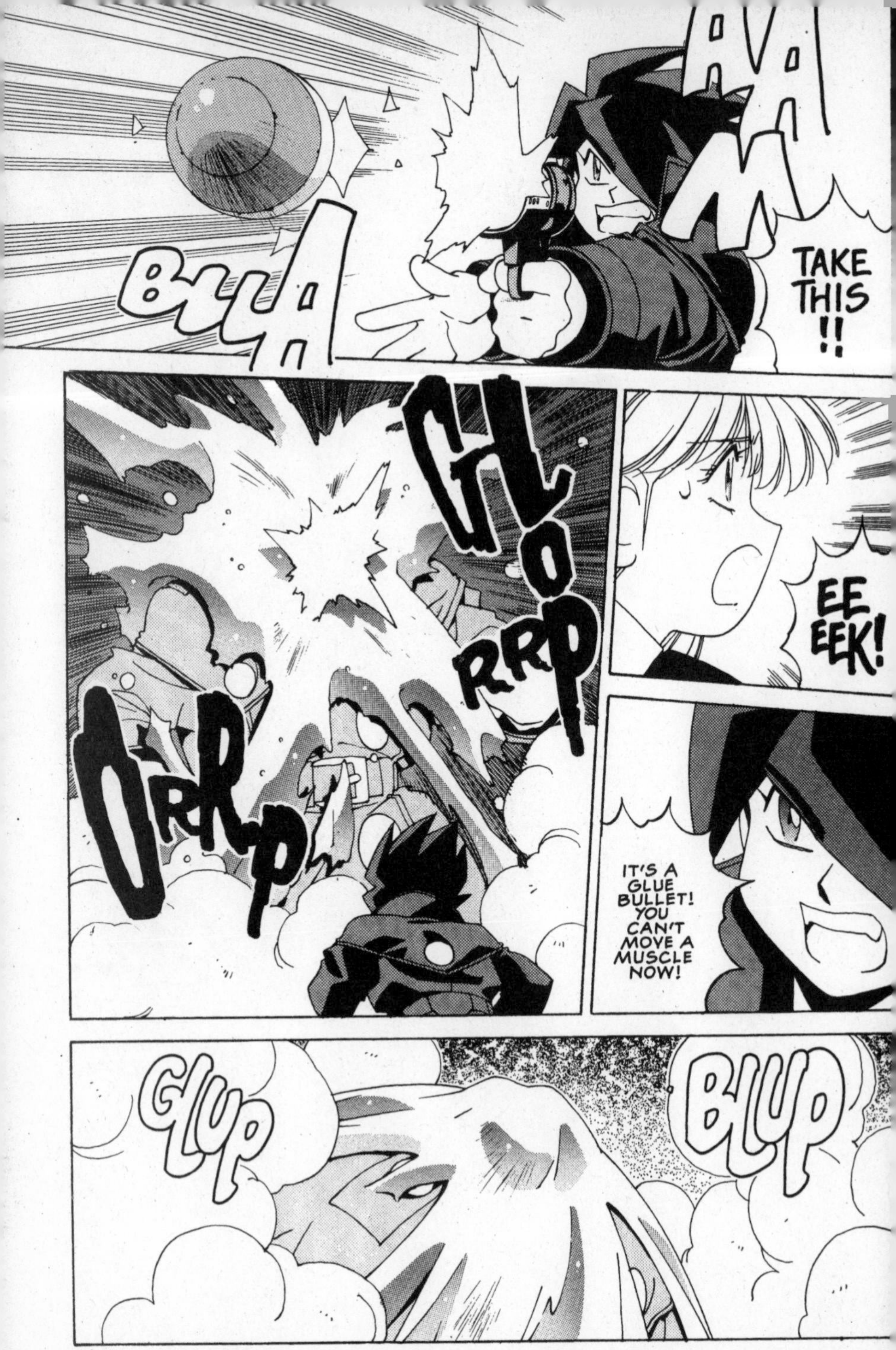
TAKE THIS !!
EE EEK!
IT'S A GLUE BULLET! YOU CAN'T MOVE A MUSCLE NOW!
GLUP
BLUP

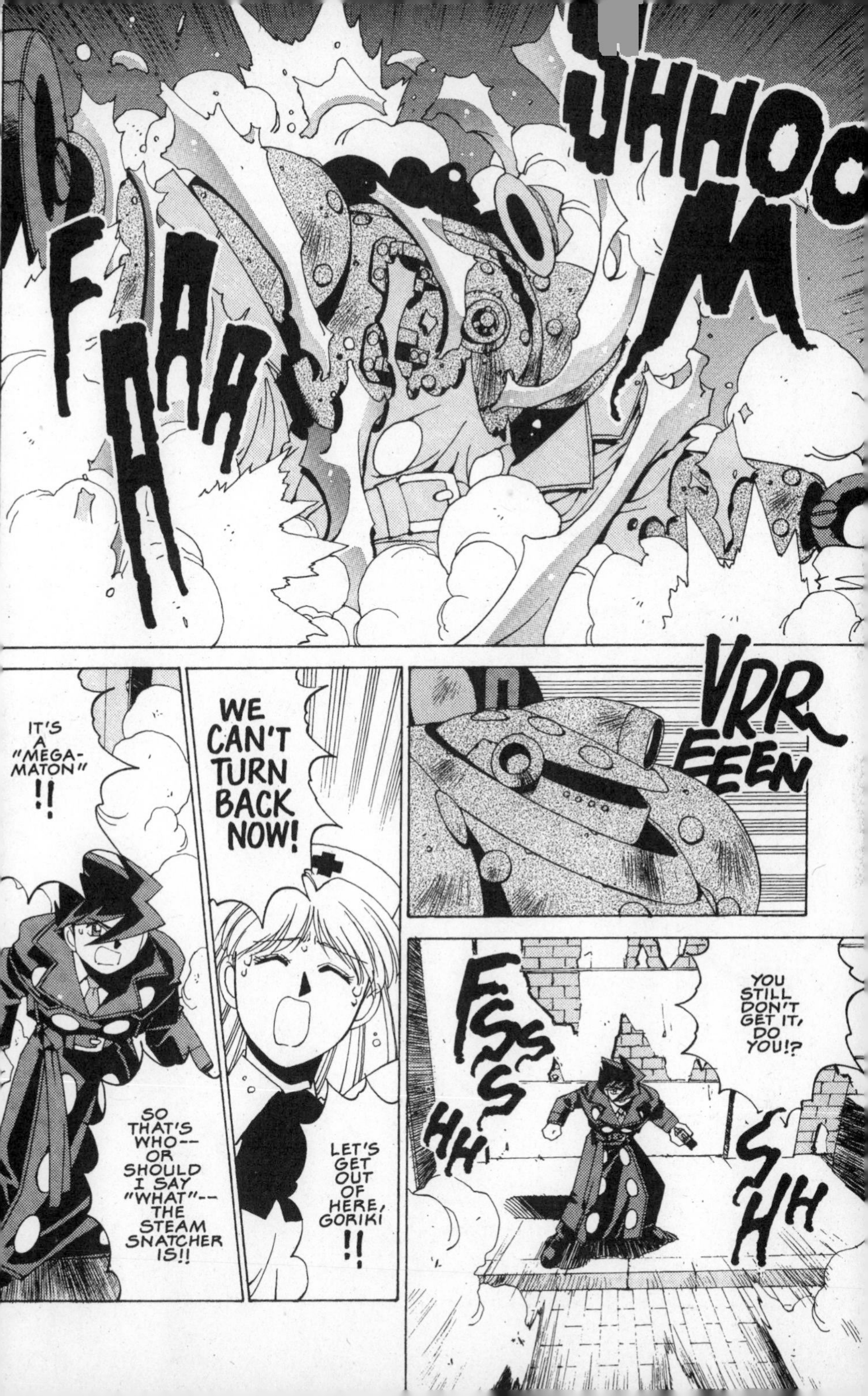
FAAAA
UHHOOM
IT'S A "MEGA-MATON"!!
SO THAT'S WHO-- OR SHOULD I SAY "WHAT"-- THE STEAM SNATCHER IS!!
WE CAN'T TURN BACK NOW!
LET'S GET OUT OF HERE, GORIKI!!
VRREEEN
FSSSHH
YOU STILL DON'T GET IT, DO YOU!?
SHHH

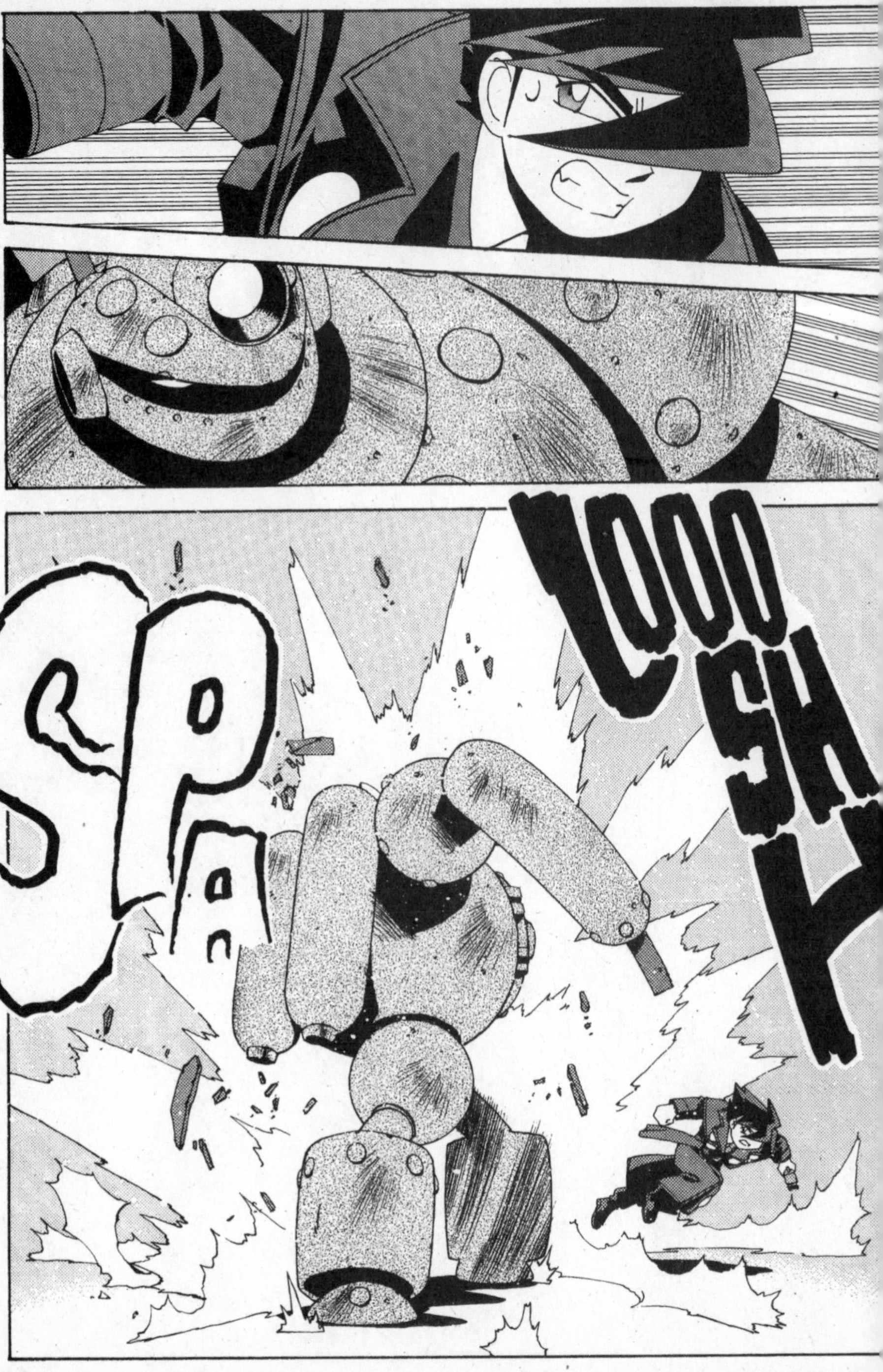
SPan

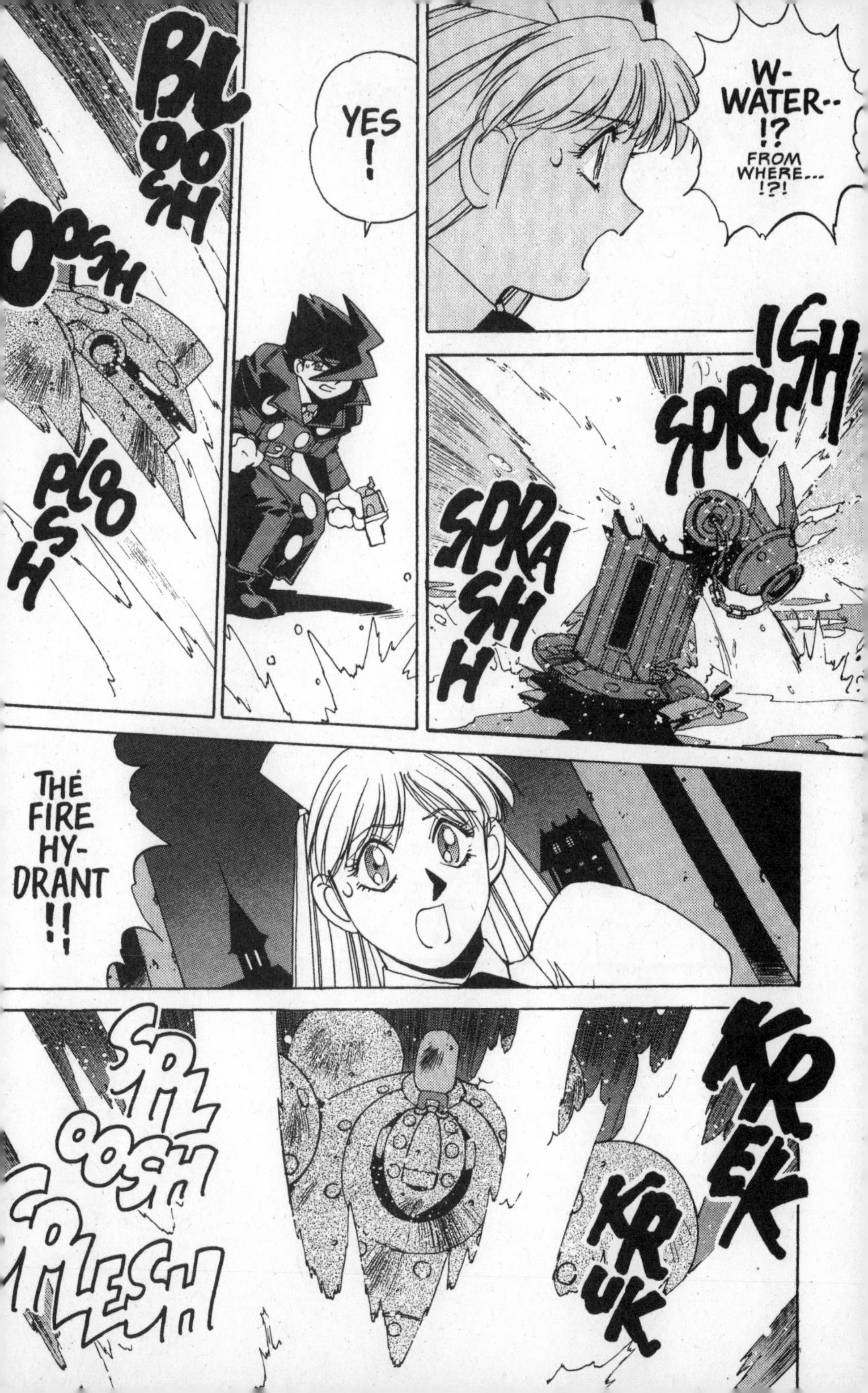
BLOOSH
OOSH
PLOOSH
YES!
W-WATER--!? FROM WHERE...!?!
SPRISH
SPRASHH
THE FIRE HY-DRANT!!
KREK
KRUK

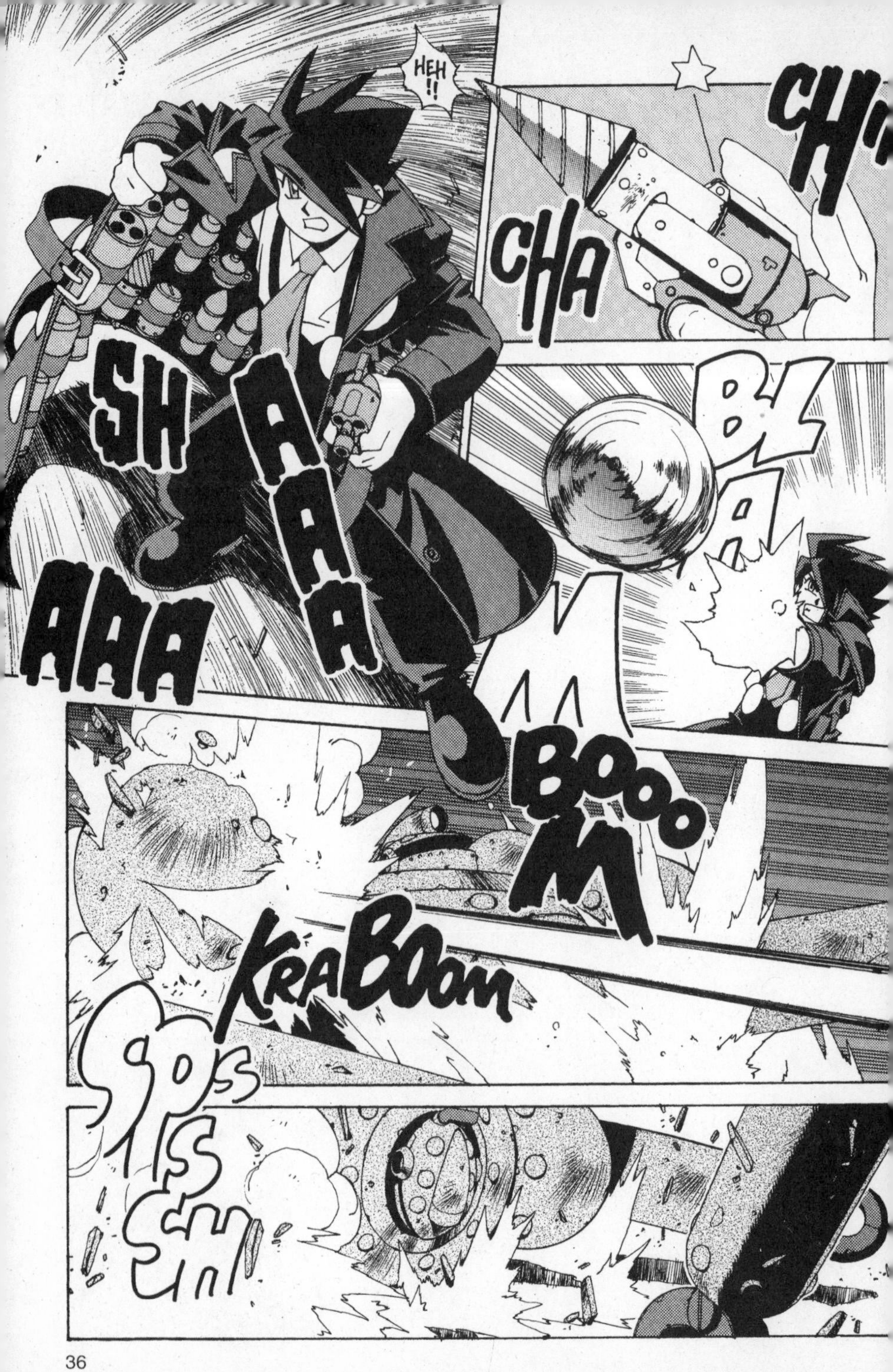
HEH!!
SHAAAAAAA
CHA
CH
BLAM
BOOOM
KRABOOM

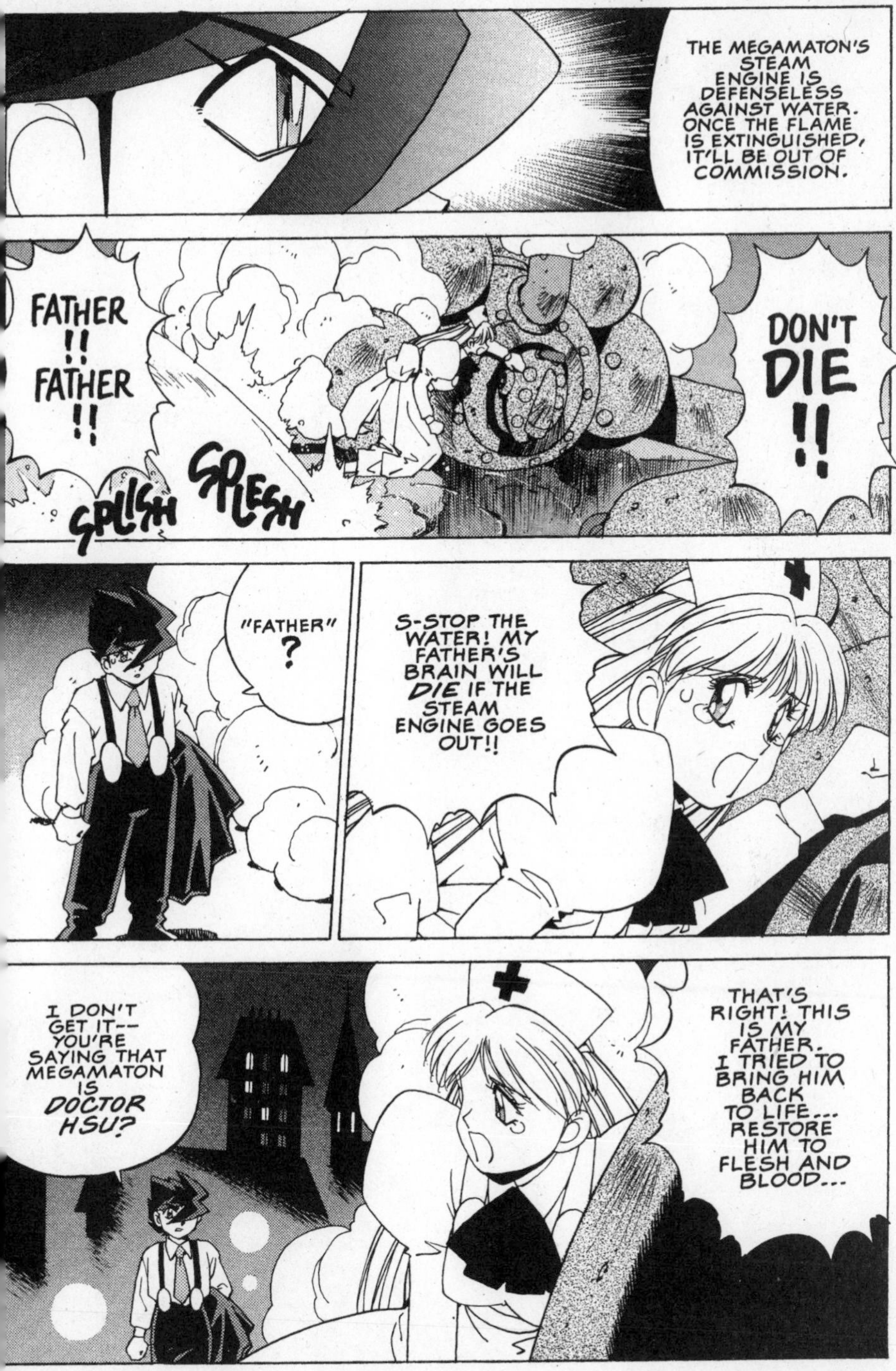
THE MEGAMATON'S STEAM ENGINE IS DEFENSELESS AGAINST WATER. ONCE THE FLAME IS EXTINGUISHED, IT'LL BE OUT OF COMMISSION.
FATHER !! FATHER !!
SPLISH
SPLESH
DON'T DIE !!
"FATHER"?
S-STOP THE WATER! MY FATHER'S BRAIN WILL *DIE* IF THE STEAM ENGINE GOES OUT!!
I DON'T GET IT-- YOU'RE SAYING THAT MEGAMATON IS *DOCTOR HSU?*
THAT'S RIGHT! THIS IS MY FATHER. I TRIED TO BRING HIM BACK TO LIFE... RESTORE HIM TO FLESH AND BLOOD...

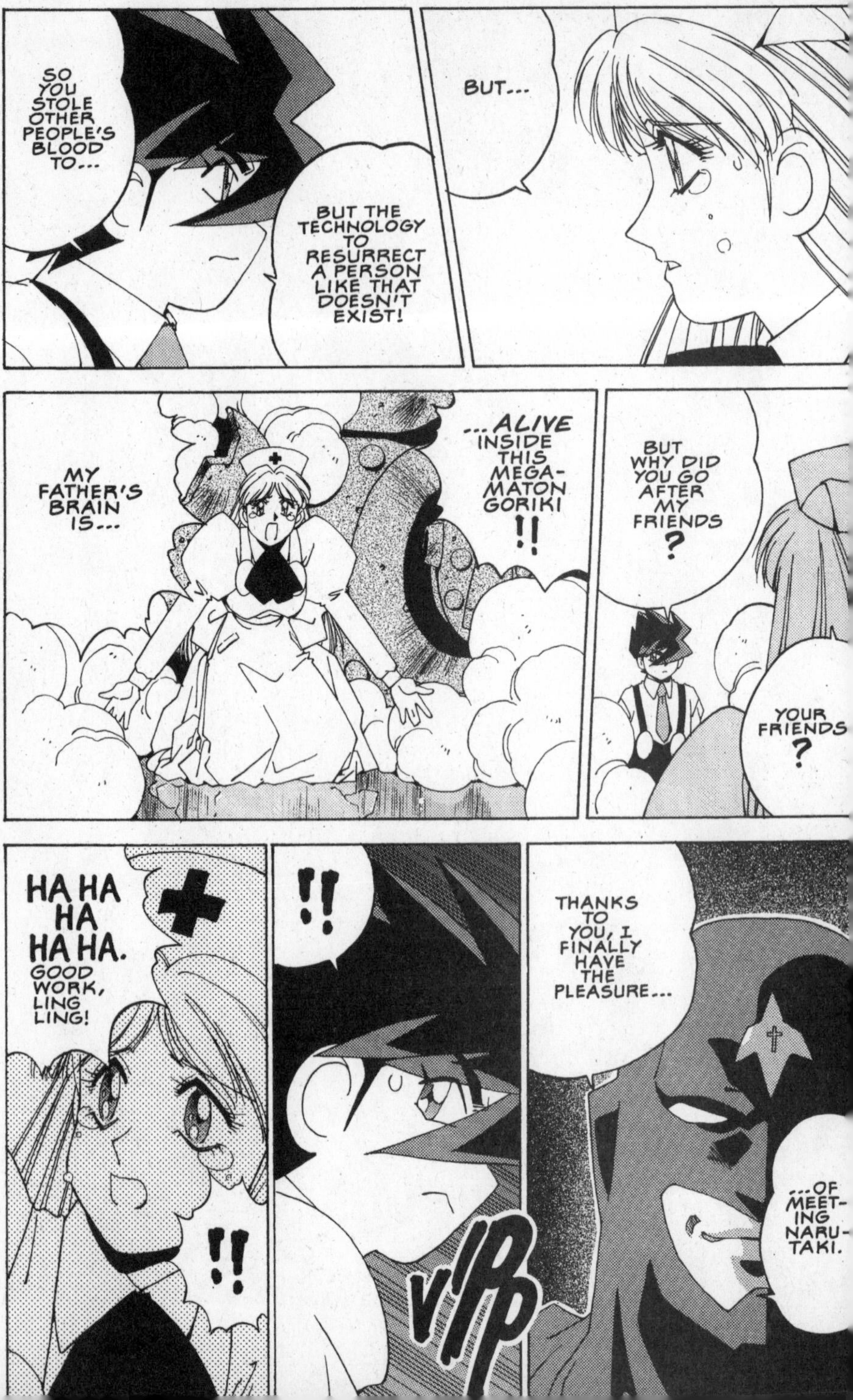
SO YOU STOLE OTHER PEOPLE'S BLOOD TO...
BUT THE TECHNOLOGY TO RESURRECT A PERSON LIKE THAT DOESN'T EXIST!
BUT...
MY FATHER'S BRAIN IS...
...ALIVE INSIDE THIS MEGA-MATON GORIKI!!
BUT WHY DID YOU GO AFTER MY FRIENDS?
YOUR FRIENDS?
HA HA HA HA HA HA. GOOD WORK, LING LING!
!!
!!
THANKS TO YOU, I FINALLY HAVE THE PLEASURE...
...OF MEETING NARUTAKI.
VIP

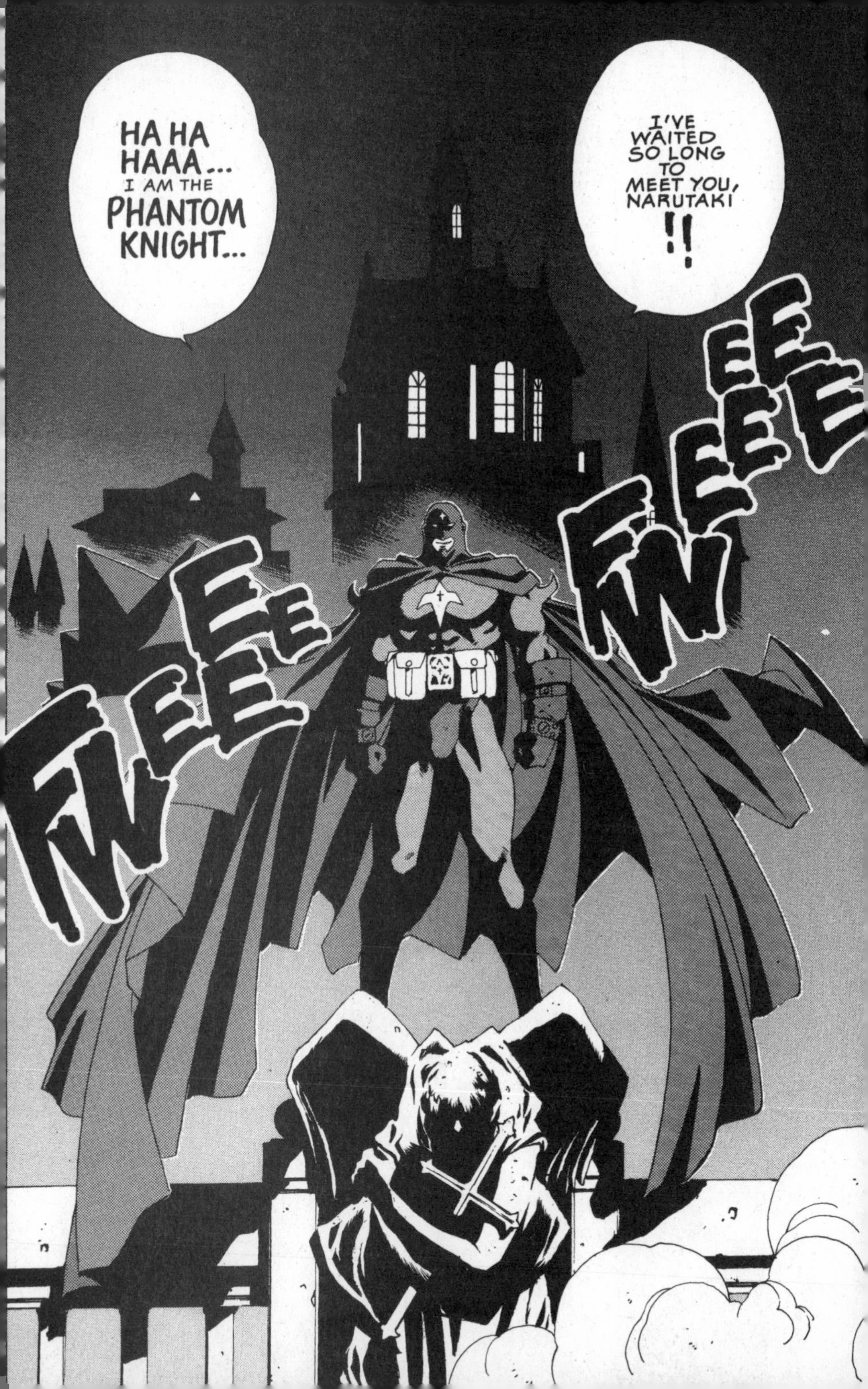
I'VE WAITED SO LONG TO MEET YOU, NARUTAKI !!
HA HA HAAA... I AM THE PHANTOM KNIGHT...
FWEEEE
FWEEEEEE

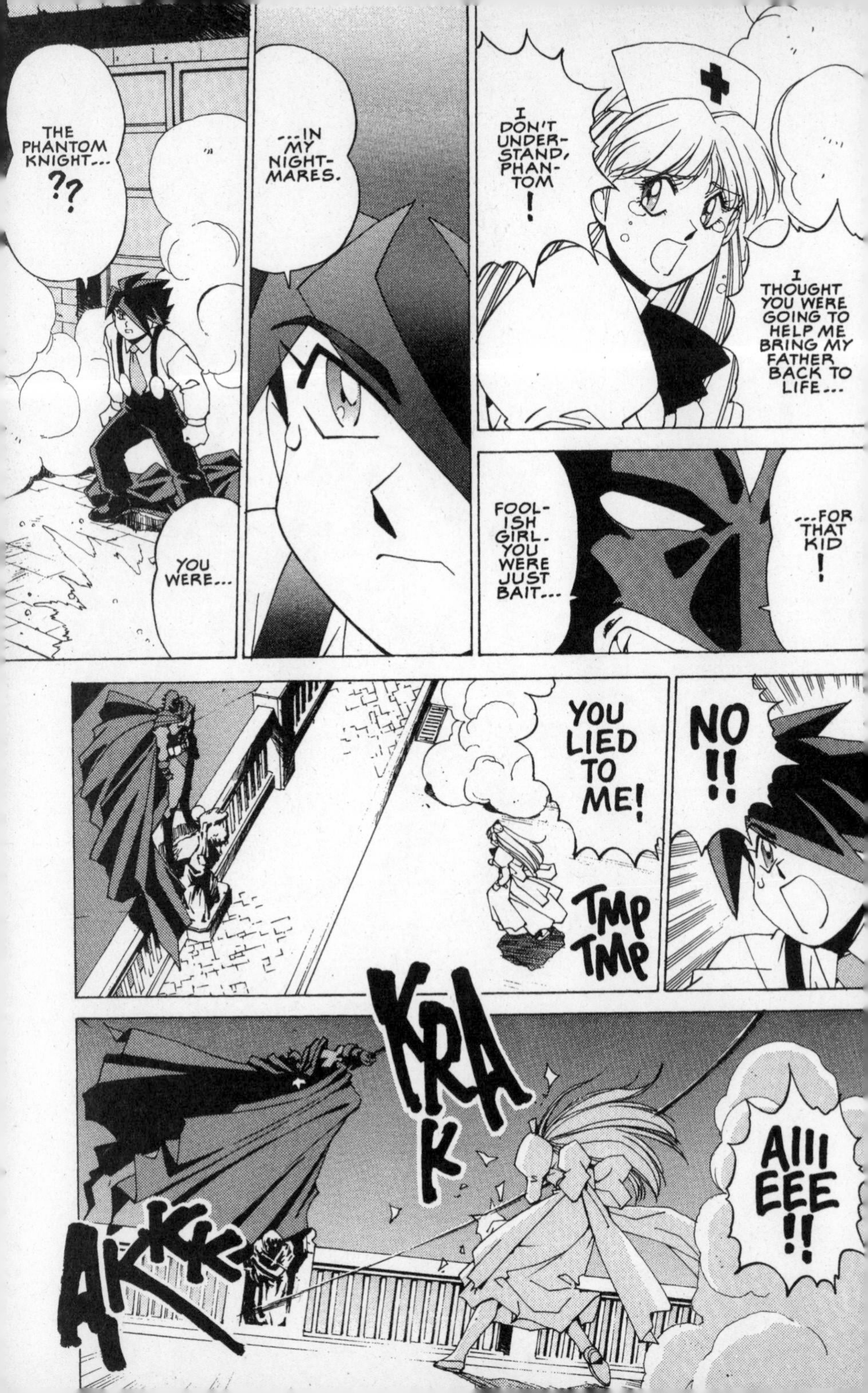
THE PHANTOM KNIGHT...
??
YOU WERE...
...IN MY NIGHT-MARES.
I DON'T UNDER-STAND, PHAN-TOM!
I THOUGHT YOU WERE GOING TO HELP ME BRING MY FATHER BACK TO LIFE...
FOOL-ISH GIRL. YOU WERE JUST BAIT...
...FOR THAT KID!
YOU LIED TO ME!
TMP TMP
NO!!
KRAK
AIII EEE!!
AKKK

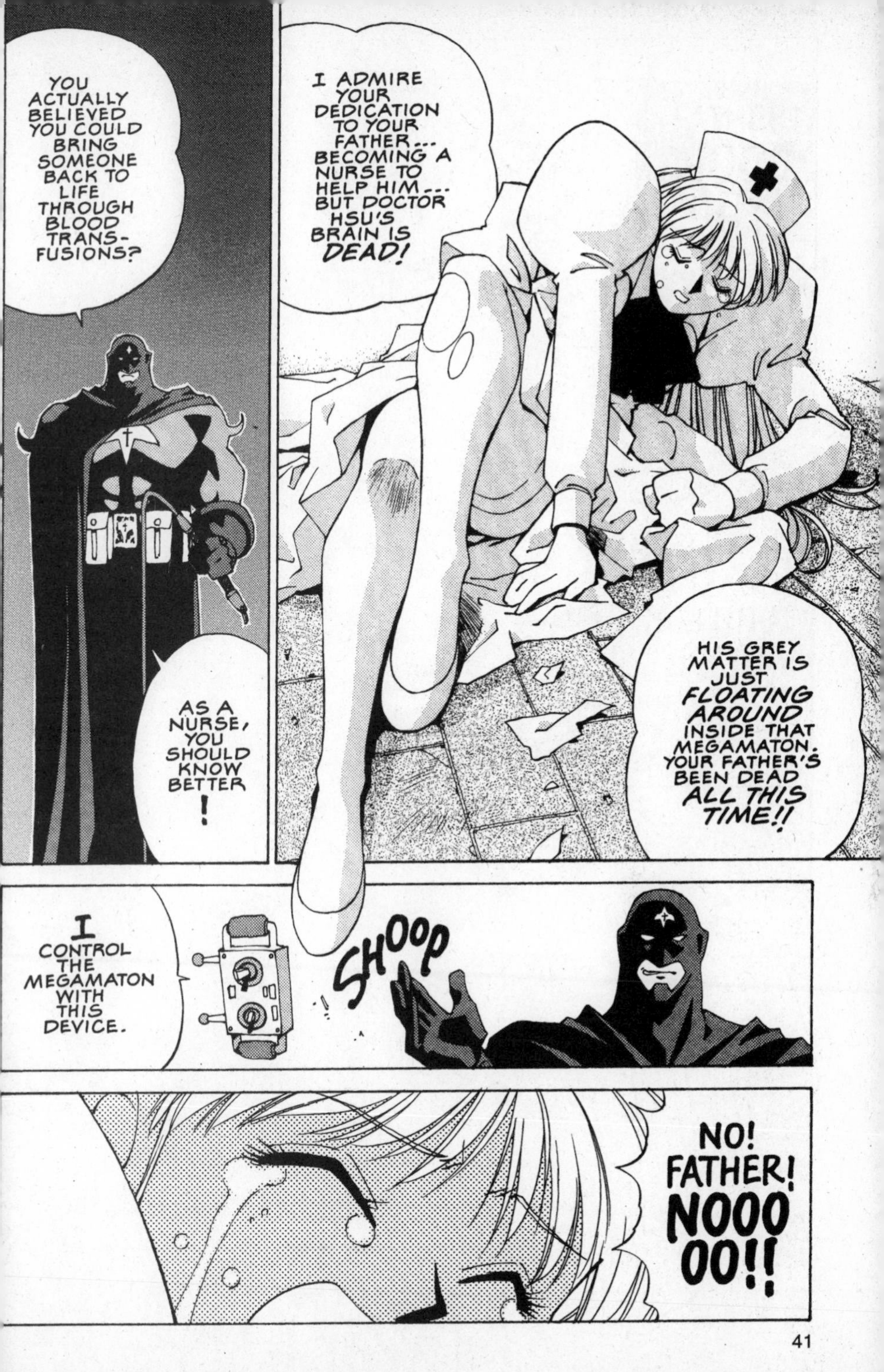
YOU ACTUALLY BELIEVED YOU COULD BRING SOMEONE BACK TO LIFE THROUGH BLOOD TRANS-FUSIONS?
AS A NURSE, YOU SHOULD KNOW BETTER!
I ADMIRE YOUR DEDICATION TO YOUR FATHER... BECOMING A NURSE TO HELP HIM... BUT DOCTOR HSU'S BRAIN IS DEAD!
HIS GREY MATTER IS JUST FLOATING AROUND INSIDE THAT MEGAMATON. YOUR FATHER'S BEEN DEAD ALL THIS TIME!!
I CONTROL THE MEGAMATON WITH THIS DEVICE.
SHOOP
NO! FATHER! NOOOOO!!

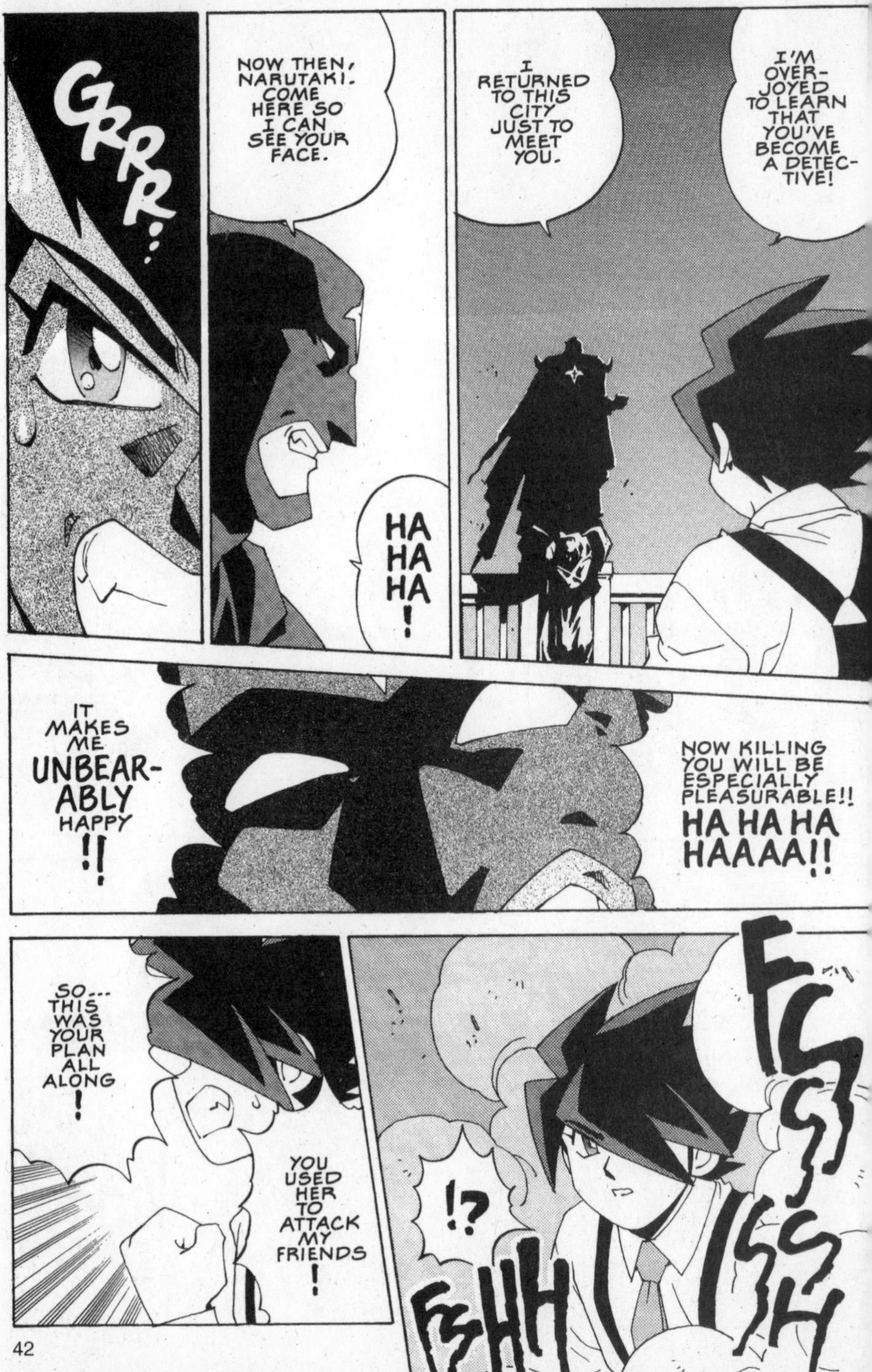
GRRR...
NOW THEN, NARUTAKI. COME HERE SO I CAN SEE YOUR FACE.
HA HA HA!
I RETURNED TO THIS CITY JUST TO MEET YOU.
I'M OVERJOYED TO LEARN THAT YOU'VE BECOME A DETECTIVE!
IT MAKES ME UNBEARABLY HAPPY!!
NOW KILLING YOU WILL BE ESPECIALLY PLEASURABLE!! HA HA HA HAAAA!!
SO... THIS WAS YOUR PLAN ALL ALONG!
YOU USED HER TO ATTACK MY FRIENDS!
FSSSSH
!?
FSHH

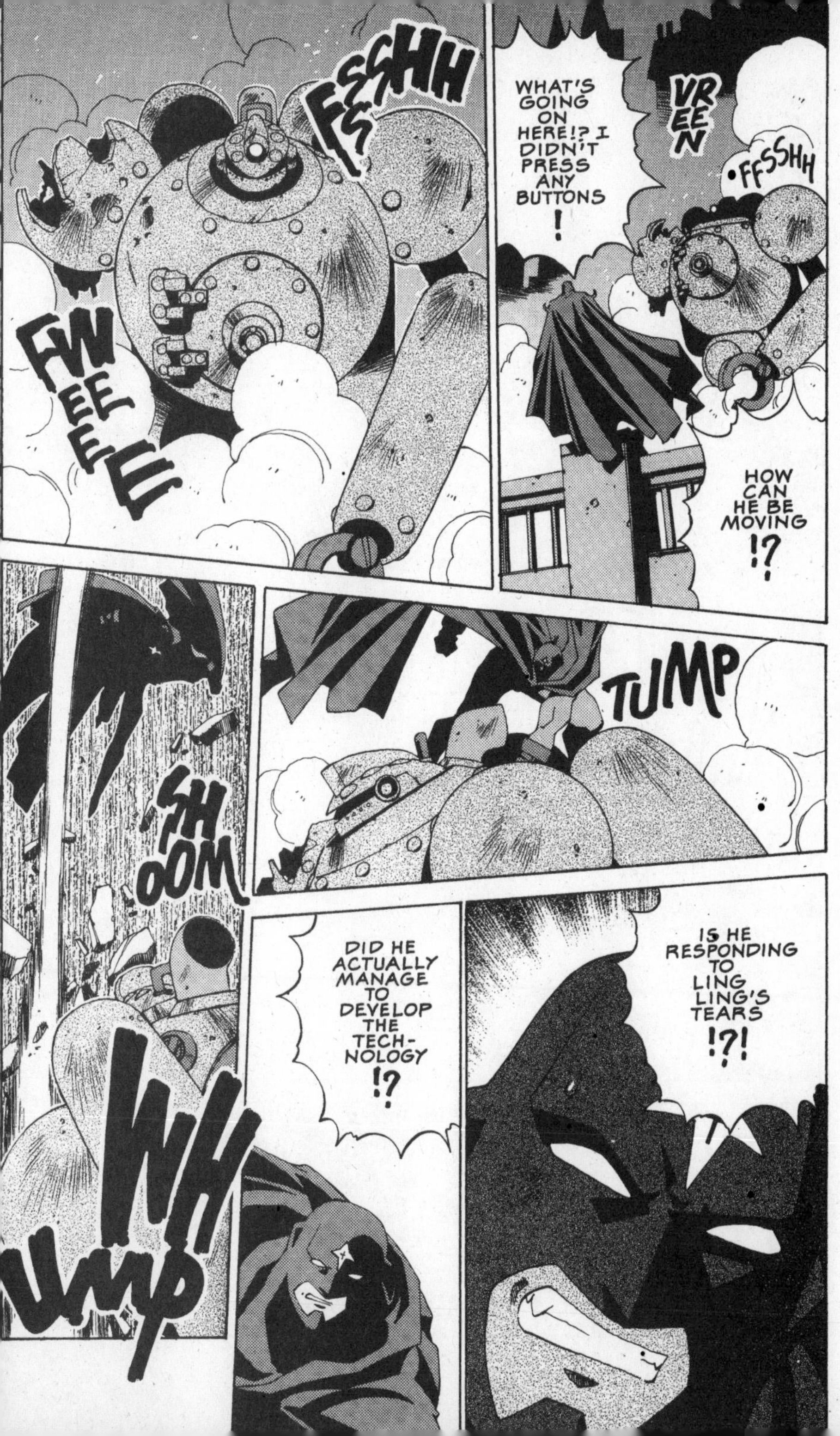
FSSHH
FWEEEE
WHAT'S GOING ON HERE!? I DIDN'T PRESS ANY BUTTONS!
VREEN
FFSSHH
HOW CAN HE BE MOVING!?
SHOOM
WHUMP
TUMP
DID HE ACTUALLY MANAGE TO DEVELOP THE TECH-NOLOGY!?
IS HE RESPONDING TO LING LING'S TEARS!?!

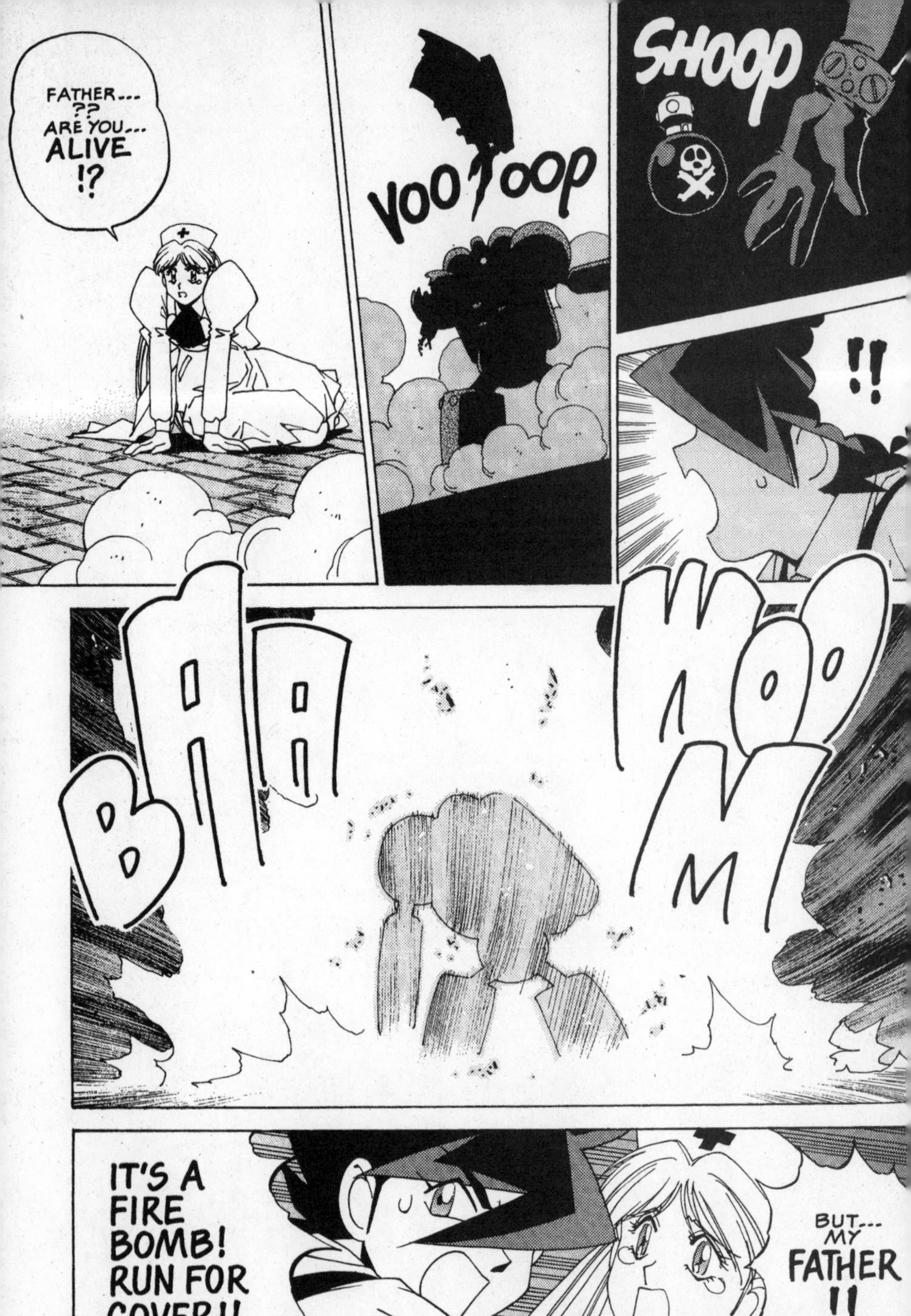
FATHER... ?? ARE YOU... ALIVE !?
VOOOOP
SHOOP
!!
BAAAA
WOOOM
IT'S A FIRE BOMB! RUN FOR COVER!!
BUT... MY FATHER !!

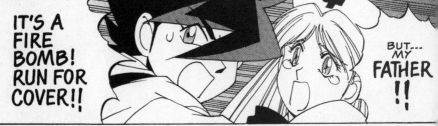

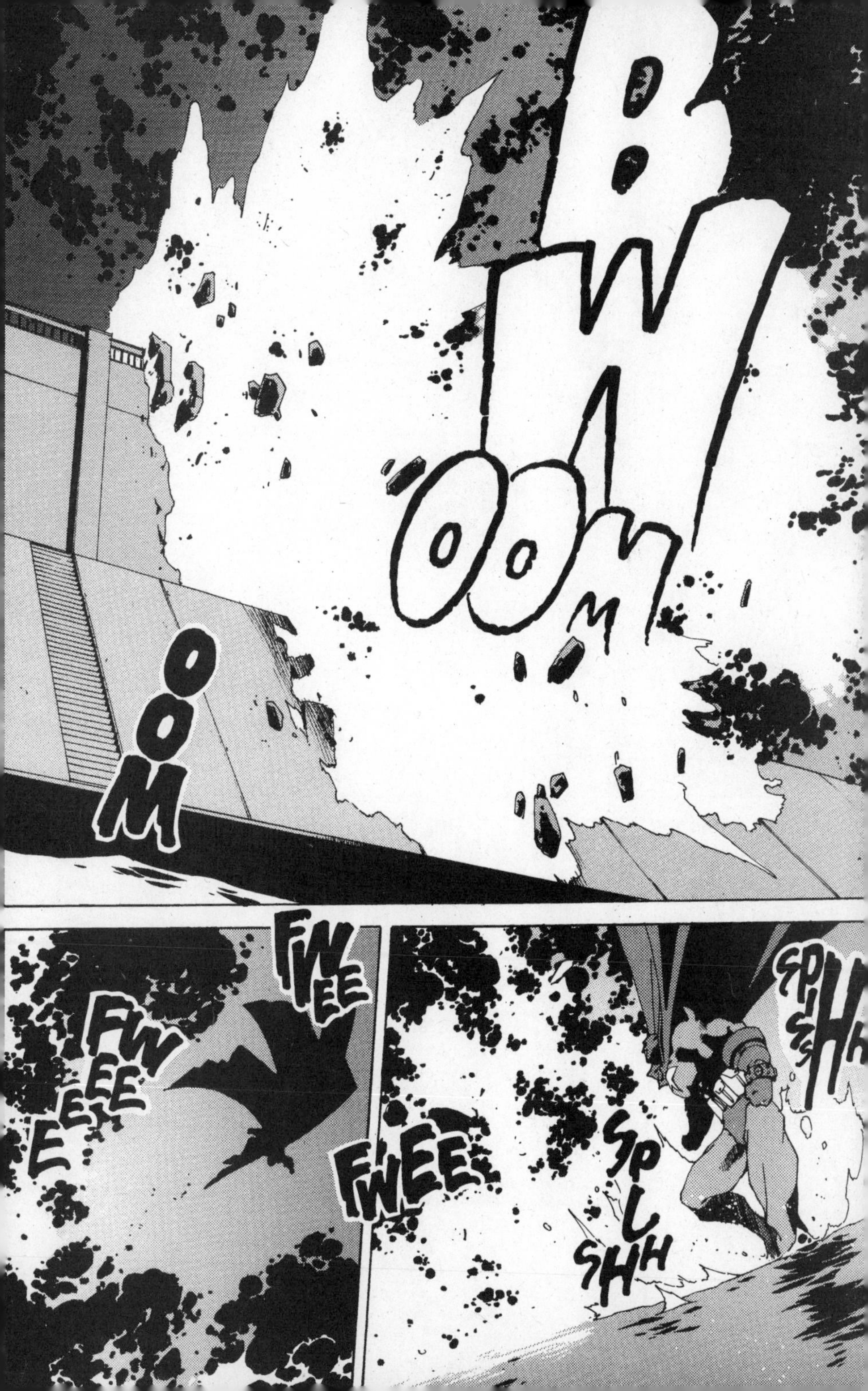
BWAOOM
OOM
FWEE
FWEEEEE
FWEE
SPLSHH
SPISSHH

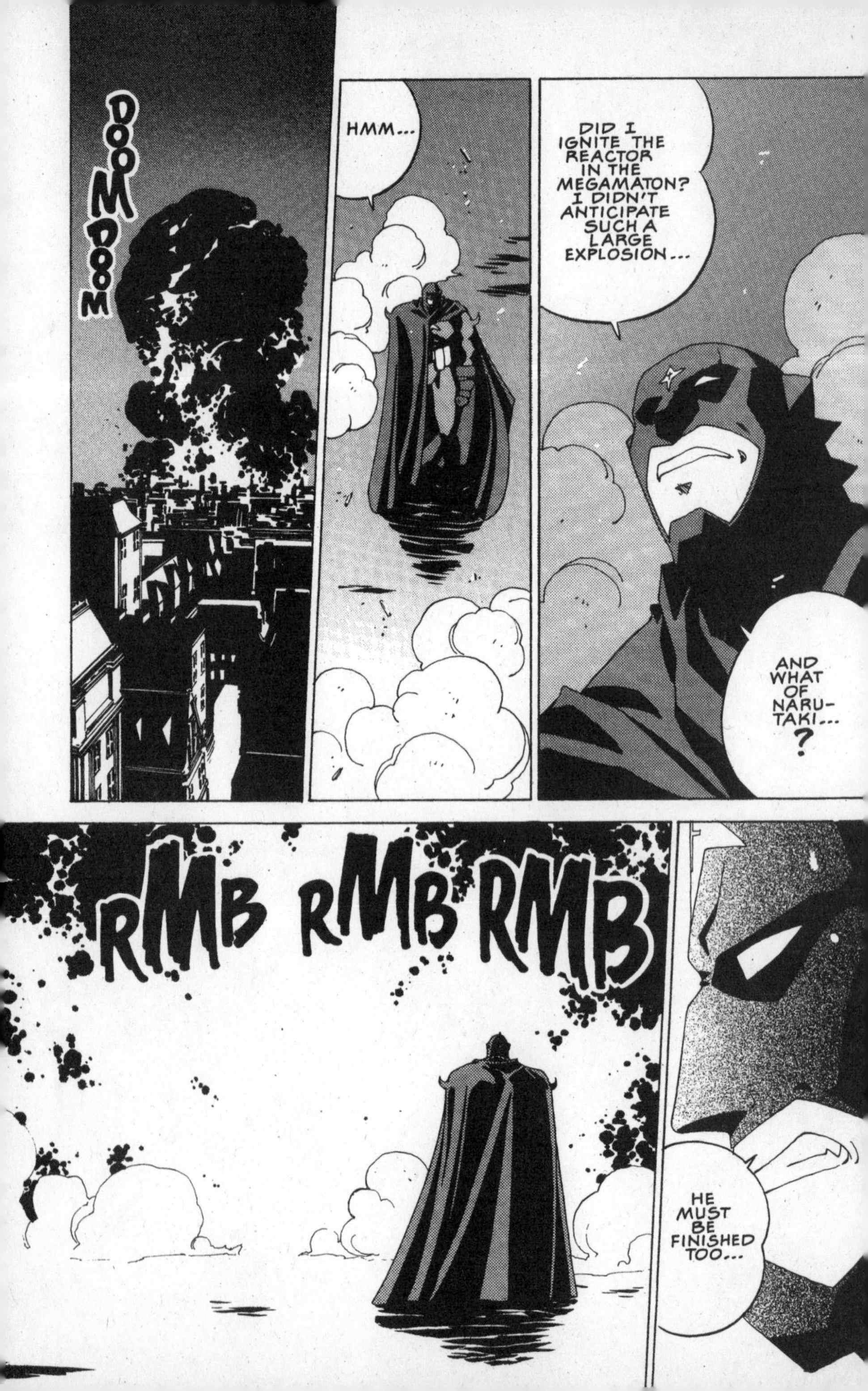
DOOM DOOM
HMM...
DID I IGNITE THE REACTOR IN THE MEGAMATON? I DIDN'T ANTICIPATE SUCH A LARGE EXPLOSION...
AND WHAT OF NARU-TAKI...?
RMB RMB RMB
HE MUST BE FINISHED TOO...

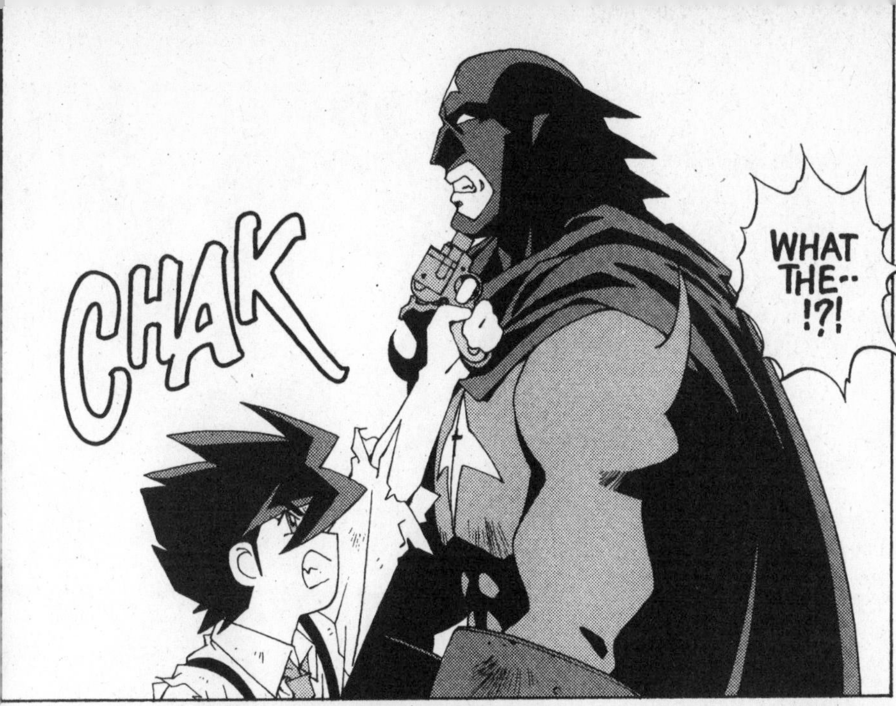
CHAK
WHAT THE-- !?!

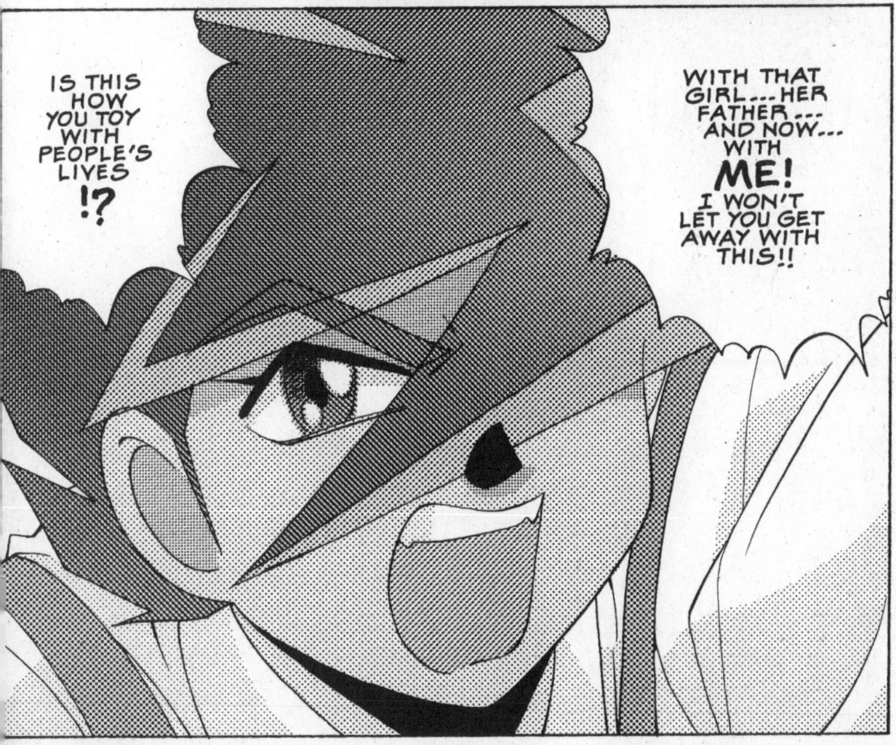
IS THIS HOW YOU TOY WITH PEOPLE'S LIVES !?
WITH THAT GIRL... HER FATHER... AND NOW... WITH ME! I WON'T LET YOU GET AWAY WITH THIS!!

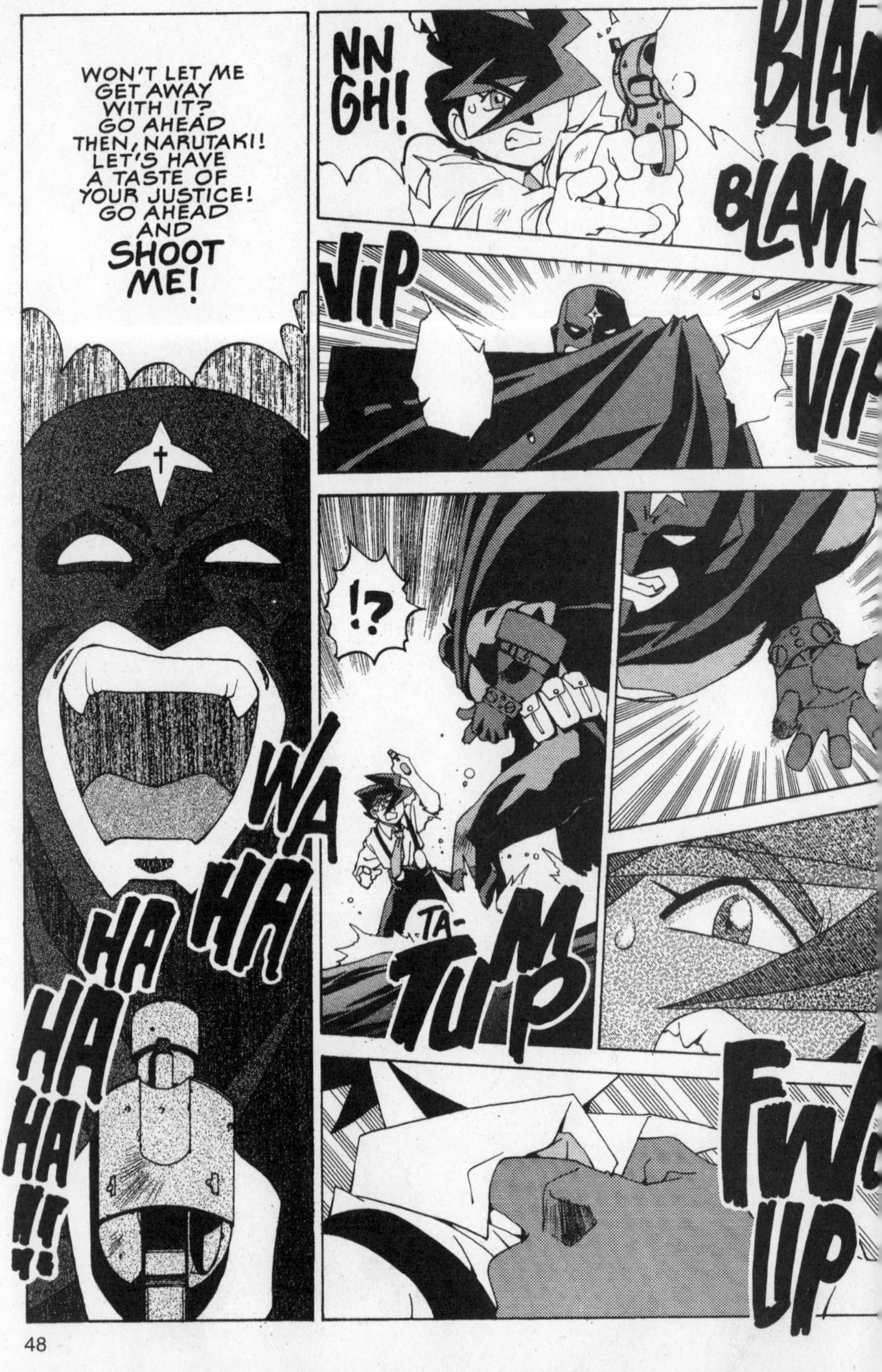
WON'T LET ME GET AWAY WITH IT? GO AHEAD THEN, NARUTAKI! LET'S HAVE A TASTE OF YOUR JUSTICE! GO AHEAD AND SHOOT ME!
WA HA HA HA HA HA!!
NNGH!
BLAM BLAM
VIP
VIP
!?
TA-TUMP
FWUP

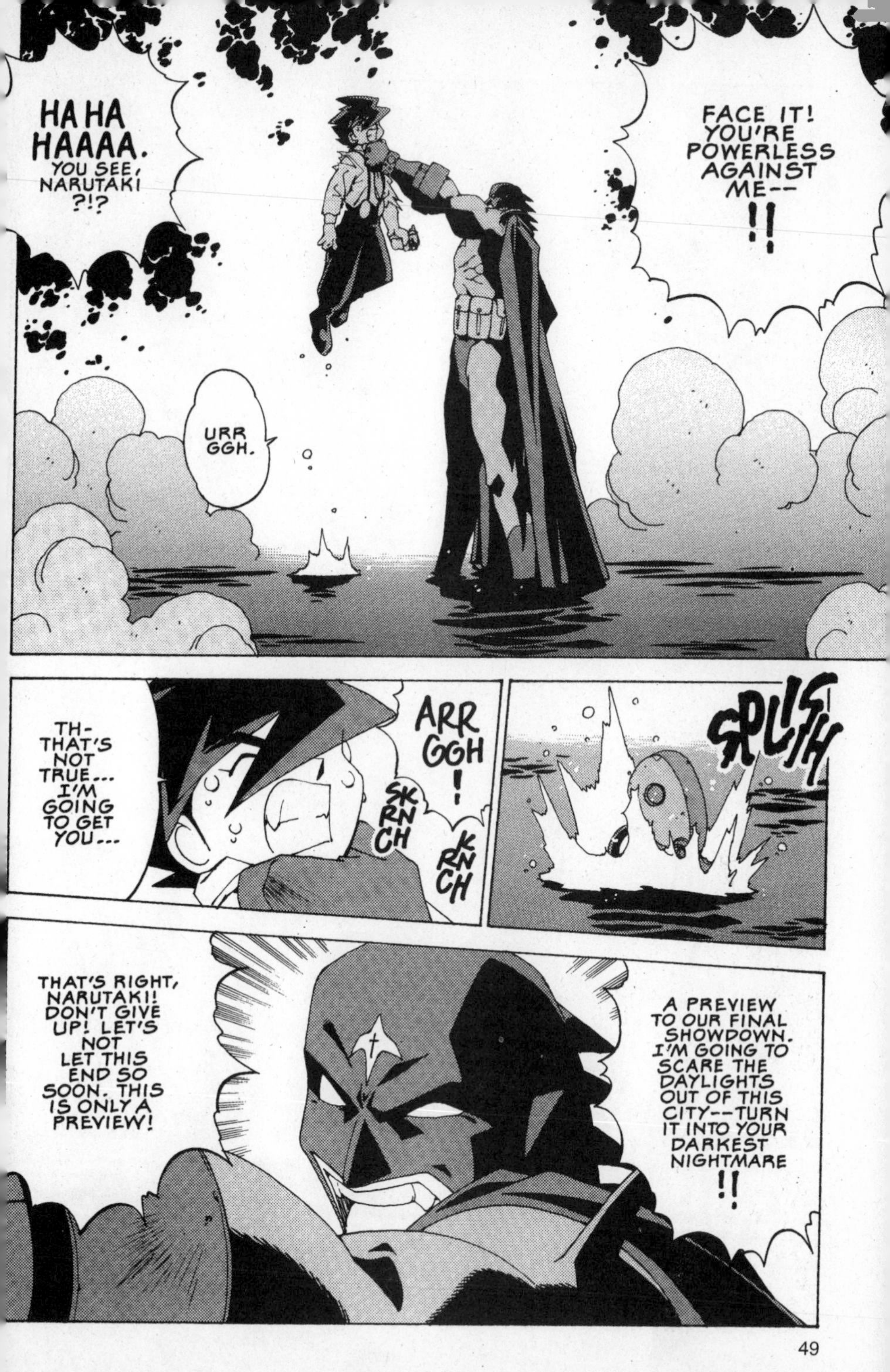
HA HA HAAAA. YOU SEE, NARUTAKI ?!?
FACE IT! YOU'RE POWERLESS AGAINST ME-- !!
URR GGH.
TH- THAT'S NOT TRUE... I'M GOING TO GET YOU...
ARR GGH !
SK RN CH
K RN CH
SPLISH
THAT'S RIGHT, NARUTAKI! DON'T GIVE UP! LET'S NOT LET THIS END SO SOON. THIS IS ONLY A PREVIEW!
A PREVIEW TO OUR FINAL SHOWDOWN. I'M GOING TO SCARE THE DAYLIGHTS OUT OF THIS CITY--TURN IT INTO YOUR DARKEST NIGHTMARE !!

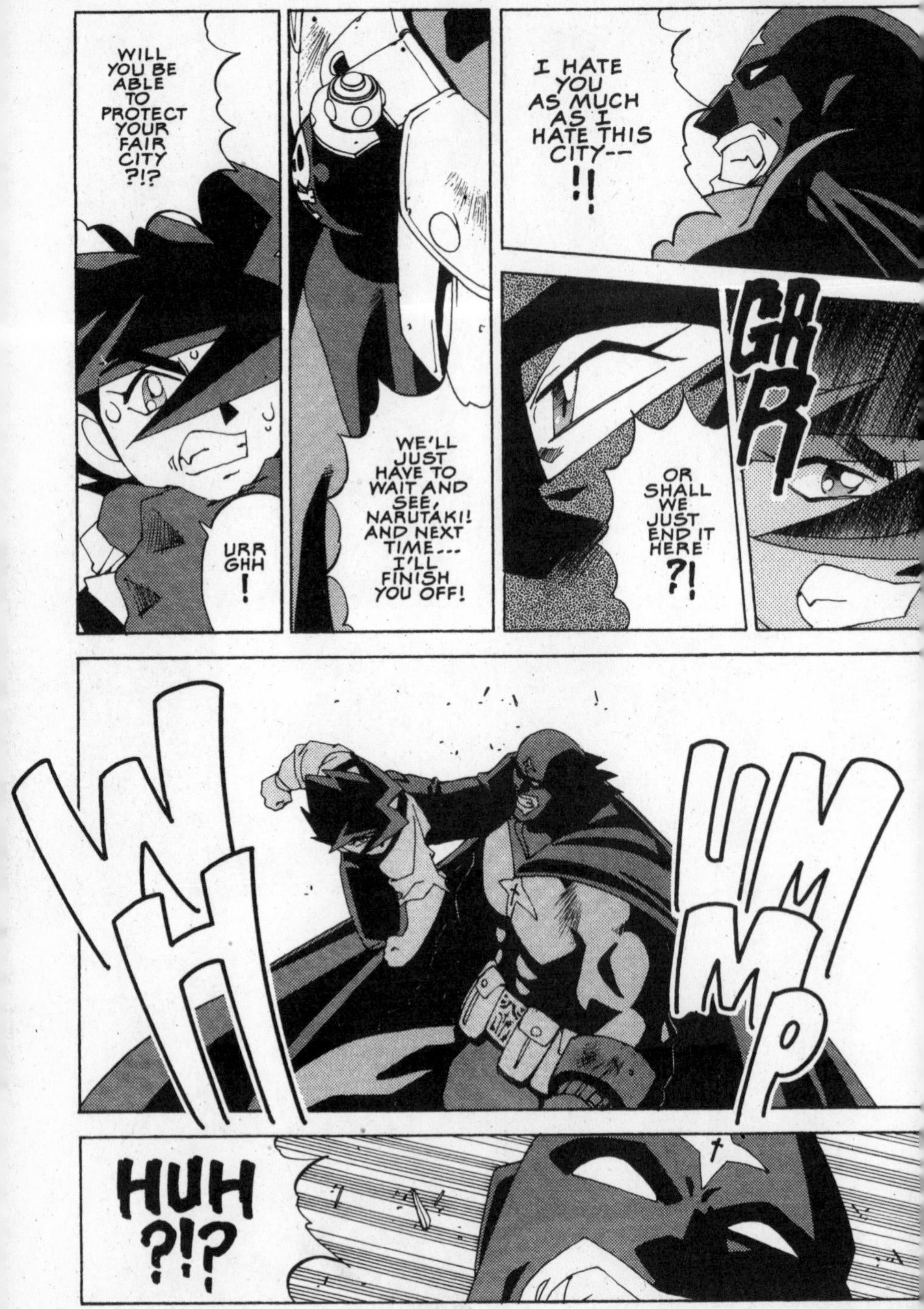
WILL YOU BE ABLE TO PROTECT YOUR FAIR CITY ?!?
URR GHH !
WE'LL JUST HAVE TO WAIT AND SEE, NARUTAKI! AND NEXT TIME--- I'LL FINISH YOU OFF!
I HATE YOU AS MUCH AS I HATE THIS CITY-- !!
OR SHALL WE JUST END IT HERE ?!
GRR
WHUMMMP
HUH ?!?

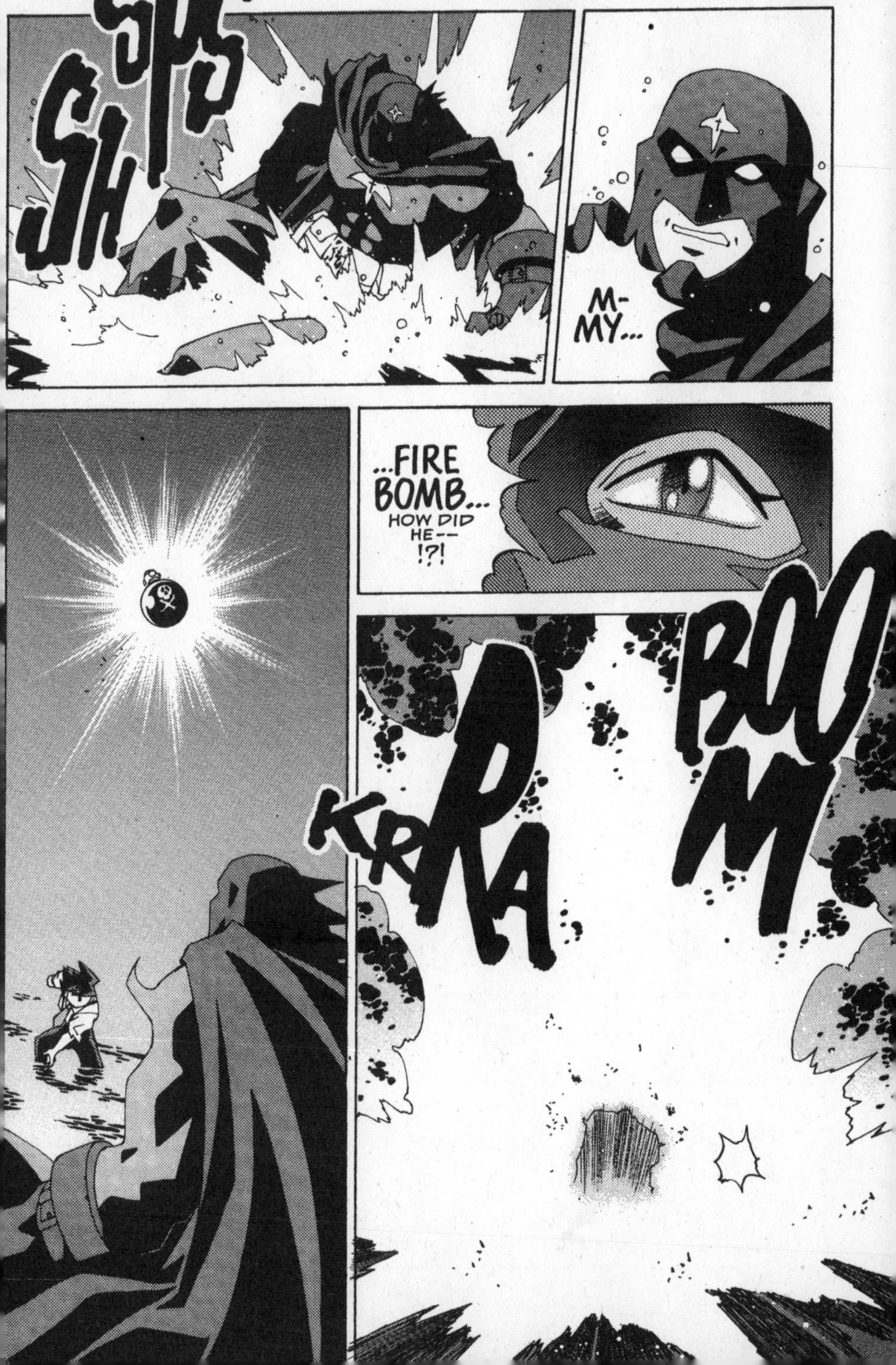
SHPS
M-MY...
...FIRE BOMB...
HOW DID HE--
!?!
KRRA
BOOM

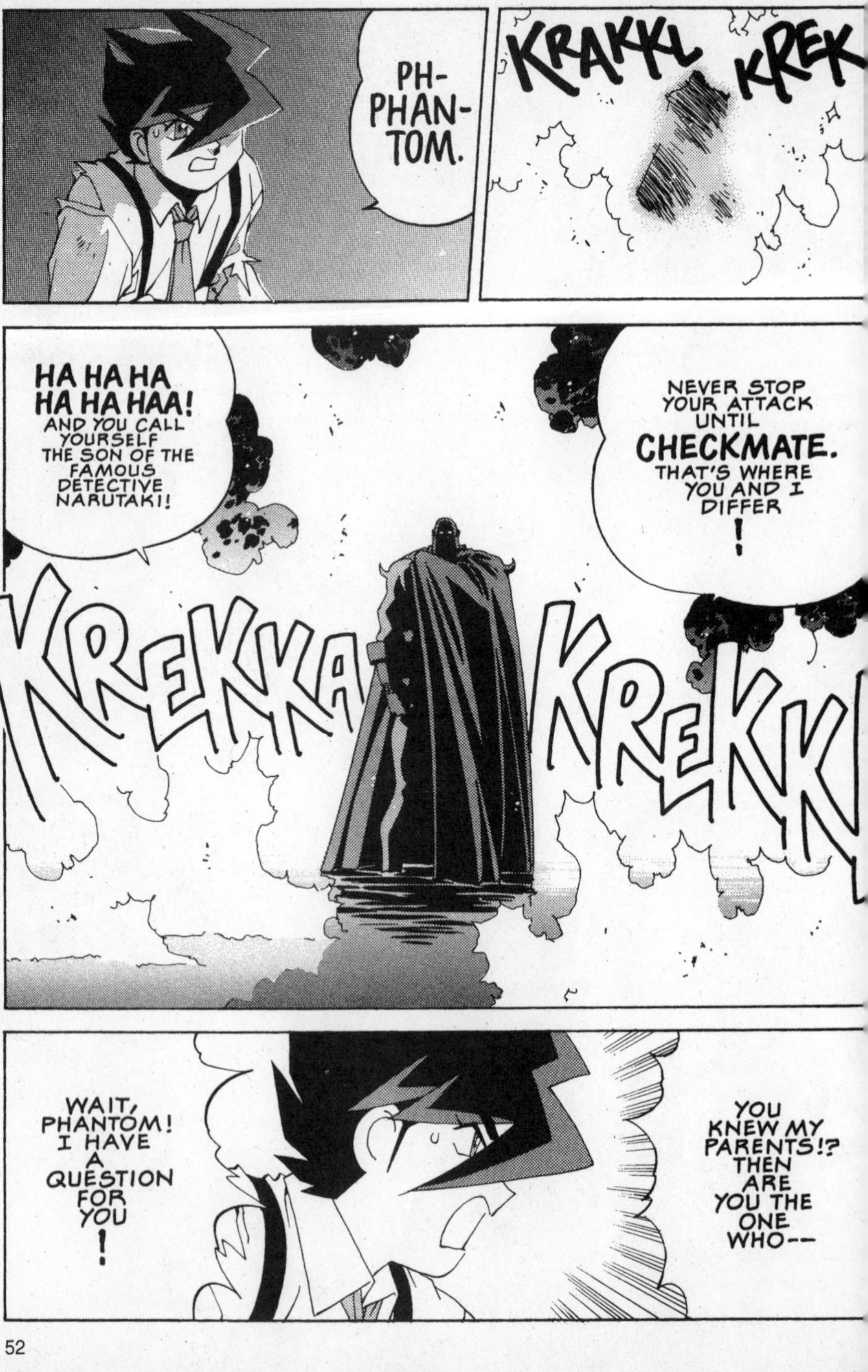
PH- PHAN- TOM.
KRAKKL KREK
HA HA HA HA HA HAA! AND YOU CALL YOURSELF THE SON OF THE FAMOUS DETECTIVE NARUTAKI!
NEVER STOP YOUR ATTACK UNTIL CHECKMATE. THAT'S WHERE YOU AND I DIFFER!
KREKKA KREKK
WAIT, PHANTOM! I HAVE A QUESTION FOR YOU!
YOU KNEW MY PARENTS!? THEN ARE YOU THE ONE WHO--

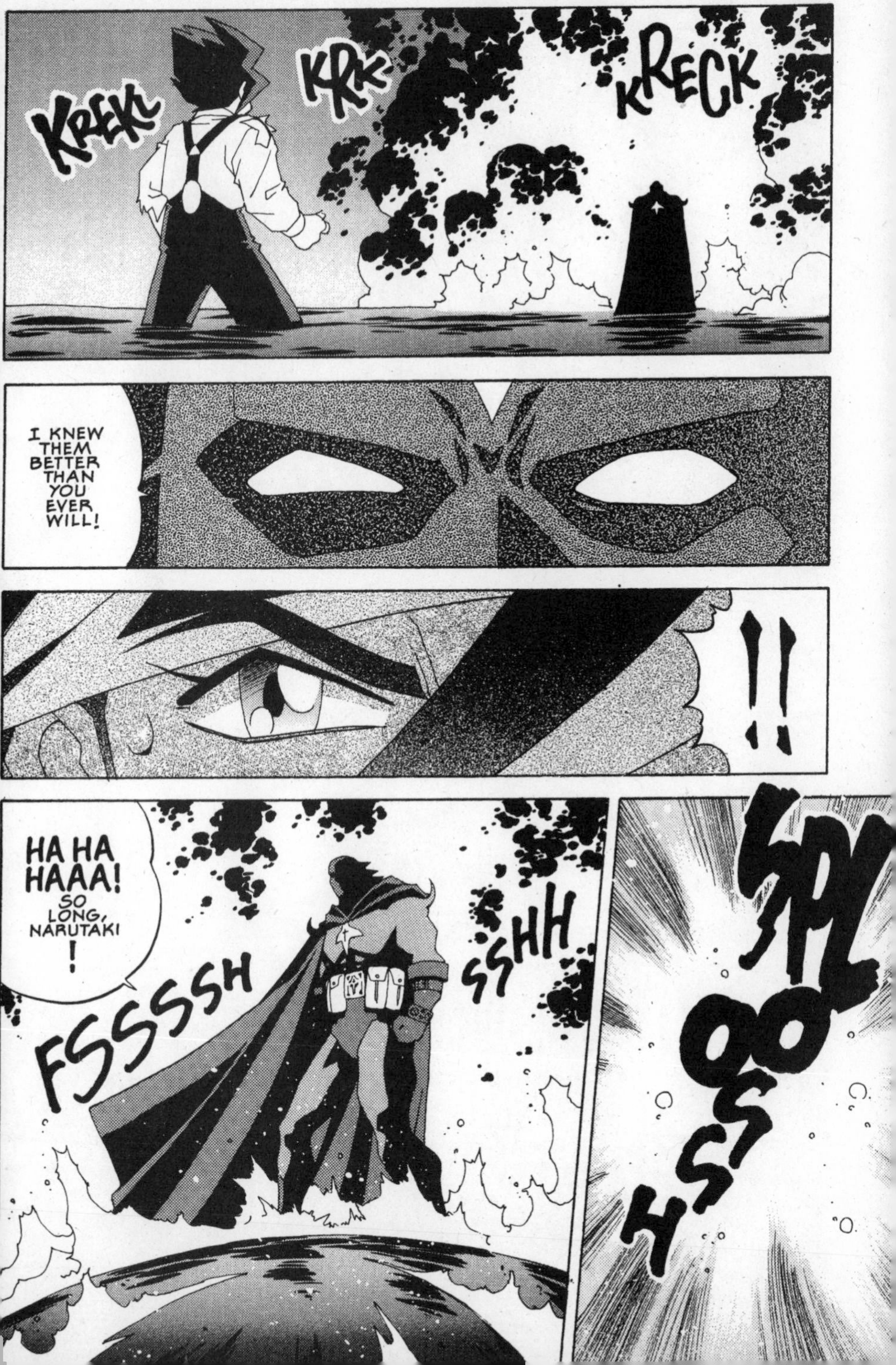
KREKL
KRK
KRECK
I KNEW THEM BETTER THAN YOU EVER WILL!
!!
HA HA HAAA! SO LONG, NARUTAKI !
FSSSSH
SSHH
SPLOOSSH

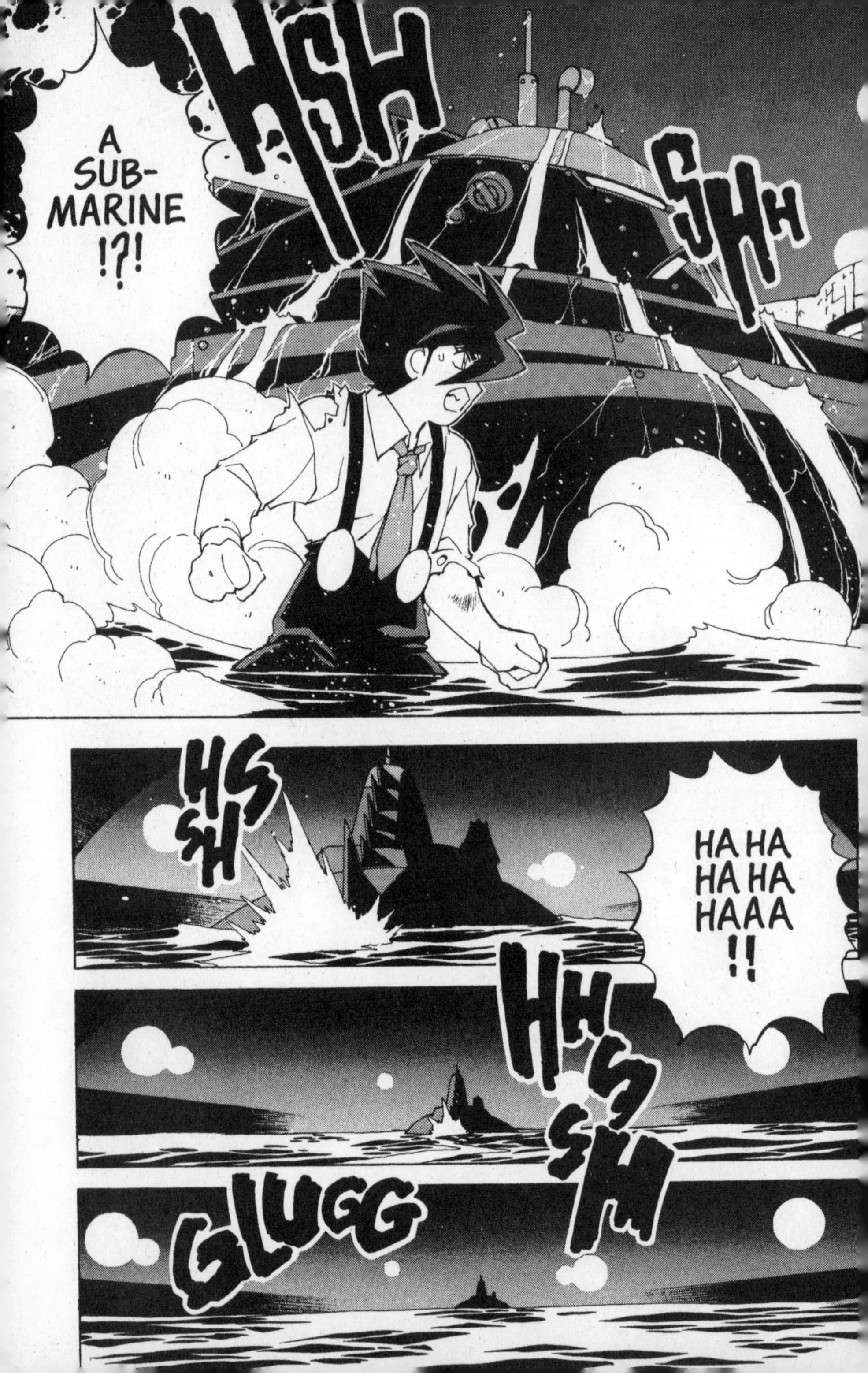

A SUB-MARINE !?!
HSH
SHH
HS SH
HA HA HA HA HAAA !!
HHS SH
GLUGG

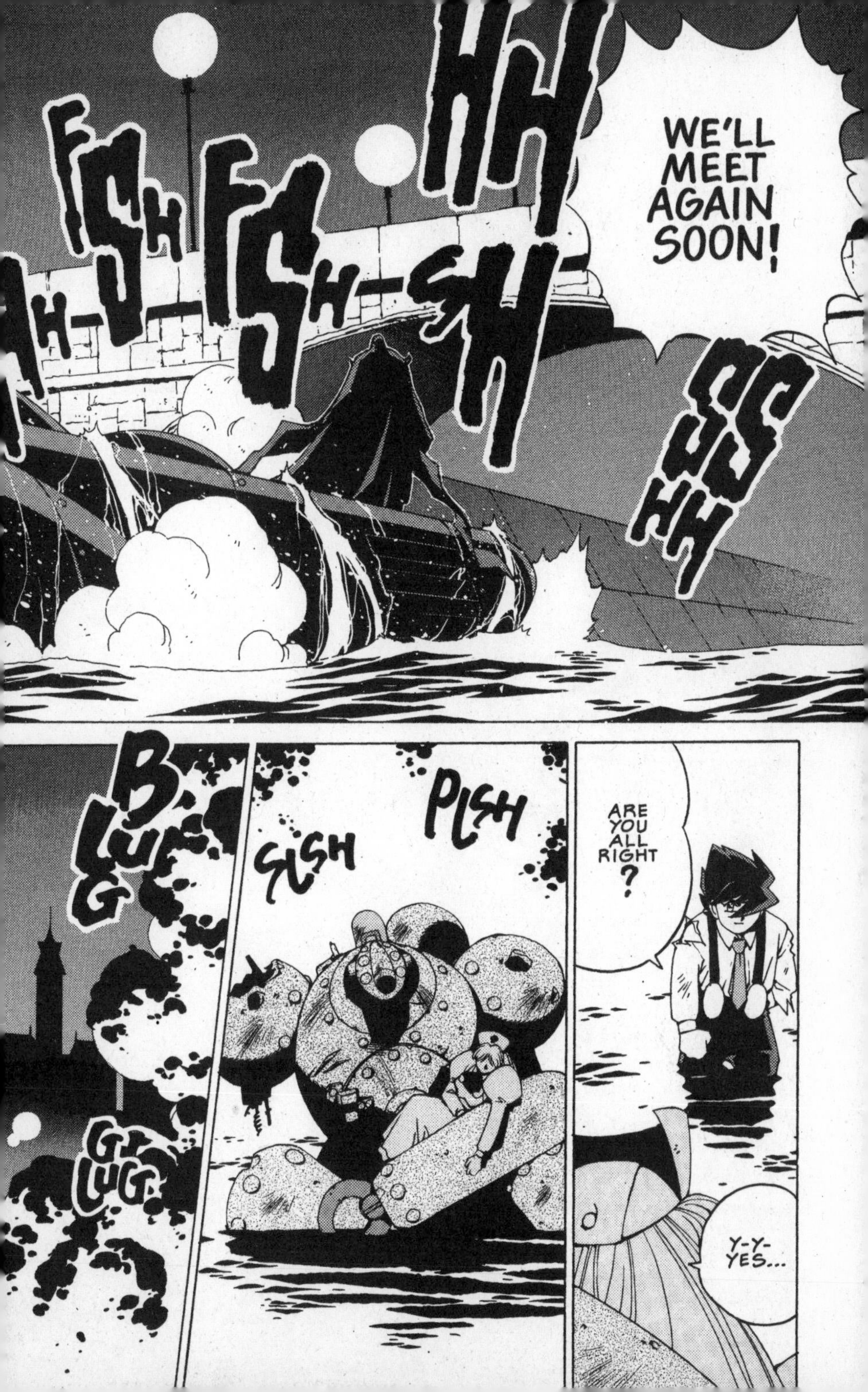
WE'LL MEET AGAIN SOON!
PLSH
ARE YOU ALL RIGHT?
Y-Y-YES...

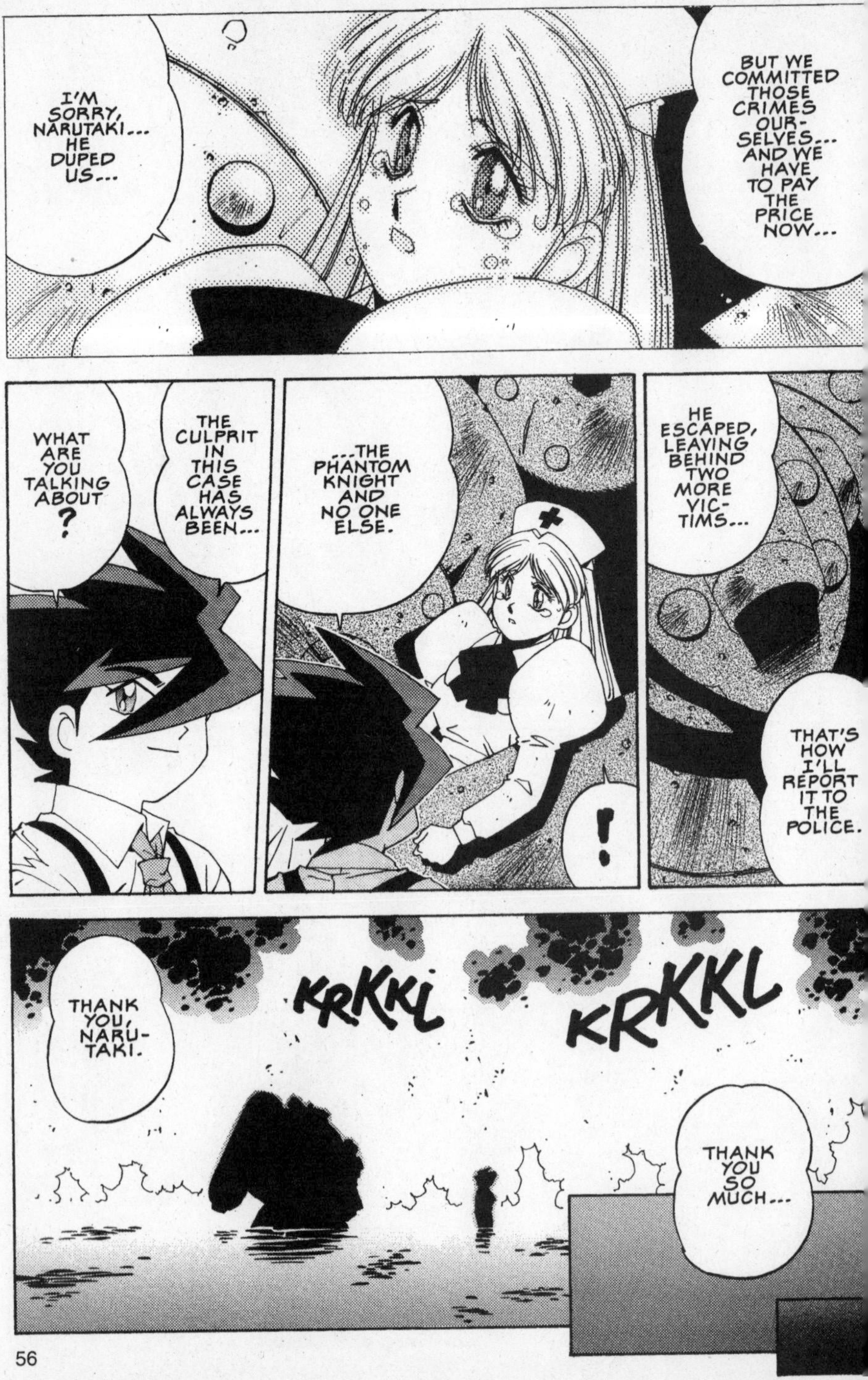
I'M SORRY, NARUTAKI... HE DUPED US...
BUT WE COMMITTED THOSE CRIMES OUR-SELVES... AND WE HAVE TO PAY THE PRICE NOW...
WHAT ARE YOU TALKING ABOUT?
THE CULPRIT IN THIS CASE HAS ALWAYS BEEN...
...THE PHANTOM KNIGHT AND NO ONE ELSE.
!
HE ESCAPED, LEAVING BEHIND TWO MORE VIC-TIMS...
THAT'S HOW I'LL REPORT IT TO THE POLICE.
THANK YOU, NARU-TAKI.
KRKKL
KRKKL
THANK YOU SO MUCH...

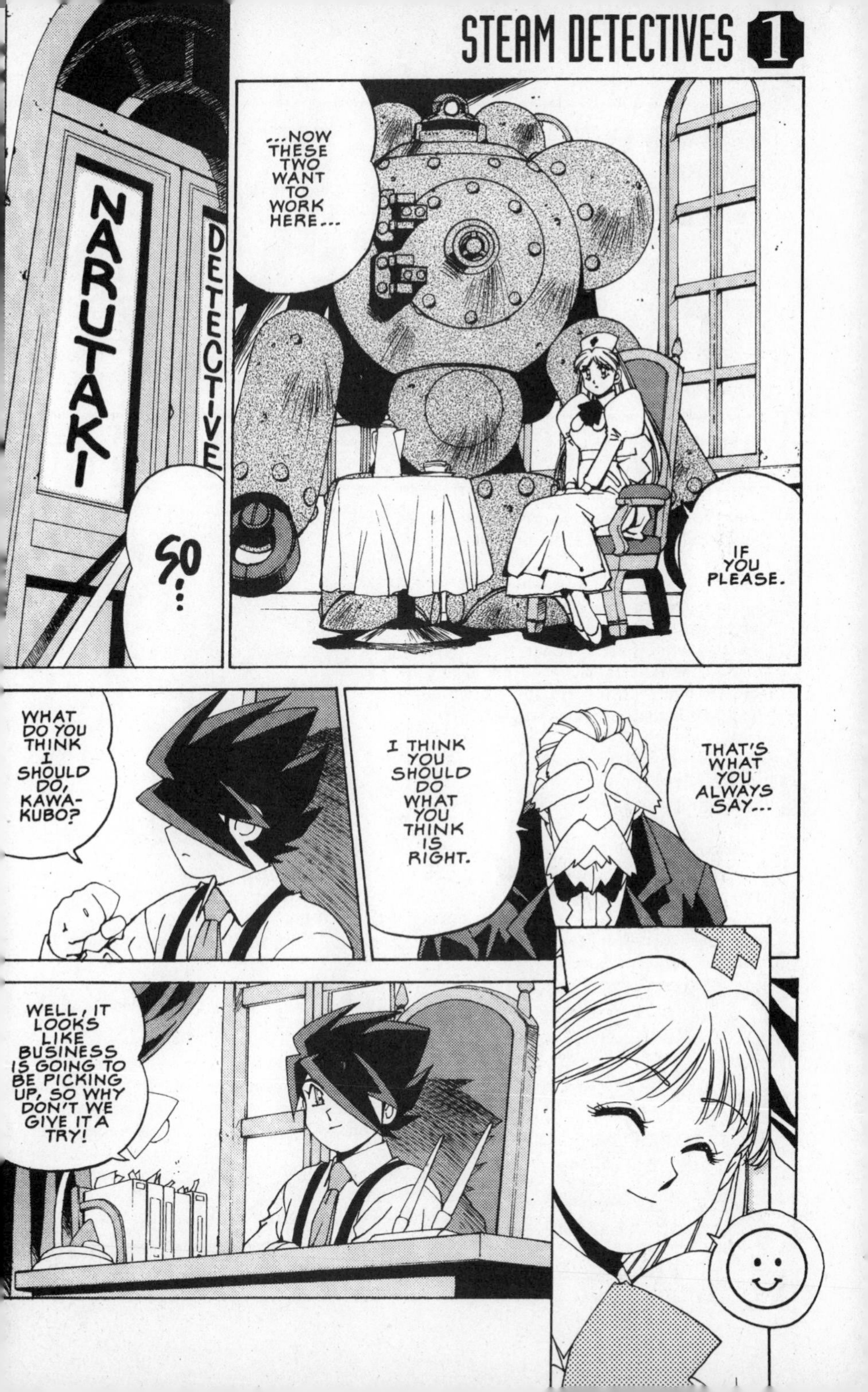
NARUTAKI
DETECTIVE
SO...?
...NOW THESE TWO WANT TO WORK HERE...
IF YOU PLEASE.
WHAT DO YOU THINK I SHOULD DO, KAWA-KUBO?
I THINK YOU SHOULD DO WHAT YOU THINK IS RIGHT.
THAT'S WHAT YOU ALWAYS SAY...
WELL, IT LOOKS LIKE BUSINESS IS GOING TO BE PICKING UP, SO WHY DON'T WE GIVE IT A TRY!

STEAM DETECTIVES PRESS

PHANTOM KNIGHT'S SUBMARINE SECRET!

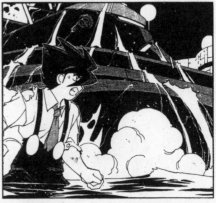

How can a submarine submerge in such shallow water? If we take a close look at the frame on the right, we see that Narutaki is only knee-deep in water. Consequently, it's natural to surmise that the canal is at most waist-deep. How can anything, let alone a submarine, surface from such a shallow canal? How did the Phantom Knight's submersible manage such a feat?

The key to this mystery lies in the design of the canals. The explanation is quite simple, in fact. The center trough running through the canals is extremely deep, approximately twenty meters. The Phantom Knight's submarine entered the canal through this passage. Canals run throughout the city. Without canals, this city would never have come into being. The canals provide vital routes for transporting cargo, not to mention the water absolutely necessary for the city's steam technology. Wait, weren't we talking about the submarine? Oops, sorry!

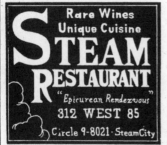

NARUTAKI DETECTIVE AGENCY HIRES NEW ASSISTANT!

Since the Phantom Knight was revealed to be the perpetrator behind the Steam Snatcher incidents, Ling Ling Hsu, his most recent victim, has joined the Narutaki Detective Agency as Narutaki's administrative assistant. Given her background as a nurse, daredevil Narutaki will undoubtedly be relying heavily on her services. The Steam Megamaton, named "Goriki," has also joined the agency. Goriki is the creation of the late Dr. Hsu.

Volume 001 • Issued by Steam Press Co., Ltd.

CASE 2

THE GREAT STEAM TRANSPORT

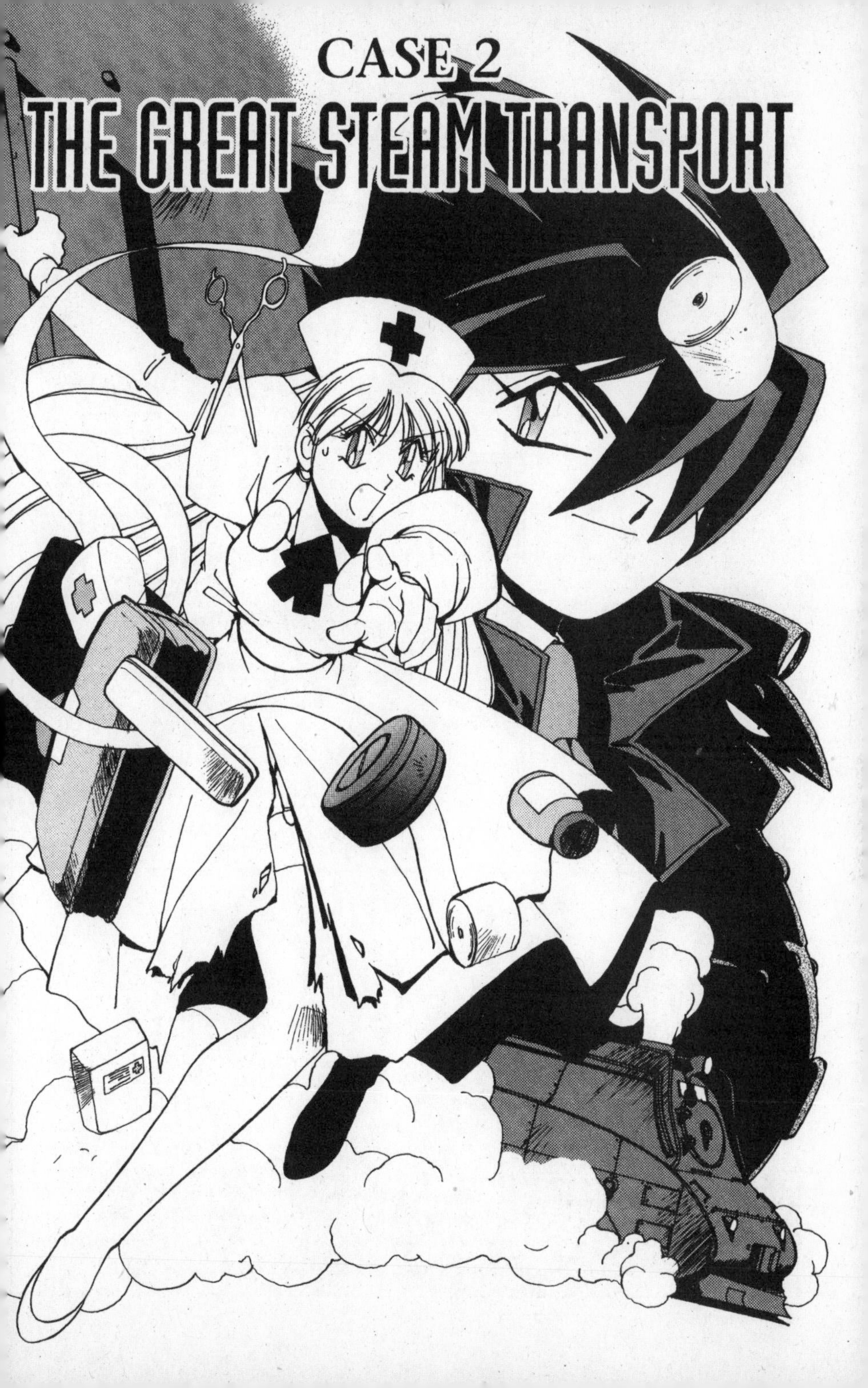

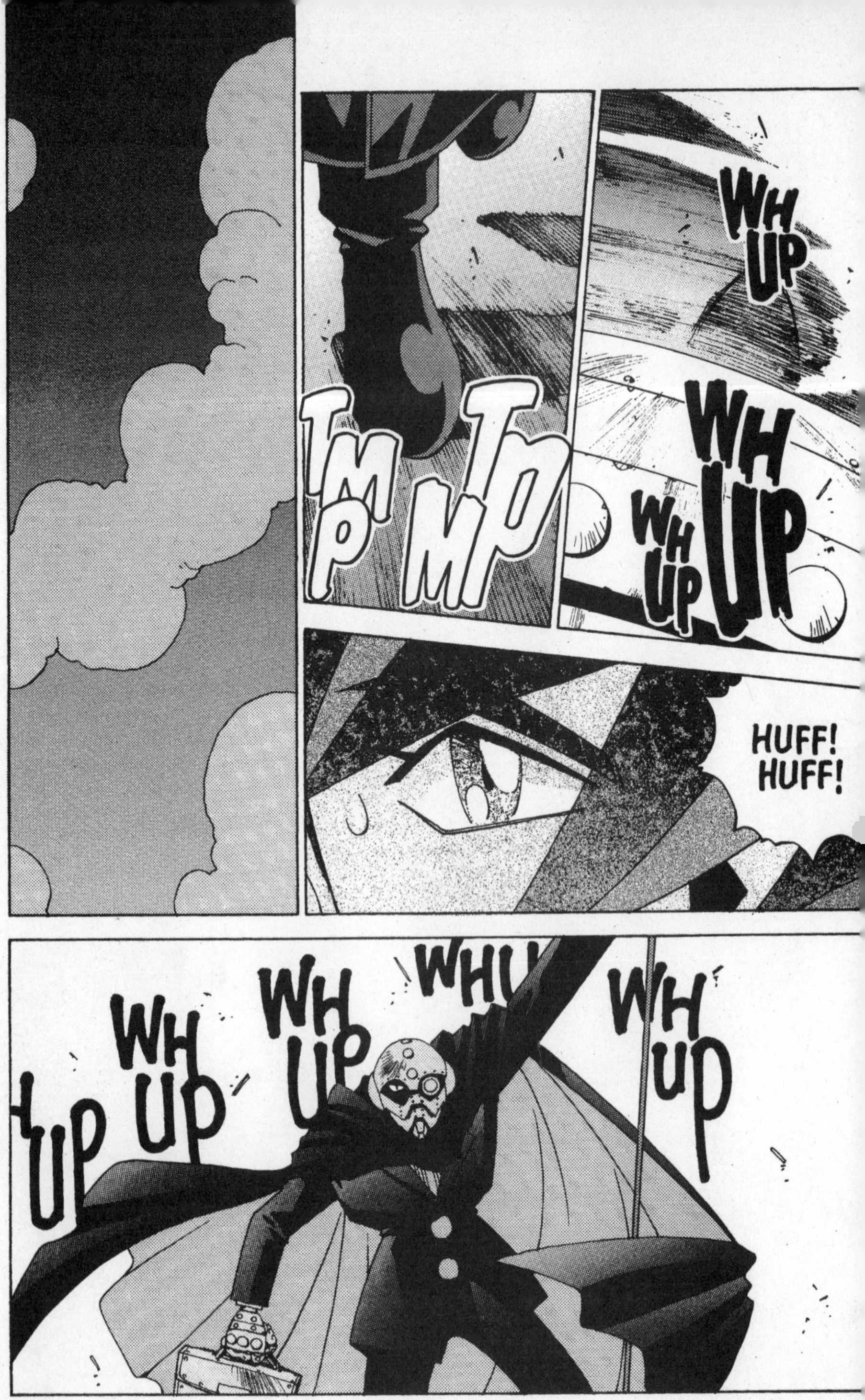
TMP TMP
WH UP
WH UP
WH UP
HUFF! HUFF!
UP
WH UP
WH UP
WH UP

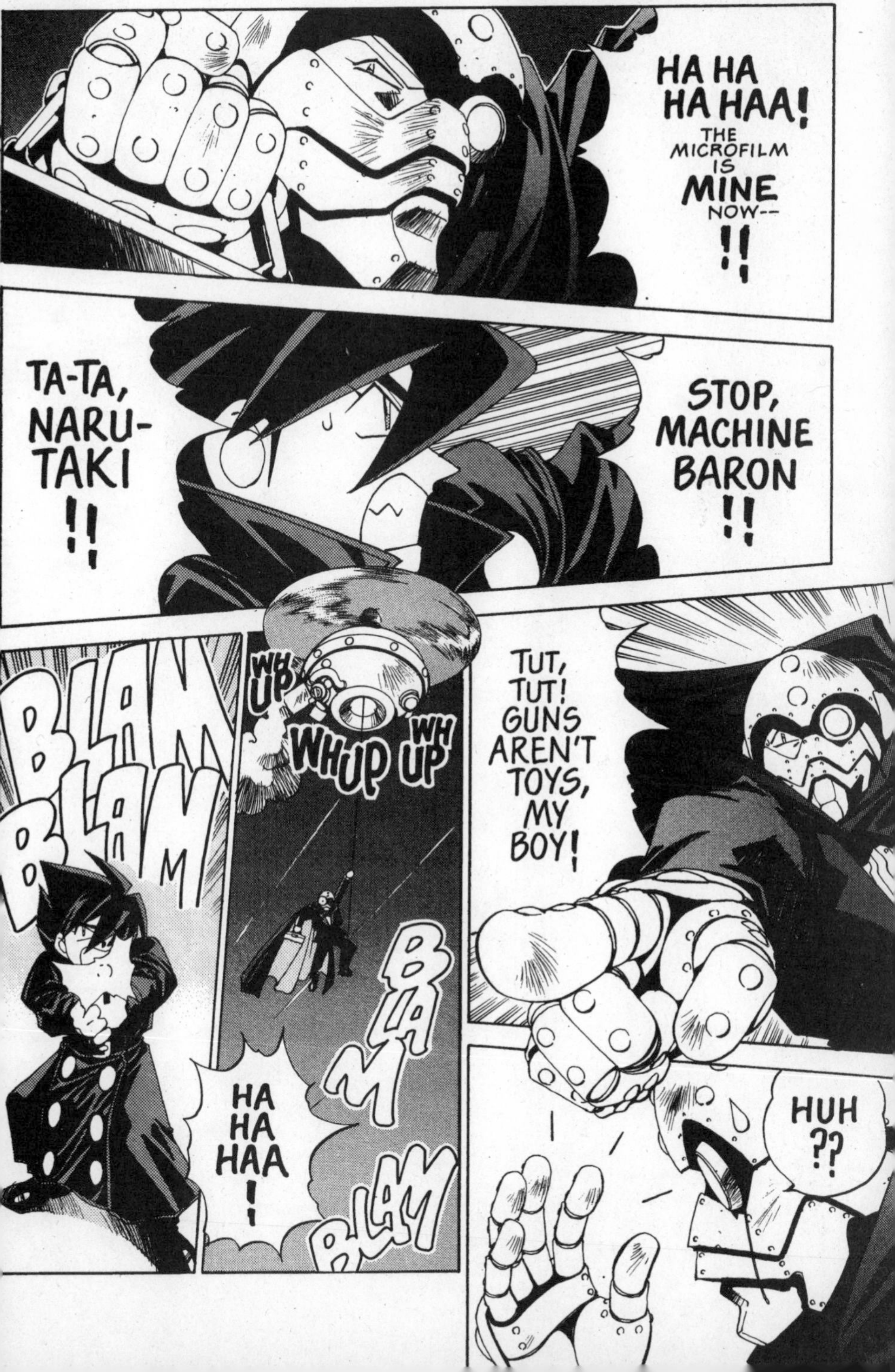
HA HA HA HAA!
THE MICROFILM IS MINE NOW-- !!
TA-TA, NARU-TAKI !!
STOP, MACHINE BARON !!
BLAM
BLAM
WHUP
WHUP
WHUP
BAM
HA HA HAA !
BLAM
TUT, TUT! GUNS AREN'T TOYS, MY BOY!
HUH ??

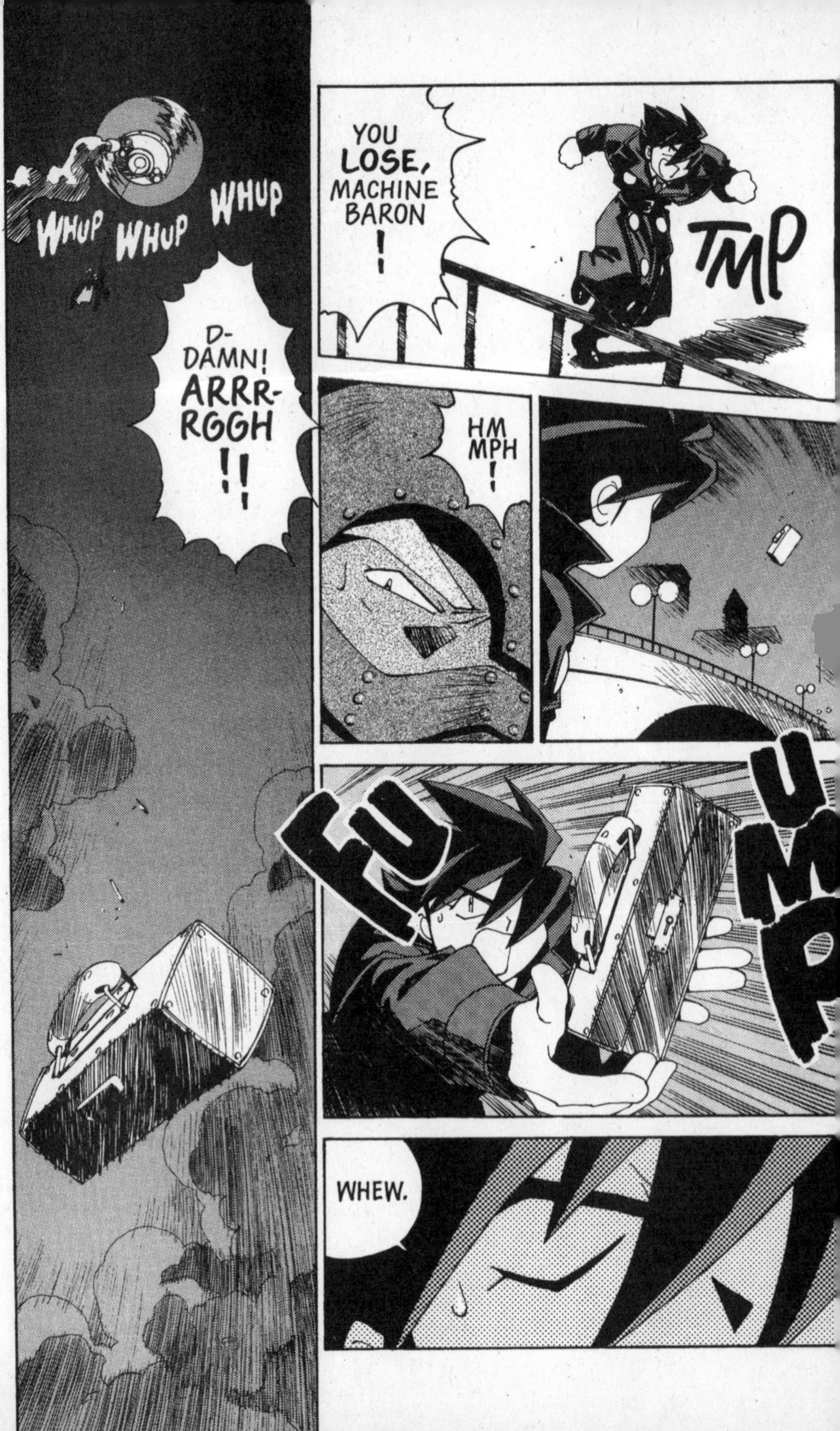
WHUP WHUP WHUP
D-DAMN! ARRR-RGGH!!
YOU LOSE, MACHINE BARON!
TMP
HMMPH!
FU
UMMP
WHEW.

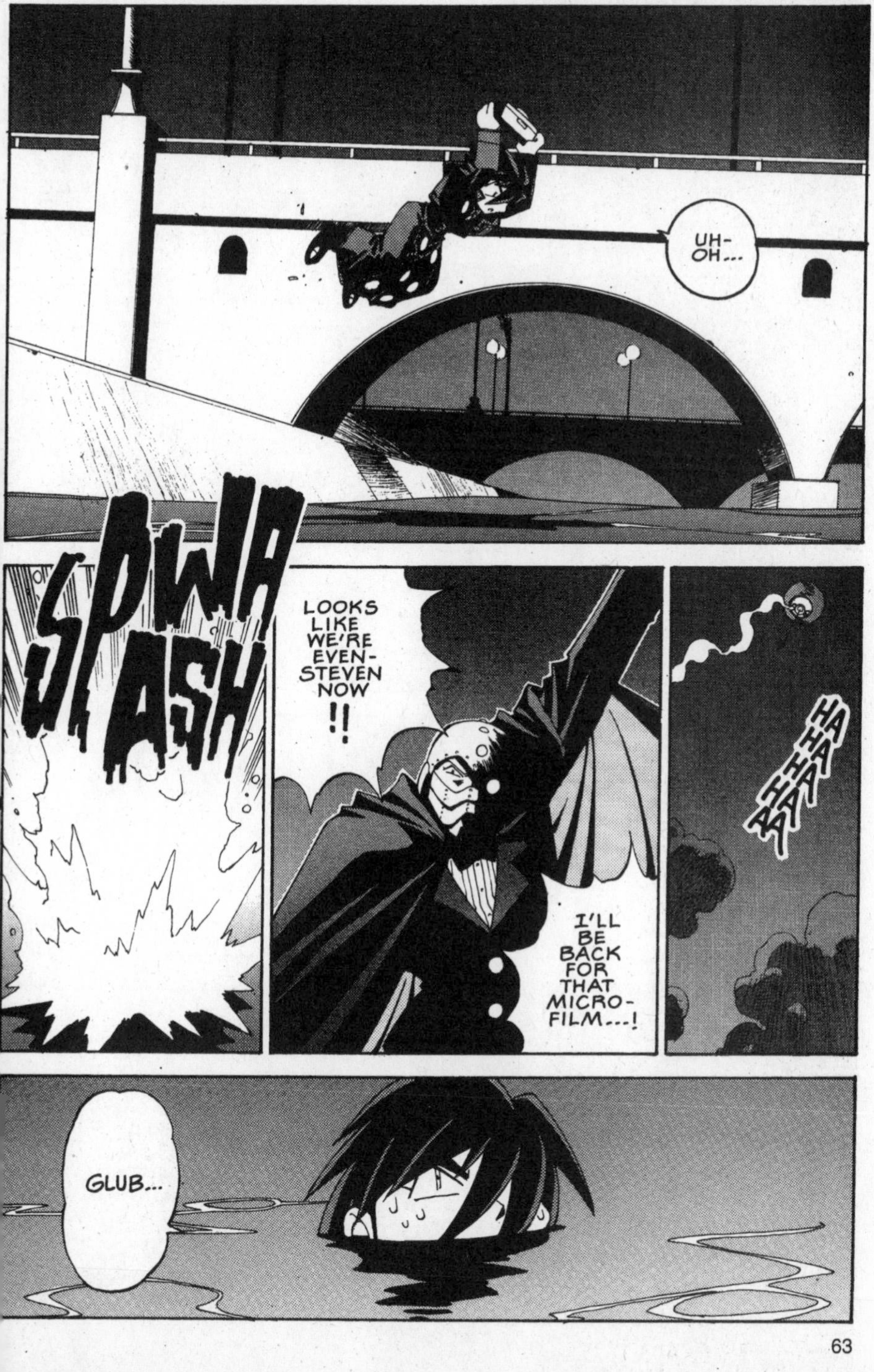
UH-OH...
SPWAA
LOOKS LIKE WE'RE EVEN-STEVEN NOW !!
I'LL BE BACK FOR THAT MICRO-FILM...!
HAHAHAHAA
GLUB...

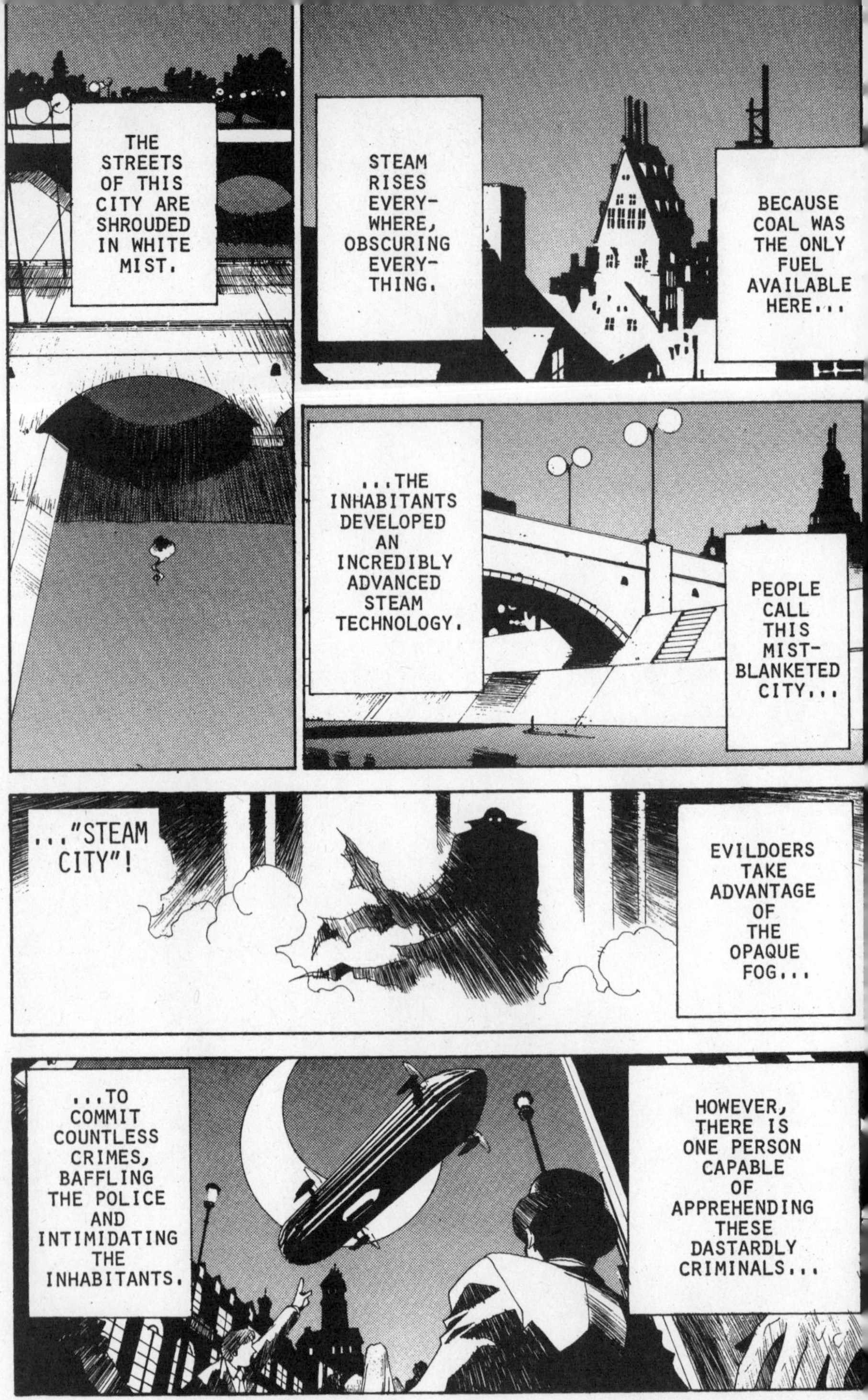
THE STREETS OF THIS CITY ARE SHROUDED IN WHITE MIST.
STEAM RISES EVERY-WHERE, OBSCURING EVERY-THING.
BECAUSE COAL WAS THE ONLY FUEL AVAILABLE HERE...
...THE INHABITANTS DEVELOPED AN INCREDIBLY ADVANCED STEAM TECHNOLOGY.
PEOPLE CALL THIS MIST-BLANKETED CITY...
..."STEAM CITY"!
EVILDOERS TAKE ADVANTAGE OF THE OPAQUE FOG...
...TO COMMIT COUNTLESS CRIMES, BAFFLING THE POLICE AND INTIMIDATING THE INHABITANTS.
HOWEVER, THERE IS ONE PERSON CAPABLE OF APPREHENDING THESE DASTARDLY CRIMINALS...

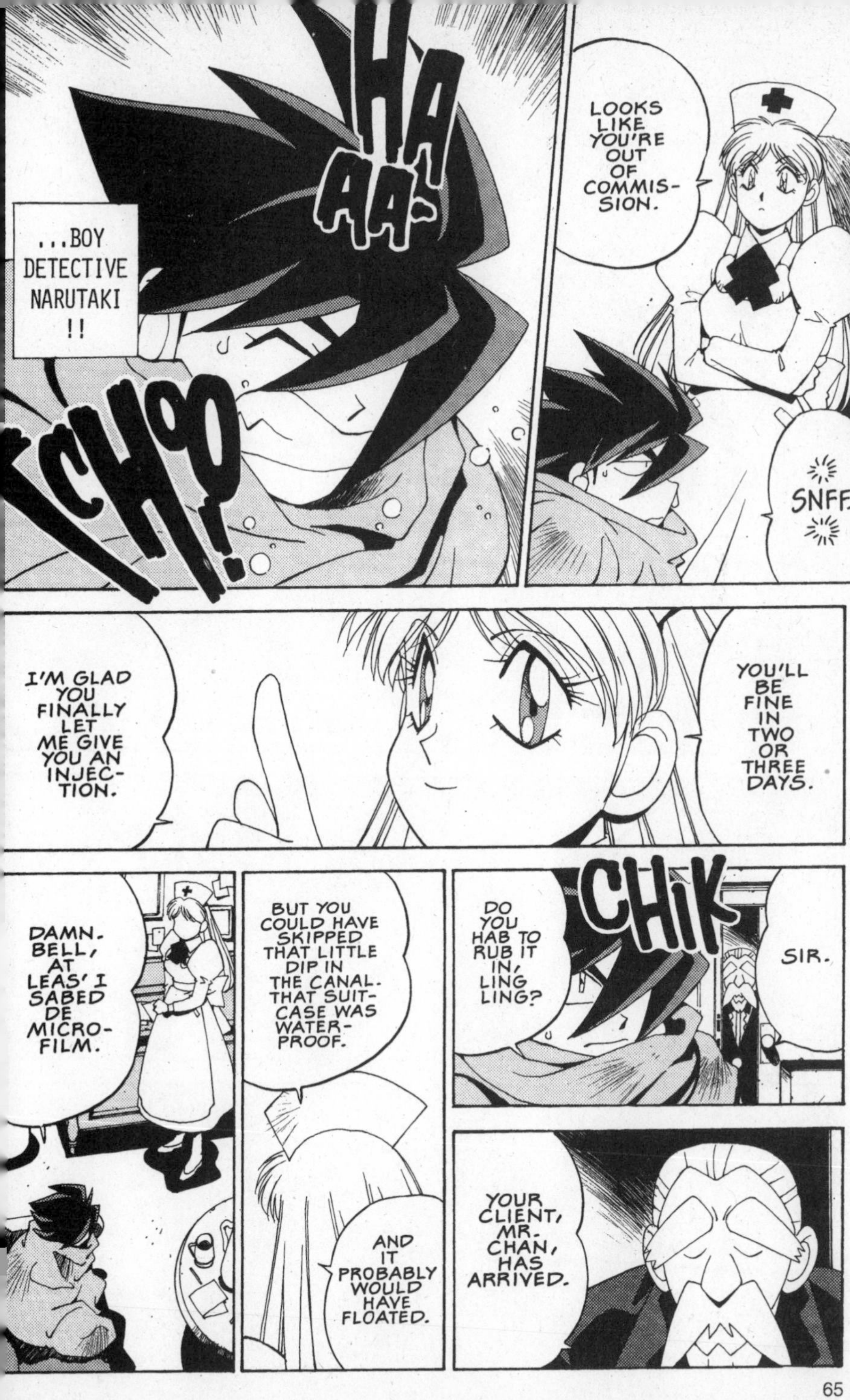
...BOY DETECTIVE NARUTAKI !!
HA AA
ACHOO!!
LOOKS LIKE YOU'RE OUT OF COMMISSION.
SNFF.
I'M GLAD YOU FINALLY LET ME GIVE YOU AN INJECTION.
YOU'LL BE FINE IN TWO OR THREE DAYS.
DAMN. BELL, AT LEAS' I SABED DE MICROFILM.
BUT YOU COULD HAVE SKIPPED THAT LITTLE DIP IN THE CANAL. THAT SUITCASE WAS WATERPROOF.
AND IT PROBABLY WOULD HAVE FLOATED.
DO YOU HAB TO RUB IT IN, LING LING?
CHIK
SIR.
YOUR CLIENT, MR. CHAN, HAS ARRIVED.

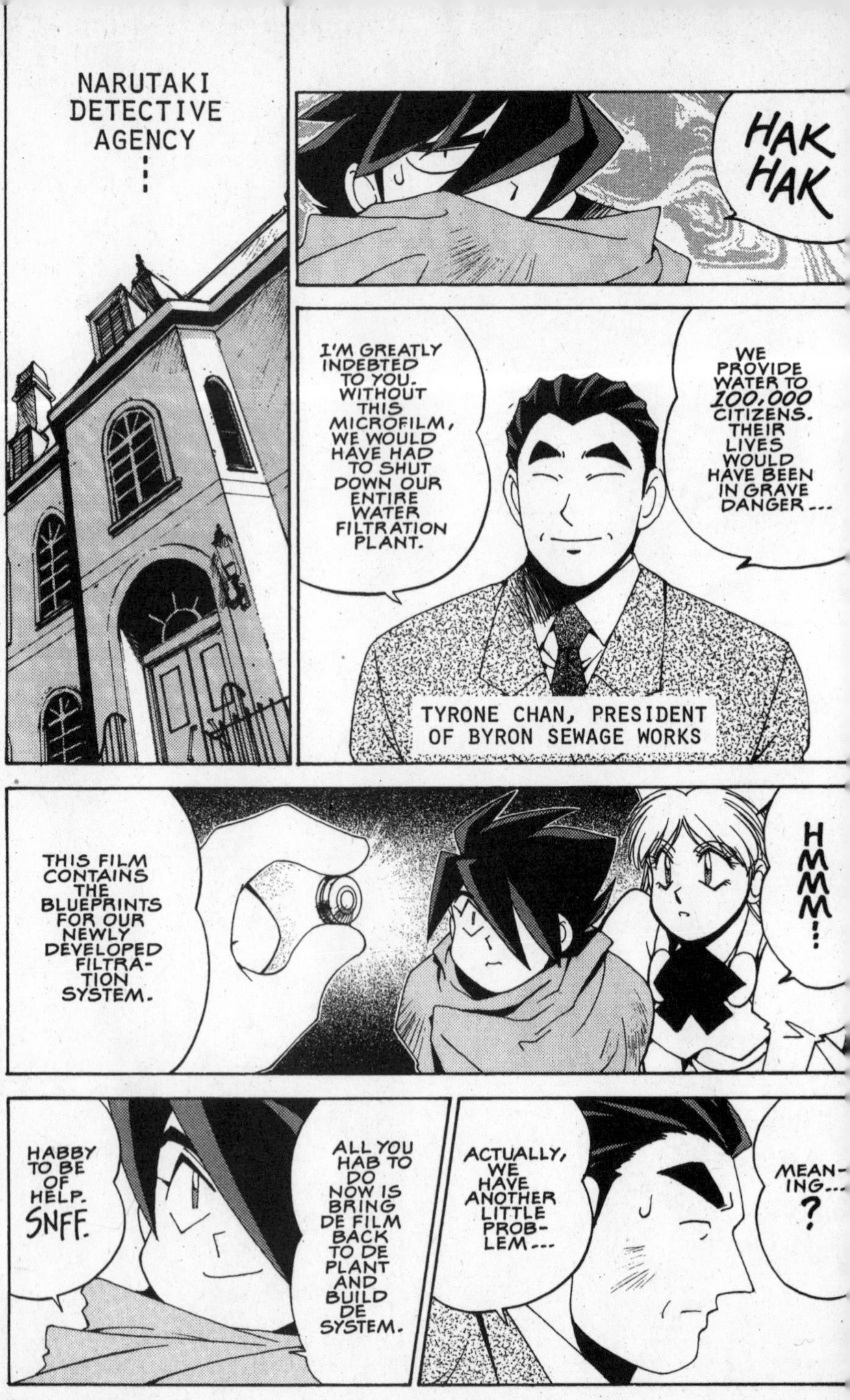

NARUTAKI DETECTIVE AGENCY ⋮
HAK HAK
I'M GREATLY INDEBTED TO YOU. WITHOUT THIS MICROFILM, WE WOULD HAVE HAD TO SHUT DOWN OUR ENTIRE WATER FILTRATION PLANT.
WE PROVIDE WATER TO 100,000 CITIZENS. THEIR LIVES WOULD HAVE BEEN IN GRAVE DANGER...
TYRONE CHAN, PRESIDENT OF BYRON SEWAGE WORKS
THIS FILM CONTAINS THE BLUEPRINTS FOR OUR NEWLY DEVELOPED FILTRATION SYSTEM.
HMMM!!
HABBY TO BE OF HELP. SNFF.
ALL YOU HAB TO DO NOW IS BRING DE FILM BACK TO DE PLANT AND BUILD DE SYSTEM.
ACTUALLY, WE HAVE ANOTHER LITTLE PROBLEM...
MEANING...?

STEAM CITY

MY FILTRATION PLANT IS LOCATED 55 MILES FROM HERE, IN THE BYRON MOUNTAINS.

I CAN ONLY REACH THE PLANT BY TRAIN. IF I'M AMBUSHED ON THE WAY...

BYRON MOUNTAINS

YOU'LL NEED PROTECTION...

...EN ROUTE.

UNFORTUNATELY, I MUST REQUEST YOUR ASSISTANCE AGAIN.

THE MACHINE BARON WILL RETURN! I'M SURE OF IT!

THE MACHINE BARON LUSTS AFTER ANYTHING MECHANICAL...

ESPECIALLY UNIQUE OR RARE DEVICES.

HE'LL EVEN STEAL OUTDATED HUNKS OF JUNK.

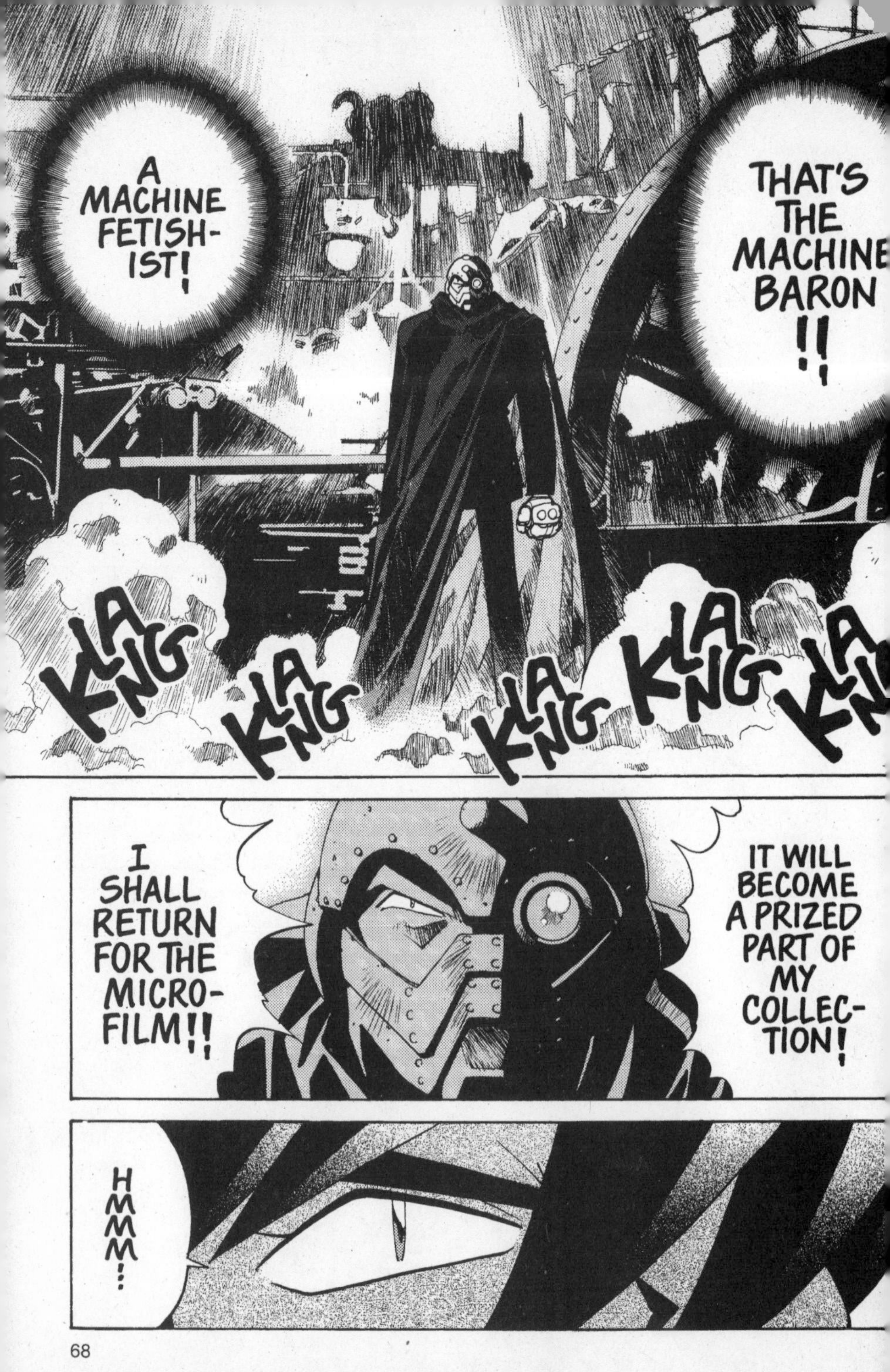
A MACHINE FETISH-IST!
THAT'S THE MACHINE BARON !!
KLANG
KLANG
KLANG
KLANG
KLANG
I SHALL RETURN FOR THE MICRO-FILM!!
IT WILL BECOME A PRIZED PART OF MY COLLEC-TION!
HMMM!

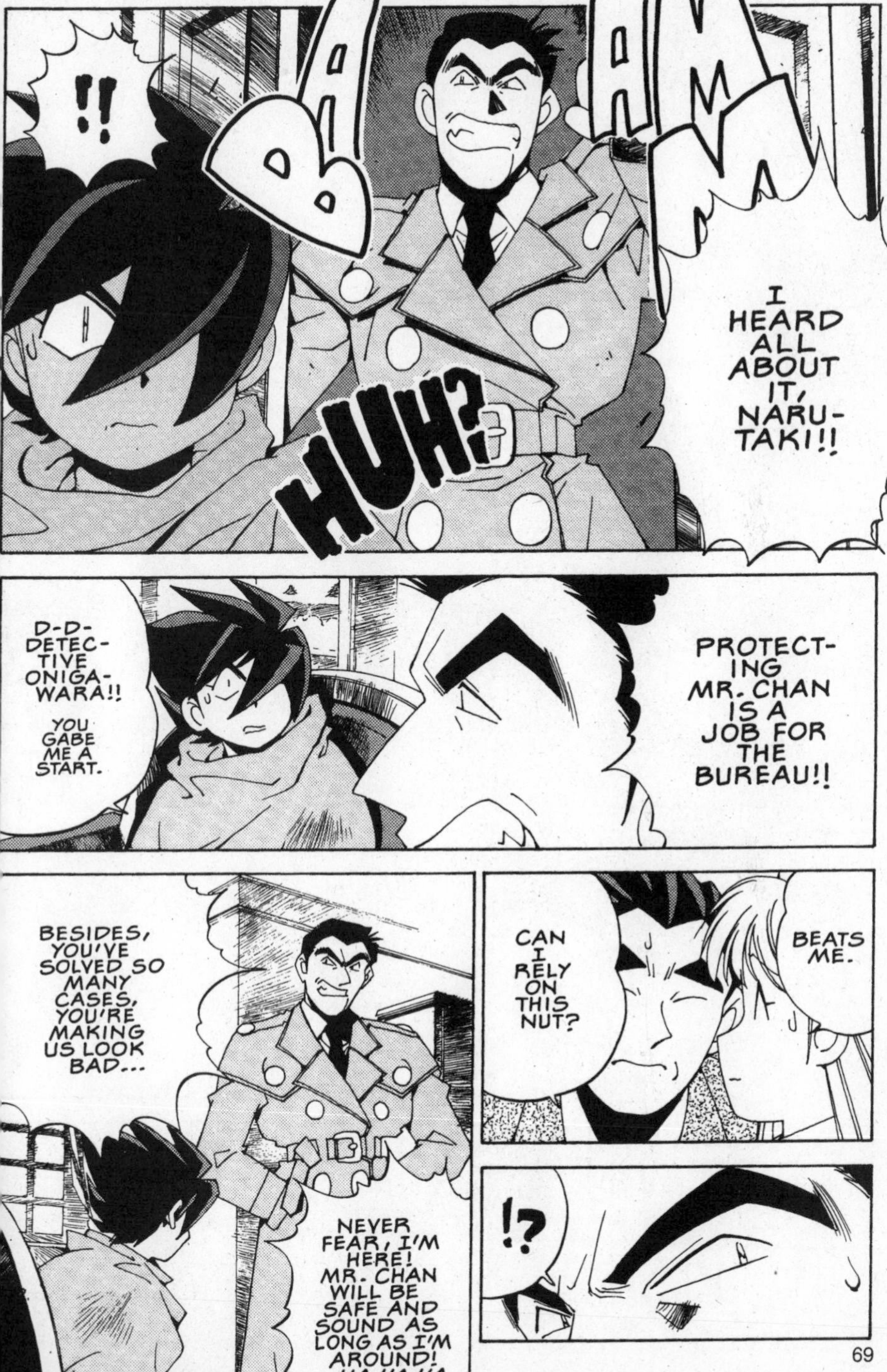
!!
HUH?
I HEARD ALL ABOUT IT, NARU-TAKI!!
D-D-DETEC-TIVE ONIGA-WARA!!
YOU GABE ME A START.
PROTECT-ING MR. CHAN IS A JOB FOR THE BUREAU!!
BESIDES, YOU'VE SOLVED SO MANY CASES, YOU'RE MAKING US LOOK BAD...
NEVER FEAR, I'M HERE! MR. CHAN WILL BE SAFE AND SOUND AS LONG AS I'M AROUND! HA HA HA HAAA!
CAN I RELY ON THIS NUT?
BEATS ME.
!?

LING LING! HOW **COULD** YOU!

BUT I--

NOT EVEN MY OWN GIRL-FRIEND TRUSTS ME...

WHOSE GIRL-FRIEND?!?

ANY-WAY... LEAVE IT TO ME!

I'LL MAKE SURE MR. CHAN MAKES IT TO BYRON !!

B-B-BUT...

!

OKAY-- I'LL ACCOM-BANY BOD OF YOU.

NGH...

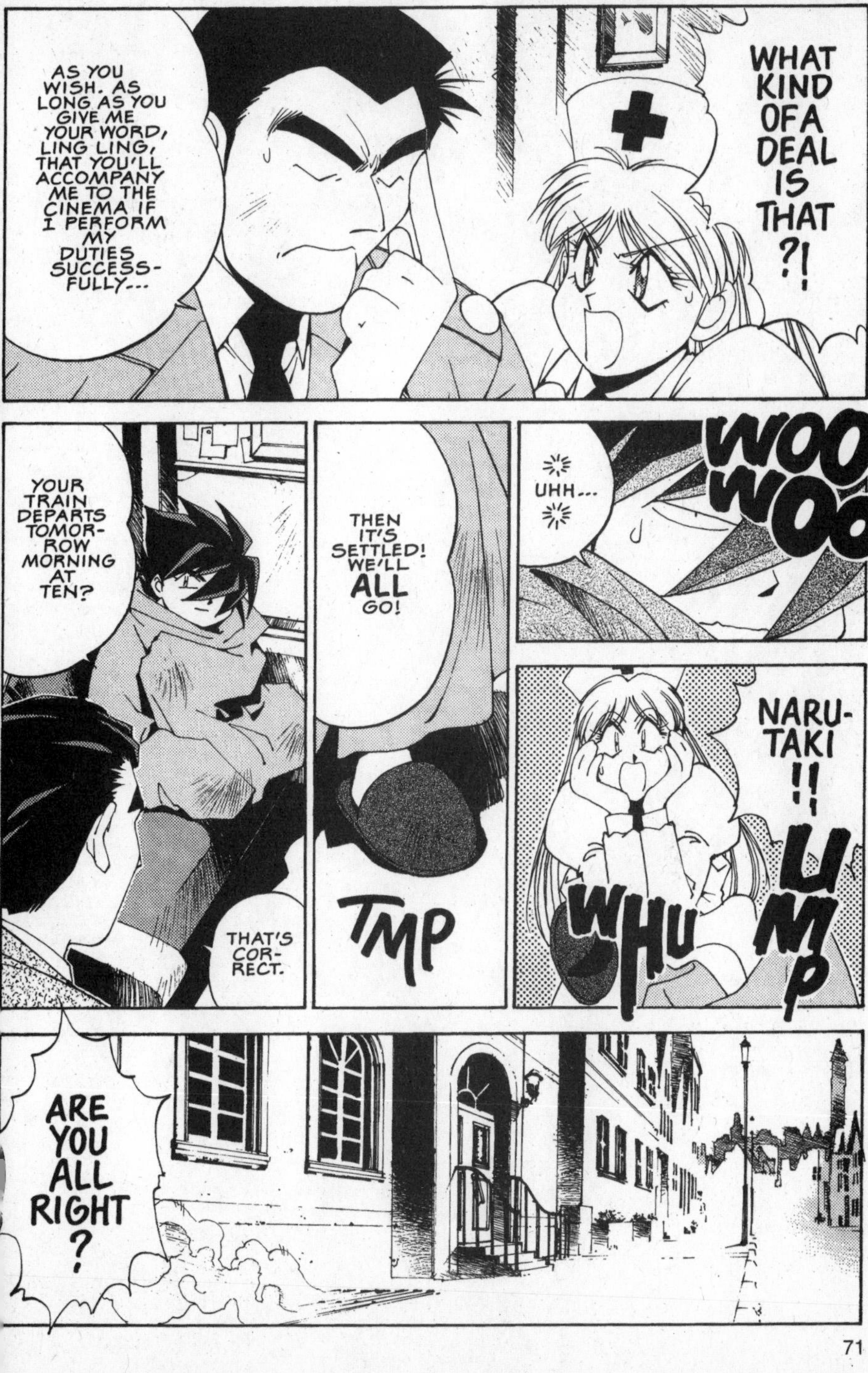
AS YOU WISH. AS LONG AS YOU GIVE ME YOUR WORD, LING LING, THAT YOU'LL ACCOMPANY ME TO THE CINEMA IF I PERFORM MY DUTIES SUCCESSFULLY...
WHAT KIND OF A DEAL IS THAT ?!
YOUR TRAIN DEPARTS TOMORROW MORNING AT TEN?
THAT'S CORRECT.
THEN IT'S SETTLED! WE'LL ALL GO!
TMP
UHH...
WOO WOO
NARUTAKI !!
WHUMP
ARE YOU ALL RIGHT ?

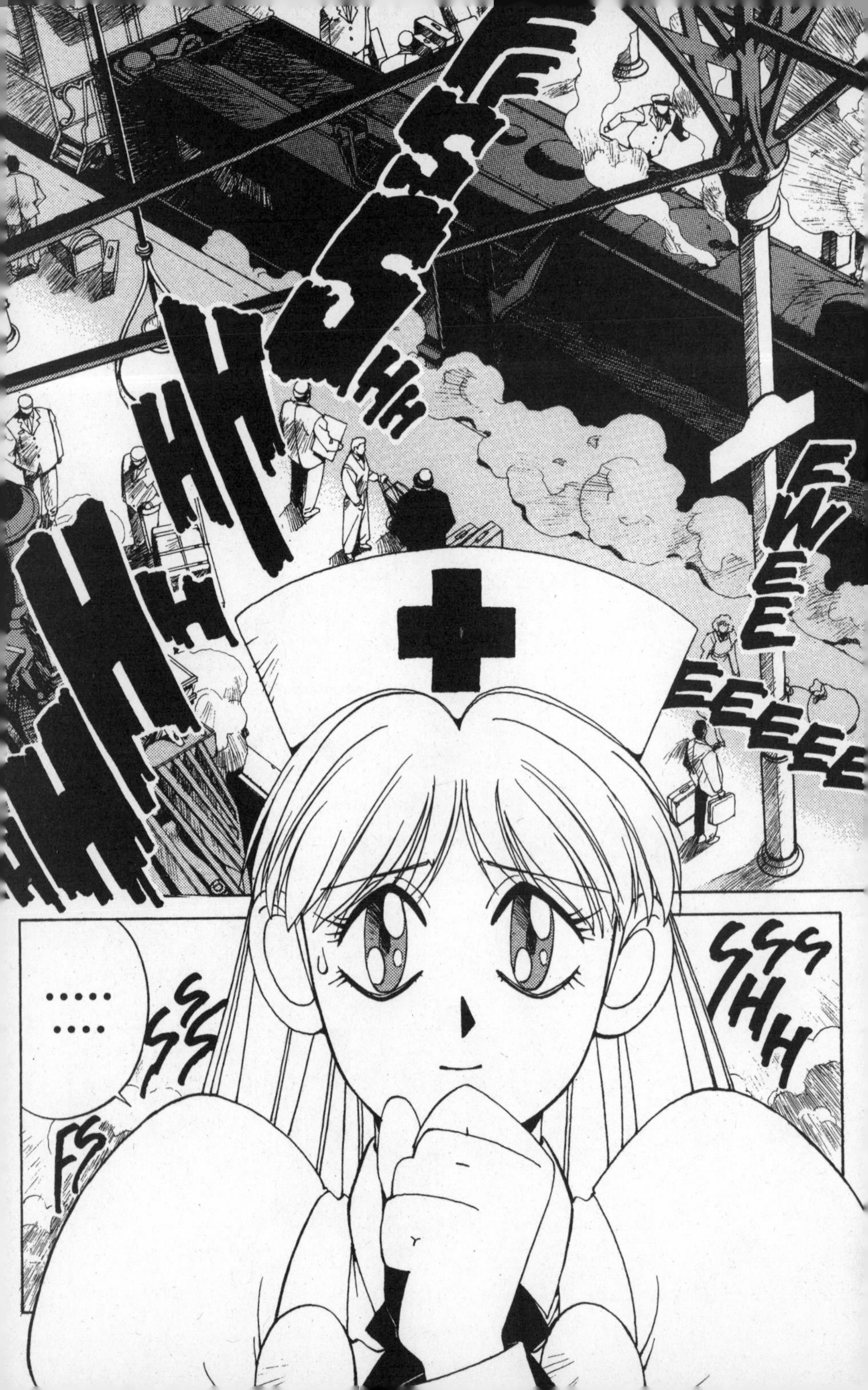
......
....
FSSS
SSSHHH

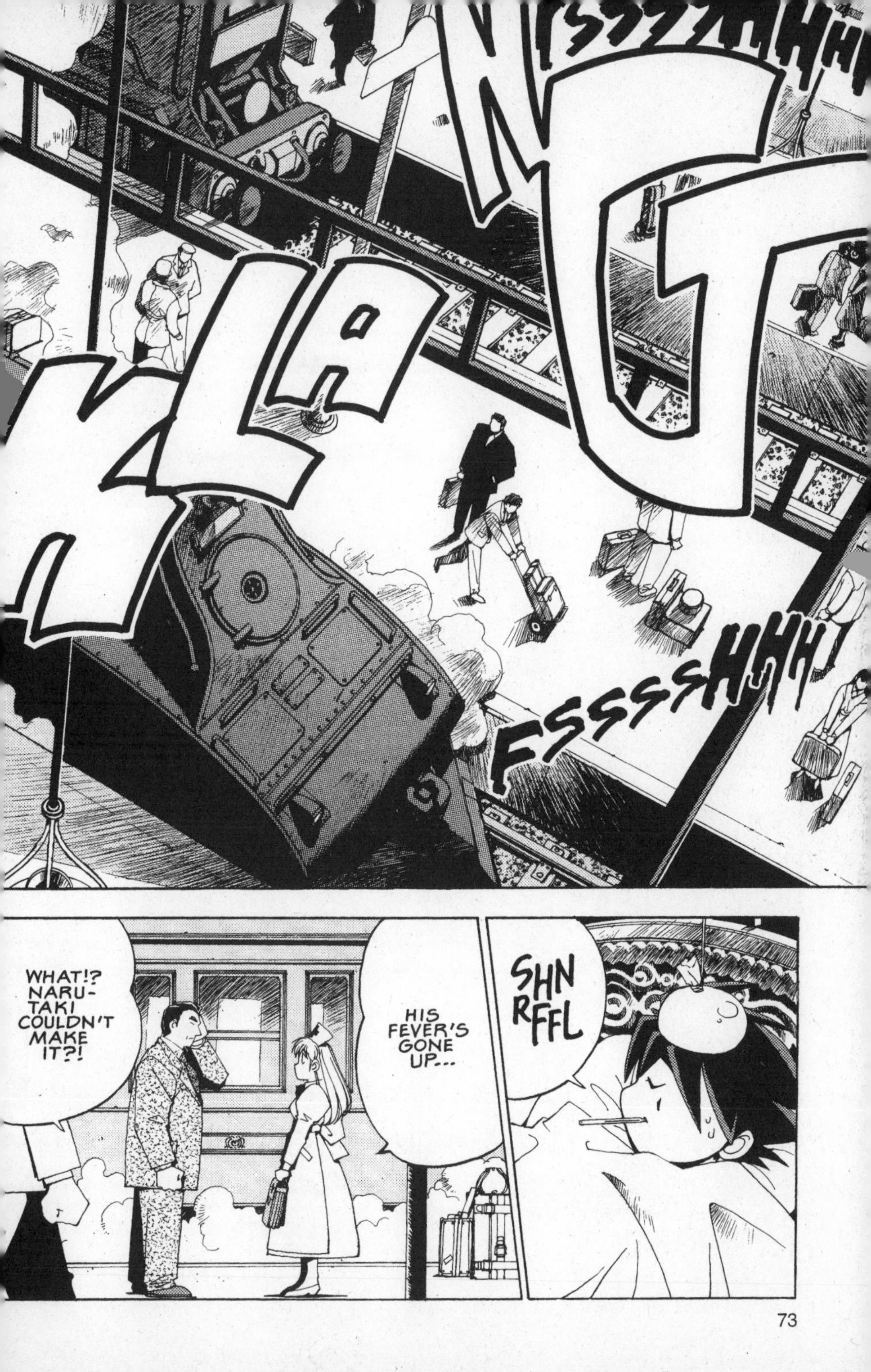
FSSSSHHHH
WHAT!? NARU-TAKI COULDN'T MAKE IT?!
HIS FEVER'S GONE UP...
SHN RFFL

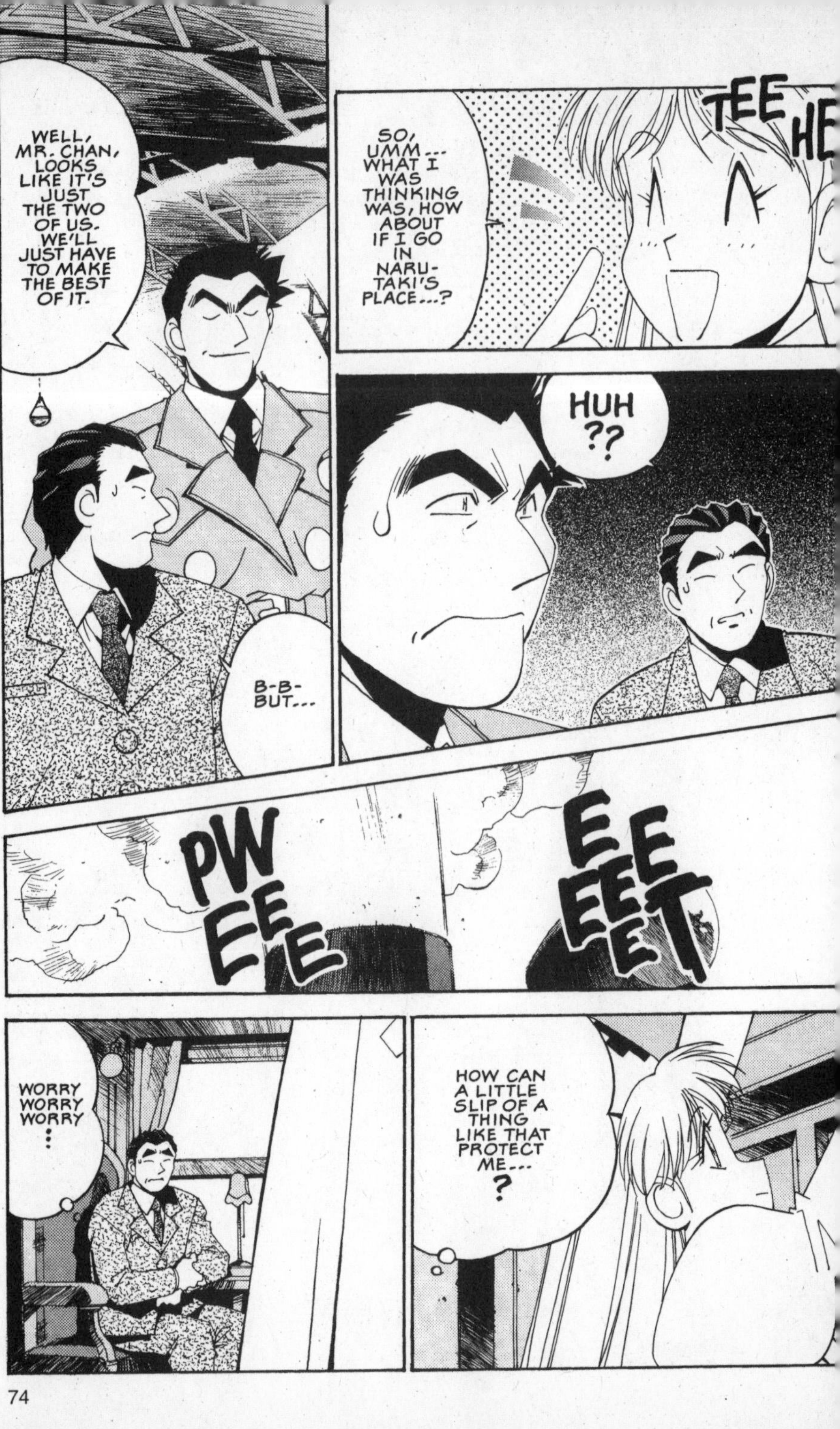
WELL, MR. CHAN, LOOKS LIKE IT'S JUST THE TWO OF US. WE'LL JUST HAVE TO MAKE THE BEST OF IT.
B-B-BUT...
SO, UMM... WHAT I WAS THINKING WAS, HOW ABOUT IF I GO IN NARU-TAKI'S PLACE...?
TEE HE
HUH ??
PWEEE EEEEET
WORRY WORRY WORRY ...
HOW CAN A LITTLE SLIP OF A THING LIKE THAT PROTECT ME...?

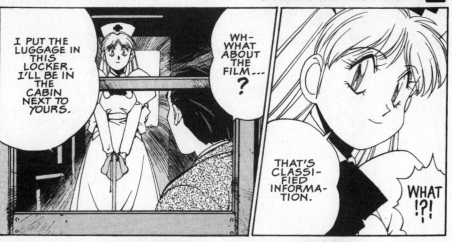

I PUT THE LUGGAGE IN THIS LOCKER. I'LL BE IN THE CABIN NEXT TO YOURS.

WH-WHAT ABOUT THE FILM...?

THAT'S CLASSIFIED INFORMATION.

WHAT!?!

NARUTAKI TOLD ME NOT TO TELL ANYONE, NOT EVEN YOU. THE LESS PEOPLE WHO KNOW ITS WHEREABOUTS, THE BETTER!

REST ASSURED THAT IT'S IN A SAFE PLACE. I HID IT MYSELF!

THAT'S WHAT I'M WORRIED ABOUT...

HUF HFF

WE'LL BE DEPARTING MOMENTARILY.

OH, OKAY...

MY TICKET...

CHK

!

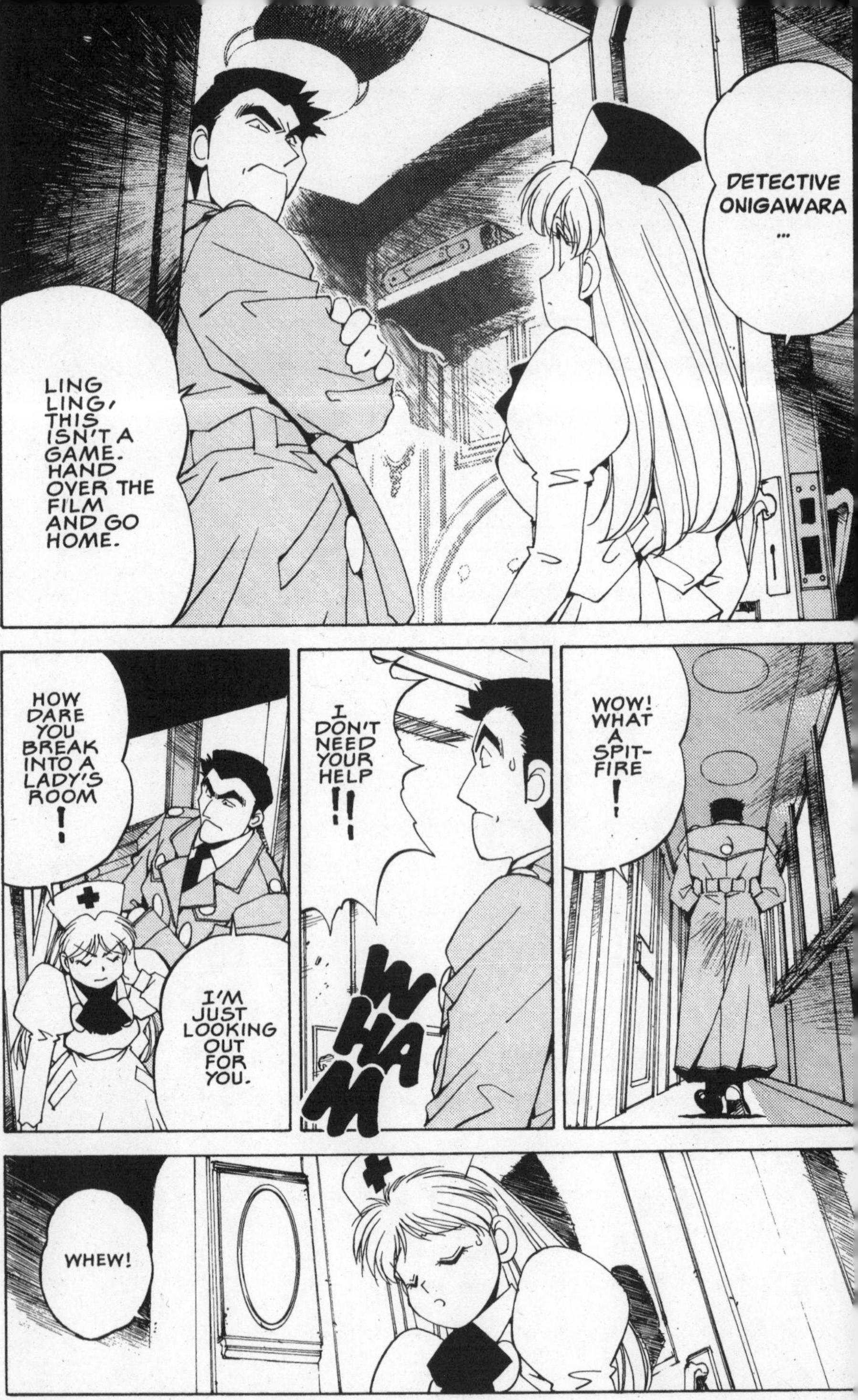
DETECTIVE ONIGAWARA ...
LING LING, THIS ISN'T A GAME. HAND OVER THE FILM AND GO HOME.
HOW DARE YOU BREAK INTO A LADY'S ROOM!
I'M JUST LOOKING OUT FOR YOU.
I DON'T NEED YOUR HELP!!
WHAM
WOW! WHAT A SPIT-FIRE!
WHEW!

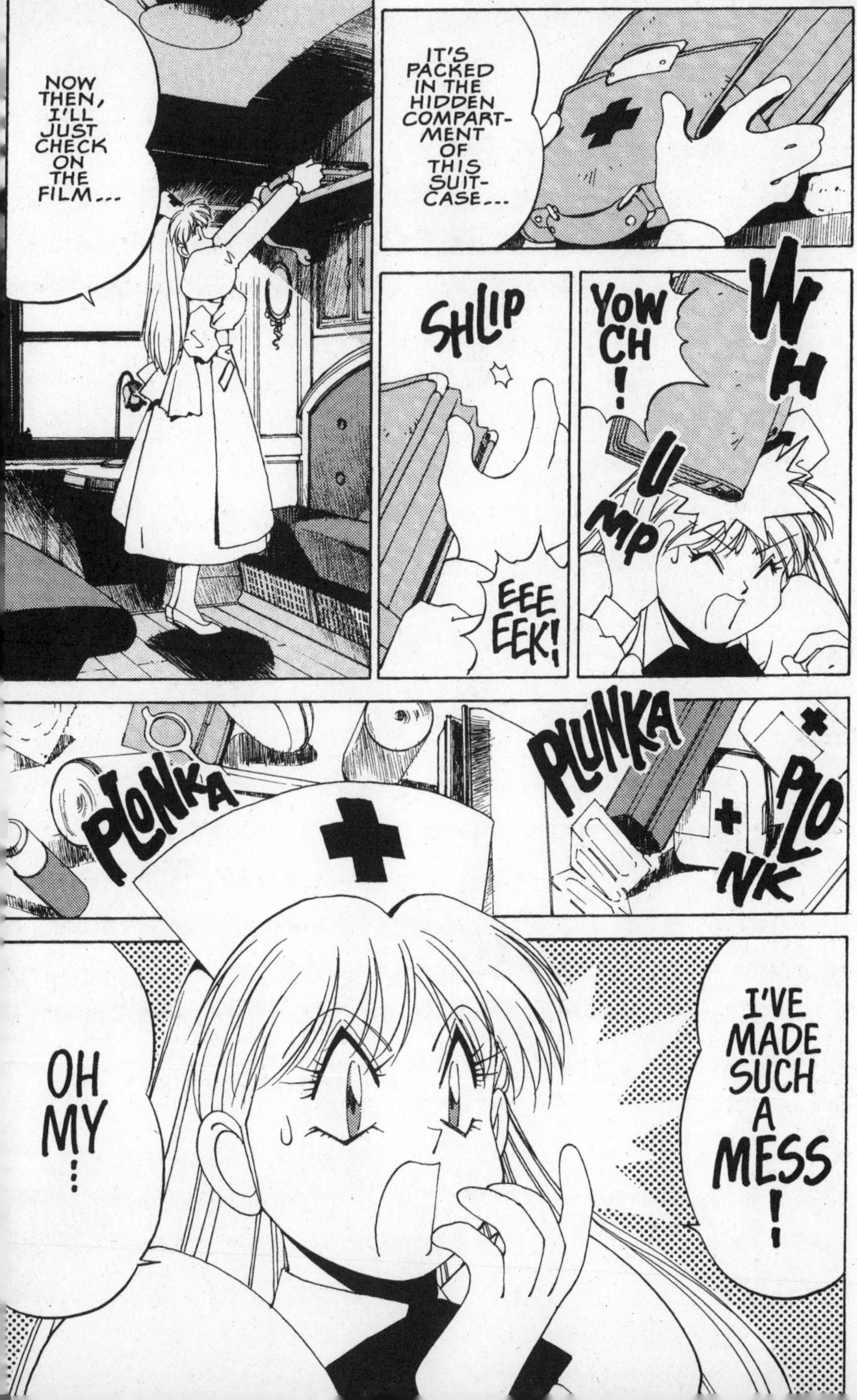
NOW THEN, I'LL JUST CHECK ON THE FILM...
IT'S PACKED IN THE HIDDEN COMPARTMENT OF THIS SUITCASE...
SHLIP
EEE EEEK!
YOWCH!
WHUMP
PLONKA
PLUNKA
PLONK
OH MY...
I'VE MADE SUCH A MESS!

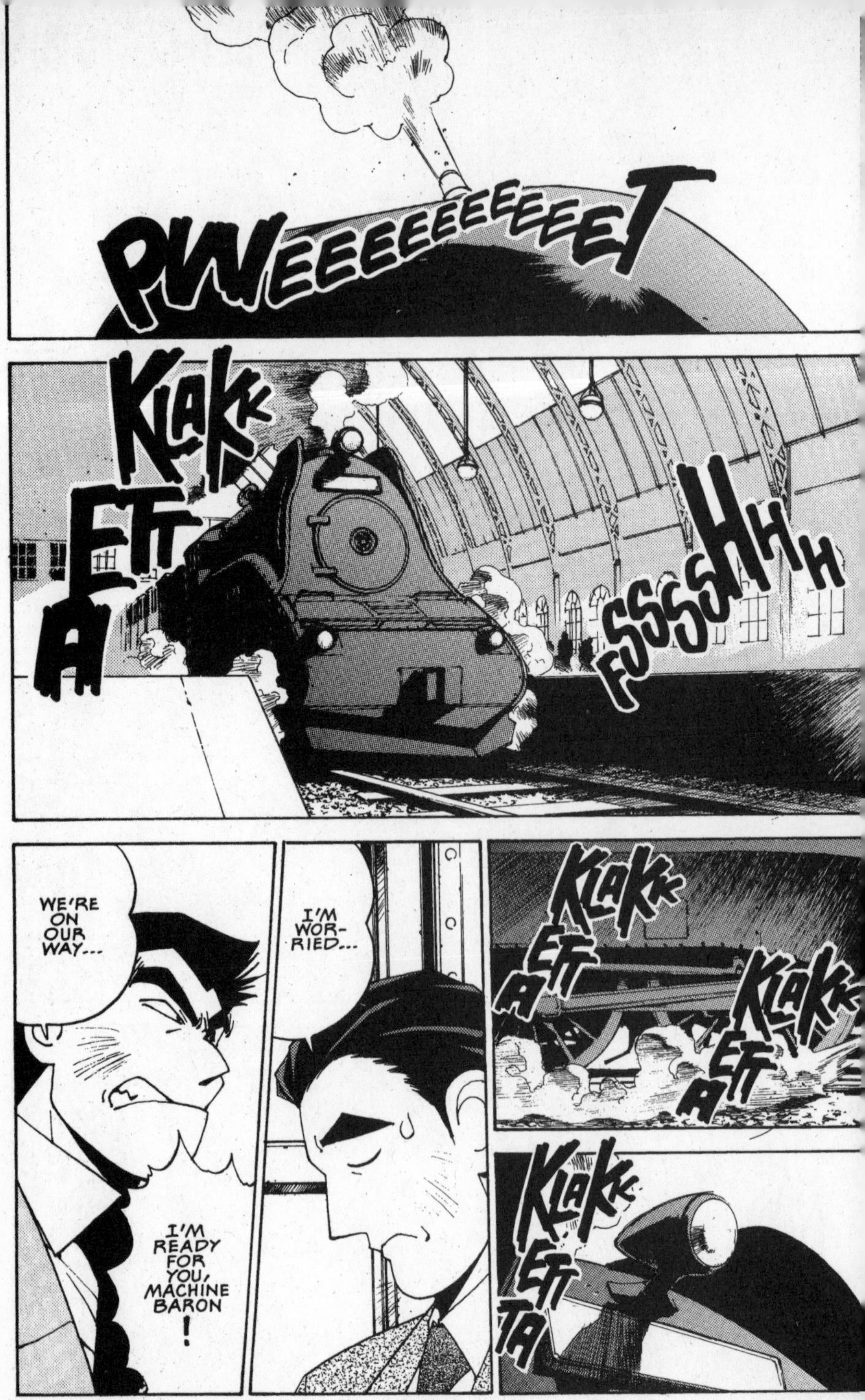

PWEEEEEEEEEEET
KLAKK
ETT
A
FSSSSHHHH
WE'RE ON OUR WAY...
I'M READY FOR YOU, MACHINE BARON!
I'M WOR-RIED...
KLAKK
ETT
A
KLAKK
ETT
A
KLAKK
ETT
TA

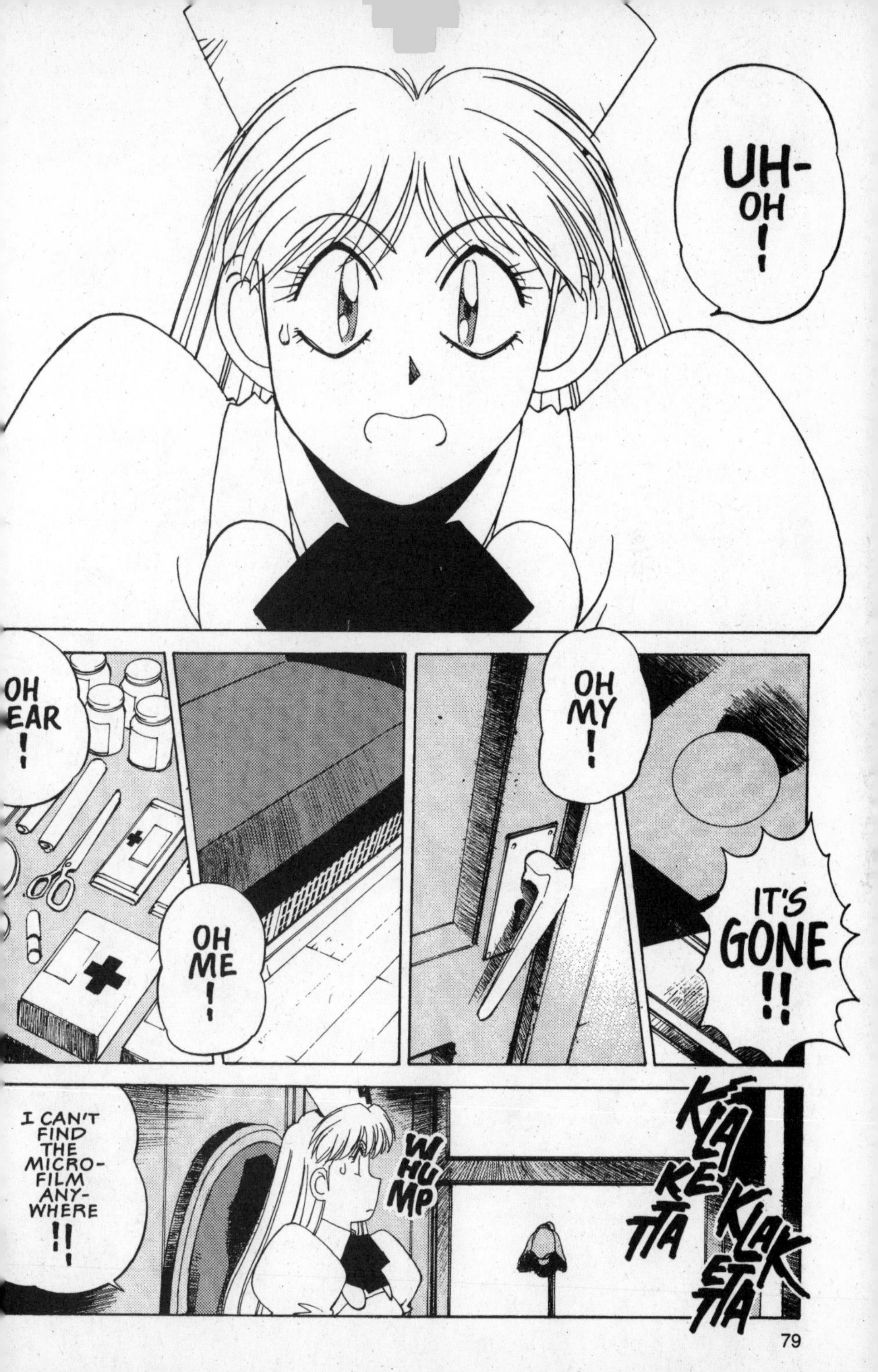
UH-OH!
OH EAR!
OH ME!
OH MY!
IT'S GONE!!
I CAN'T FIND THE MICRO-FILM ANY-WHERE!!
WHUMP
KLAKETA KLAKETA

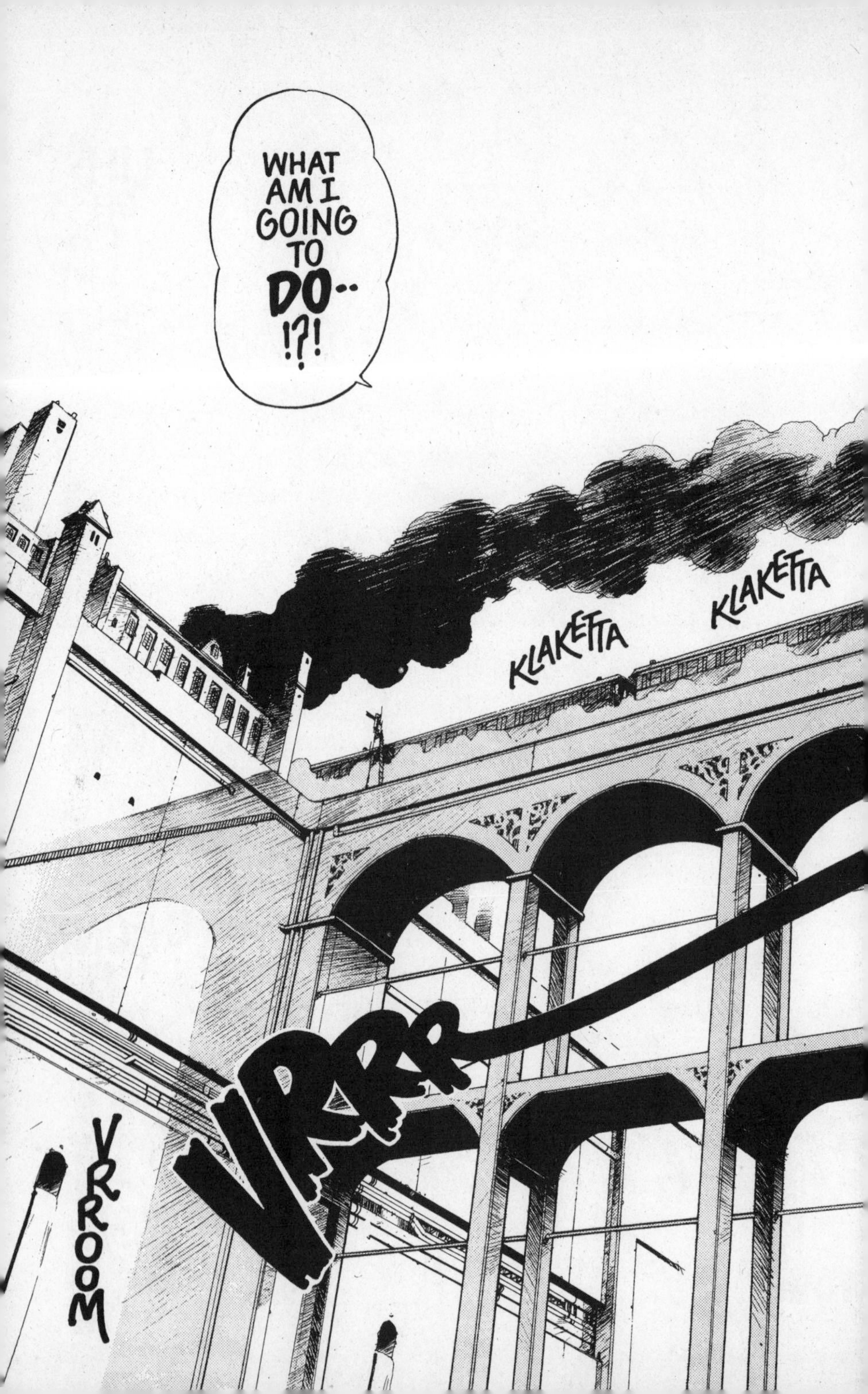
WHAT AM I GOING TO DO.. !?!
KLAKETTA
KLAKETTA
VRRR
VRROOM

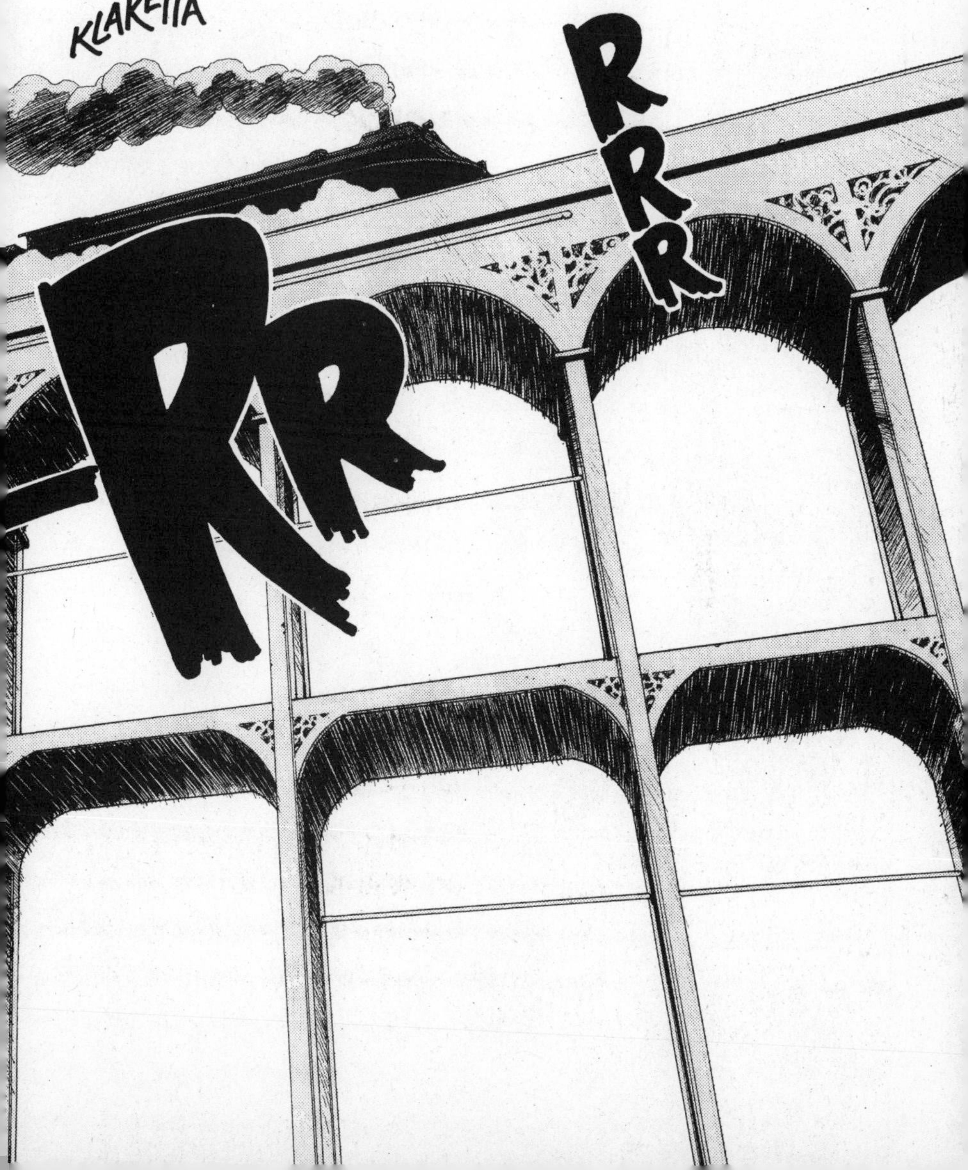
KLAKETTA
RRRR
RR

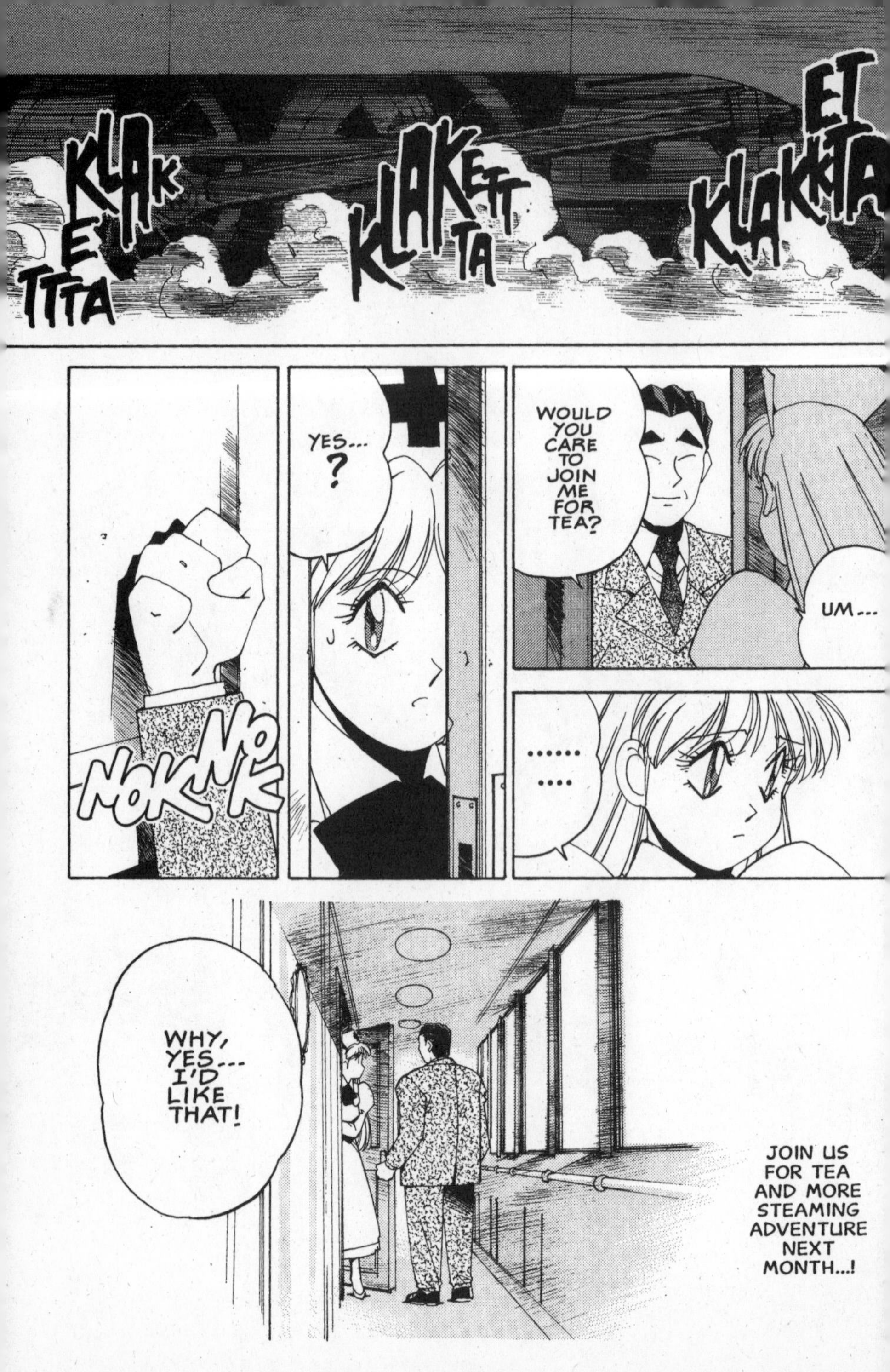
KLAK E TTTA
KLAKETT TA
KLAKKTA ET
NOK NOK
YES... ?
WOULD YOU CARE TO JOIN ME FOR TEA?
UM...
....
WHY, YES... I'D LIKE THAT!
JOIN US FOR TEA AND MORE STEAMING ADVENTURE NEXT MONTH...!

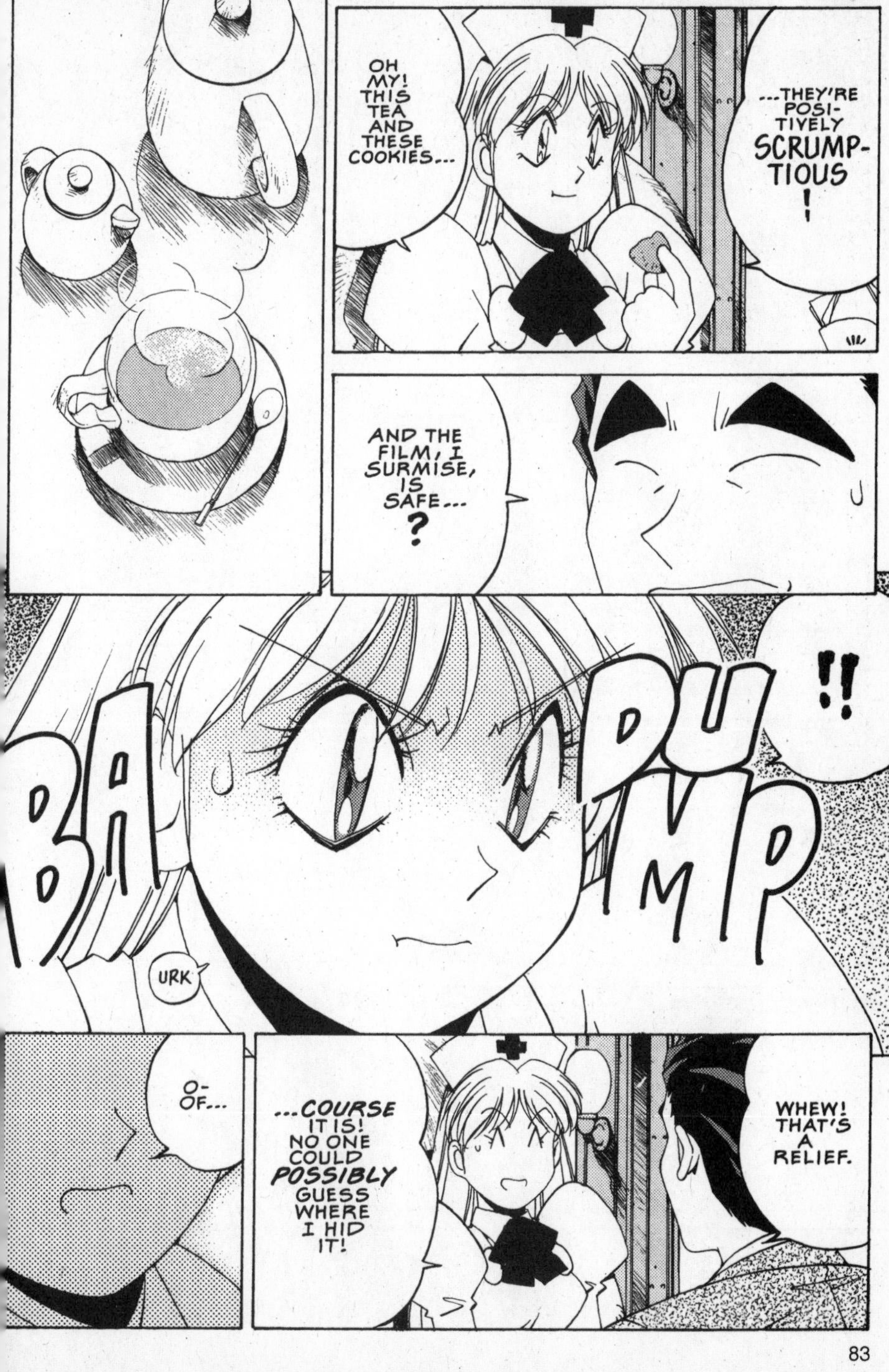
OH MY! THIS TEA AND THESE COOKIES...
...THEY'RE POSITIVELY SCRUMPTIOUS!
AND THE FILM, I SURMISE, IS SAFE...?
BA
DUMP
MP
!!
URK
O-OF...
...COURSE IT IS! NO ONE COULD POSSIBLY GUESS WHERE I HID IT!
WHEW! THAT'S A RELIEF.

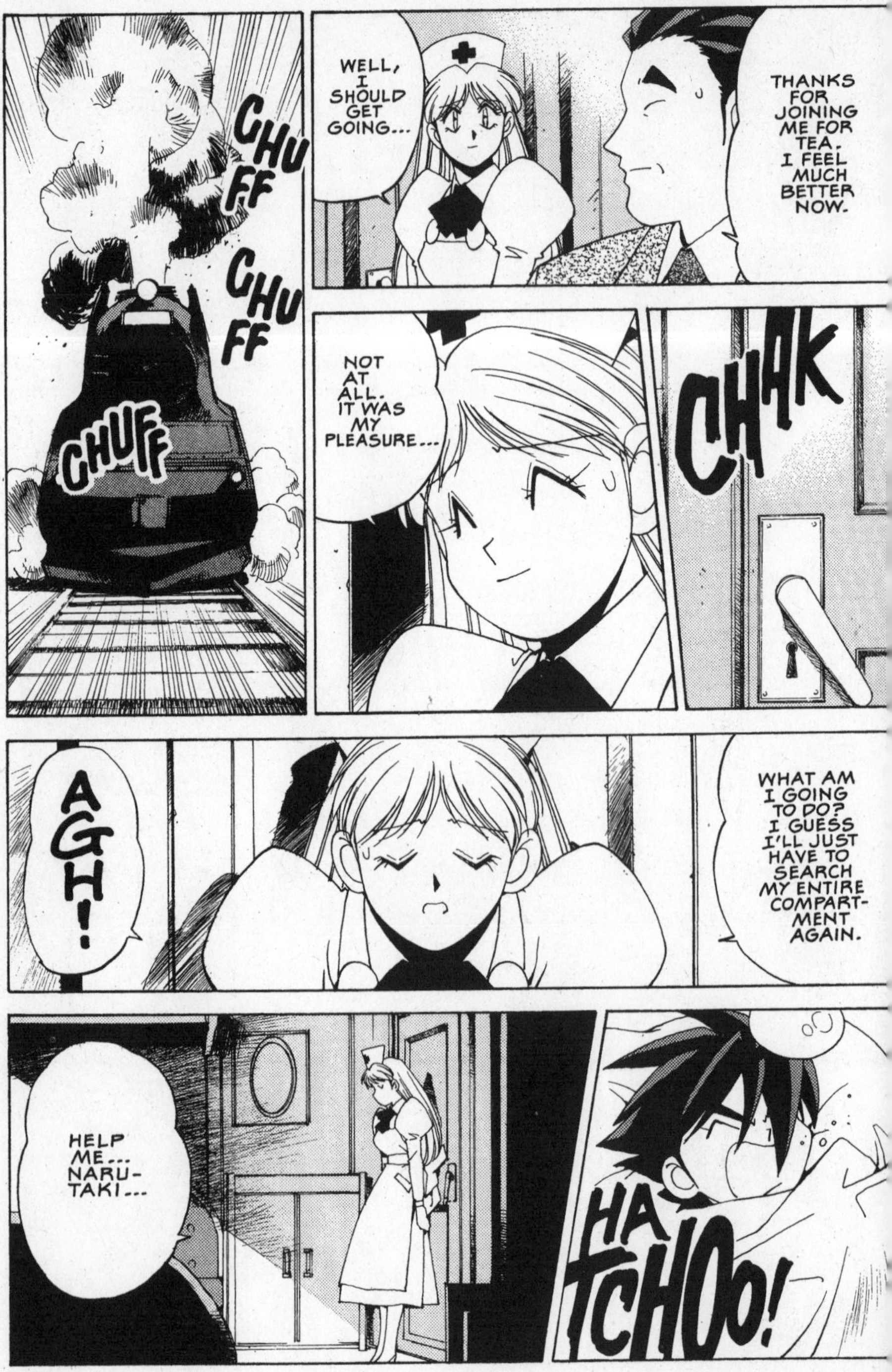
CHUFF
CHUFF
CHUFF
WELL, I SHOULD GET GOING...
THANKS FOR JOINING ME FOR TEA. I FEEL MUCH BETTER NOW.
NOT AT ALL. IT WAS MY PLEASURE...
CHAK
AGH!
WHAT AM I GOING TO DO? I GUESS I'LL JUST HAVE TO SEARCH MY ENTIRE COMPART-MENT AGAIN.
HELP ME... NARU-TAKI...
HATCHOO!

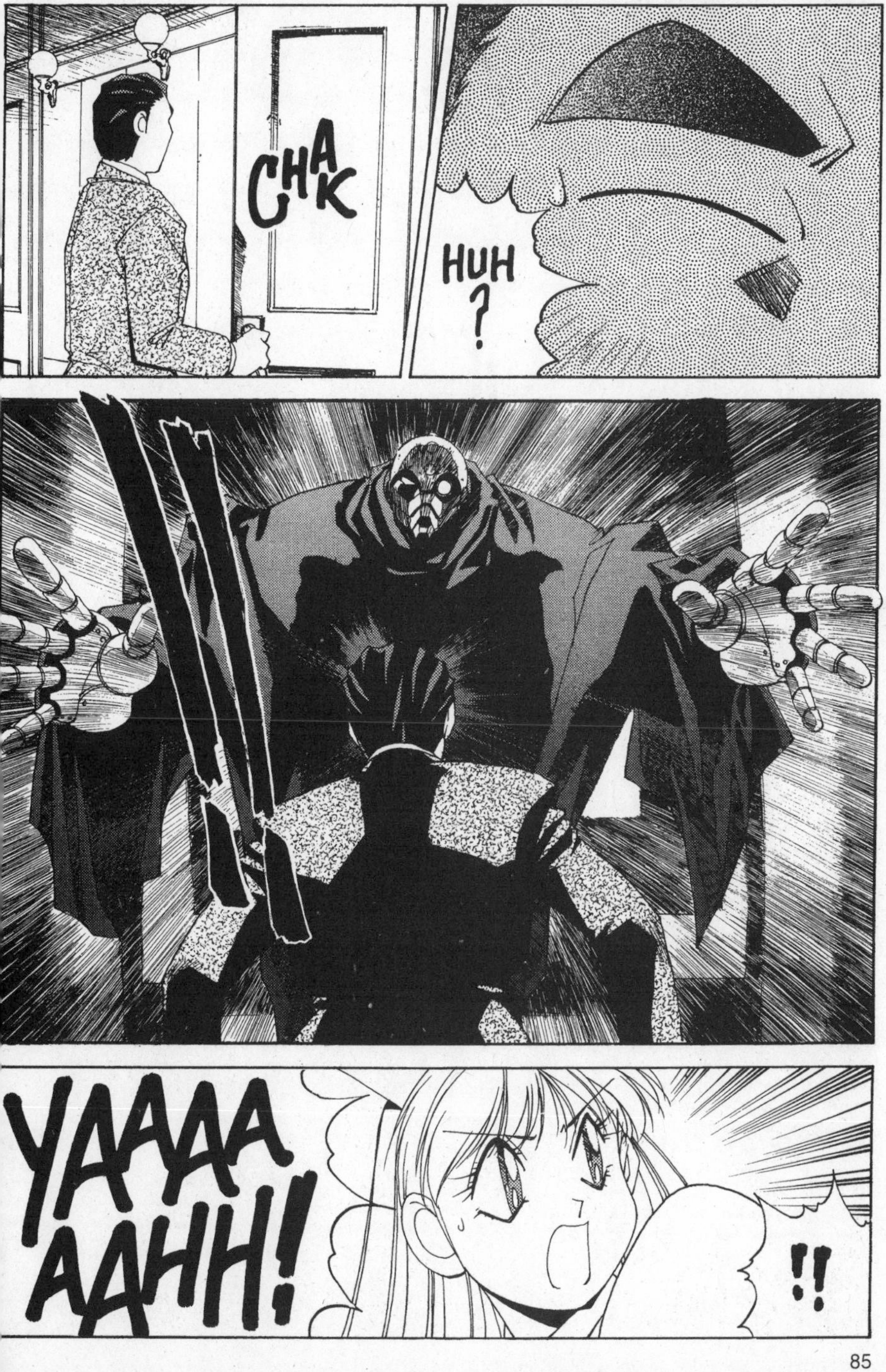
CHAK
HUH?
YAAAAAHH!
!!

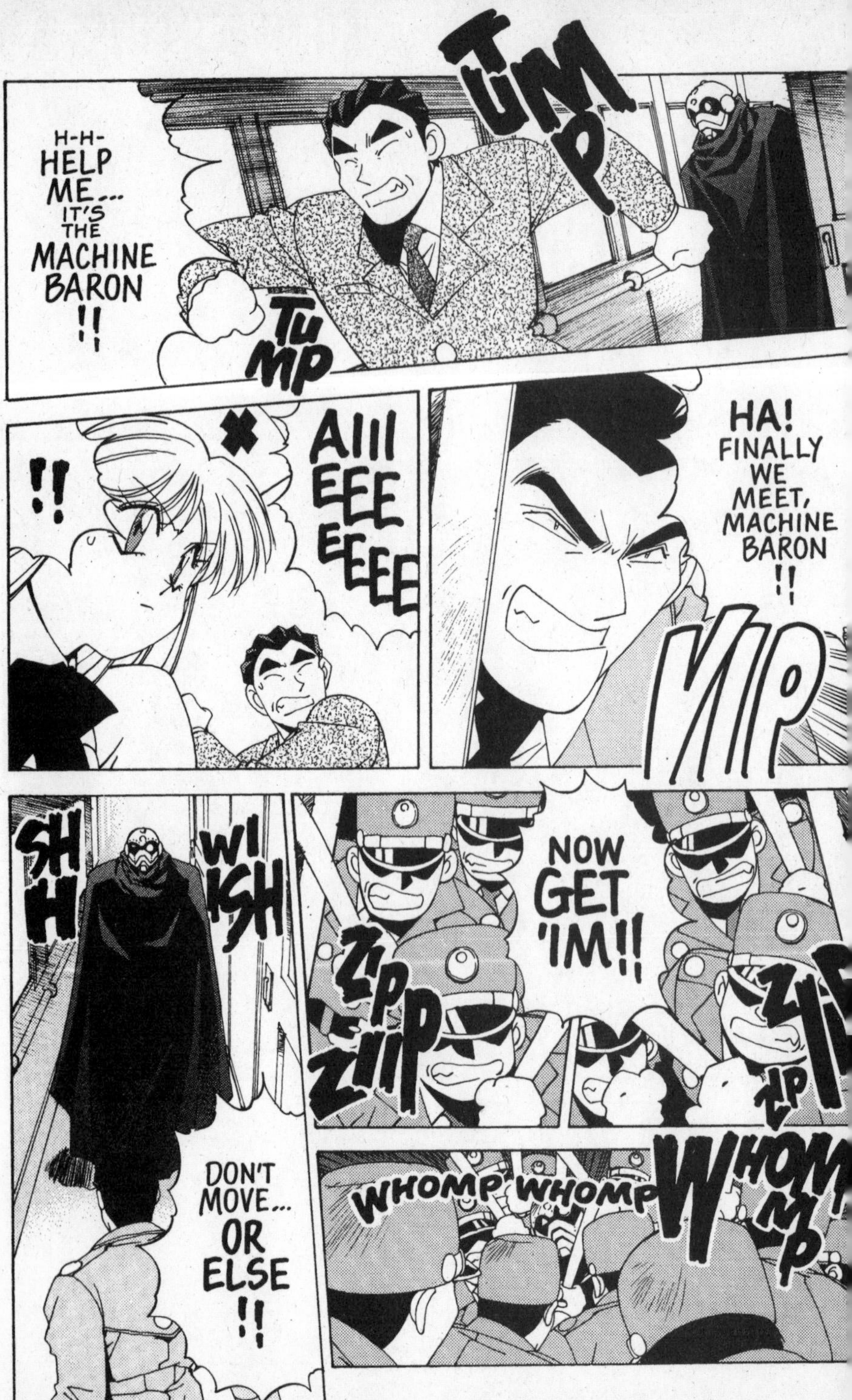
TUMP
H-H-HELP ME... IT'S THE MACHINE BARON !!
TUMP
HA! FINALLY WE MEET, MACHINE BARON !!
VIP
AIIIEEEEEEEE
!!
NOW GET 'IM!!
ZIPP ZIIP
SHH
WISH
WHOMP WHOMP WHOMP
DON'T MOVE... OR ELSE !!

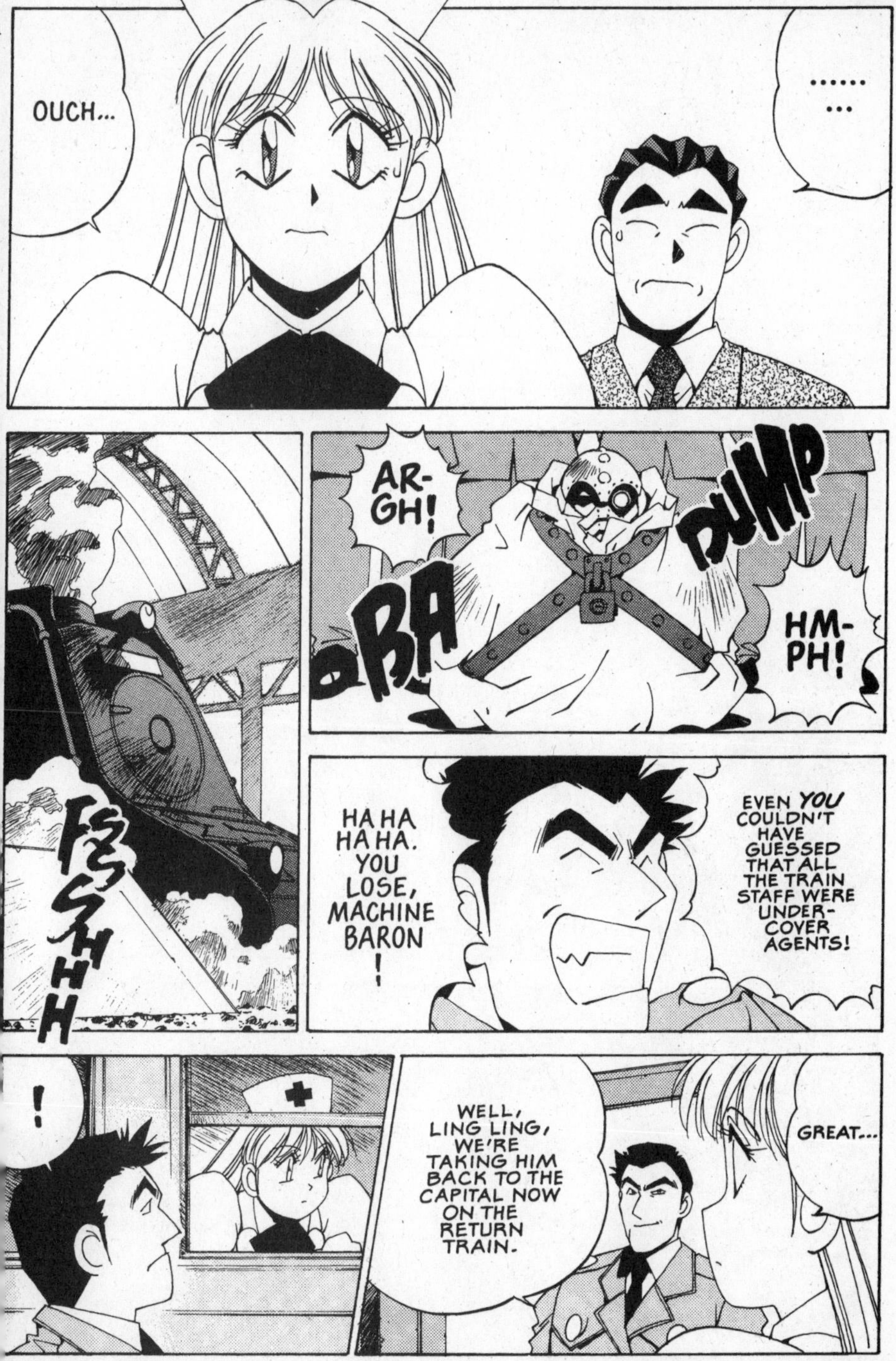
OUCH...
....
FSSHHHH
AR-GH!
BA
DUMP
HM-PH!
HA HA HA HA. YOU LOSE, MACHINE BARON!
EVEN YOU COULDN'T HAVE GUESSED THAT ALL THE TRAIN STAFF WERE UNDER-COVER AGENTS!
!
WELL, LING LING, WE'RE TAKING HIM BACK TO THE CAPITAL NOW ON THE RETURN TRAIN.
GREAT...

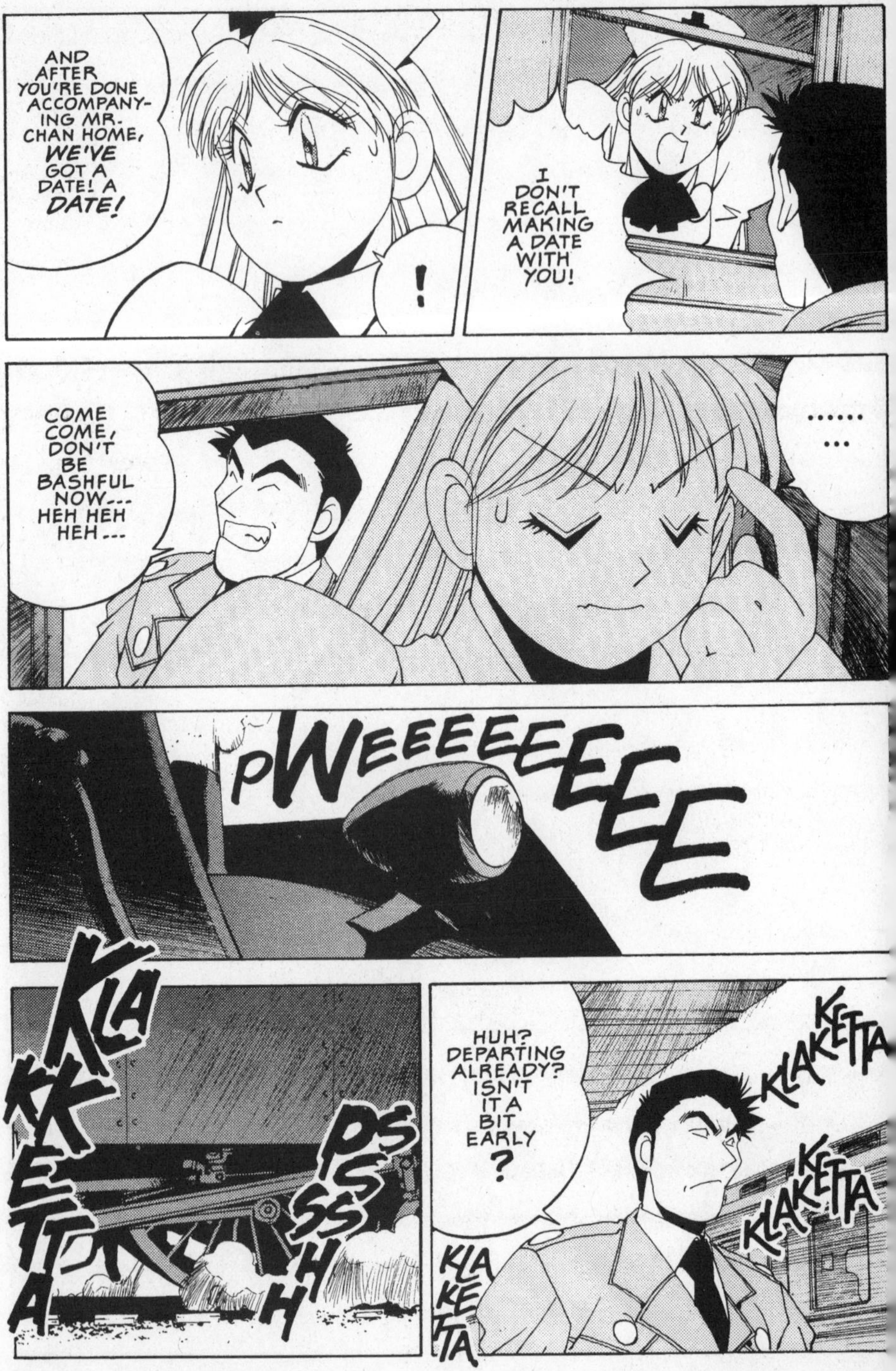
AND AFTER YOU'RE DONE ACCOMPANYING MR. CHAN HOME, WE'VE GOT A DATE! A DATE!
!
I DON'T RECALL MAKING A DATE WITH YOU!
COME COME, DON'T BE BASHFUL NOW... HEH HEH HEH...
....
PWEEEEEEEEE
KLAKKETTA
PSSSSHHH
HUH? DEPARTING ALREADY? ISN'T IT A BIT EARLY?
KLAKETTA
KLAKETTA
KLAKETTA

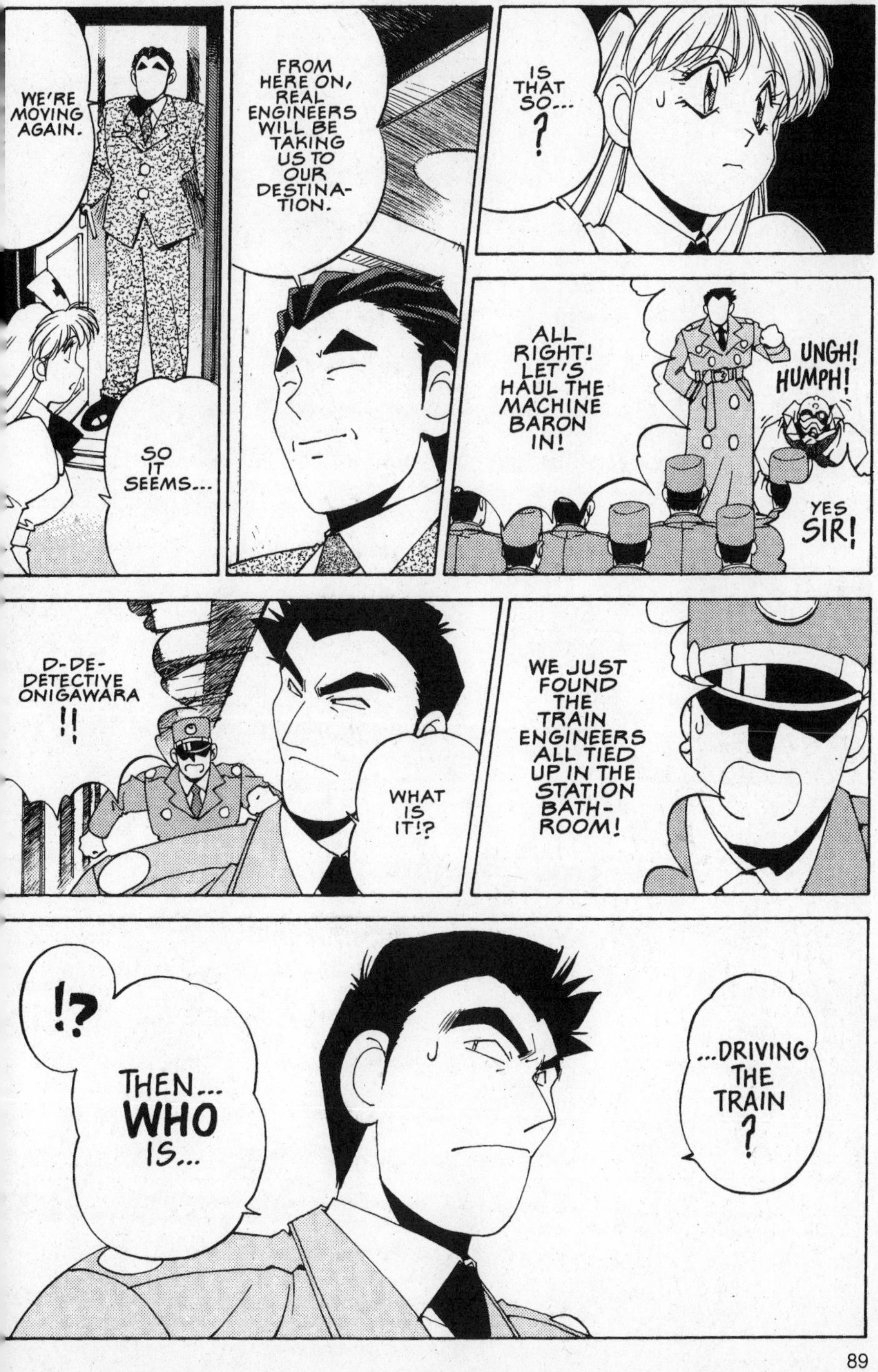
WE'RE MOVING AGAIN.
SO IT SEEMS...
FROM HERE ON, REAL ENGINEERS WILL BE TAKING US TO OUR DESTINA-TION.
IS THAT SO...?
ALL RIGHT! LET'S HAUL THE MACHINE BARON IN!
UNGH! HUMPH!
YES SIR!
D-DE-DETECTIVE ONIGAWARA!!
WHAT IS IT!?
WE JUST FOUND THE TRAIN ENGINEERS ALL TIED UP IN THE STATION BATH-ROOM!
!?
THEN... WHO IS...
...DRIVING THE TRAIN?

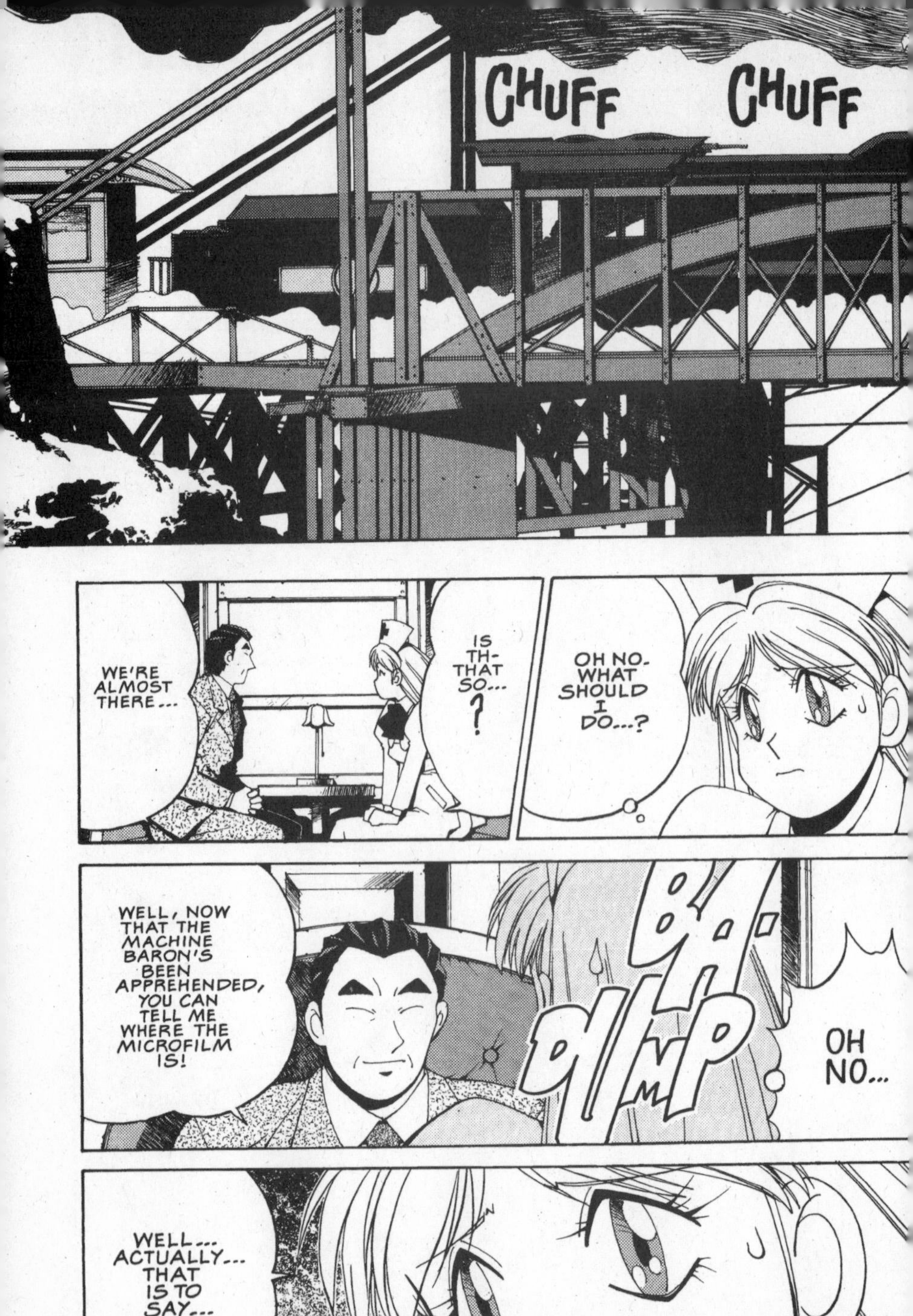
CHUFF CHUFF
WE'RE ALMOST THERE...
IS TH-THAT SO...?
OH NO. WHAT SHOULD I DO...?
WELL, NOW THAT THE MACHINE BARON'S BEEN APPREHENDED, YOU CAN TELL ME WHERE THE MICROFILM IS!
BA-DUMP
OH NO...
WELL... ACTUALLY... THAT IS TO SAY...

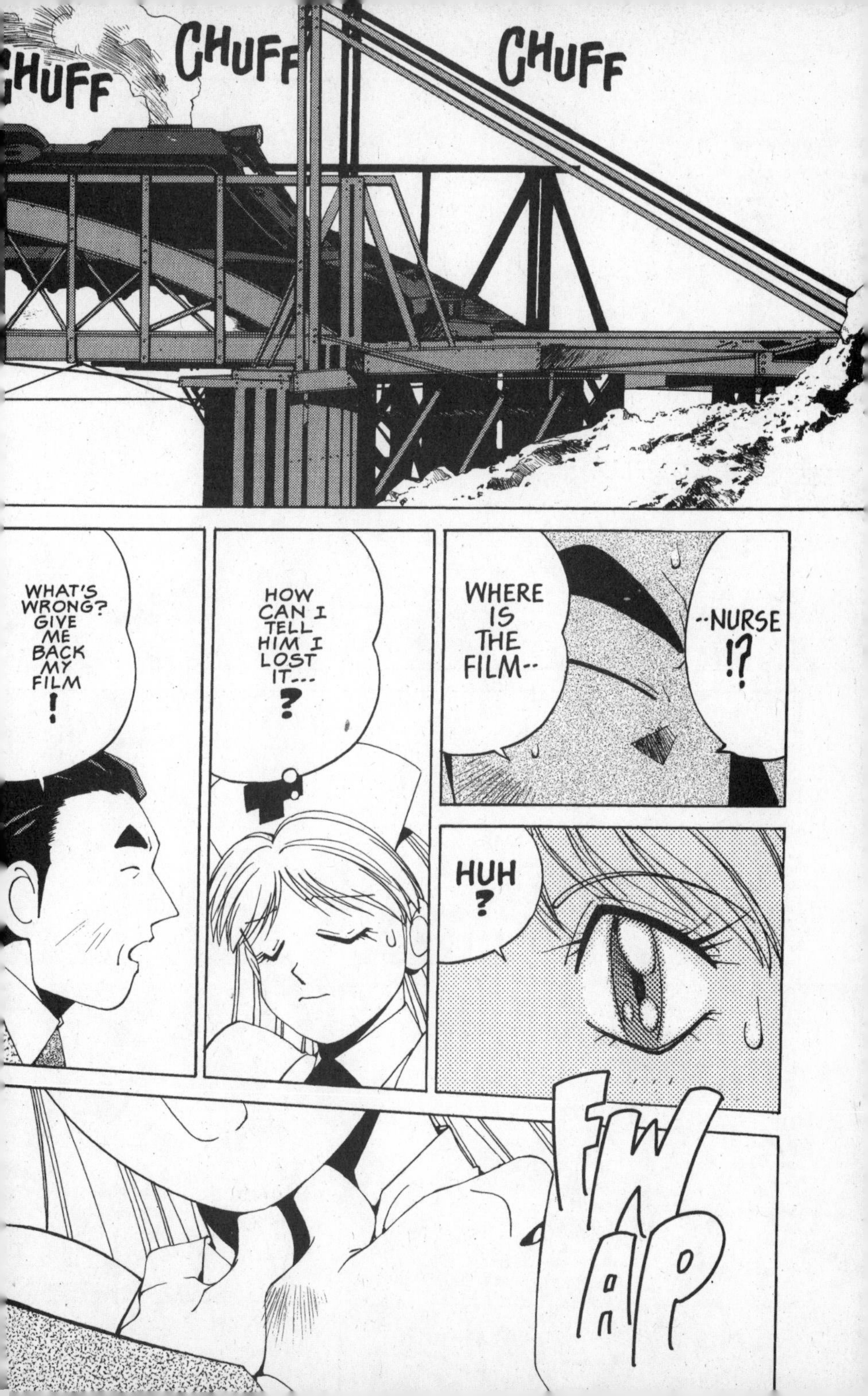

CHUFF
CHUFF
CHUFF
WHAT'S WRONG? GIVE ME BACK MY FILM!
HOW CAN I TELL HIM I LOST IT...?
WHERE IS THE FILM--
--NURSE!?
HUH?
FWAP

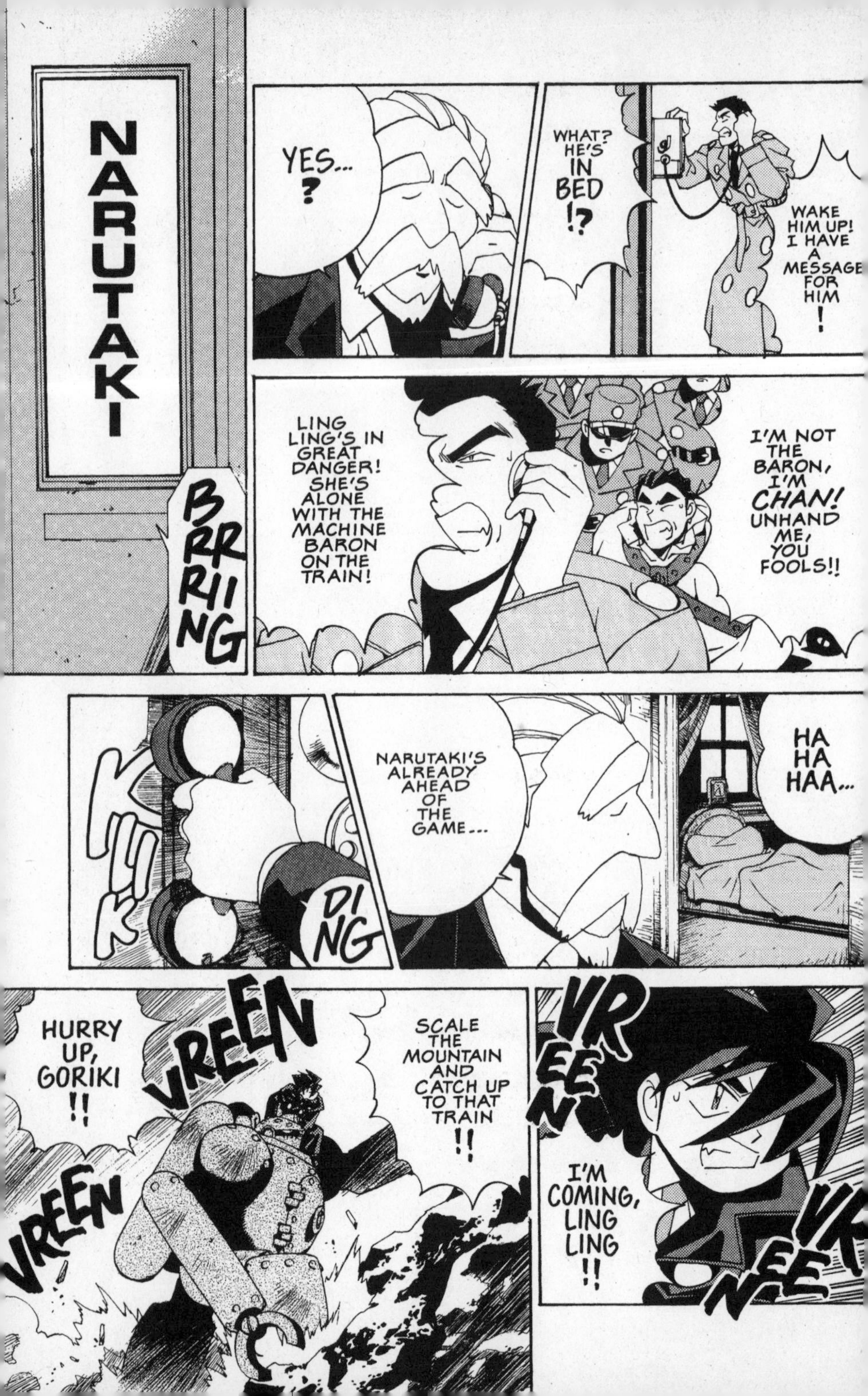
NARUTAKI
BRRRIING
YES...?
WHAT? HE'S IN BED!?
WAKE HIM UP! I HAVE A MESSAGE FOR HIM!
LING LING'S IN GREAT DANGER! SHE'S ALONE WITH THE MACHINE BARON ON THE TRAIN!
I'M NOT THE BARON, I'M CHAN! UNHAND ME, YOU FOOLS!!
KLIK
DING
NARUTAKI'S ALREADY AHEAD OF THE GAME...
HA HA HAA...
HURRY UP, GORIKI!!
VREEN
VREEN
SCALE THE MOUNTAIN AND CATCH UP TO THAT TRAIN!!
VREEN
I'M COMING, LING LING!!
VREEN

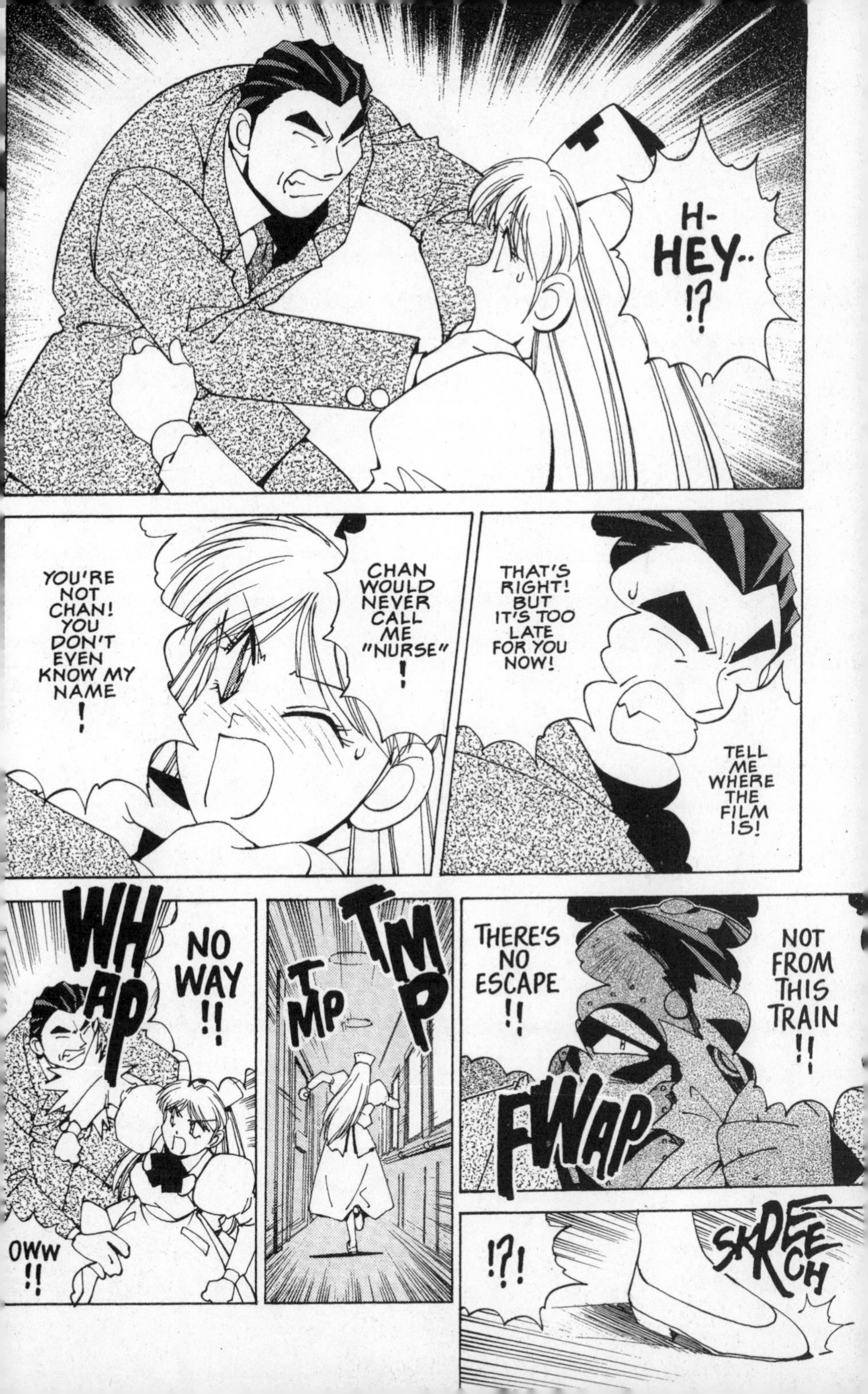
H-
HEY..
!?
YOU'RE NOT CHAN! YOU DON'T EVEN KNOW MY NAME !
CHAN WOULD NEVER CALL ME "NURSE" !
THAT'S RIGHT! BUT IT'S TOO LATE FOR YOU NOW!
TELL ME WHERE THE FILM IS!
WHAP
NO WAY !!
OWW !!
TMP
TMP
THERE'S NO ESCAPE !!
NOT FROM THIS TRAIN !!
FWAP
!?!
SKREECH

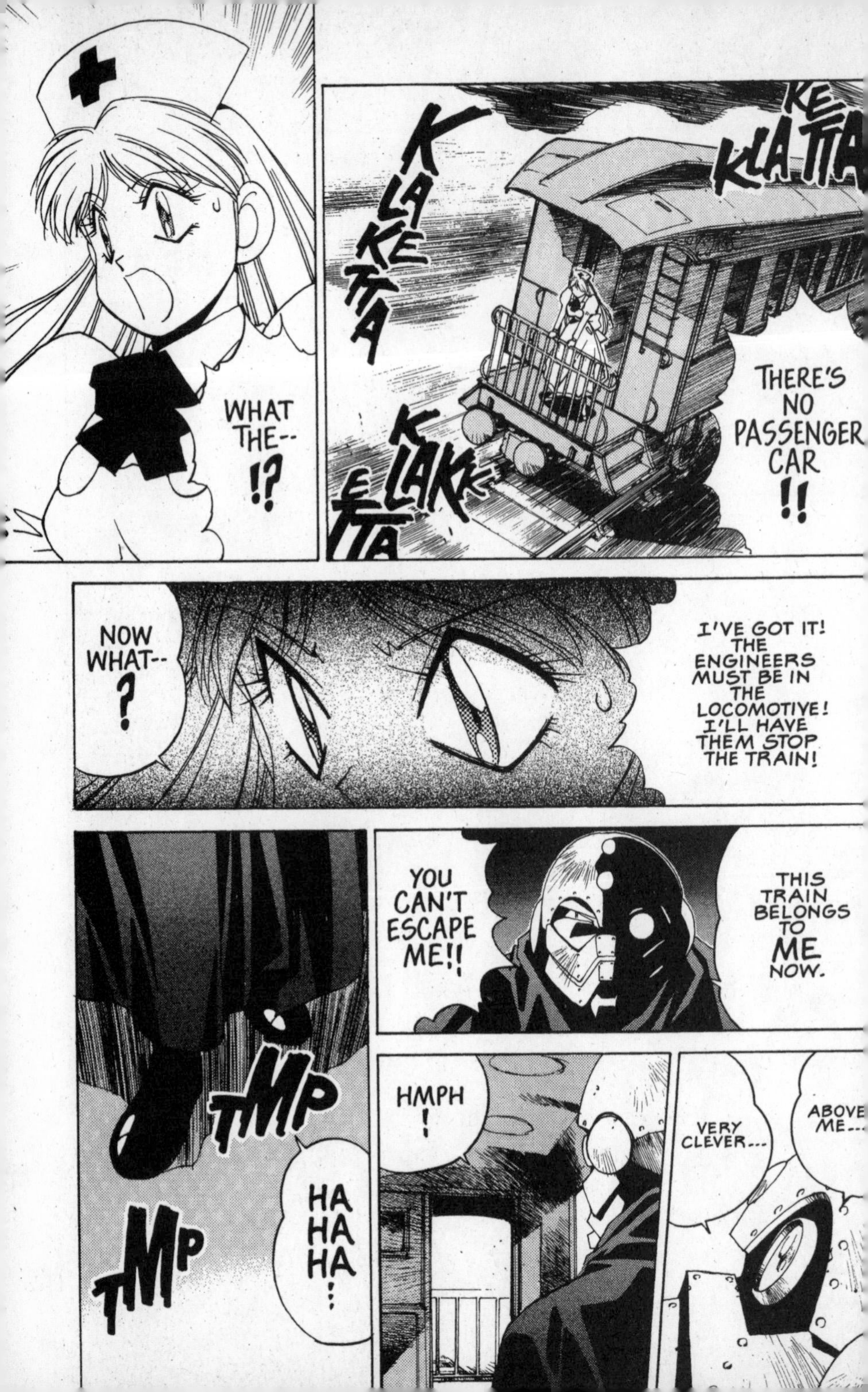
WHAT THE-- !?
KLAKETTA
KE KLATTA
KLAKK
ETTA
THERE'S NO PASSENGER CAR !!
NOW WHAT-- ?
I'VE GOT IT! THE ENGINEERS MUST BE IN THE LOCOMOTIVE! I'LL HAVE THEM STOP THE TRAIN!
TMP
TMP
HA HA HA HA!
YOU CAN'T ESCAPE ME!!
THIS TRAIN BELONGS TO ME NOW.
HMPH!
VERY CLEVER...
ABOVE ME...

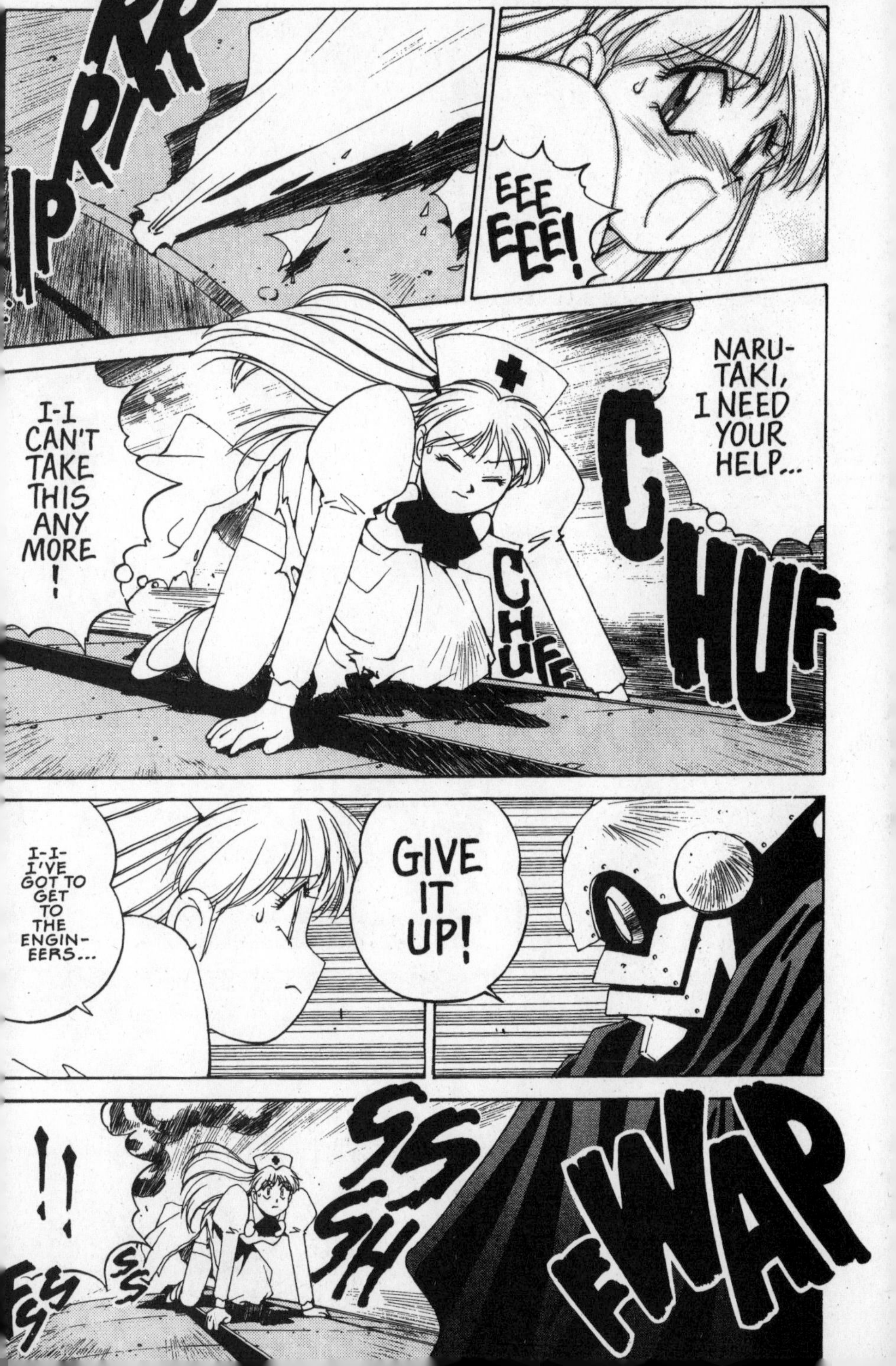
RRRIIIP
EEE EEE!
I-I CAN'T TAKE THIS ANY MORE!
NARU-TAKI, I NEED YOUR HELP...
CHUFF
CHUF
I-I-I'VE GOT TO GET TO THE ENGIN-EERS...
GIVE IT UP!
!!
SSSSH
FWAP
SSS
SSS

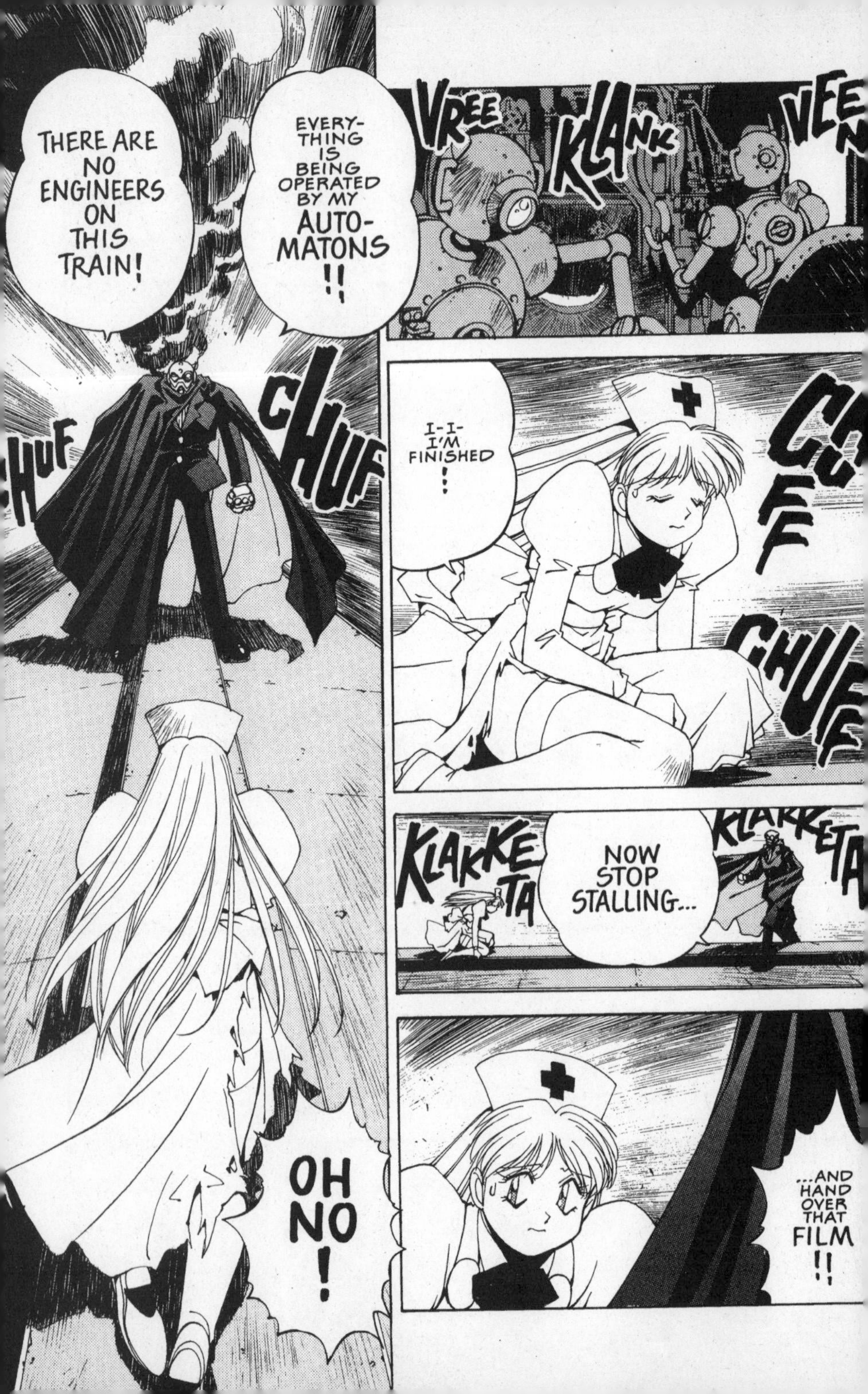
THERE ARE NO ENGINEERS ON THIS TRAIN!
EVERY-THING IS BEING OPERATED BY MY AUTO-MATONS!!
CHUF
CHUF
OH NO!
VREE
KLANK
VEEN
I-I-I'M FINISHED!
CHUF
NOW STOP STALLING...
...AND HAND OVER THAT FILM!!

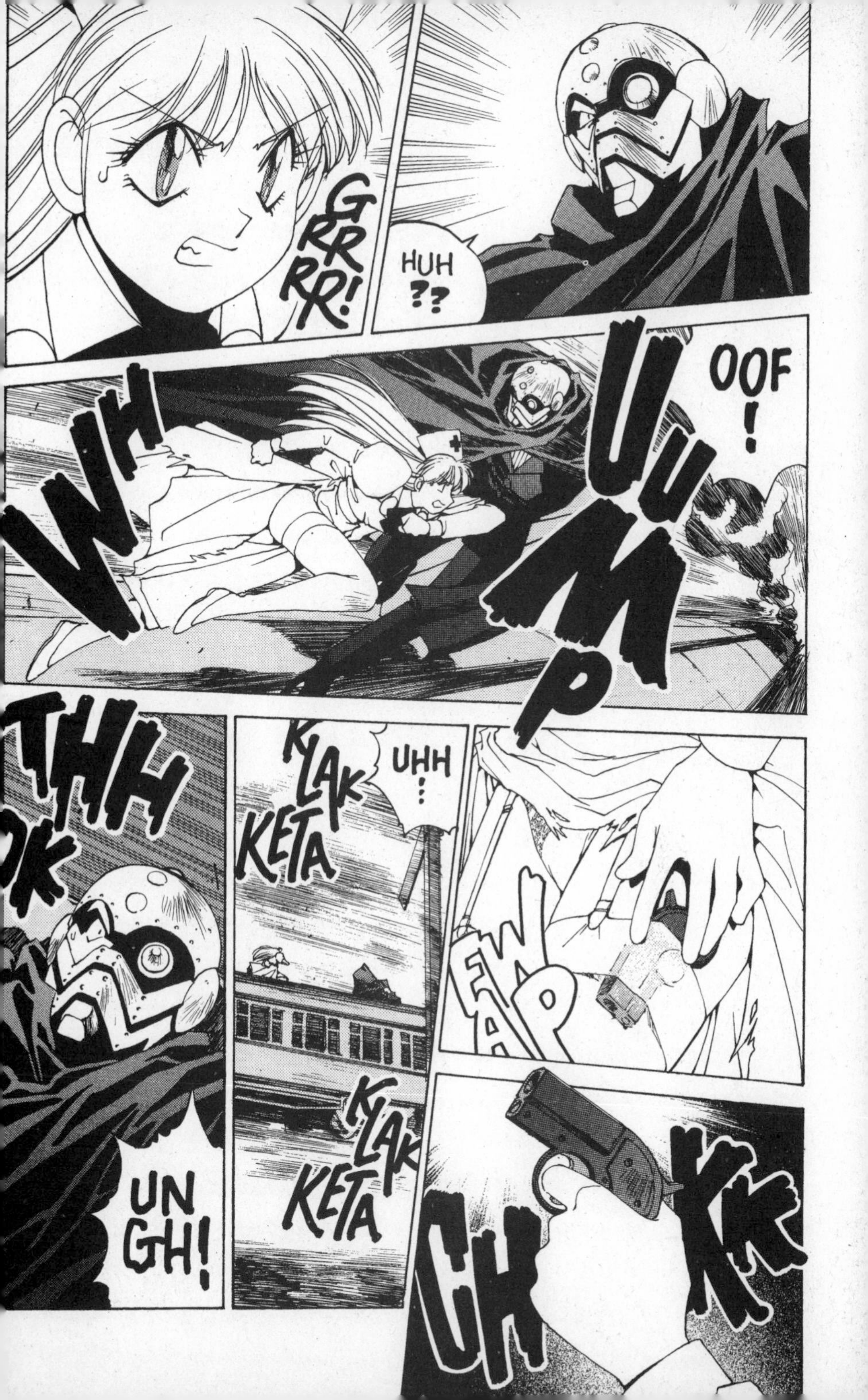
GRRRRR!
HUH ??
WHUUMP
OOF !
THHOK
UNGH!
KLAK KETA
UHH ...
KLAK KETA
FWAP
CHKK

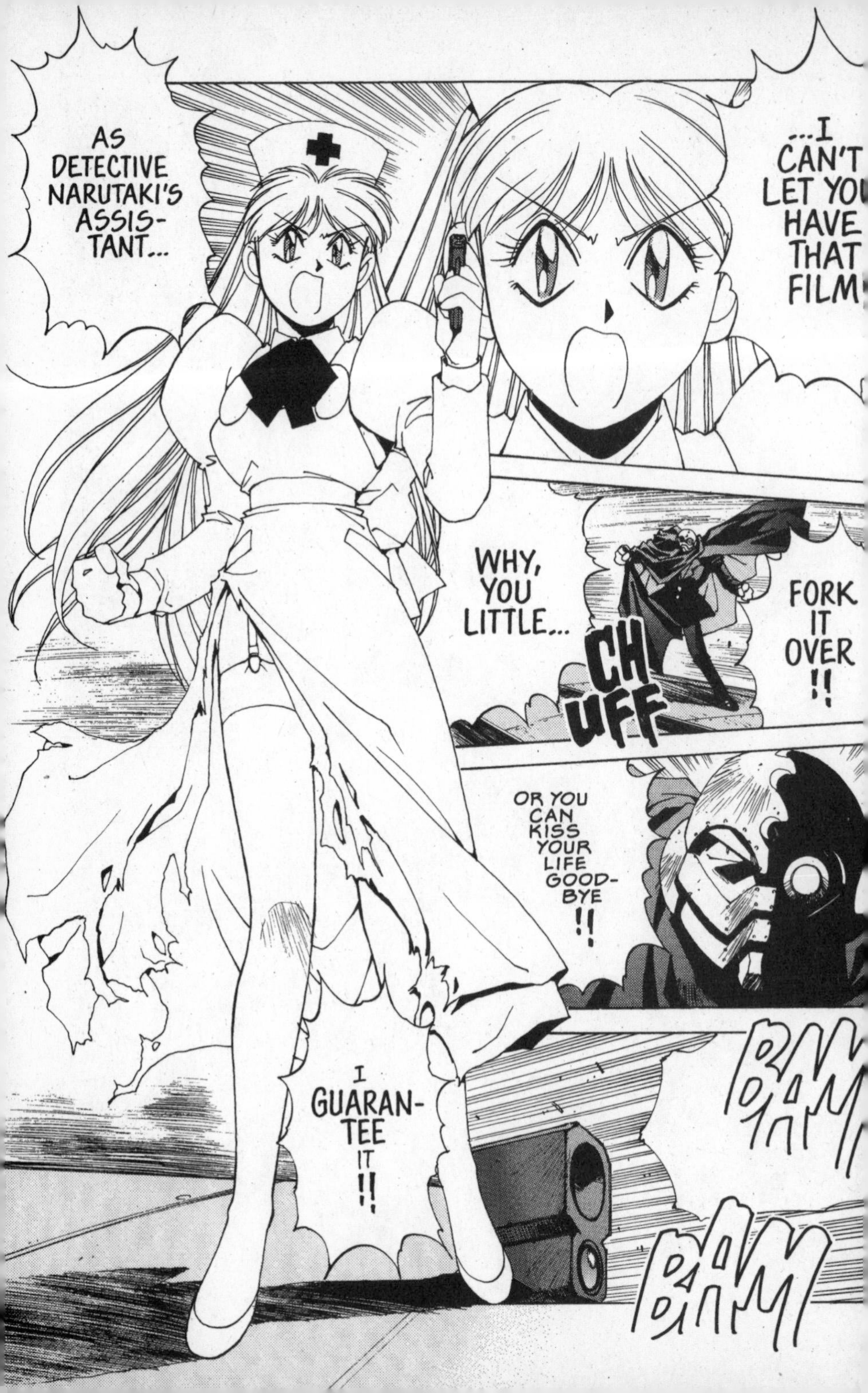
AS DETECTIVE NARUTAKI'S ASSIS-TANT...
I GUARAN-TEE IT!!
...I CAN'T LET YOU HAVE THAT FILM
WHY, YOU LITTLE...
CH UFF
FORK IT OVER!!
OR YOU CAN KISS YOUR LIFE GOOD-BYE!!
BAM
BAM

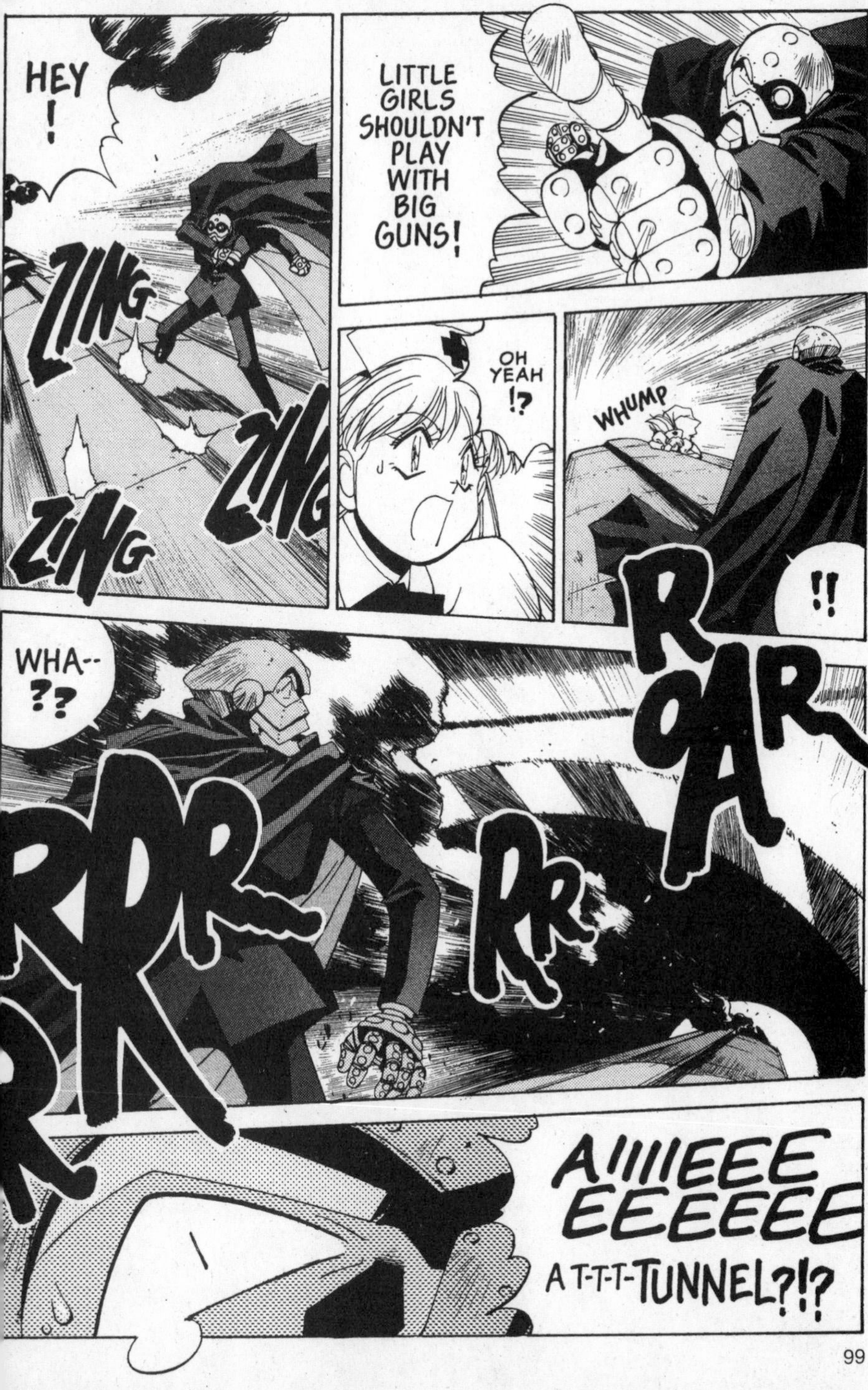
HEY!
ZING
ZING
ZING
LITTLE GIRLS SHOULDN'T PLAY WITH BIG GUNS!
OH YEAH !?
WHUMP
!!
WHA-- ??
RRRR
RRR
ROAR
AIIIIEEE EEEEEE
A T-T-T-TUNNEL?!?

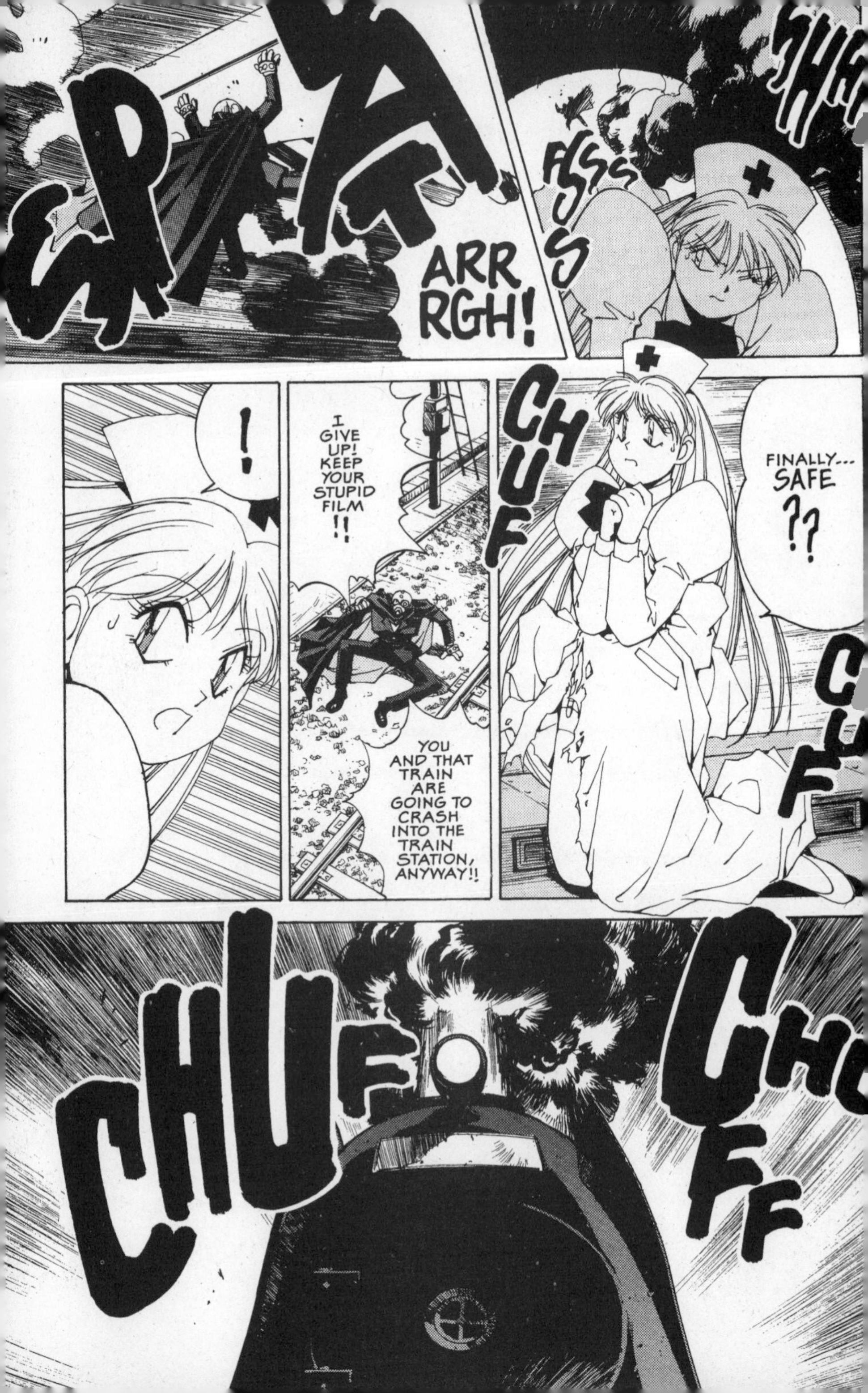
SPLAT
ARR RGH!
FSSSS
SHH
!
I GIVE UP! KEEP YOUR STUPID FILM !!
YOU AND THAT TRAIN ARE GOING TO CRASH INTO THE TRAIN STATION, ANYWAY!!
CHUF
FINALLY... SAFE ??
CHUF
CHUF
CHUFF

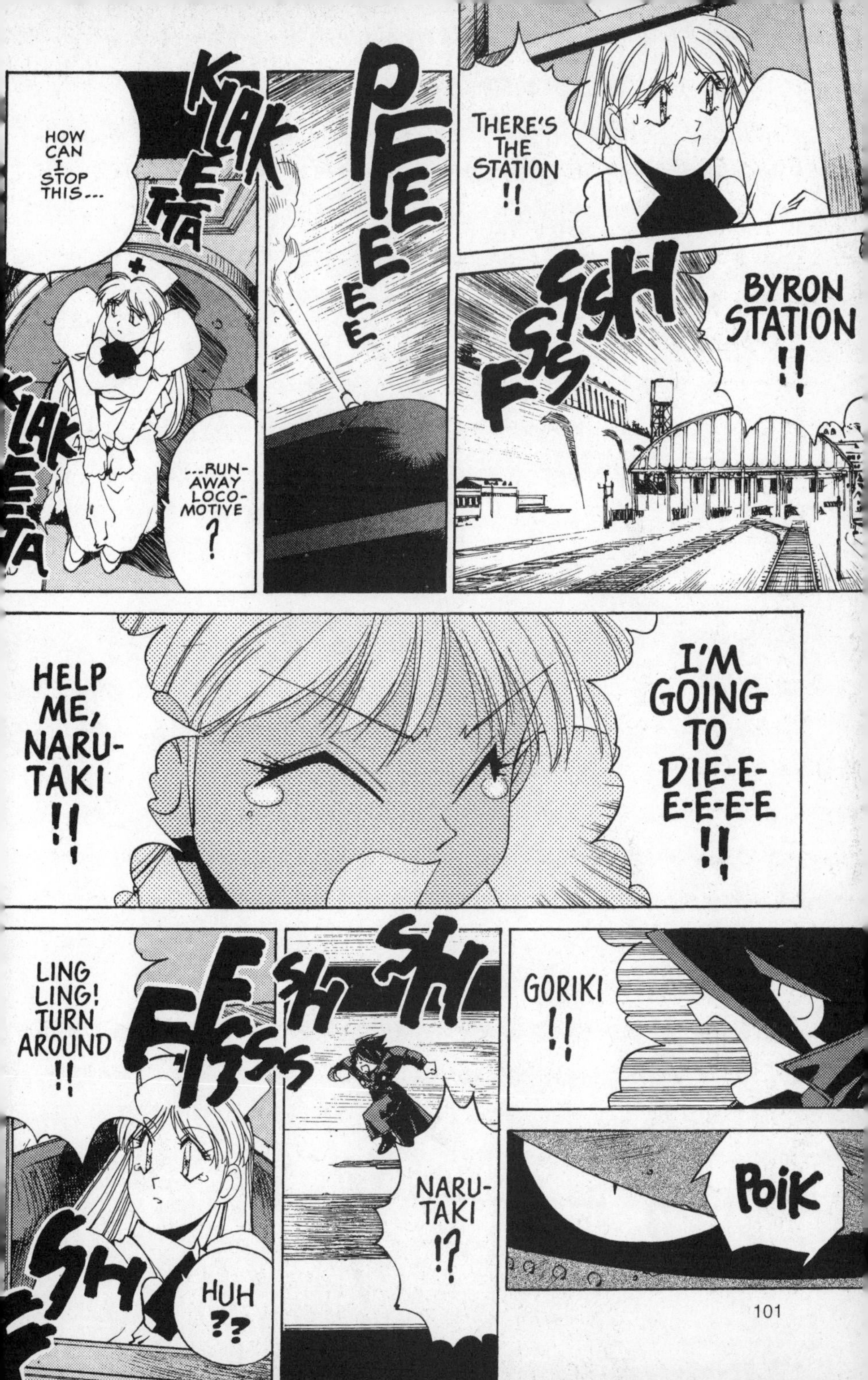
HOW CAN I STOP THIS...
KLAK ETTA
KLAK ETTA
...RUNAWAY LOCOMOTIVE?
PFEEEE
THERE'S THE STATION!!
FSSSH
BYRON STATION!!
HELP ME, NARUTAKI!!
I'M GOING TO DIE-E-E-E-E-E!!
LING LING! TURN AROUND!!
FSSS
SH
HUH??
SH SH
NARUTAKI!?
GORIKI!!
POIK

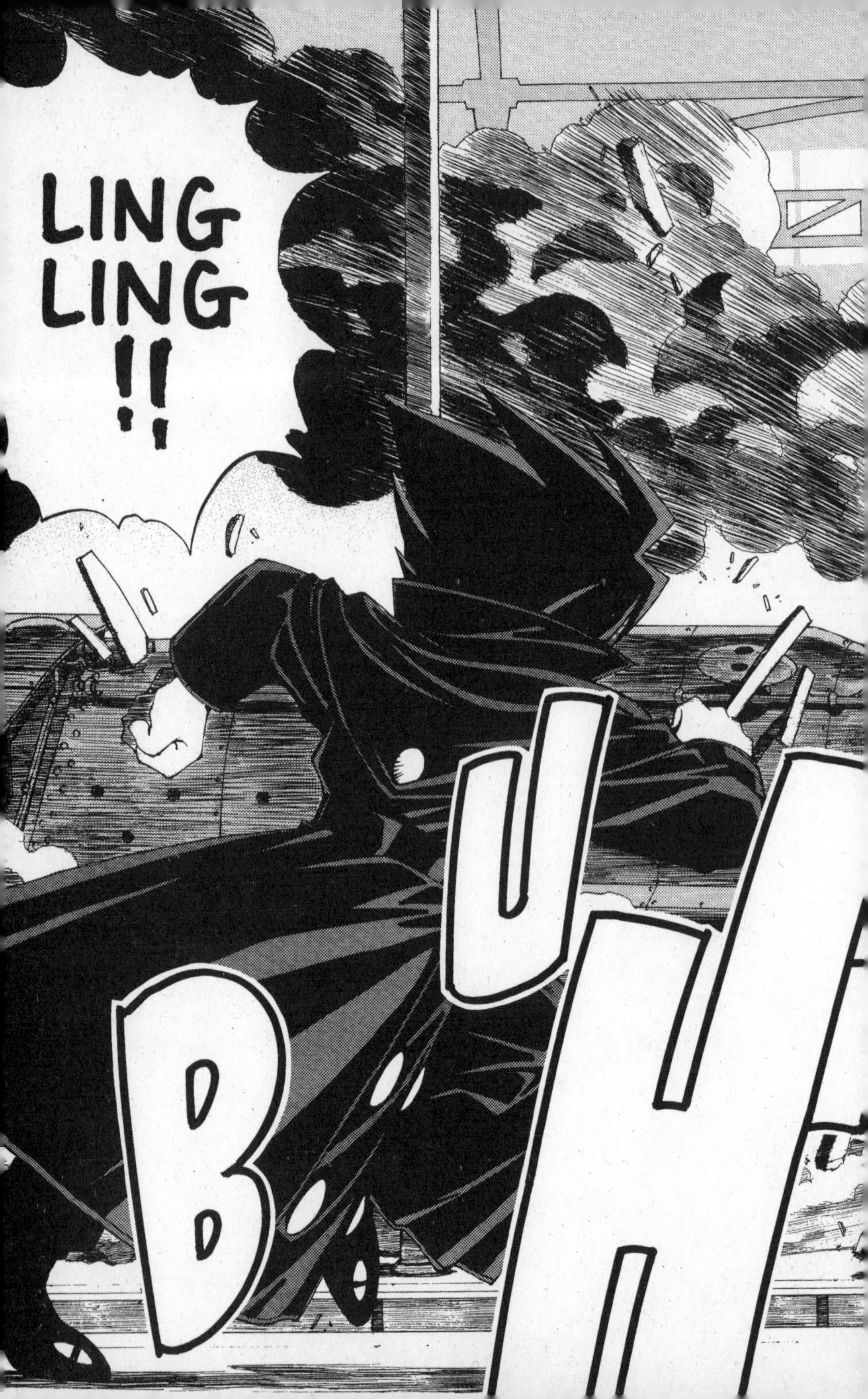
LING LING !!
BUH

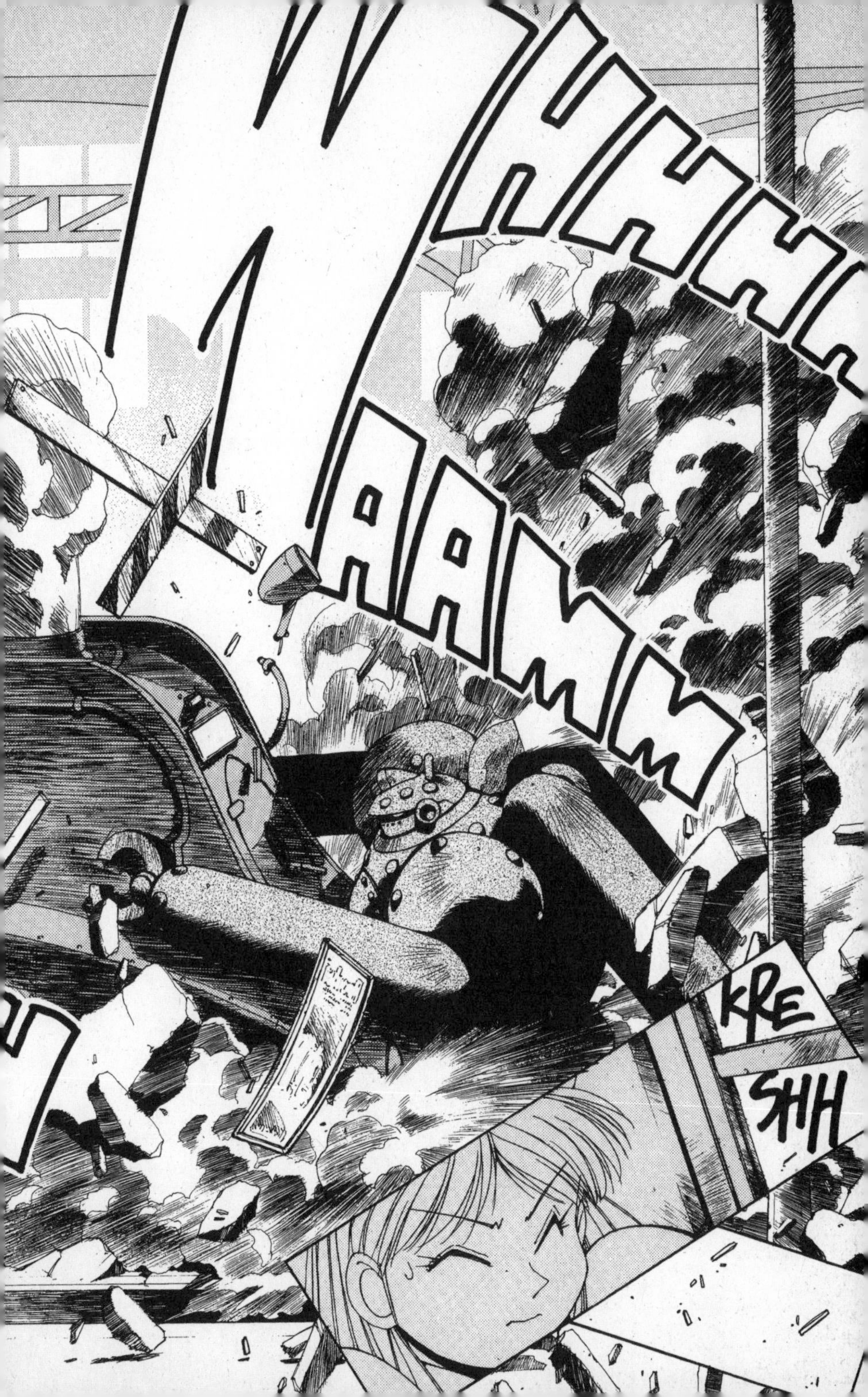
KRE
SHH

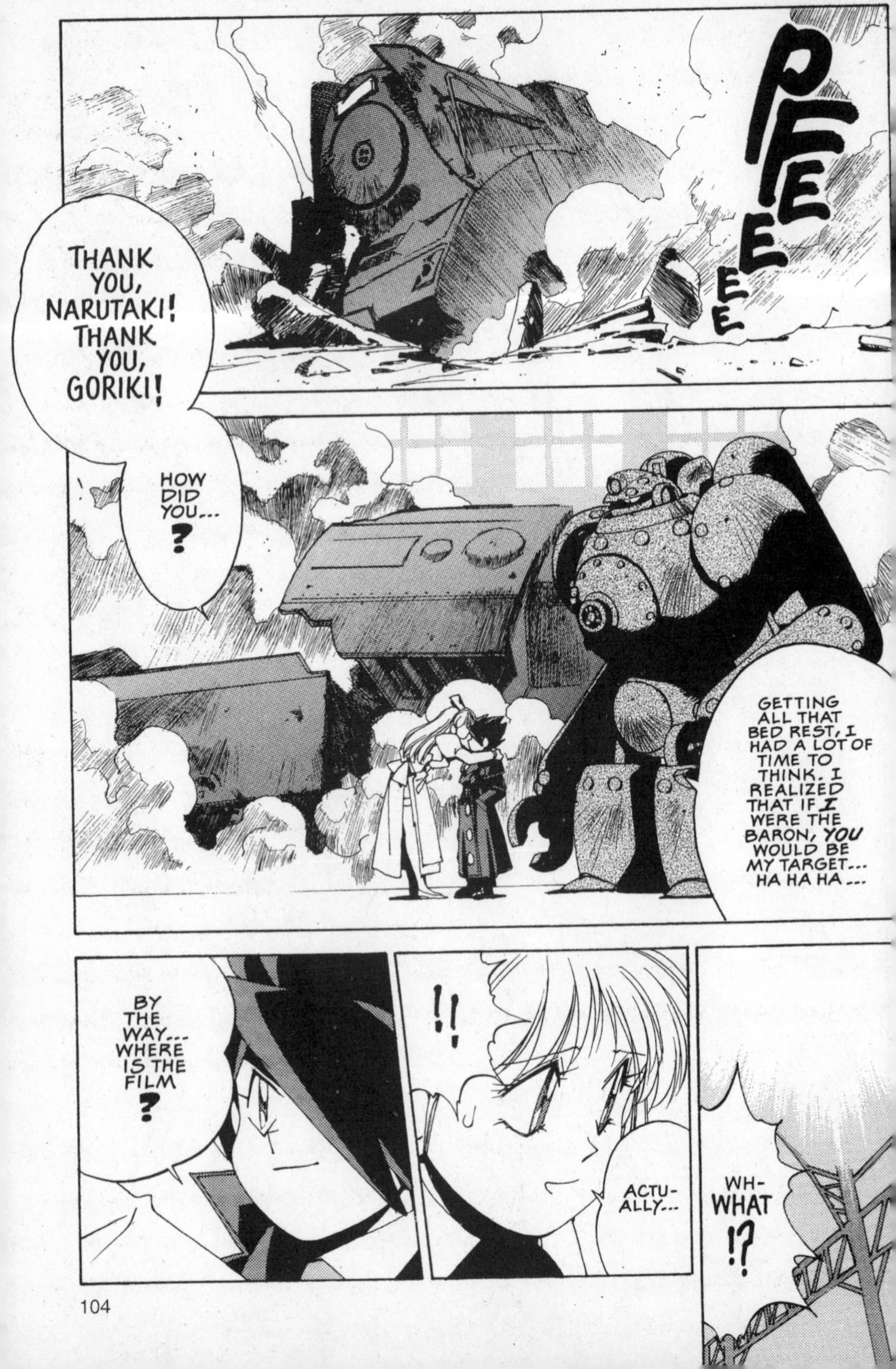
THANK YOU, NARUTAKI! THANK YOU, GORIKI!
PFEEEEE
HOW DID YOU...?
GETTING ALL THAT BED REST, I HAD A LOT OF TIME TO THINK. I REALIZED THAT IF I WERE THE BARON, YOU WOULD BE MY TARGET... HA HA HA...
BY THE WAY... WHERE IS THE FILM?
!!
ACTU-ALLY...
WH-WHAT !?

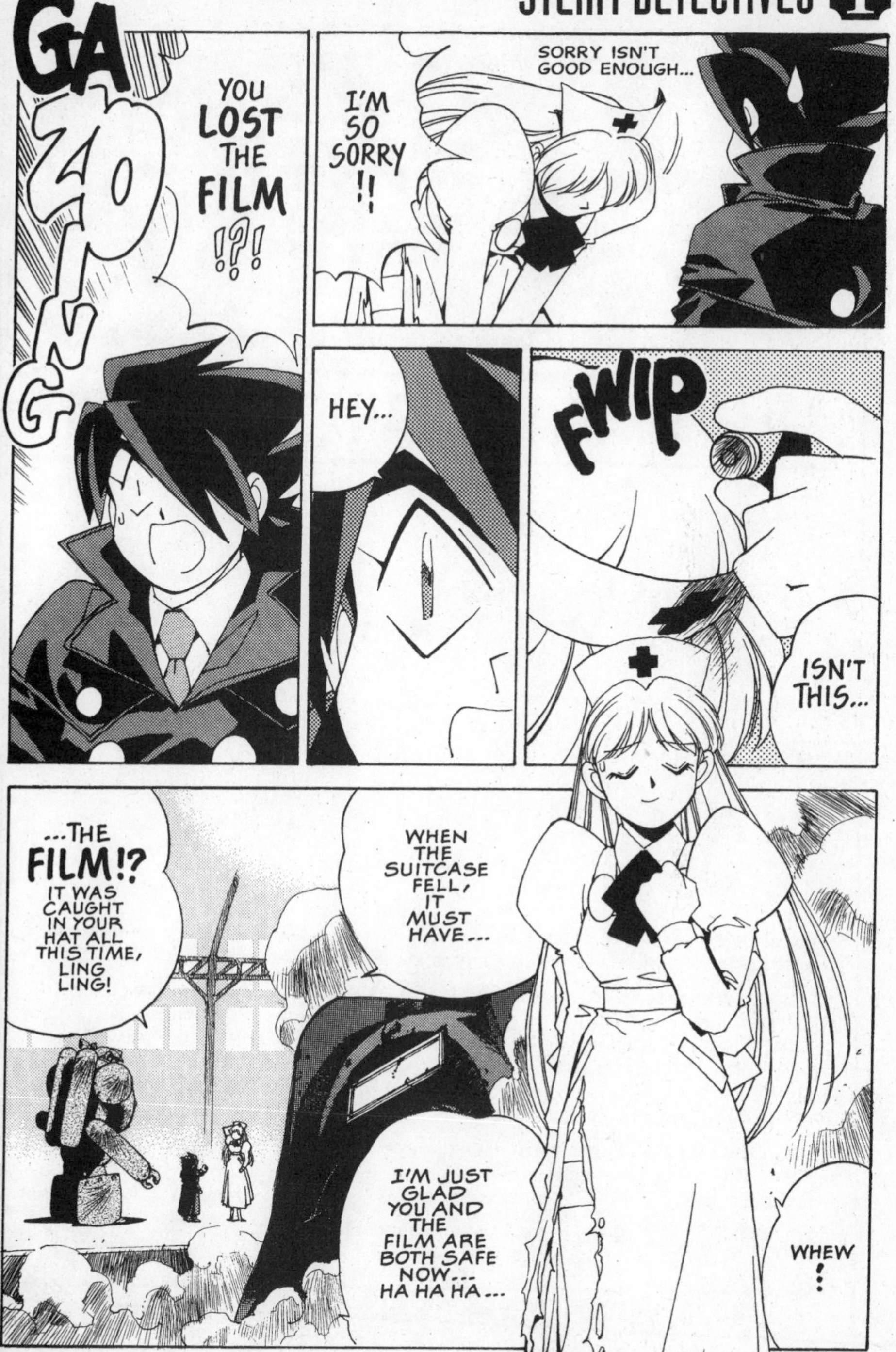
GAZOING
YOU LOST THE FILM !?!
I'M SO SORRY !!
SORRY ISN'T GOOD ENOUGH...
HEY...
FWIP
ISN'T THIS...
...THE FILM!? IT WAS CAUGHT IN YOUR HAT ALL THIS TIME, LING LING!
WHEN THE SUITCASE FELL, IT MUST HAVE...
I'M JUST GLAD YOU AND THE FILM ARE BOTH SAFE NOW... HA HA HA...
WHEW !

STEAM DETECTIVES PRESS

SPECIAL PROFILE: NARUTAKI'S GUN

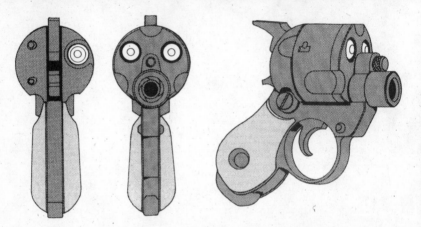

The illustration above depicts Narutaki's custom-made gun. The manufacturer remains unknown, but its technology is extremely advanced.

According to confirmed sources, the gun is a basic model equipped with multiple features. The "Wire Gun Feature" shoots a wire rope for scaling walls, the "Glue Feature" stops criminals in their tracks, the "Drill Gun Feature" can drill holes through metal sheets up to 50 millimeters thick, and the "Fire Extinguisher Feature" can put out towering flames. And that's only to mention a few of the gun's incredible capabilities!

The bullets in the chamber are also equipped with special features. The "Metal-Sheet Bullet" causes radio interference, the "Smoke Bullet" explodes into a cloud of smoke, and the "Explosive Bullet" bursts into fireworks.

This small multipurpose weapon is indispensable to Narutaki in his daily battle for justice on the streets of Steam City.

Volume 002 • Issued by Steam Press Co., Ltd.

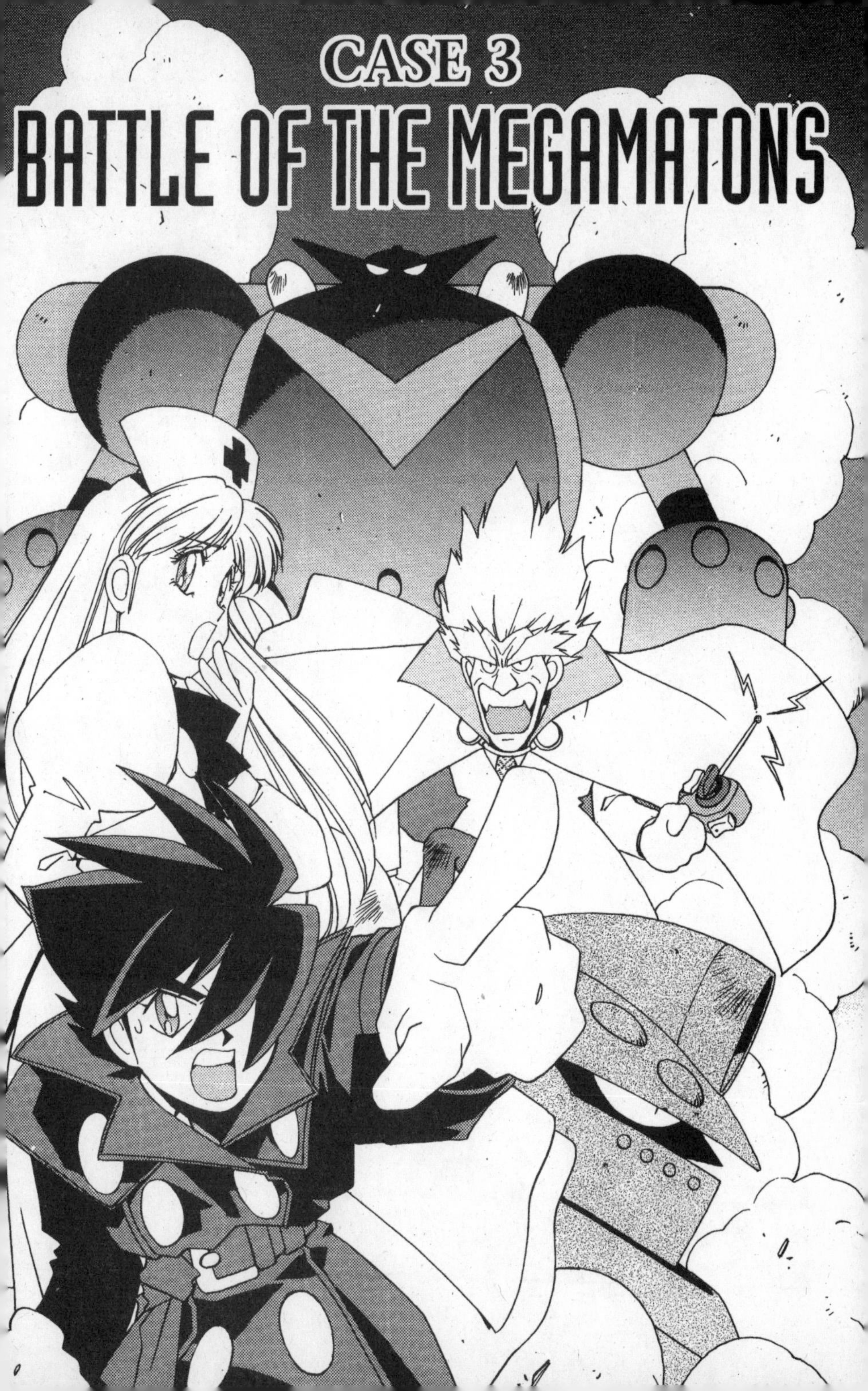
CASE 3
BATTLE OF THE MEGAMATONS

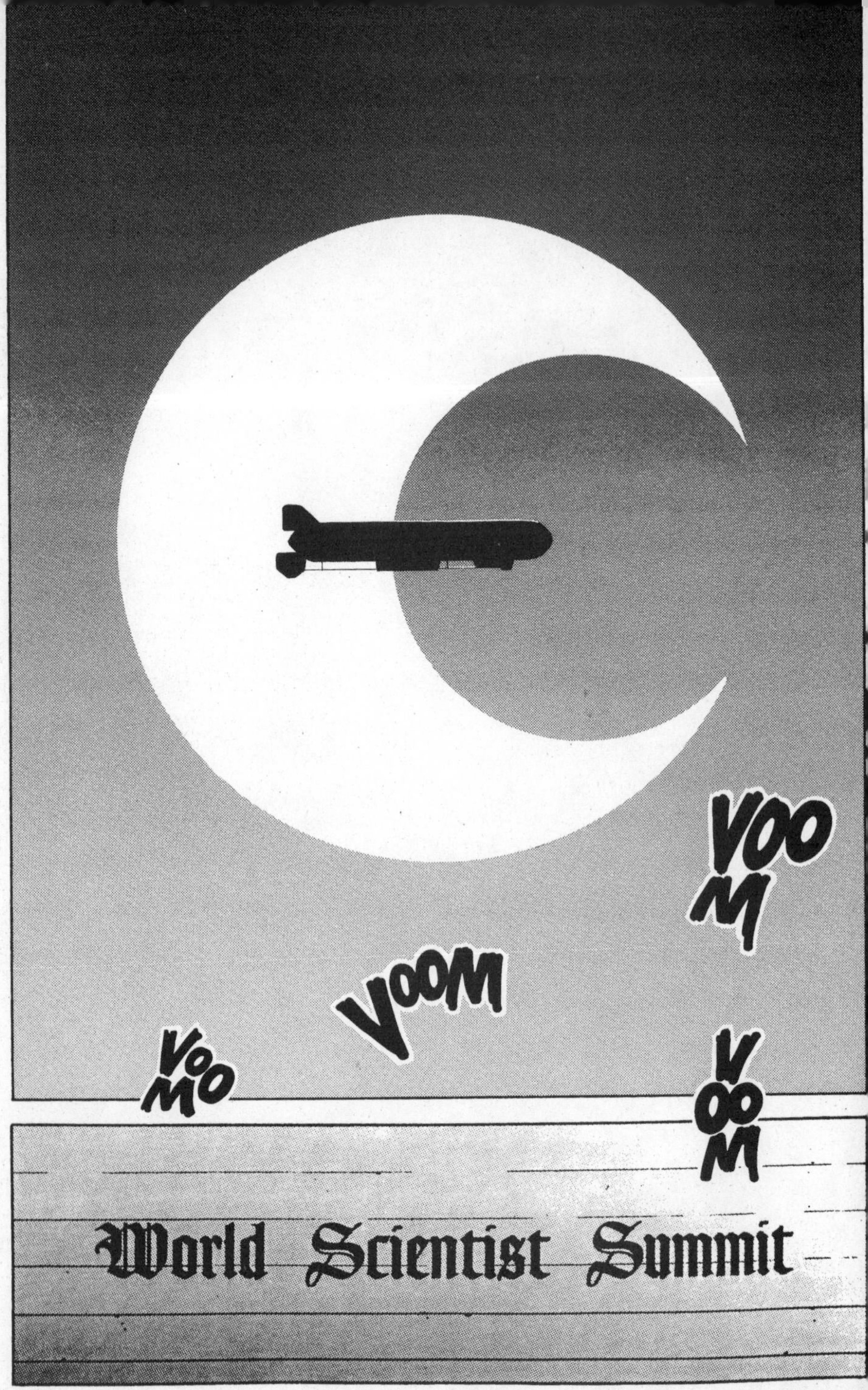

VOOM
VOOM
VOOMO
VOOM
World Scientist Summit

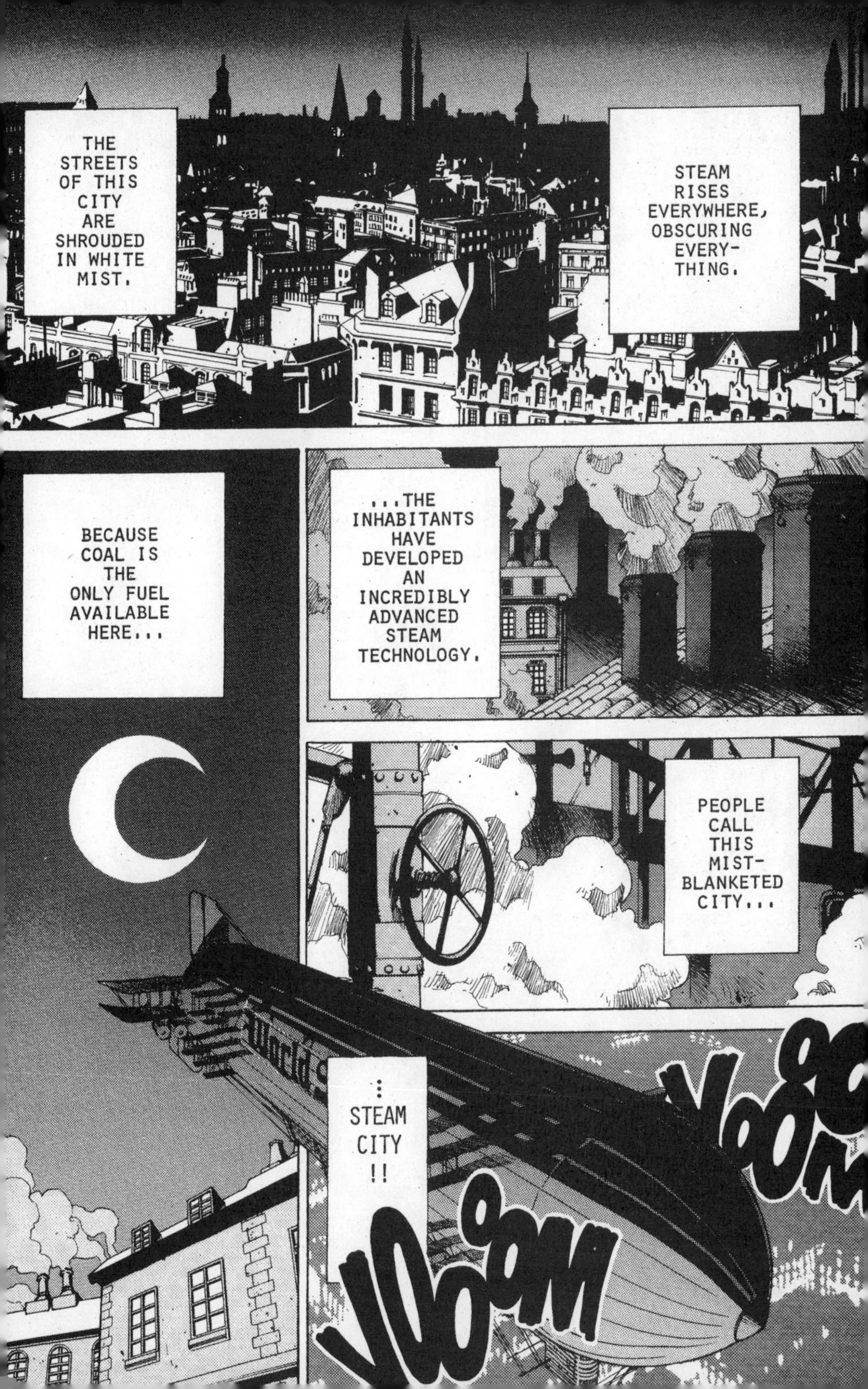
THE STREETS OF THIS CITY ARE SHROUDED IN WHITE MIST.
STEAM RISES EVERYWHERE, OBSCURING EVERY-THING.
BECAUSE COAL IS THE ONLY FUEL AVAILABLE HERE...
...THE INHABITANTS HAVE DEVELOPED AN INCREDIBLY ADVANCED STEAM TECHNOLOGY.
PEOPLE CALL THIS MIST-BLANKETED CITY...
... STEAM CITY !!
VOOOOM
VOOOOM

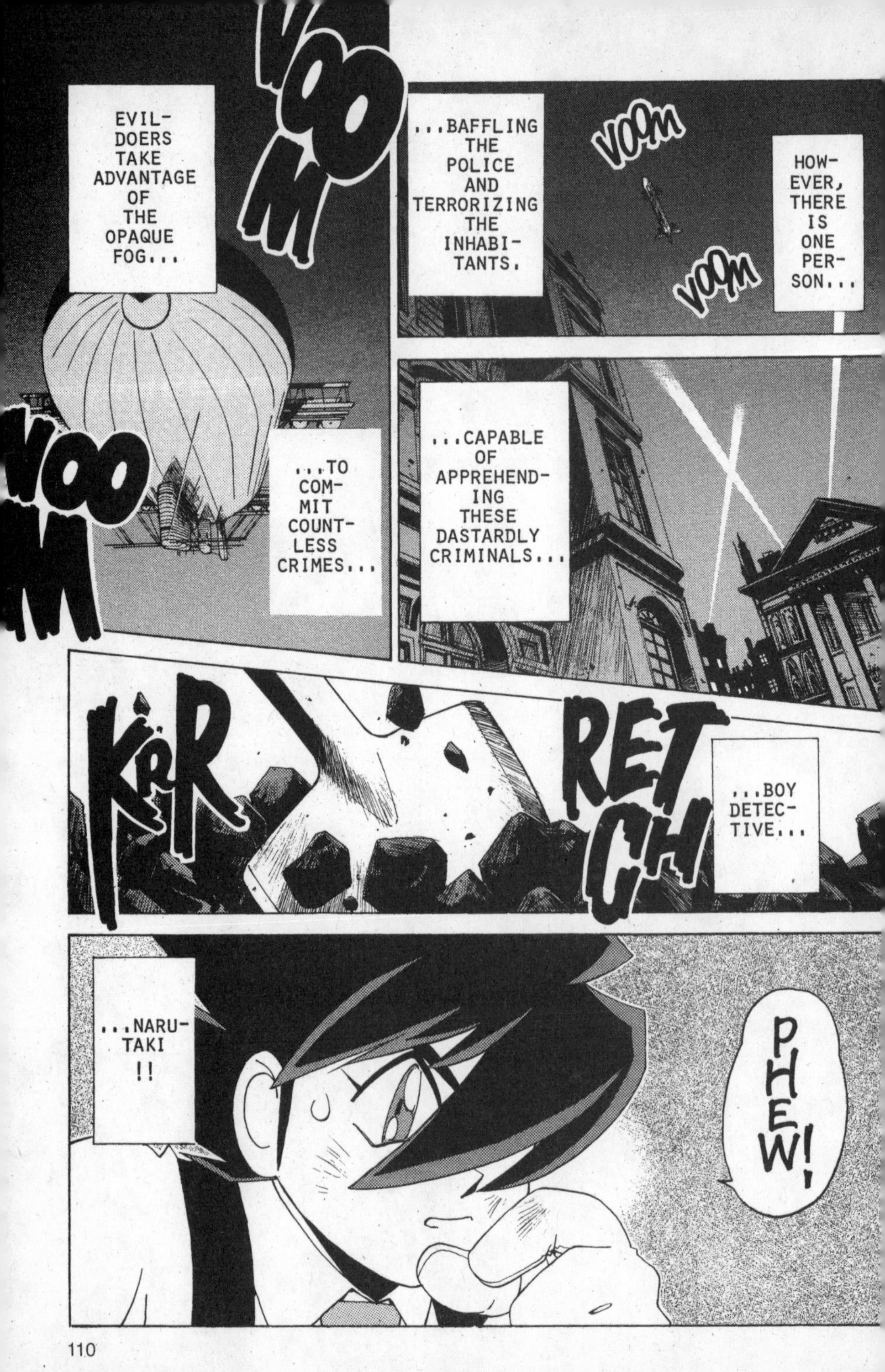
EVIL-DOERS TAKE ADVANTAGE OF THE OPAQUE FOG...
VOOM
WOOM
...TO COMMIT COUNTLESS CRIMES...
...BAFFLING THE POLICE AND TERRORIZING THE INHABITANTS.
VOOM
VOOM
HOWEVER, THERE IS ONE PERSON...
...CAPABLE OF APPREHENDING THESE DASTARDLY CRIMINALS...
KRR
RETCH
...BOY DETECTIVE...
...NARUTAKI !!
PHEW!

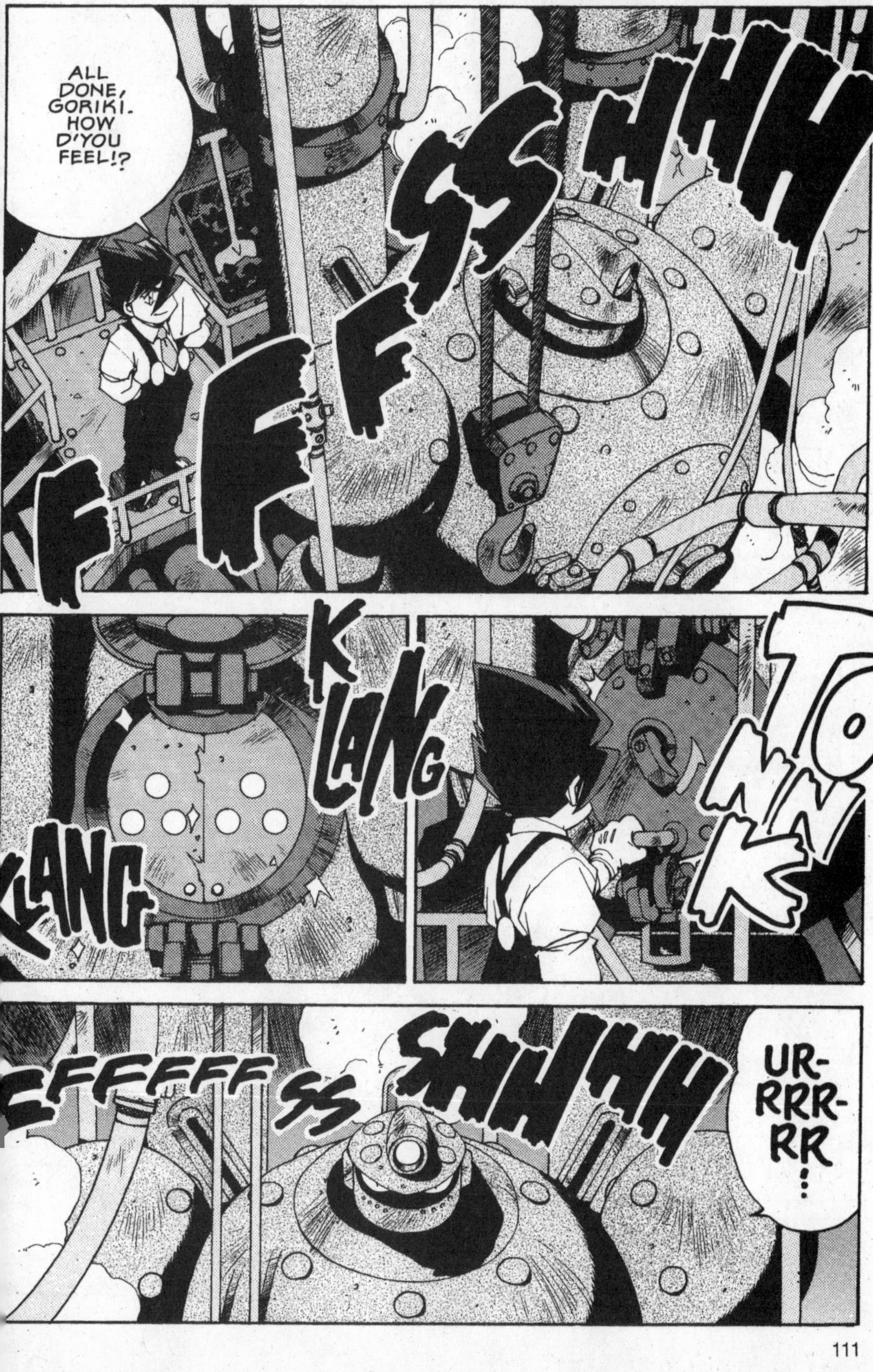
ALL DONE, GORIKI. HOW D'YOU FEEL!?
FFFSSHHHHH
KLANG
KLANG
TONNNK
FFFFFFSS
SHHHHHH
UR-RRR-RR...!

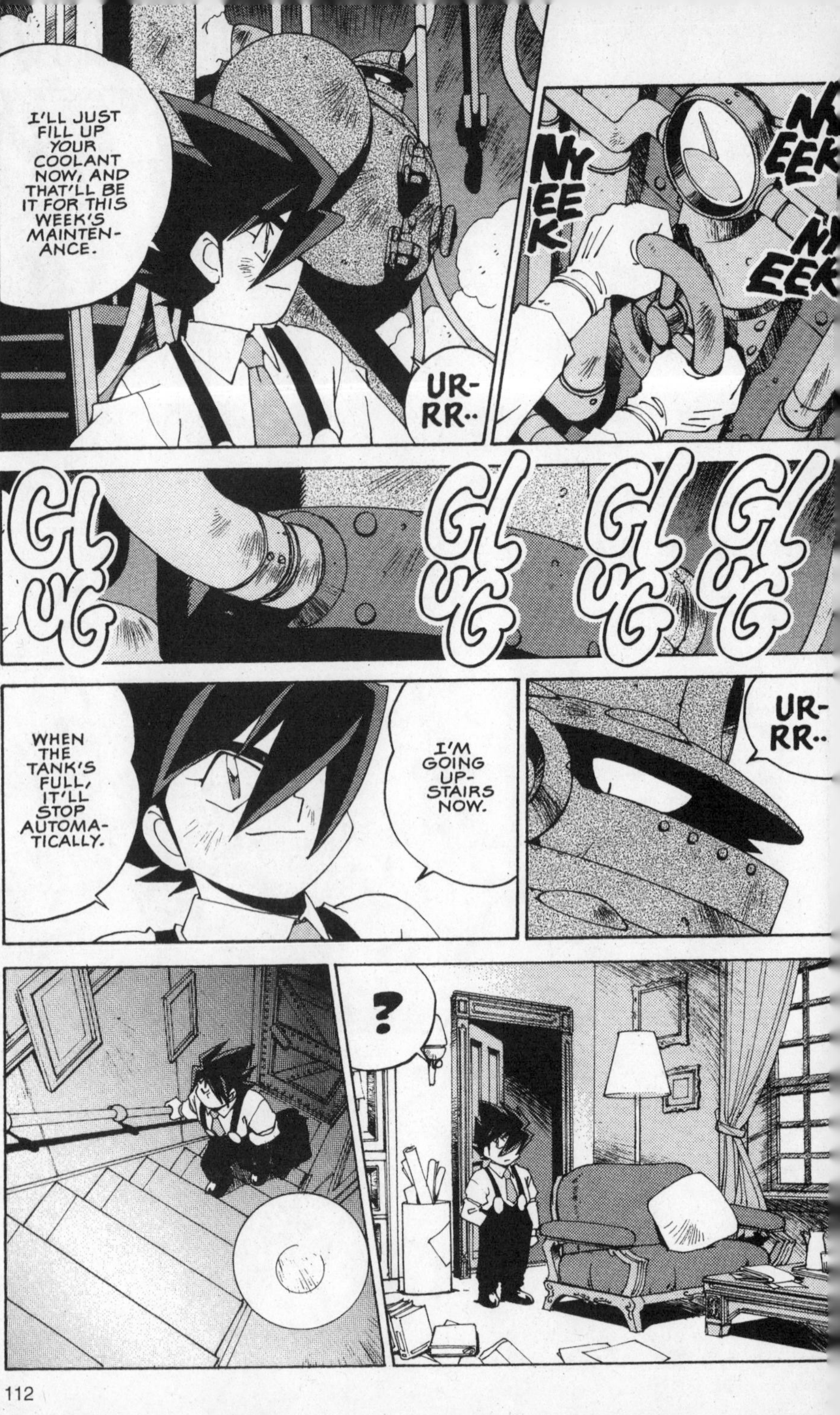
I'LL JUST FILL UP YOUR COOLANT NOW, AND THAT'LL BE IT FOR THIS WEEK'S MAINTEN-ANCE.
UR-RR..
NYEEK
GLUG
GLUG
GLUG
GLUG
WHEN THE TANK'S FULL, IT'LL STOP AUTOMA-TICALLY.
I'M GOING UP-STAIRS NOW.
UR-RR..
?

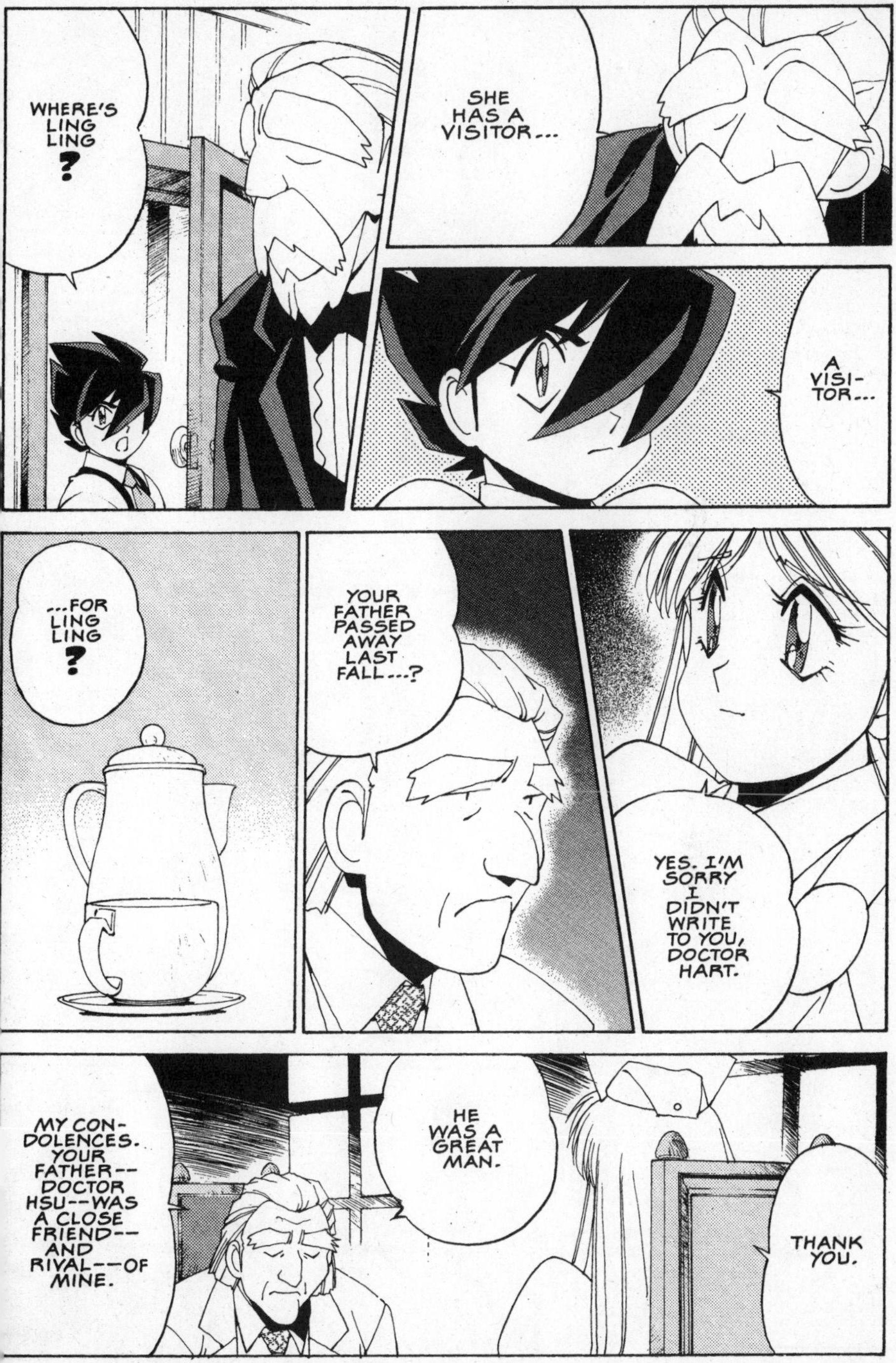
WHERE'S LING LING ?
SHE HAS A VISITOR...
A VISI- TOR...
...FOR LING LING ?
YOUR FATHER PASSED AWAY LAST FALL...?
YES. I'M SORRY I DIDN'T WRITE TO YOU, DOCTOR HART.
MY CON- DOLENCES. YOUR FATHER--DOCTOR HSU--WAS A CLOSE FRIEND--AND RIVAL--OF MINE.
HE WAS A GREAT MAN.
THANK YOU.

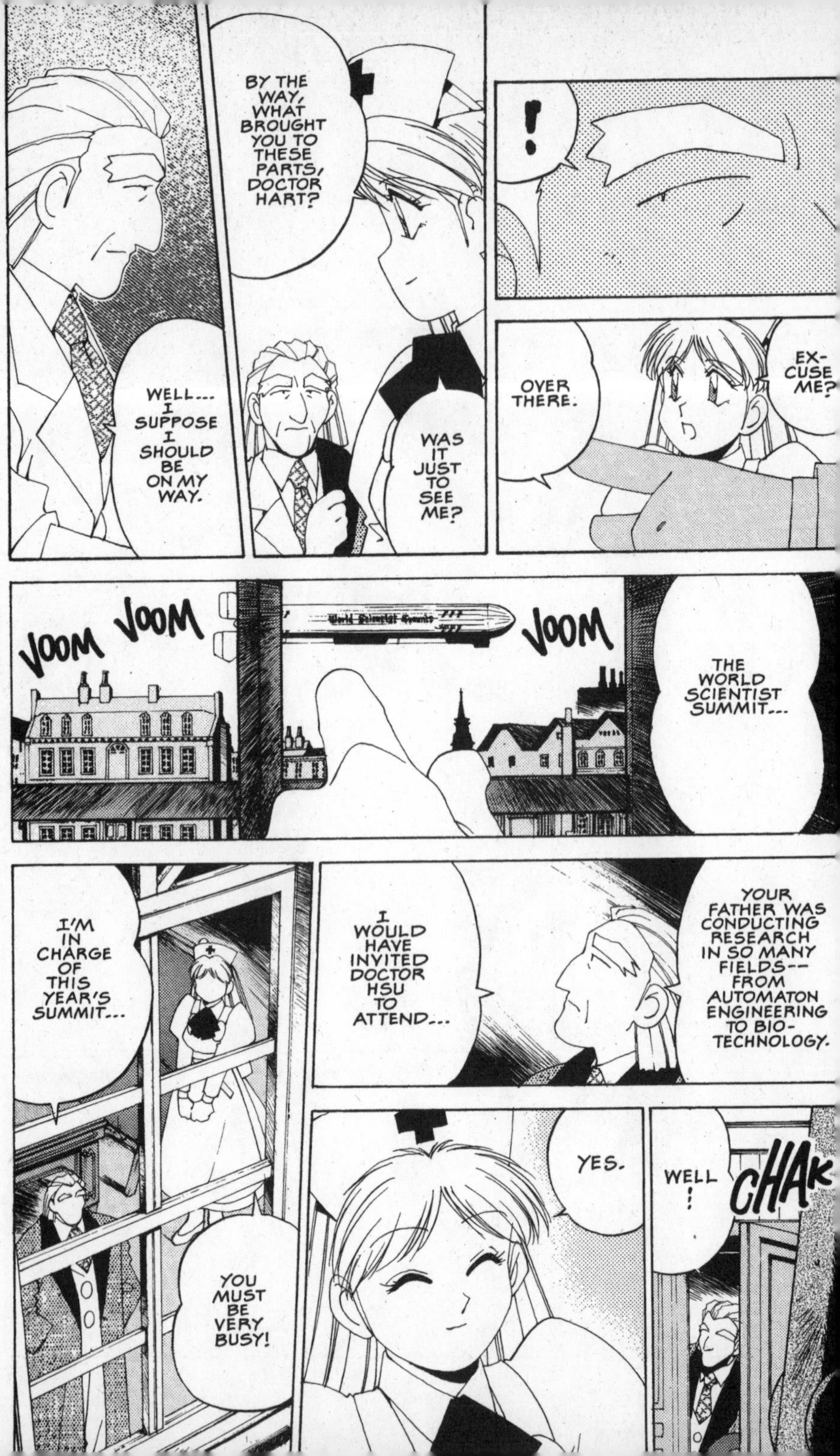
WELL... I SUPPOSE I SHOULD BE ON MY WAY.
BY THE WAY, WHAT BROUGHT YOU TO THESE PARTS, DOCTOR HART?
WAS IT JUST TO SEE ME?
!
OVER THERE.
EXCUSE ME?
VOOM
VOOM
VOOM
THE WORLD SCIENTIST SUMMIT...
I'M IN CHARGE OF THIS YEAR'S SUMMIT...
YOU MUST BE VERY BUSY!
I WOULD HAVE INVITED DOCTOR HSU TO ATTEND...
YOUR FATHER WAS CONDUCTING RESEARCH IN SO MANY FIELDS-- FROM AUTOMATON ENGINEERING TO BIO-TECHNOLOGY.
YES.
WELL!
CHAK

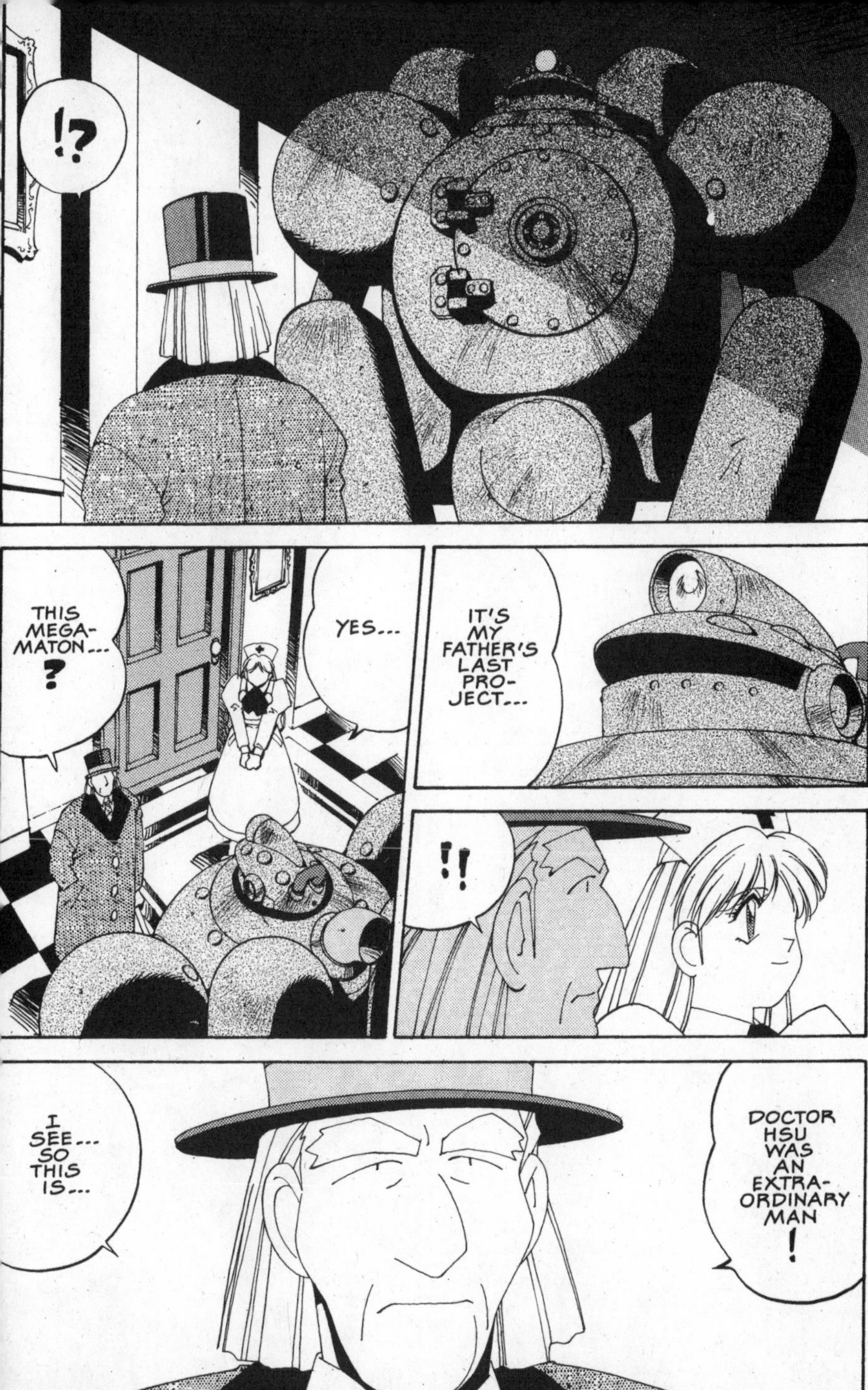
!?
THIS MEGA-MATON...?
YES...
IT'S MY FATHER'S LAST PROJECT...
!!
I SEE... SO THIS IS...
DOCTOR HSU WAS AN EXTRA-ORDINARY MAN!

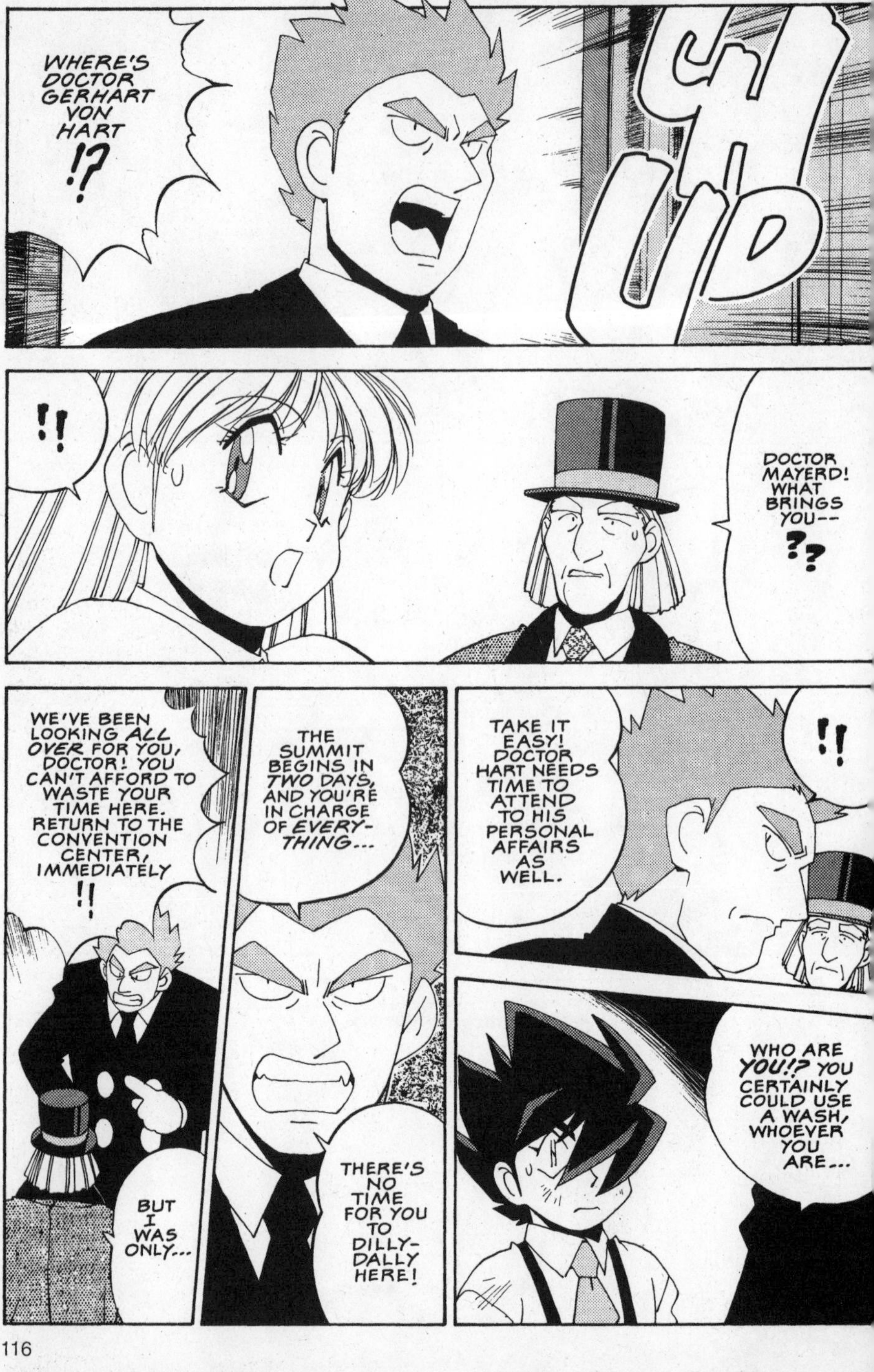
WHERE'S DOCTOR GERHART VON HART !?
!!
DOCTOR MAYERD! WHAT BRINGS YOU-- ??
WE'VE BEEN LOOKING *ALL OVER* FOR YOU, DOCTOR! YOU CAN'T AFFORD TO WASTE YOUR TIME HERE. RETURN TO THE CONVENTION CENTER, IMMEDIATELY !!
BUT I WAS ONLY...
THE SUMMIT BEGINS IN *TWO DAYS,* AND YOU'RE IN CHARGE OF *EVERYTHING...*
THERE'S NO TIME FOR YOU TO DILLY-DALLY HERE!
TAKE IT EASY! DOCTOR HART NEEDS TIME TO ATTEND TO HIS PERSONAL AFFAIRS AS WELL.
!!
WHO ARE *YOU!?* YOU CERTAINLY COULD USE A WASH, WHOEVER YOU ARE...

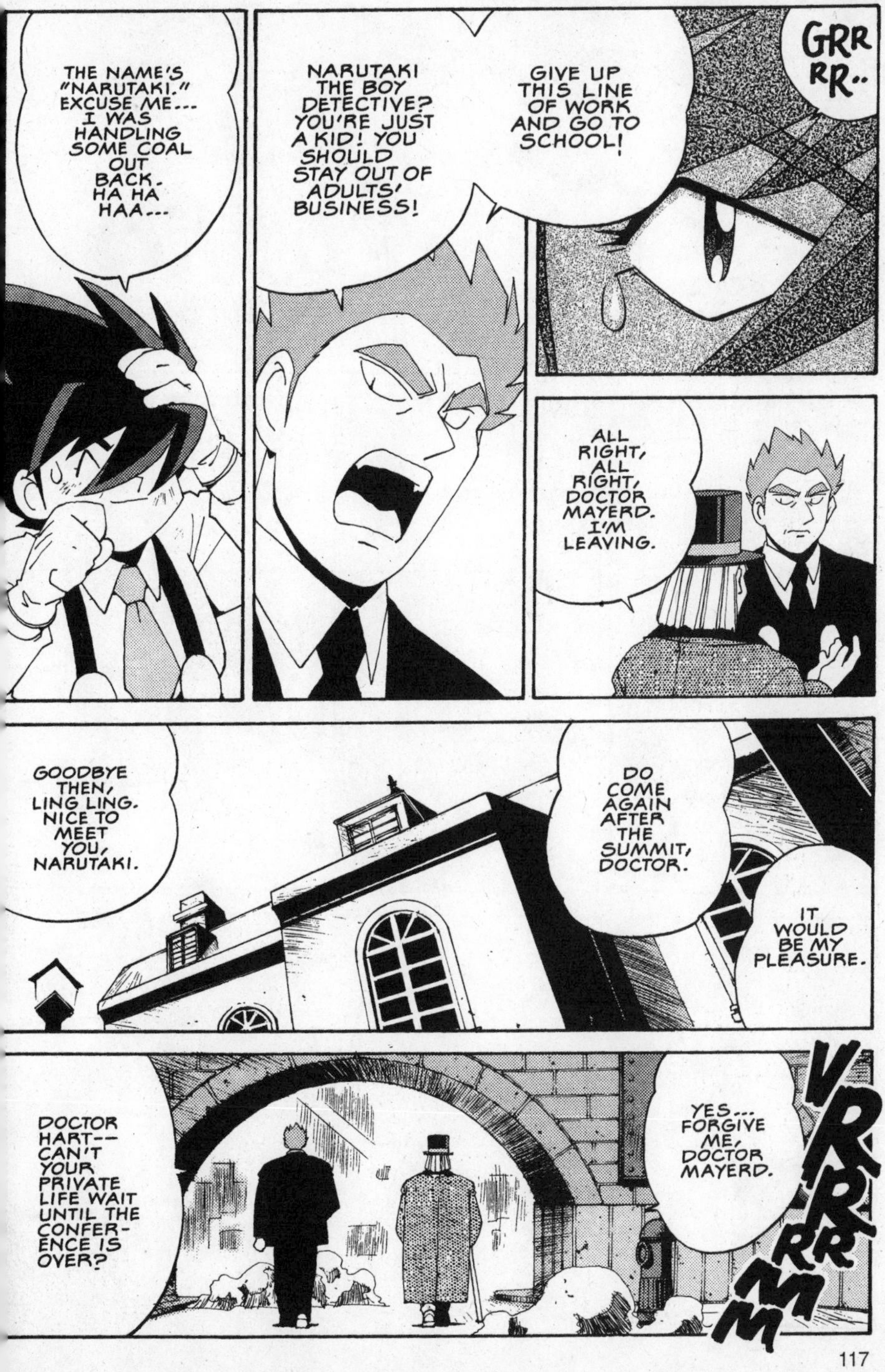
THE NAME'S "NARUTAKI." EXCUSE ME... I WAS HANDLING SOME COAL OUT BACK. HA HA HAA...
NARUTAKI THE BOY DETECTIVE? YOU'RE JUST A KID! YOU SHOULD STAY OUT OF ADULTS' BUSINESS!
GIVE UP THIS LINE OF WORK AND GO TO SCHOOL!
GRRRR..
ALL RIGHT, ALL RIGHT, DOCTOR MAYERD. I'M LEAVING.
GOODBYE THEN, LING LING. NICE TO MEET YOU, NARUTAKI.
DO COME AGAIN AFTER THE SUMMIT, DOCTOR.
IT WOULD BE MY PLEASURE.
DOCTOR HART-- CAN'T YOUR PRIVATE LIFE WAIT UNTIL THE CONFER-ENCE IS OVER?
YES... FORGIVE ME, DOCTOR MAYERD.
VRRRRMM

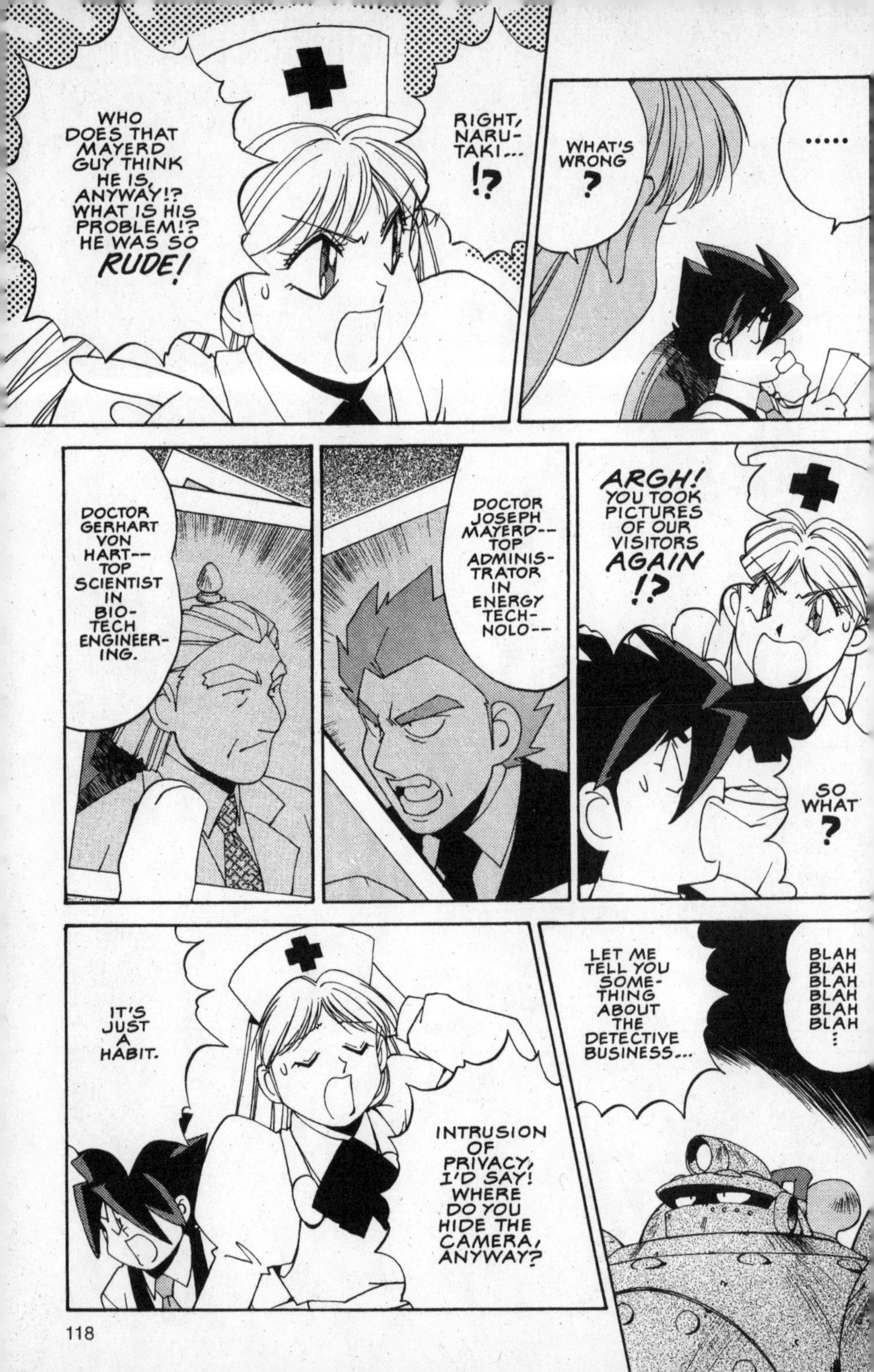

WHO DOES THAT MAYERD GUY THINK HE IS, ANYWAY!? WHAT IS HIS PROBLEM!? HE WAS SO RUDE!
RIGHT, NARU-TAKI... !?
WHAT'S WRONG ?
.....
DOCTOR GERHART VON HART-- TOP SCIENTIST IN BIO-TECH ENGINEER-ING.
DOCTOR JOSEPH MAYERD-- TOP ADMINIS-TRATOR IN ENERGY TECH-NOLO--
ARGH! YOU TOOK PICTURES OF OUR VISITORS AGAIN !?
SO WHAT ?
IT'S JUST A HABIT.
INTRUSION OF PRIVACY, I'D SAY! WHERE DO YOU HIDE THE CAMERA, ANYWAY?
LET ME TELL YOU SOME-THING ABOUT THE DETECTIVE BUSINESS...
BLAH BLAH BLAH BLAH BLAH BLAH ...

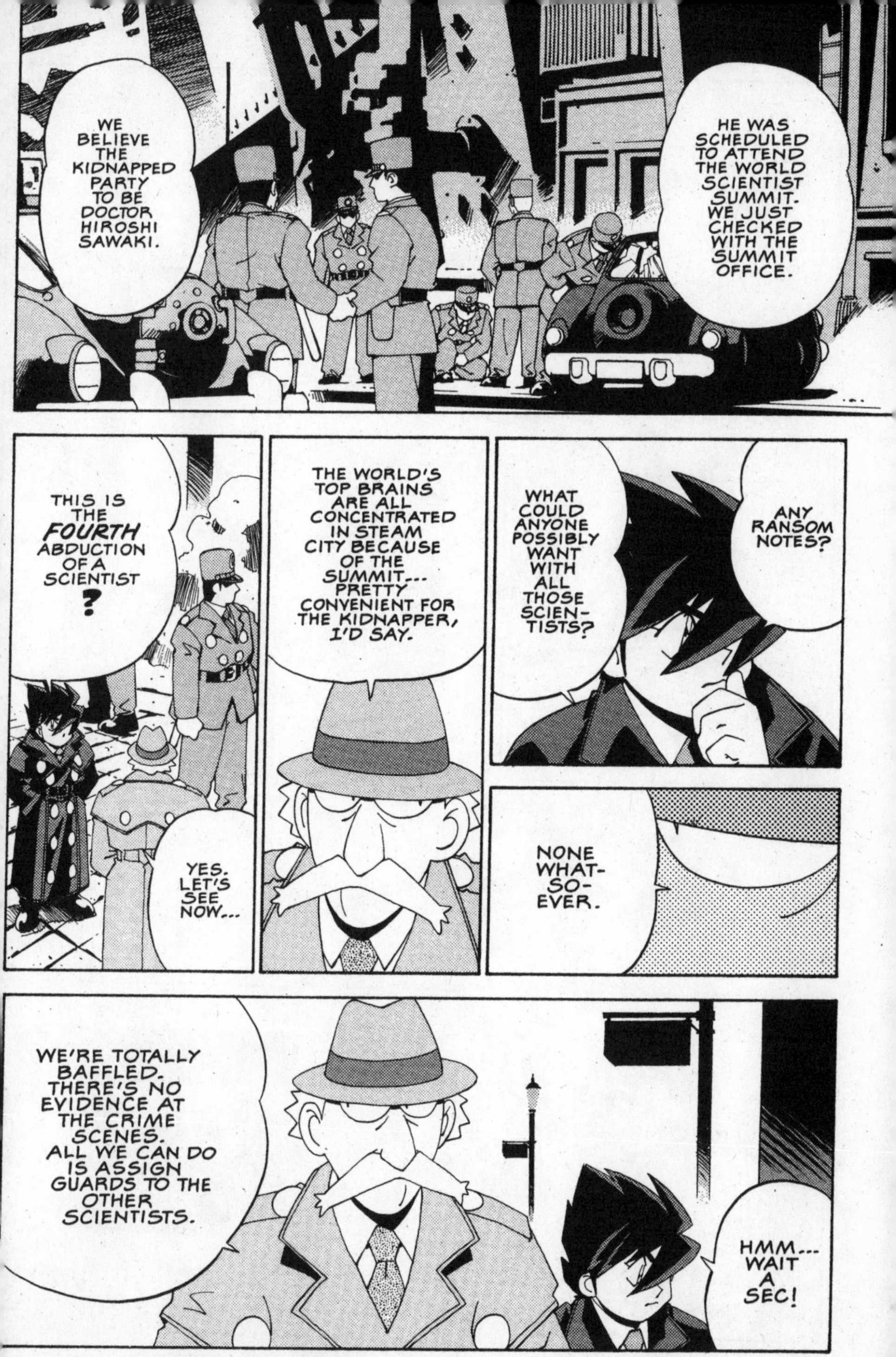
WE BELIEVE THE KIDNAPPED PARTY TO BE DOCTOR HIROSHI SAWAKI.
HE WAS SCHEDULED TO ATTEND THE WORLD SCIENTIST SUMMIT. WE JUST CHECKED WITH THE SUMMIT OFFICE.
THIS IS THE *FOURTH* ABDUCTION OF A SCIENTIST?
YES. LET'S SEE NOW...
THE WORLD'S TOP BRAINS ARE ALL CONCENTRATED IN STEAM CITY BECAUSE OF THE SUMMIT... PRETTY CONVENIENT FOR THE KIDNAPPER, I'D SAY.
WHAT COULD ANYONE POSSIBLY WANT WITH ALL THOSE SCIEN-TISTS?
ANY RANSOM NOTES?
NONE WHAT-SO-EVER.
WE'RE TOTALLY BAFFLED. THERE'S NO EVIDENCE AT THE CRIME SCENES. ALL WE CAN DO IS ASSIGN GUARDS TO THE OTHER SCIENTISTS.
HMM... WAIT A SEC!

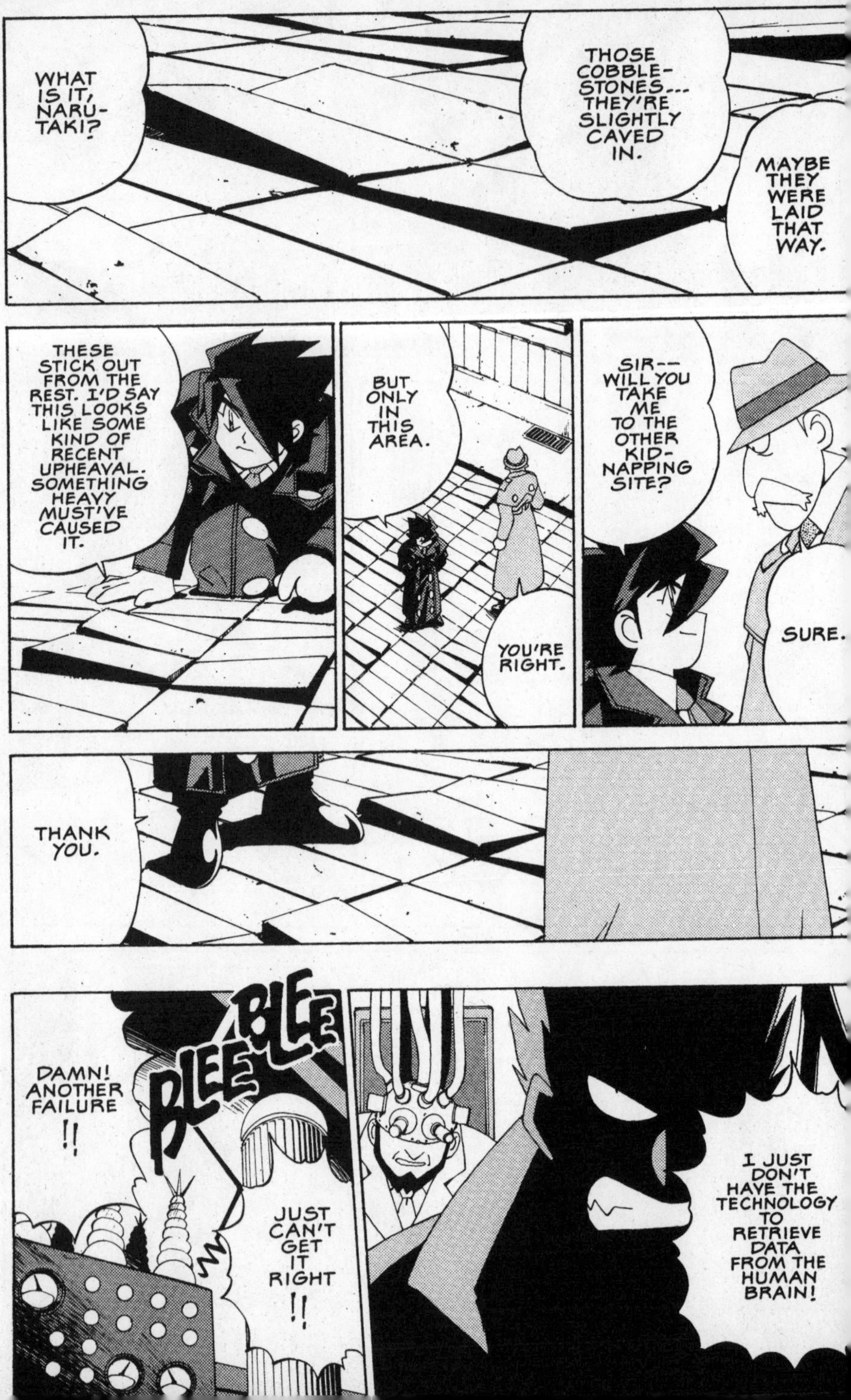
WHAT IS IT, NARU-TAKI?
THOSE COBBLE-STONES... THEY'RE SLIGHTLY CAVED IN.
MAYBE THEY WERE LAID THAT WAY.
THESE STICK OUT FROM THE REST. I'D SAY THIS LOOKS LIKE SOME KIND OF RECENT UPHEAVAL. SOMETHING HEAVY MUST'VE CAUSED IT.
BUT ONLY IN THIS AREA.
YOU'RE RIGHT.
SIR-- WILL YOU TAKE ME TO THE OTHER KID-NAPPING SITE?
SURE.
THANK YOU.
DAMN! ANOTHER FAILURE !!
BLEE BLEE BLEE
JUST CAN'T GET IT RIGHT !!
I JUST DON'T HAVE THE TECHNOLOGY TO RETRIEVE DATA FROM THE HUMAN BRAIN!

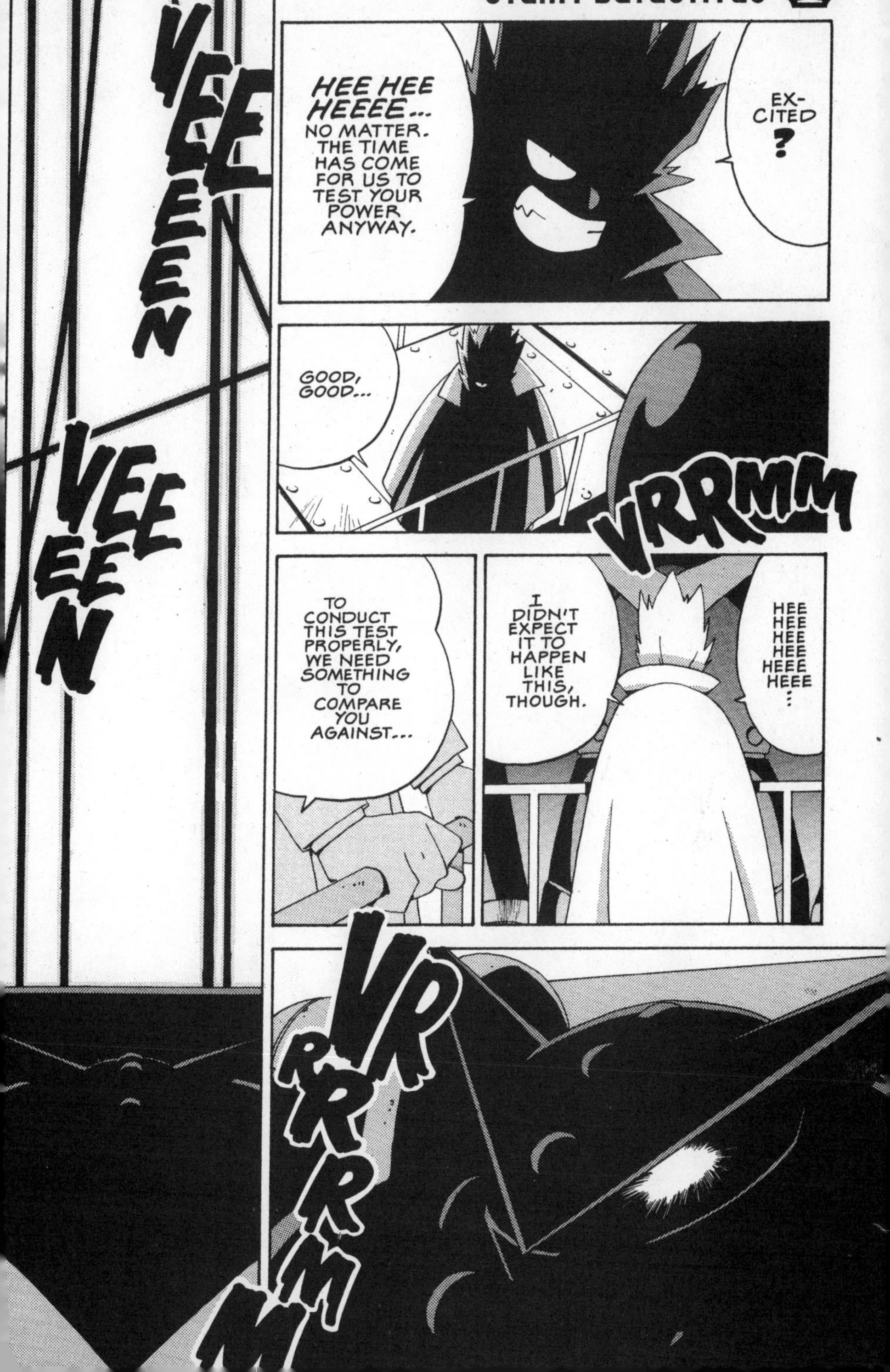
VEEEEEN
VEEEEEN
HEE HEE HEEEE... NO MATTER. THE TIME HAS COME FOR US TO TEST YOUR POWER ANYWAY.
EX-CITED?
GOOD, GOOD...
VRRMMM
TO CONDUCT THIS TEST PROPERLY, WE NEED SOMETHING TO COMPARE YOU AGAINST...
I DIDN'T EXPECT IT TO HAPPEN LIKE THIS, THOUGH.
HEE HEE HEE HEE HEEE HEEE...
VRRRRRMM

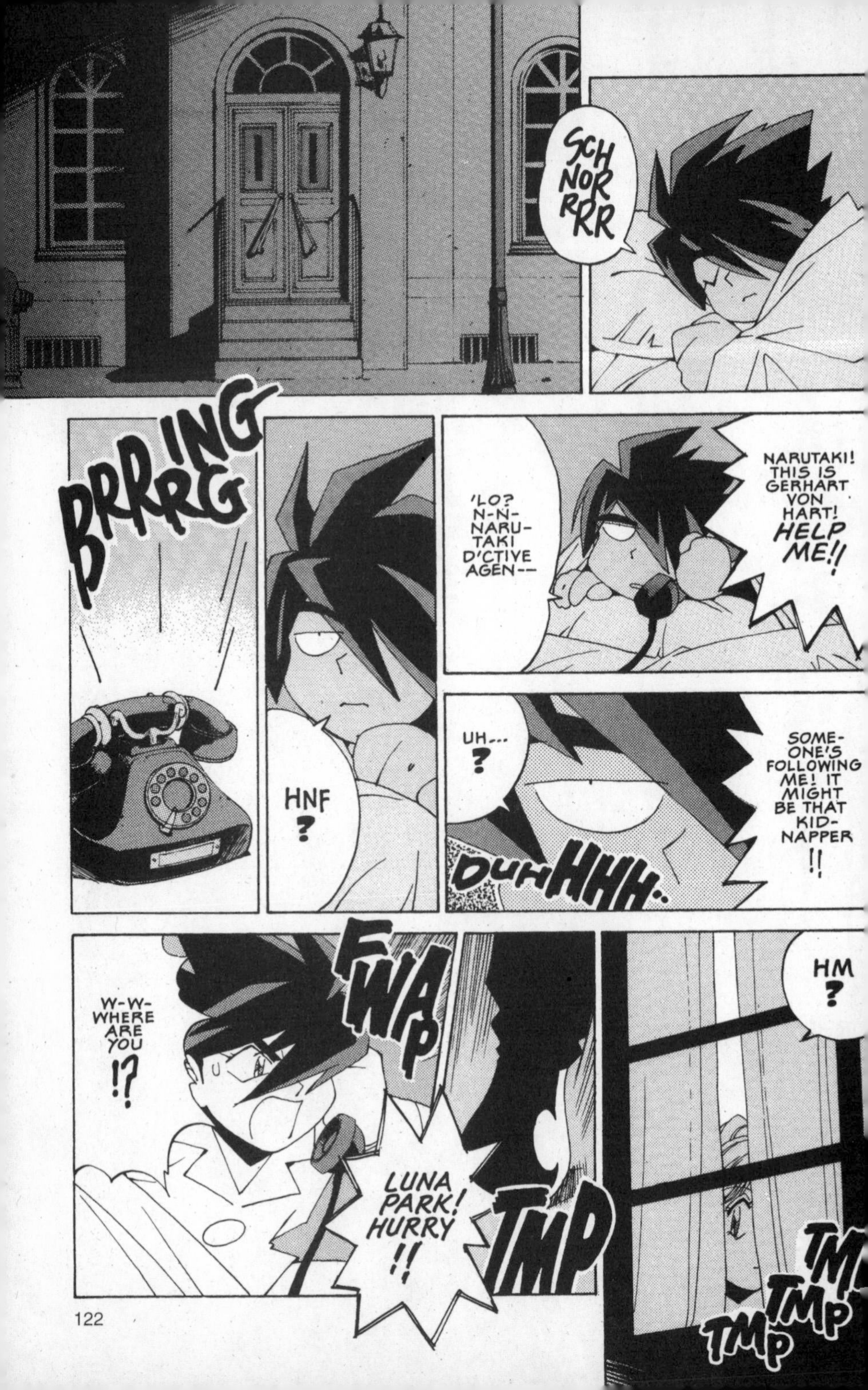
SCHNORRRR
BRRRING BRRRG
HNF ?
'LO? N-N-NARUTAKI D'CTIVE AGEN--
NARUTAKI! THIS IS GERHART VON HART! HELP ME!!
UH... ?
SOME-ONE'S FOLLOWING ME! IT MIGHT BE THAT KID-NAPPER !!
DUHHHH..
W-W-WHERE ARE YOU !?
FWAP
LUNA PARK! HURRY !!
TMP
HM ?
TMP TMP TMP

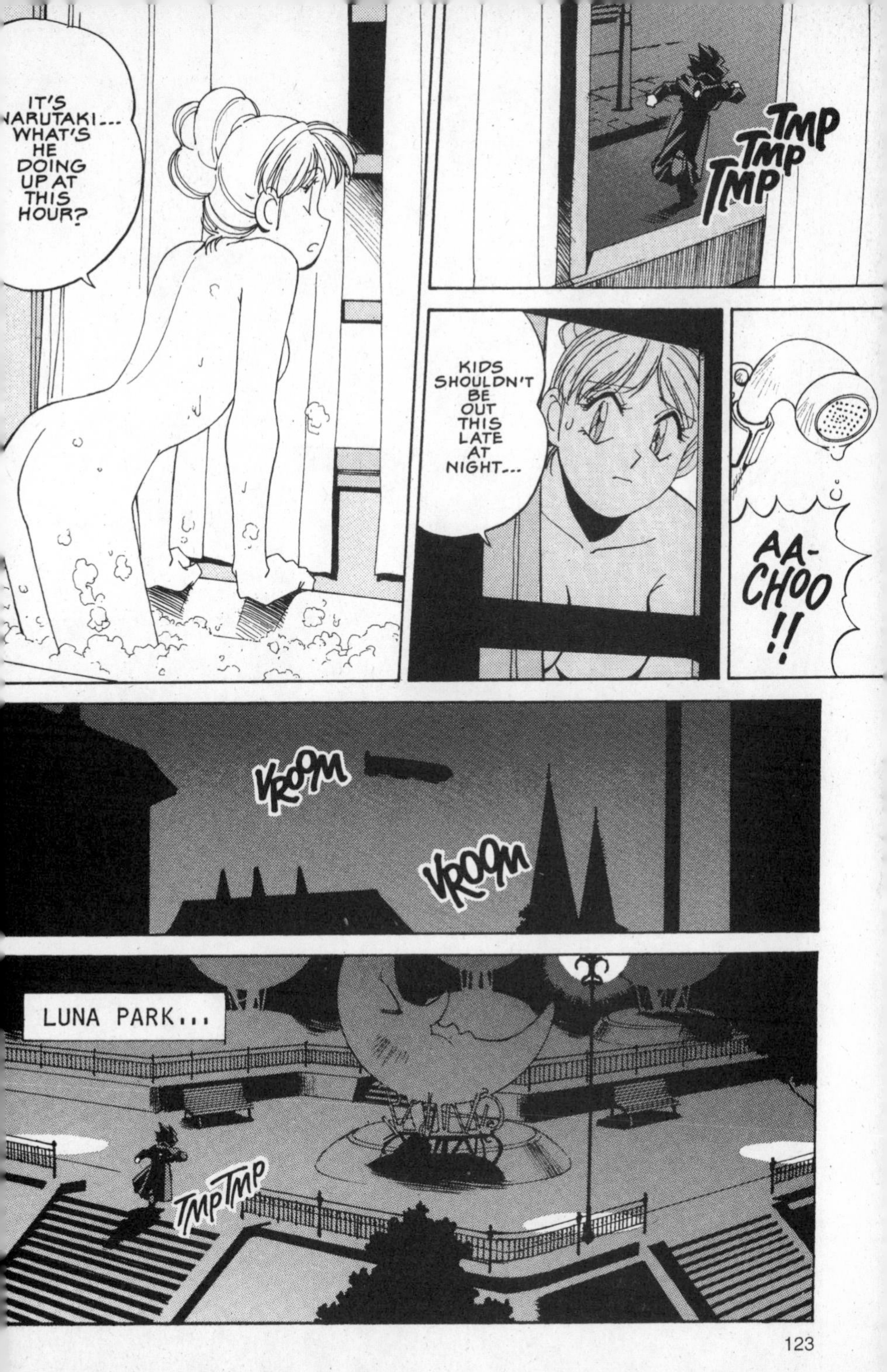
IT'S NARUTAKI... WHAT'S HE DOING UP AT THIS HOUR?
TMP TMP TMP
KIDS SHOULDN'T BE OUT THIS LATE AT NIGHT...
AA-CHOO!!
VROOM
VROOM
LUNA PARK...
TMP TMP

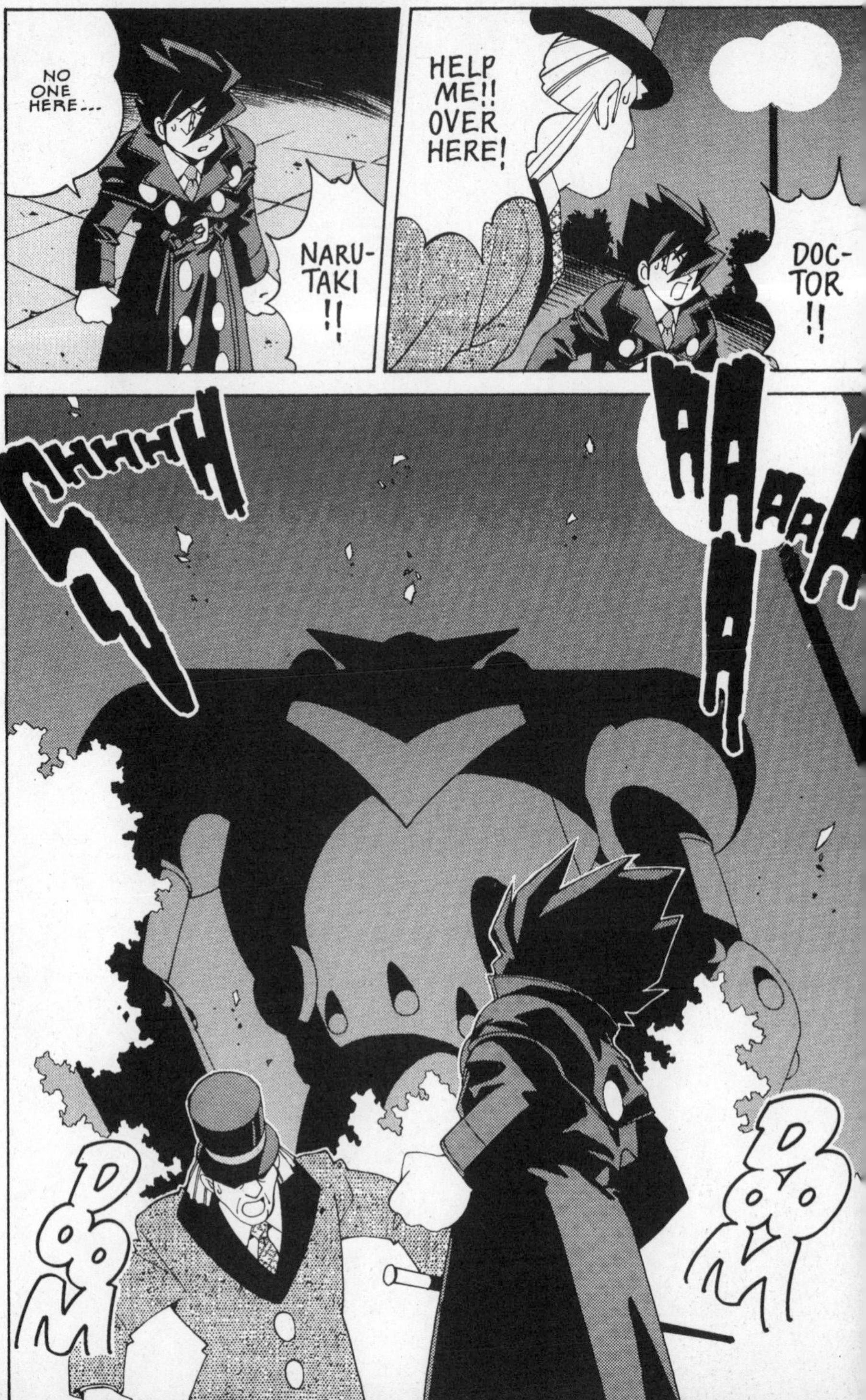

NO ONE HERE...
NARU-TAKI !!
HELP ME!! OVER HERE!
DOC-TOR !!
DOOM
DOOM

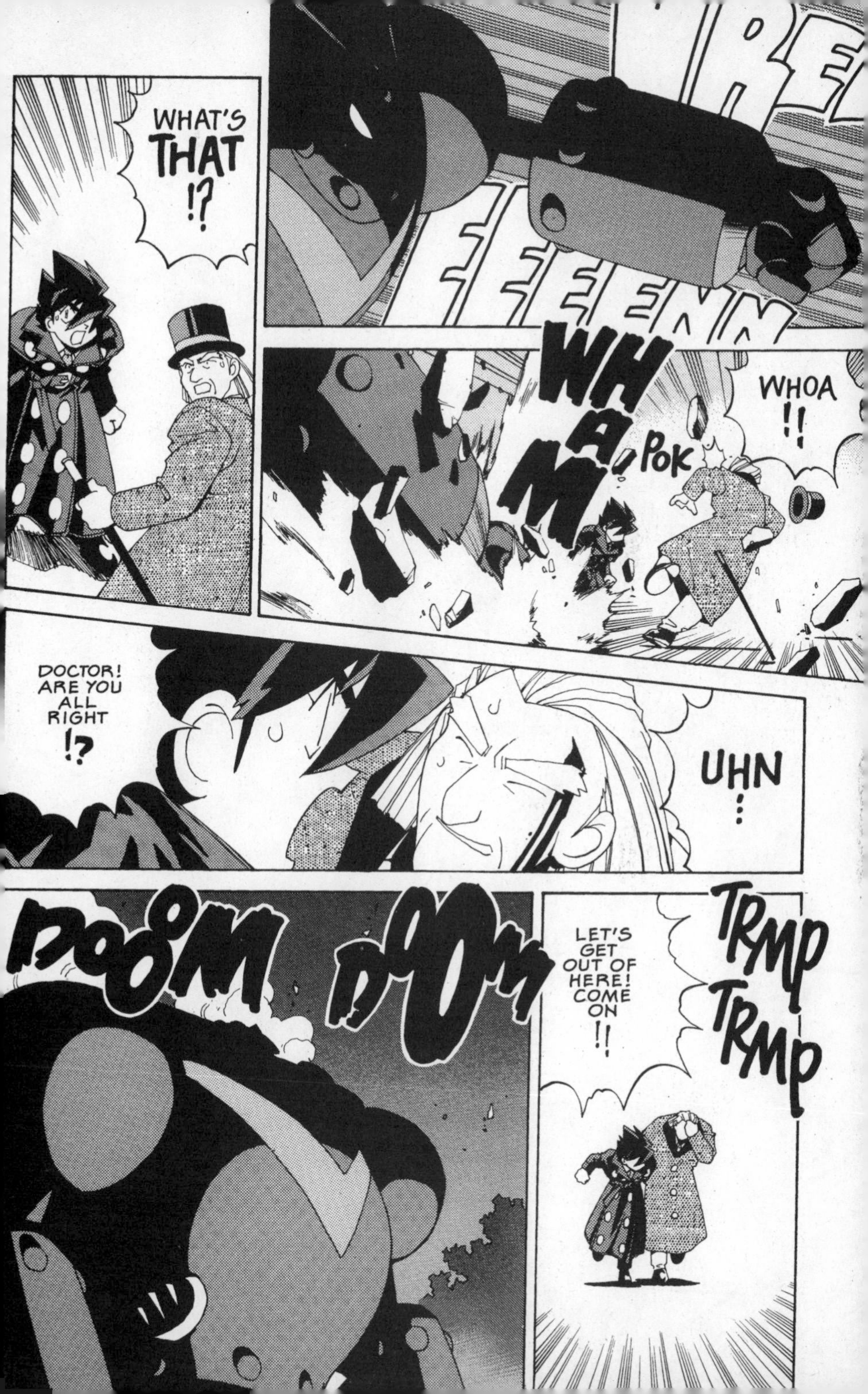
WHAT'S THAT !?
WHAM
POK
WHOA !!
DOCTOR! ARE YOU ALL RIGHT !?
UHN ...
DOOM DOOM
LET'S GET OUT OF HERE! COME ON !!
TRMP TRMP

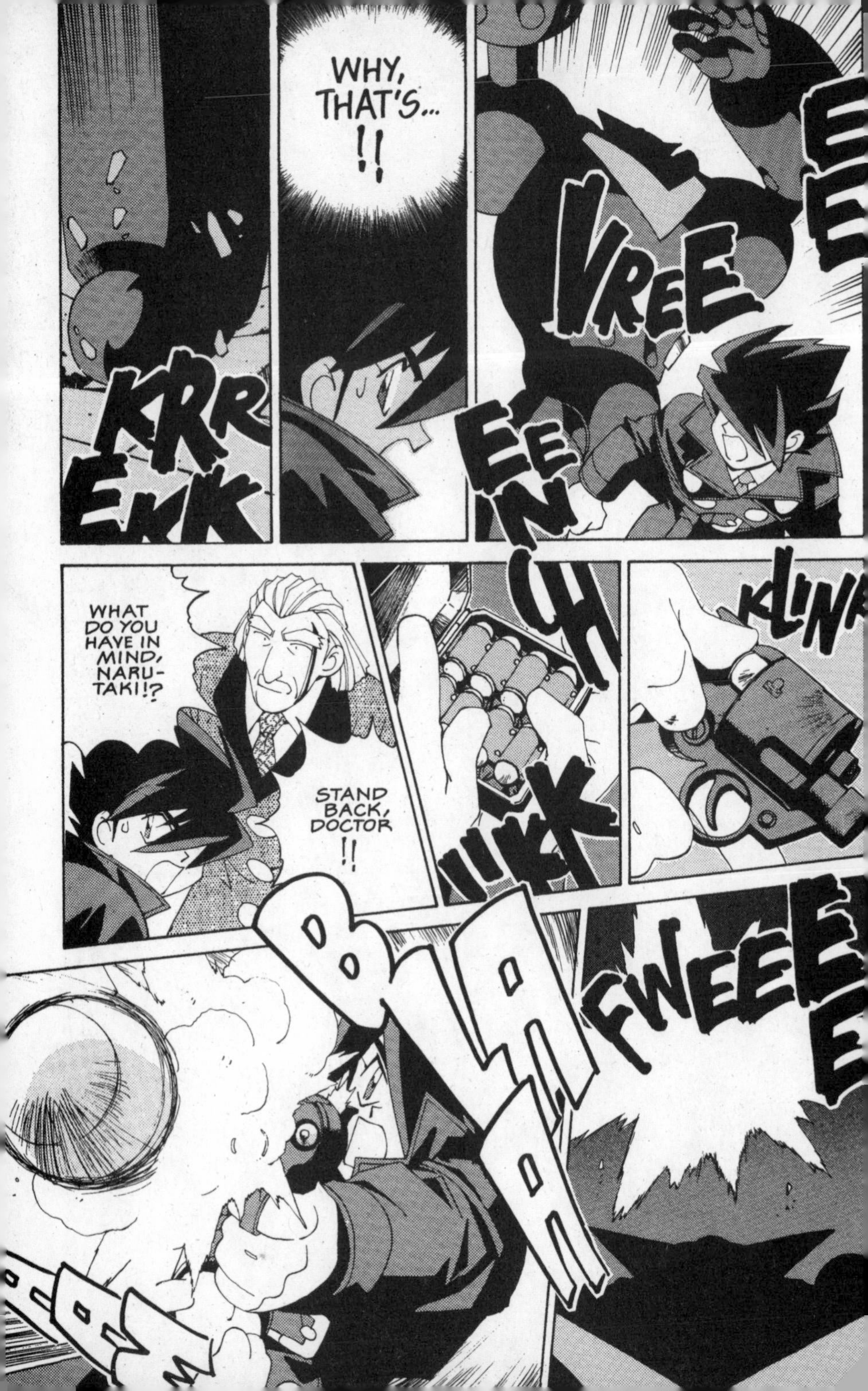
KRR EKK
WHY, THAT'S... !!
VREE
WHAT DO YOU HAVE IN MIND, NARU-TAKI!?
STAND BACK, DOCTOR !!
KLINK
FWEEE

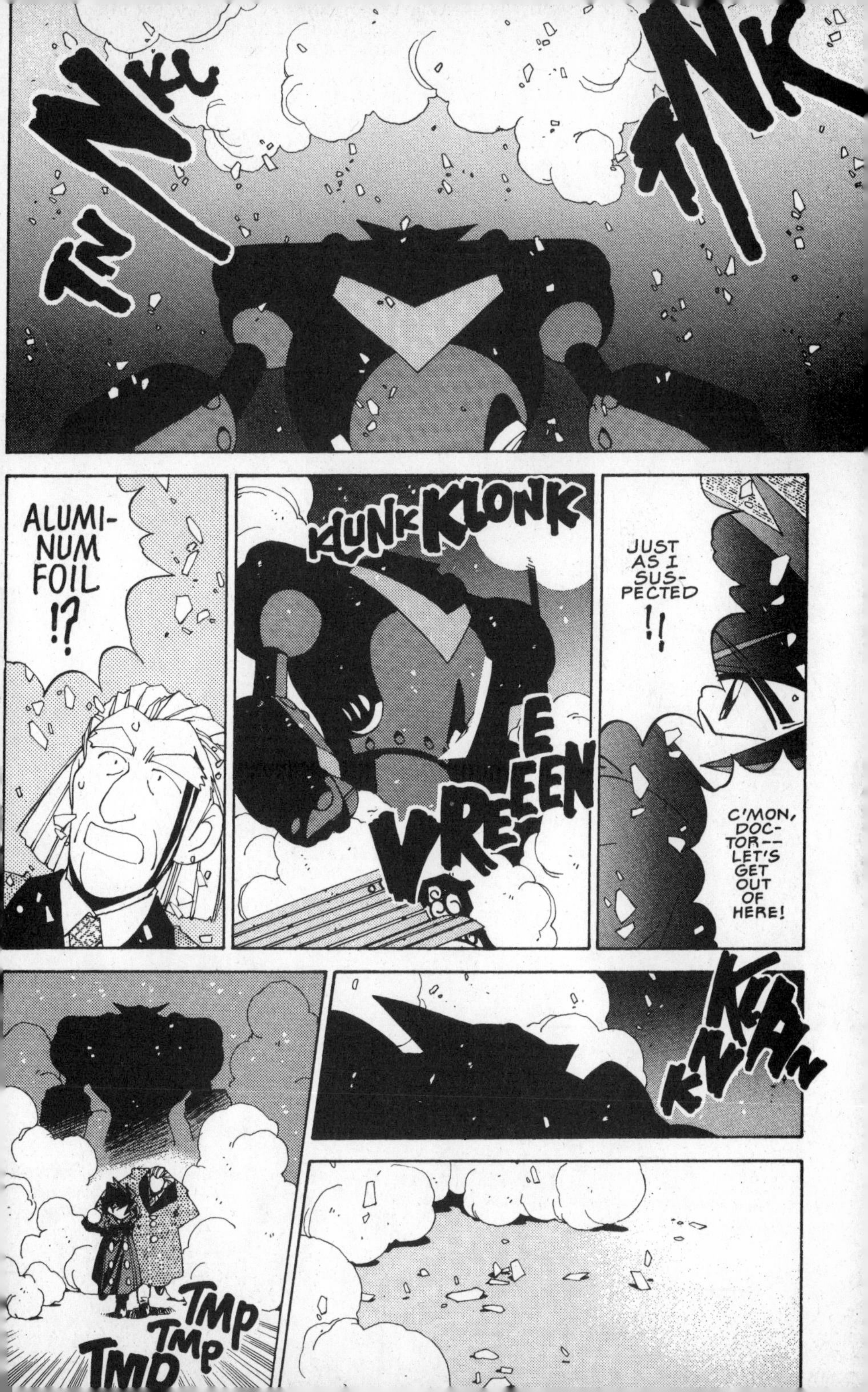
TINK
TINK
ALUMI-NUM FOIL!?
KLUNK KLONK
VREEEEN
JUST AS I SUS-PECTED!!
C'MON, DOCTOR--LET'S GET OUT OF HERE!
TMP TMP TMP

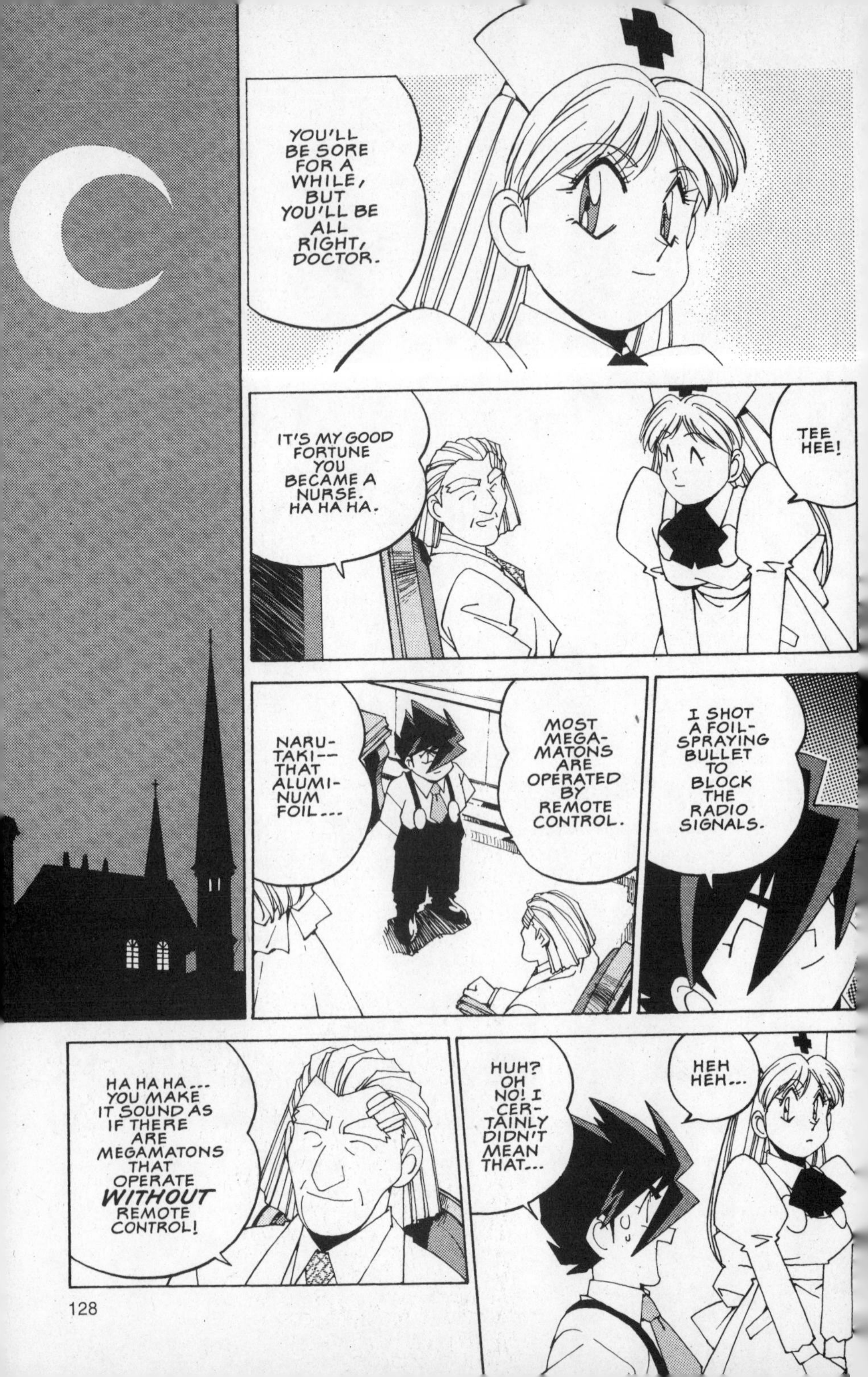
YOU'LL BE SORE FOR A WHILE, BUT YOU'LL BE ALL RIGHT, DOCTOR.
IT'S MY GOOD FORTUNE YOU BECAME A NURSE. HA HA HA.
TEE HEE!
NARU-TAKI-- THAT ALUMI-NUM FOIL...
MOST MEGA-MATONS ARE OPERATED BY REMOTE CONTROL.
I SHOT A FOIL-SPRAYING BULLET TO BLOCK THE RADIO SIGNALS.
HA HA HA... YOU MAKE IT SOUND AS IF THERE ARE MEGAMATONS THAT OPERATE ***WITHOUT*** REMOTE CONTROL!
HUH? OH NO! I CER-TAINLY DIDN'T MEAN THAT...
HEH HEH...

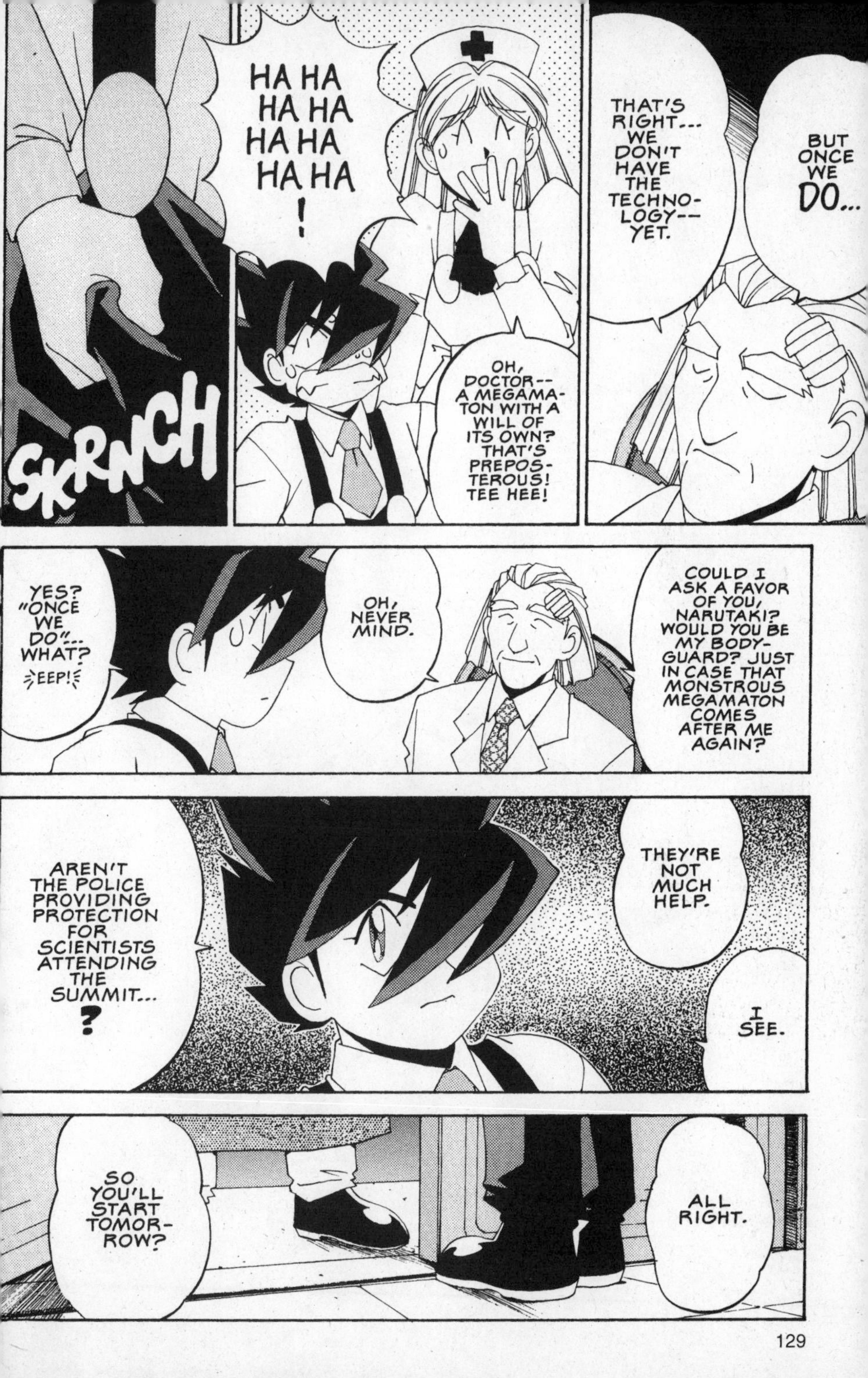
SKRNCH
HA HA HA HA HA HA HA HA !
OH, DOCTOR-- A MEGAMATON WITH A WILL OF ITS OWN? THAT'S PREPOSTEROUS! TEE HEE!
THAT'S RIGHT... WE DON'T HAVE THE TECHNOLOGY-- YET.
BUT ONCE WE DO...
YES? "ONCE WE DO"... WHAT?
EEP!
OH, NEVER MIND.
COULD I ASK A FAVOR OF YOU, NARUTAKI? WOULD YOU BE MY BODYGUARD? JUST IN CASE THAT MONSTROUS MEGAMATON COMES AFTER ME AGAIN?
AREN'T THE POLICE PROVIDING PROTECTION FOR SCIENTISTS ATTENDING THE SUMMIT...?
THEY'RE NOT MUCH HELP.
I SEE.
SO YOU'LL START TOMORROW?
ALL RIGHT.

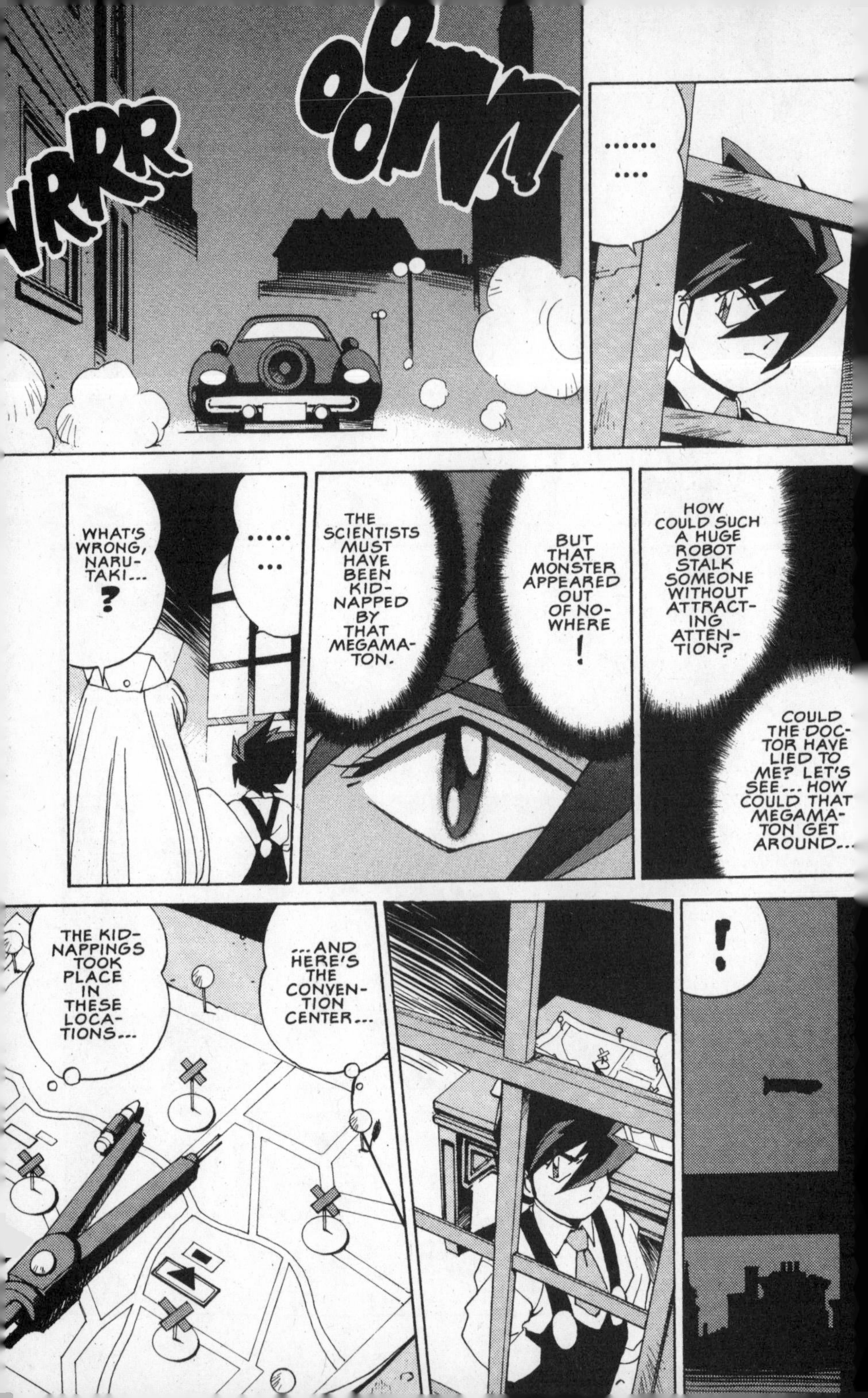
VRRR
OOOMMM
......
....
WHAT'S WRONG, NARU-TAKI...?
.....
...
THE SCIENTISTS MUST HAVE BEEN KID-NAPPED BY THAT MEGAMA-TON.
BUT THAT MONSTER APPEARED OUT OF NO-WHERE!
HOW COULD SUCH A HUGE ROBOT STALK SOMEONE WITHOUT ATTRACT-ING ATTEN-TION?
COULD THE DOC-TOR HAVE LIED TO ME? LET'S SEE... HOW COULD THAT MEGAMA-TON GET AROUND...
THE KID-NAPPINGS TOOK PLACE IN THESE LOCA-TIONS...
...AND HERE'S THE CONVEN-TION CENTER...
!

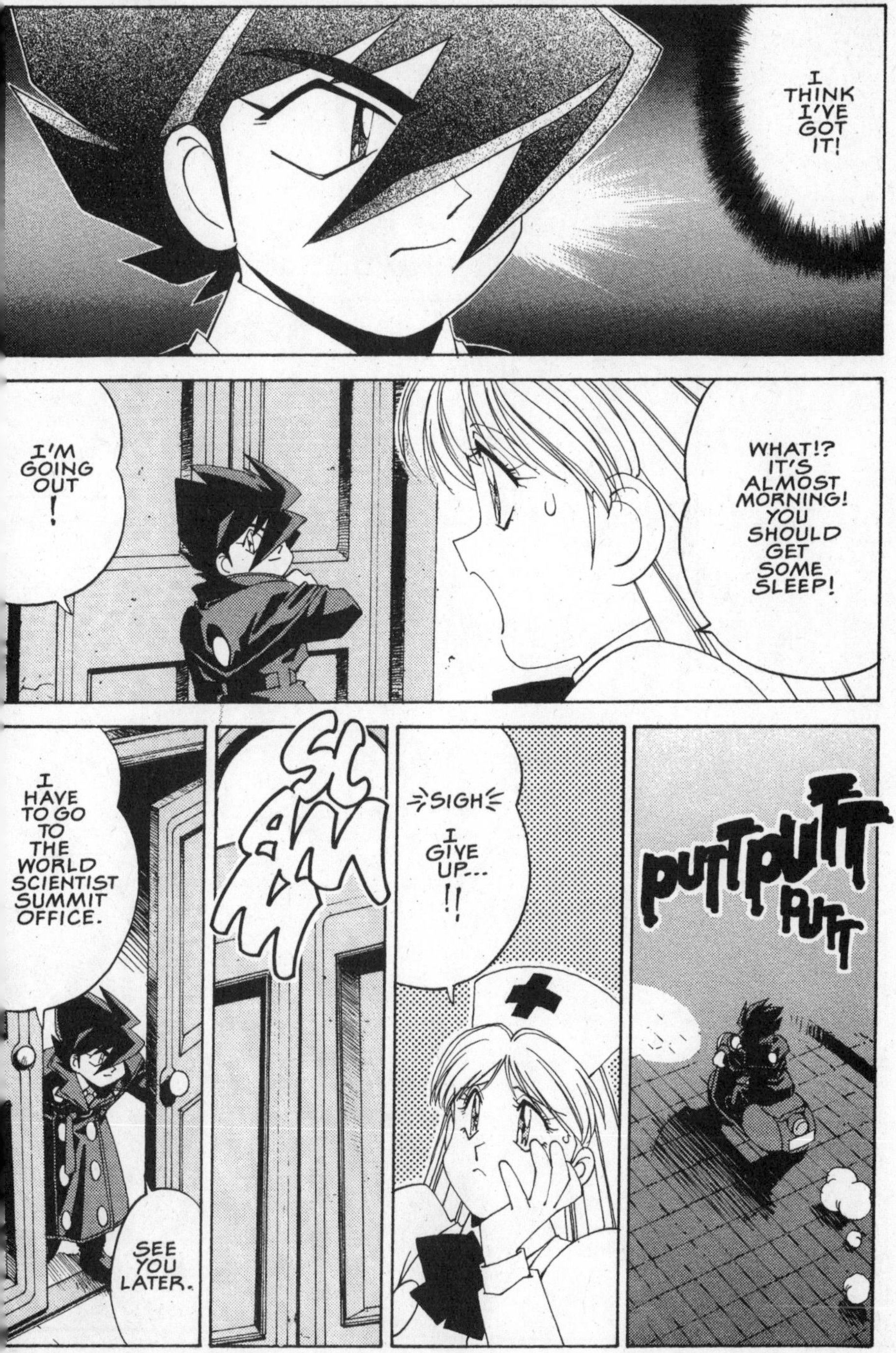
I THINK I'VE GOT IT!
I'M GOING OUT!
WHAT!? IT'S ALMOST MORNING! YOU SHOULD GET SOME SLEEP!
I HAVE TO GO TO THE WORLD SCIENTIST SUMMIT OFFICE.
SEE YOU LATER.
SLAM
SIGH
I GIVE UP...!!
PUTT PUTT PUTT

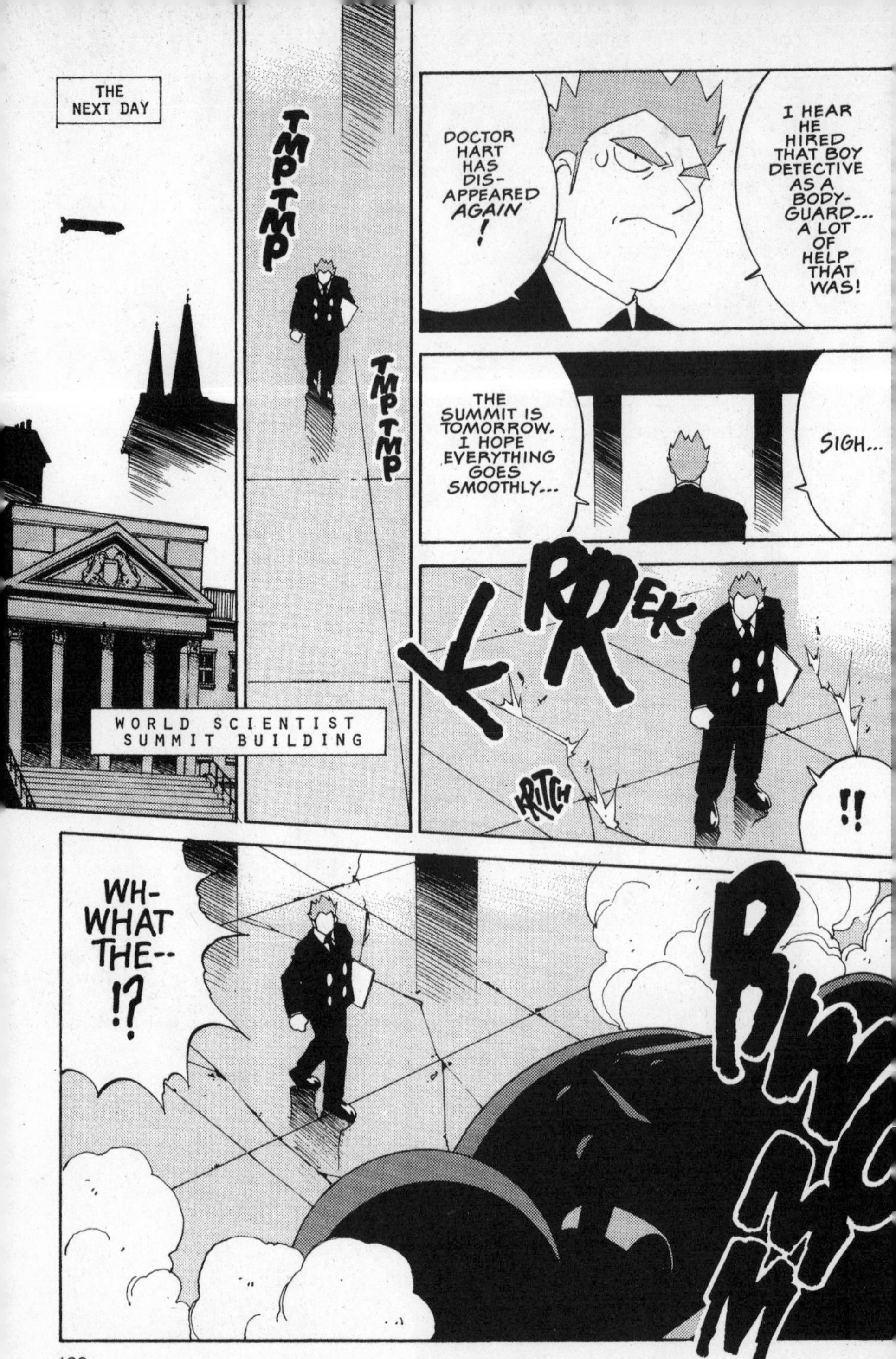
THE NEXT DAY
WORLD SCIENTIST SUMMIT BUILDING
TMPTMP
TMPTMP
DOCTOR HART HAS DIS-APPEARED AGAIN!
I HEAR HE HIRED THAT BOY DETECTIVE AS A BODY-GUARD... A LOT OF HELP THAT WAS!
THE SUMMIT IS TOMORROW. I HOPE EVERYTHING GOES SMOOTHLY...
SIGH...
KRREK
KRITCH
!!
WH-WHAT THE--!?

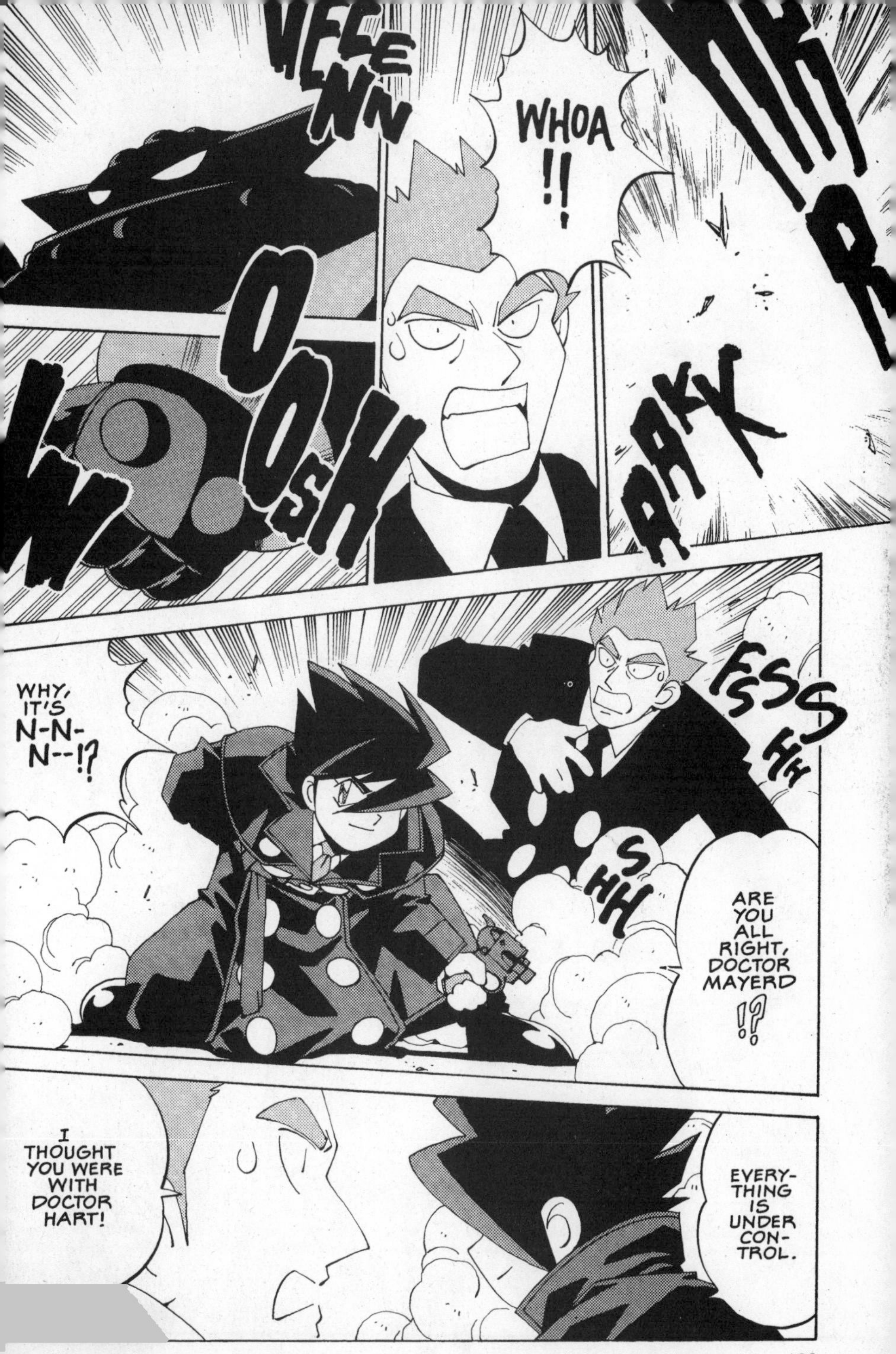

WHOA!!
WHY, IT'S N-N-N--!?
FSSS HH
SHH
ARE YOU ALL RIGHT, DOCTOR MAYERD!?
I THOUGHT YOU WERE WITH DOCTOR HART!
EVERYTHING IS UNDER CONTROL.

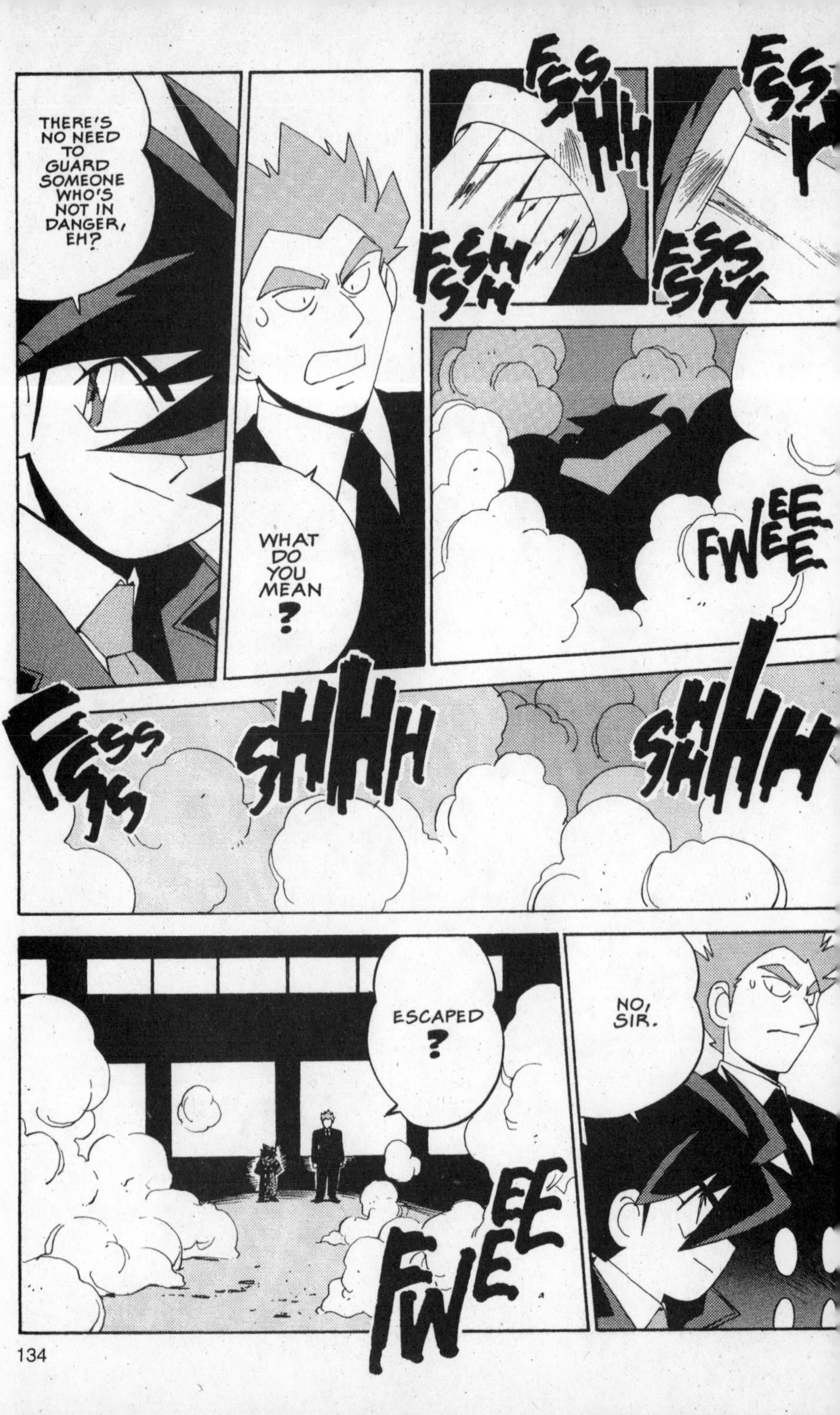
THERE'S NO NEED TO GUARD SOMEONE WHO'S NOT IN DANGER, EH?
WHAT DO YOU MEAN?
FSSHHH
FSSHH
FSSHH
FSSSHH
FWEEE
FSSSSHHHH
SHHHH
ESCAPED?
FWEEE
NO, SIR.

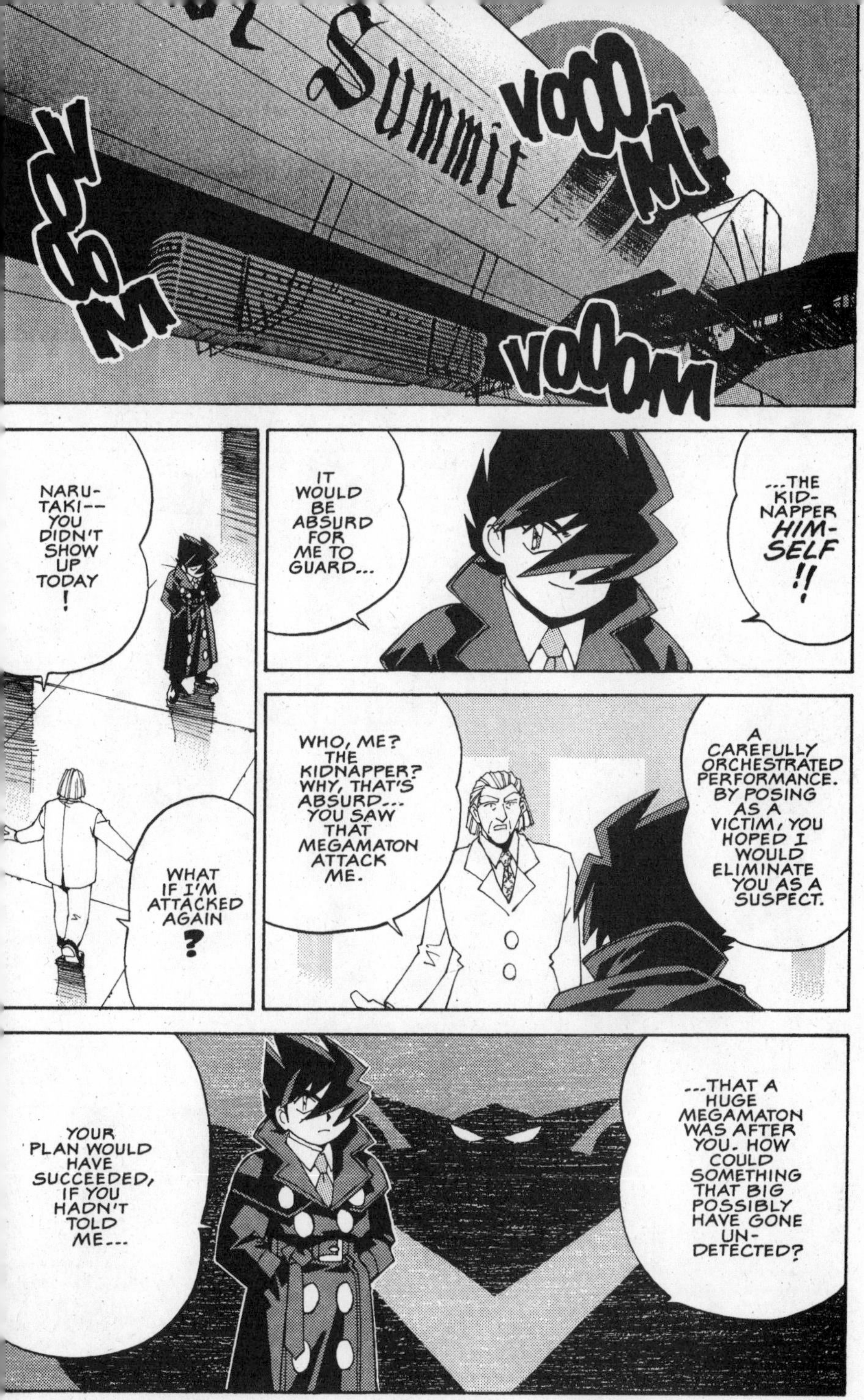
Summit
VOOOM
VOOOM
VOOOM
NARU-TAKI-- YOU DIDN'T SHOW UP TODAY!
WHAT IF I'M ATTACKED AGAIN?
IT WOULD BE ABSURD FOR ME TO GUARD...
...THE KIDNAPPER HIMSELF!!
WHO, ME? THE KIDNAPPER? WHY, THAT'S ABSURD... YOU SAW THAT MEGAMATON ATTACK ME.
A CAREFULLY ORCHESTRATED PERFORMANCE. BY POSING AS A VICTIM, YOU HOPED I WOULD ELIMINATE YOU AS A SUSPECT.
YOUR PLAN WOULD HAVE SUCCEEDED, IF YOU HADN'T TOLD ME...
...THAT A HUGE MEGAMATON WAS AFTER YOU. HOW COULD SOMETHING THAT BIG POSSIBLY HAVE GONE UN-DETECTED?

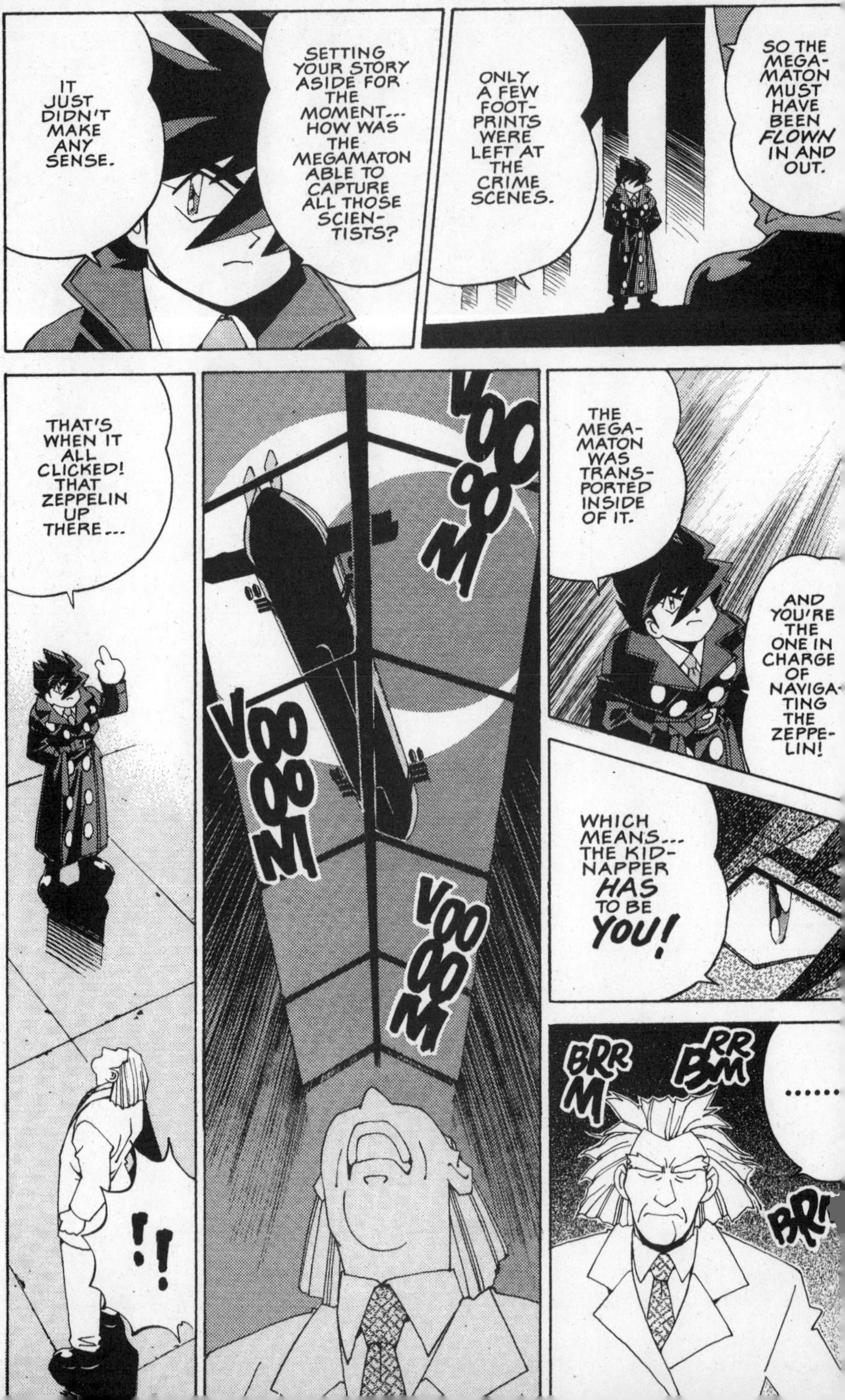
IT JUST DIDN'T MAKE ANY SENSE.
SETTING YOUR STORY ASIDE FOR THE MOMENT... HOW WAS THE MEGAMATON ABLE TO CAPTURE ALL THOSE SCIEN-TISTS?
ONLY A FEW FOOT-PRINTS WERE LEFT AT THE CRIME SCENES.
SO THE MEGA-MATON MUST HAVE BEEN *FLOWN* IN AND OUT.
THAT'S WHEN IT ALL CLICKED! THAT ZEPPELIN UP THERE...
!!
VOOOOM
VOOOOM
VOOOOM
THE MEGA-MATON WAS TRANS-PORTED INSIDE OF IT.
AND YOU'RE THE ONE IN CHARGE OF NAVIGA-TING THE ZEPPE-LIN!
WHICH MEANS... THE KID-NAPPER *HAS* TO BE *YOU!*
BRRM
BRRM
......

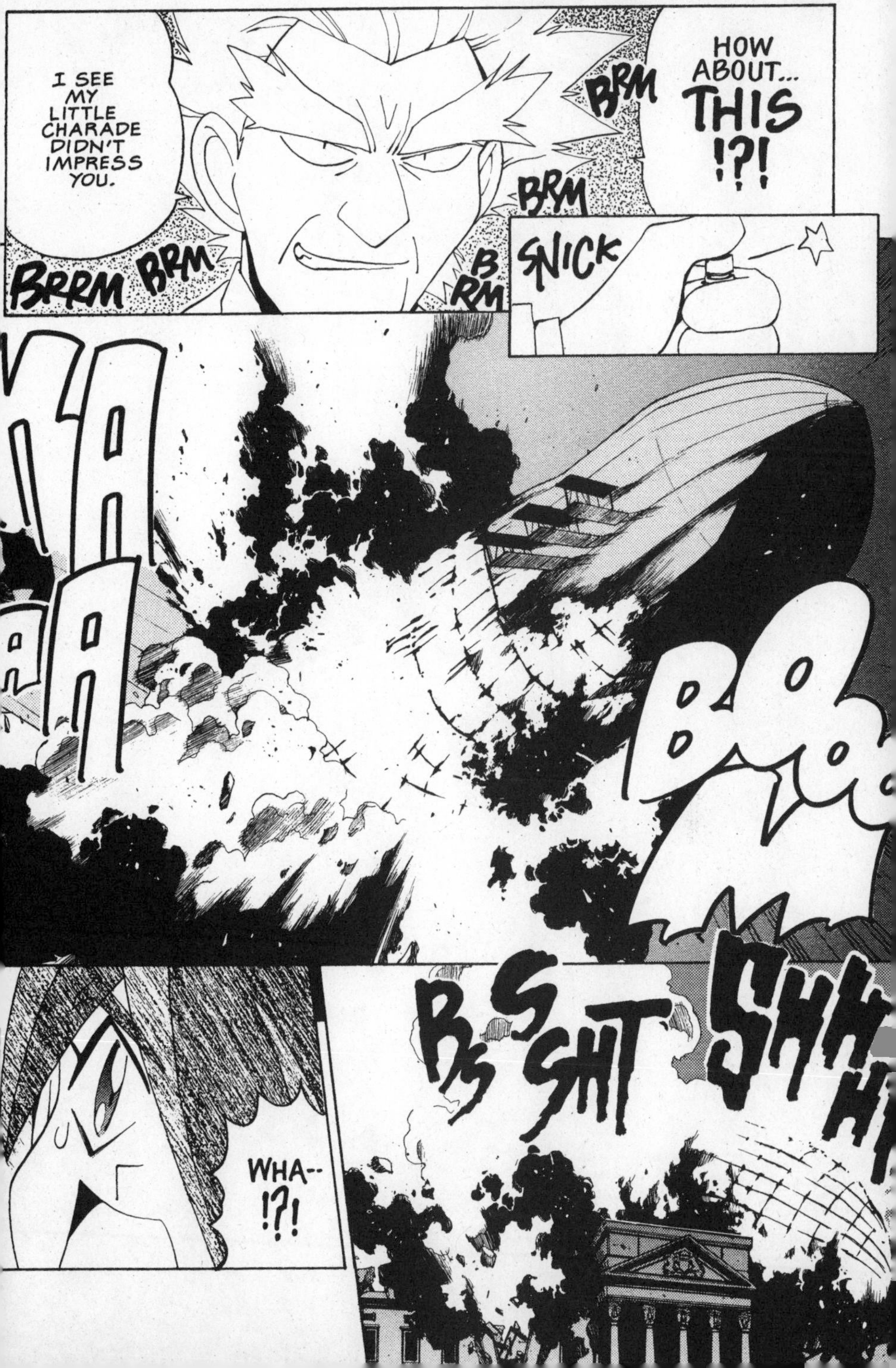
I SEE MY LITTLE CHARADE DIDN'T IMPRESS YOU.
BRRM
BRM
BRM
BRM
B RM
HOW ABOUT... THIS !?!
SNICK
WHA-- !?!
SHT

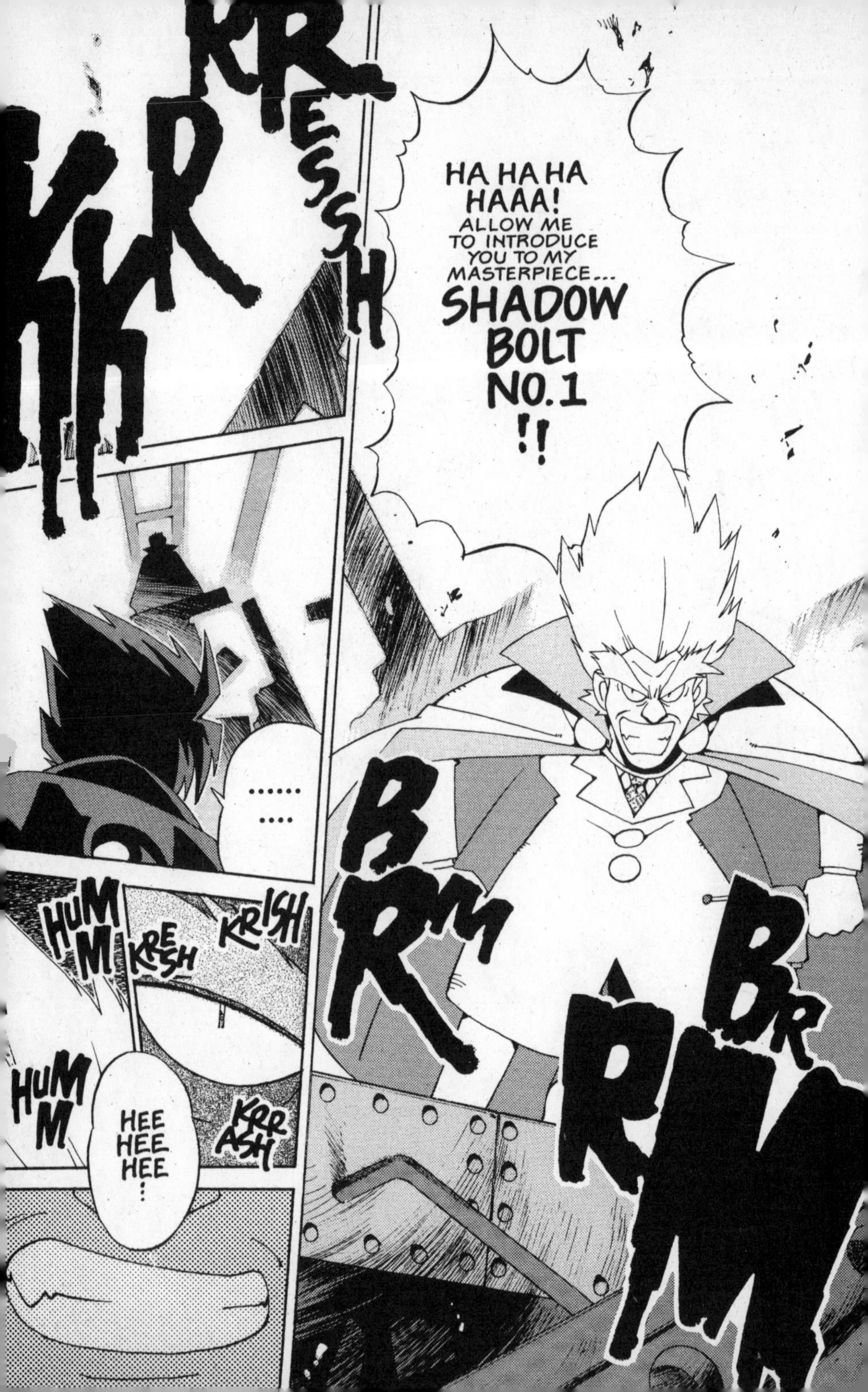
KRESSH
......
....
HUMM
KRESH
KRISH
HUMM
HEE HEE HEE...
KRRASH
HA HA HA HAAA! ALLOW ME TO INTRODUCE YOU TO MY MASTERPIECE... SHADOW BOLT NO.1 !!
BRRM
BRRM

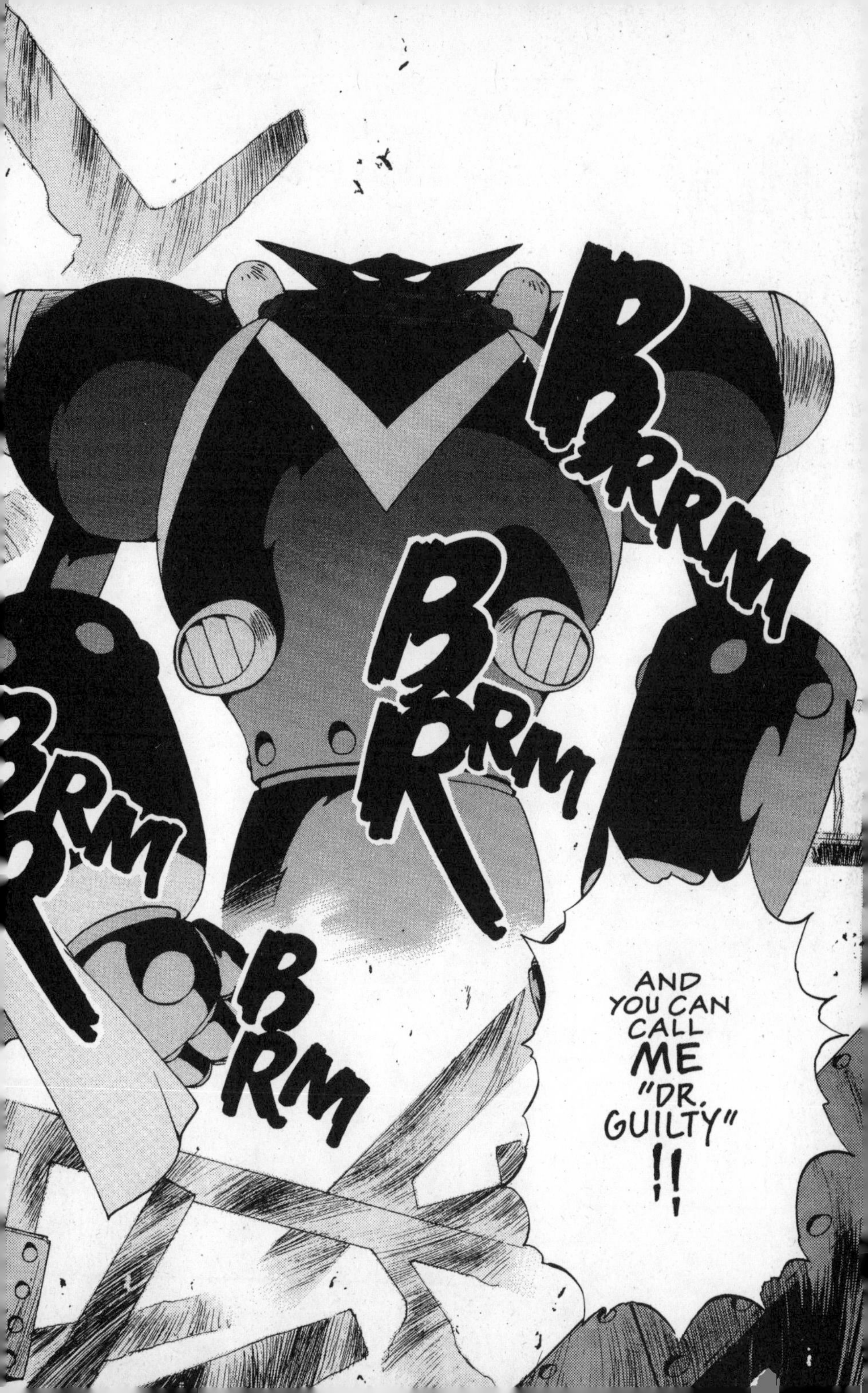
BRRRM
BRRM
BRRM
BRM
AND YOU CAN CALL ME "DR. GUILTY"!!

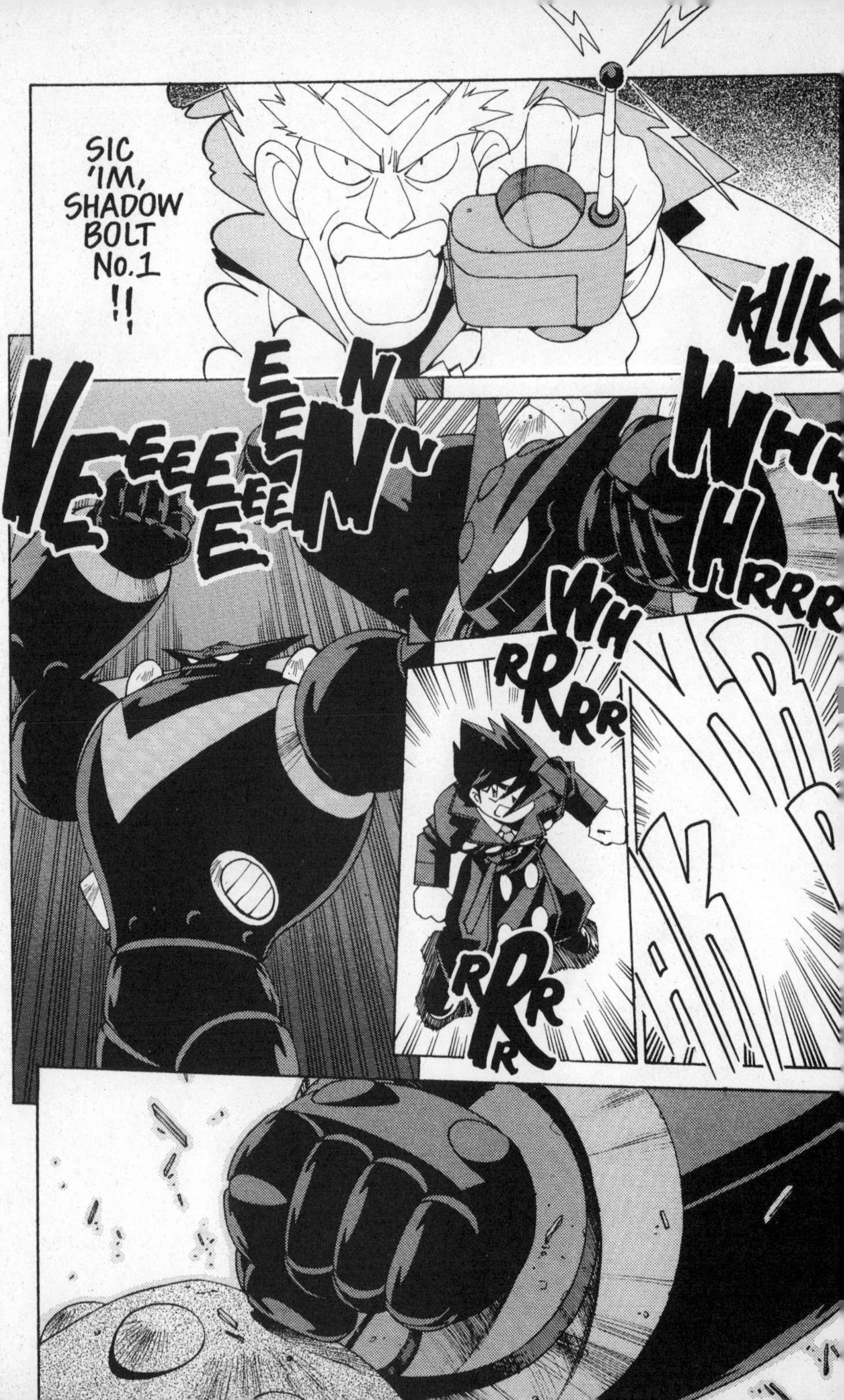
SIC 'IM, SHADOW BOLT No.1 !!
KLIK
VEEEEEEEEEEENNN
WHHHRRRR
WHRRRRR
RRRRR

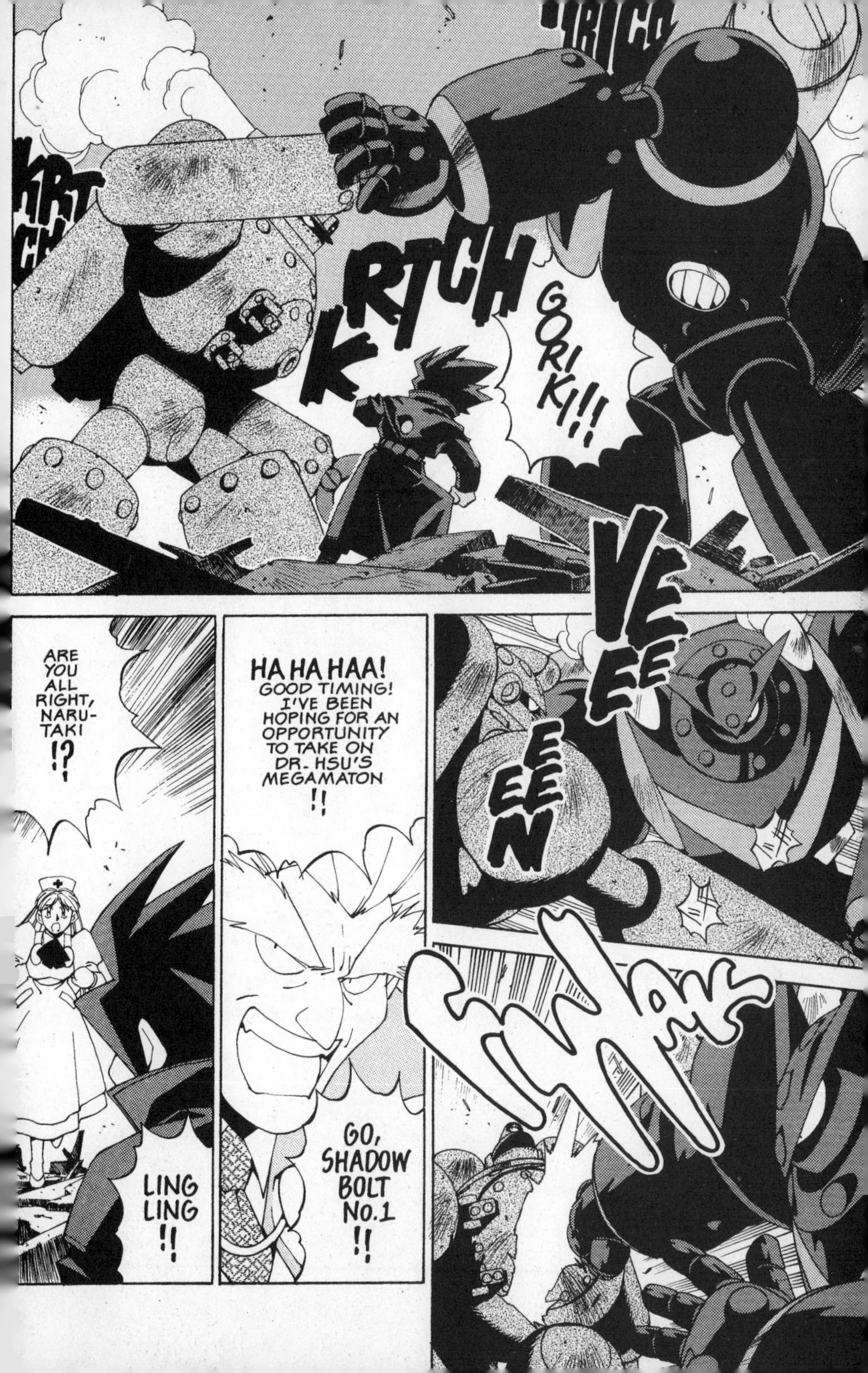
KRTCH
GORIKI!!
ARE YOU ALL RIGHT, NARUTAKI !?
LING LING !!
HA HA HAA! GOOD TIMING! I'VE BEEN HOPING FOR AN OPPORTUNITY TO TAKE ON DR. HSU'S MEGAMATON !!
GO, SHADOW BOLT No.1 !!
VEEEEEEN

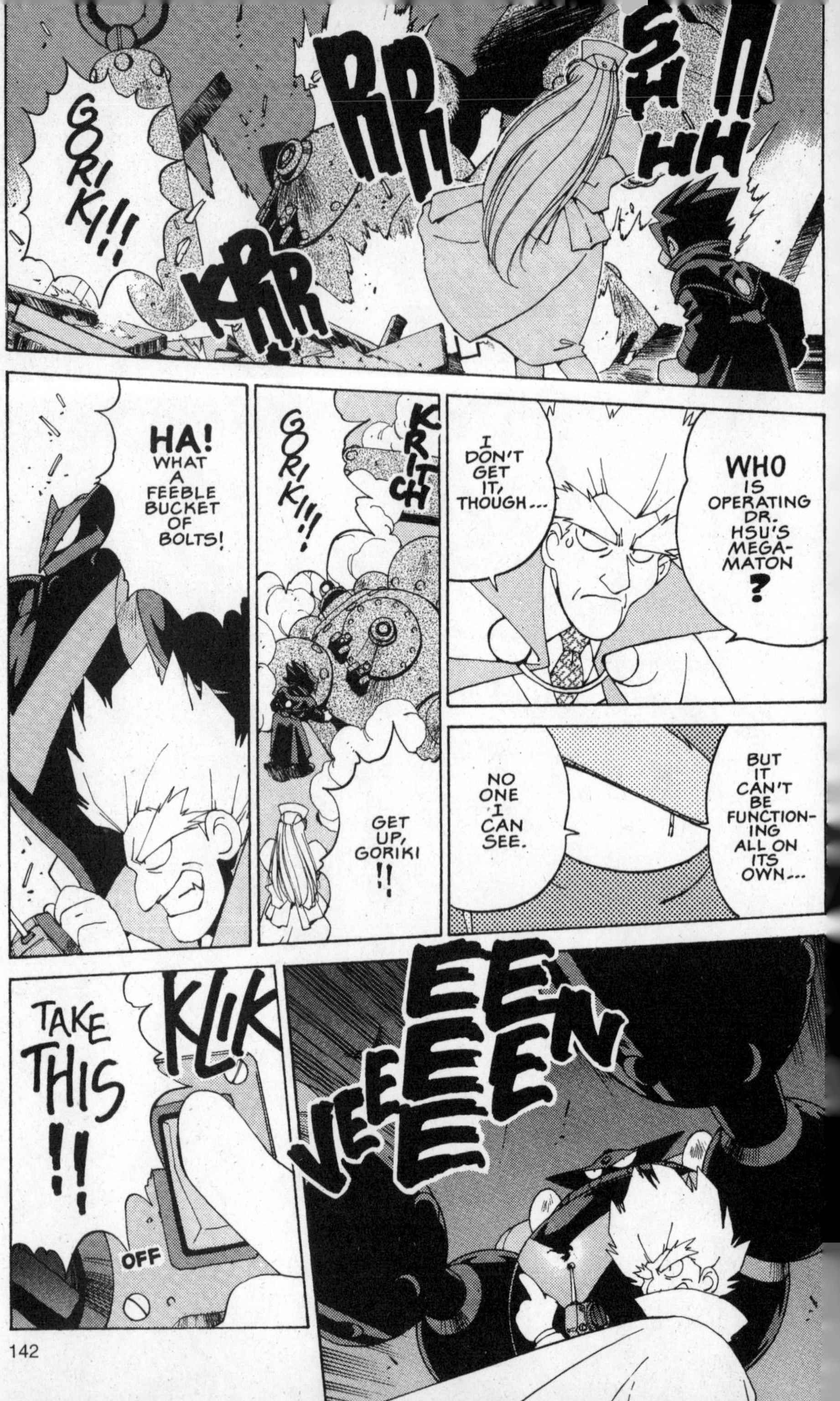

GORIKI!!!
RRRR
SHHH
KRR
HA! WHAT A FEEBLE BUCKET OF BOLTS!
GORIKI!!!
KRITCH
GET UP, GORIKI!!
I DON'T GET IT, THOUGH...
WHO IS OPERATING DR. HSU'S MEGA-MATON?
NO ONE I CAN SEE.
BUT IT CAN'T BE FUNCTION-ING ALL ON ITS OWN...
TAKE THIS!!
KLIK
OFF
VEEEEEEEN

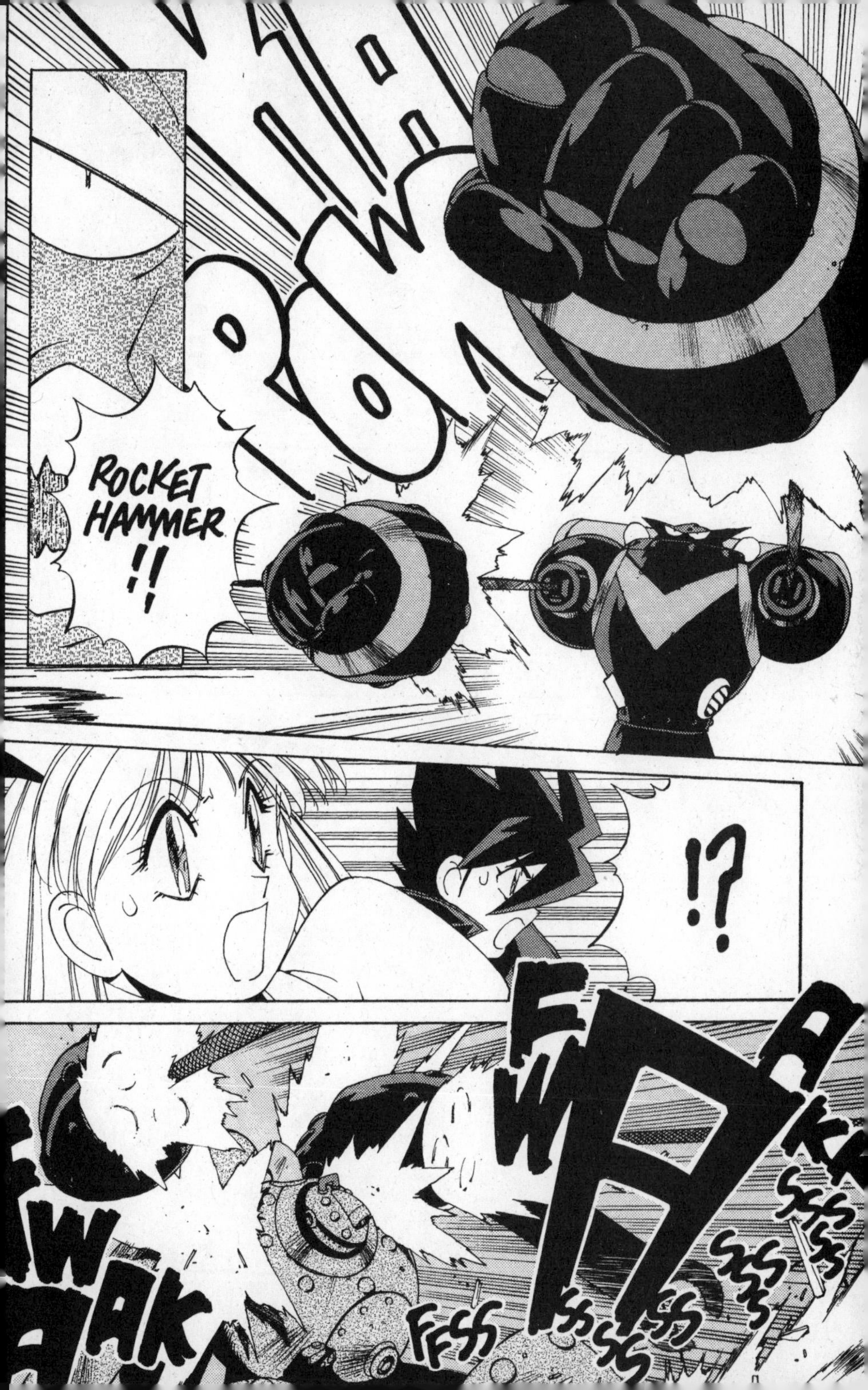
ROCKET HAMMER !!
!?
FFSS

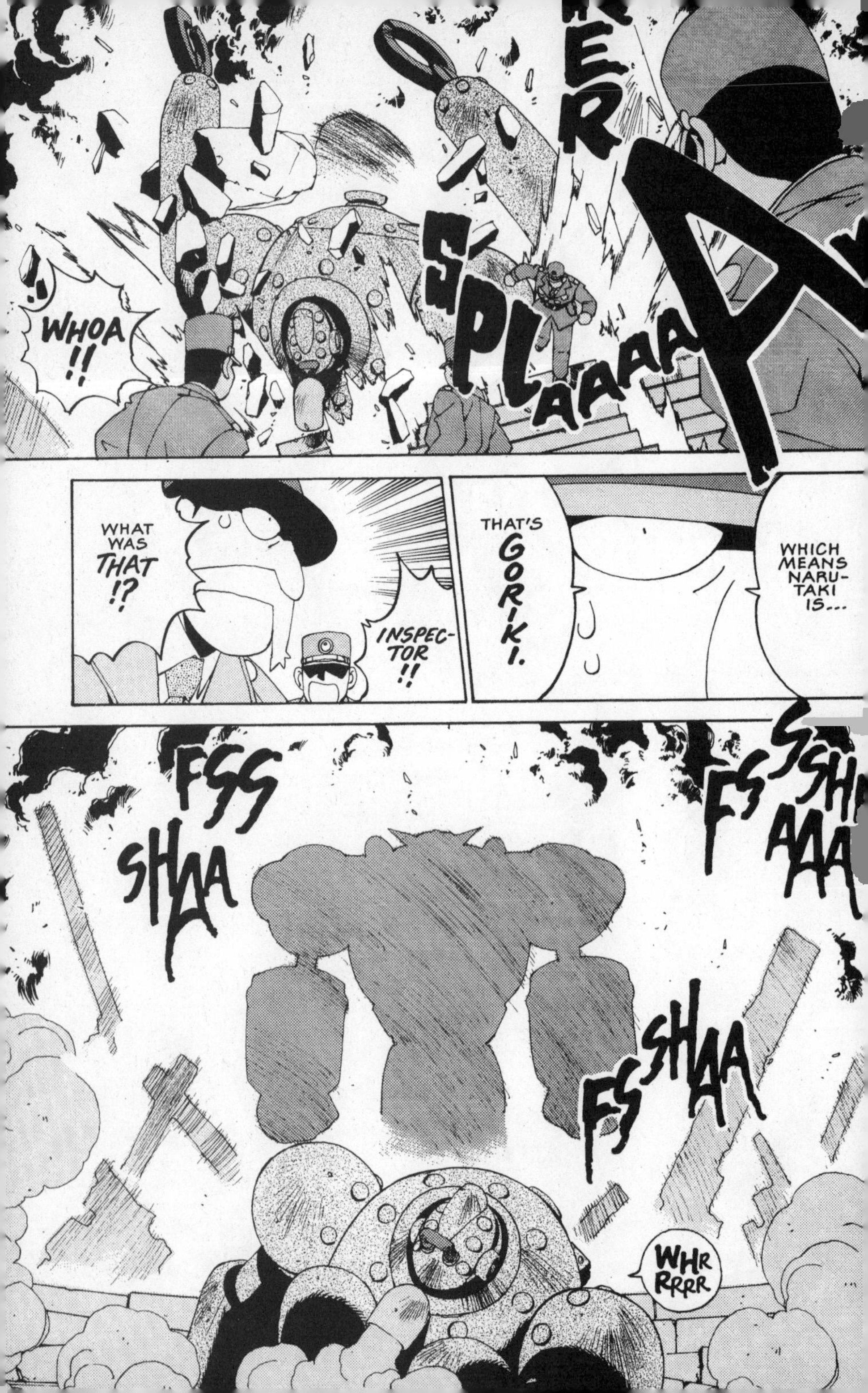
WHOA !!
SPLAAAAA
WHAT WAS THAT !?
INSPECTOR !!
THAT'S GORIKI.
WHICH MEANS NARUTAKI IS...
FSS SHAA
FS SSHAAA
FS SHAA
WHRRRRR

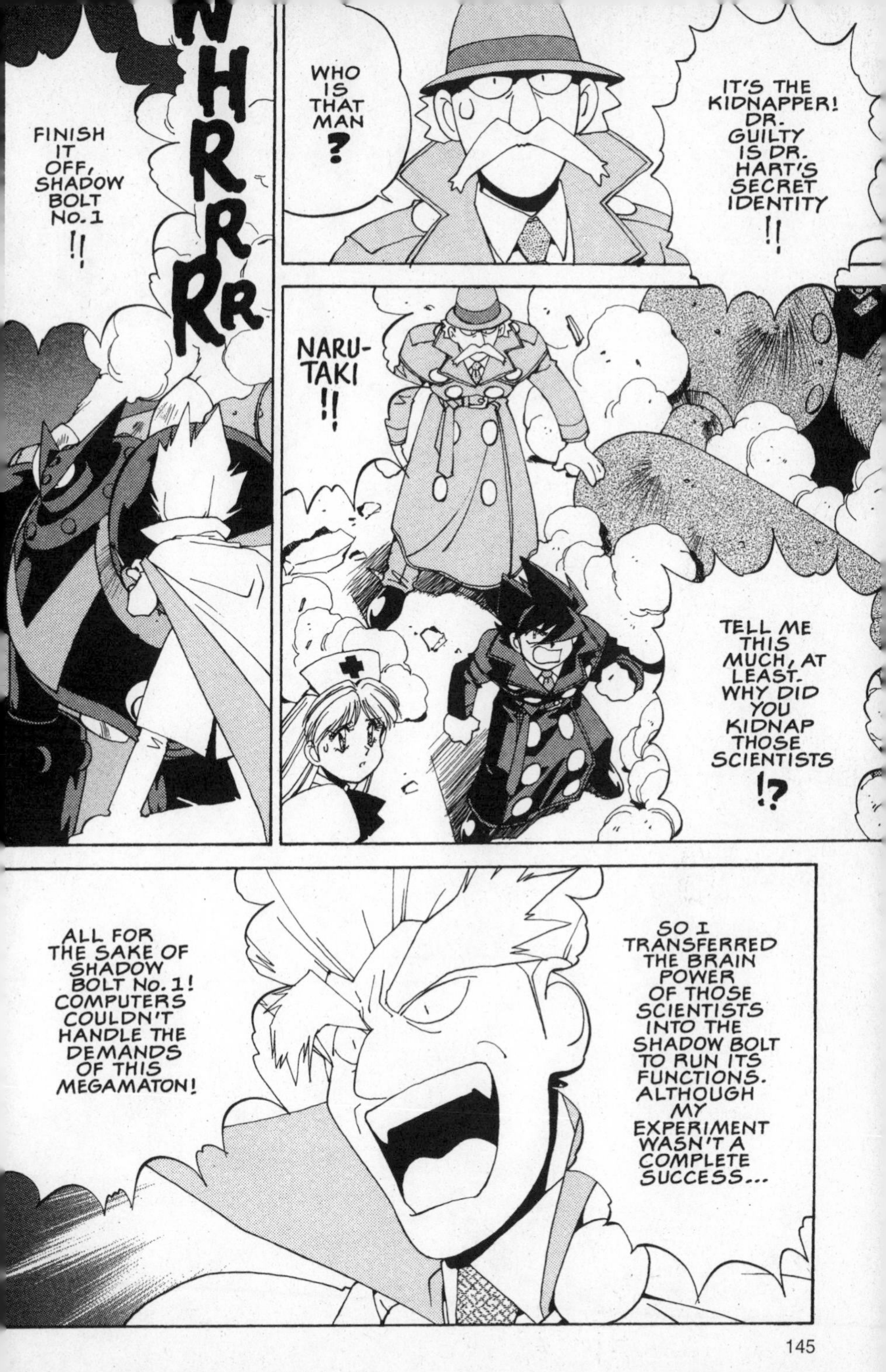
WHRRRR
FINISH IT OFF, SHADOW BOLT No. 1 !!
WHO IS THAT MAN ?
IT'S THE KIDNAPPER! DR. GUILTY IS DR. HART'S SECRET IDENTITY !!
NARU-TAKI !!
TELL ME THIS MUCH, AT LEAST. WHY DID YOU KIDNAP THOSE SCIENTISTS !?
ALL FOR THE SAKE OF SHADOW BOLT No. 1! COMPUTERS COULDN'T HANDLE THE DEMANDS OF THIS MEGAMATON!
SO I TRANSFERRED THE BRAIN POWER OF THOSE SCIENTISTS INTO THE SHADOW BOLT TO RUN ITS FUNCTIONS. ALTHOUGH MY EXPERIMENT WASN'T A COMPLETE SUCCESS...

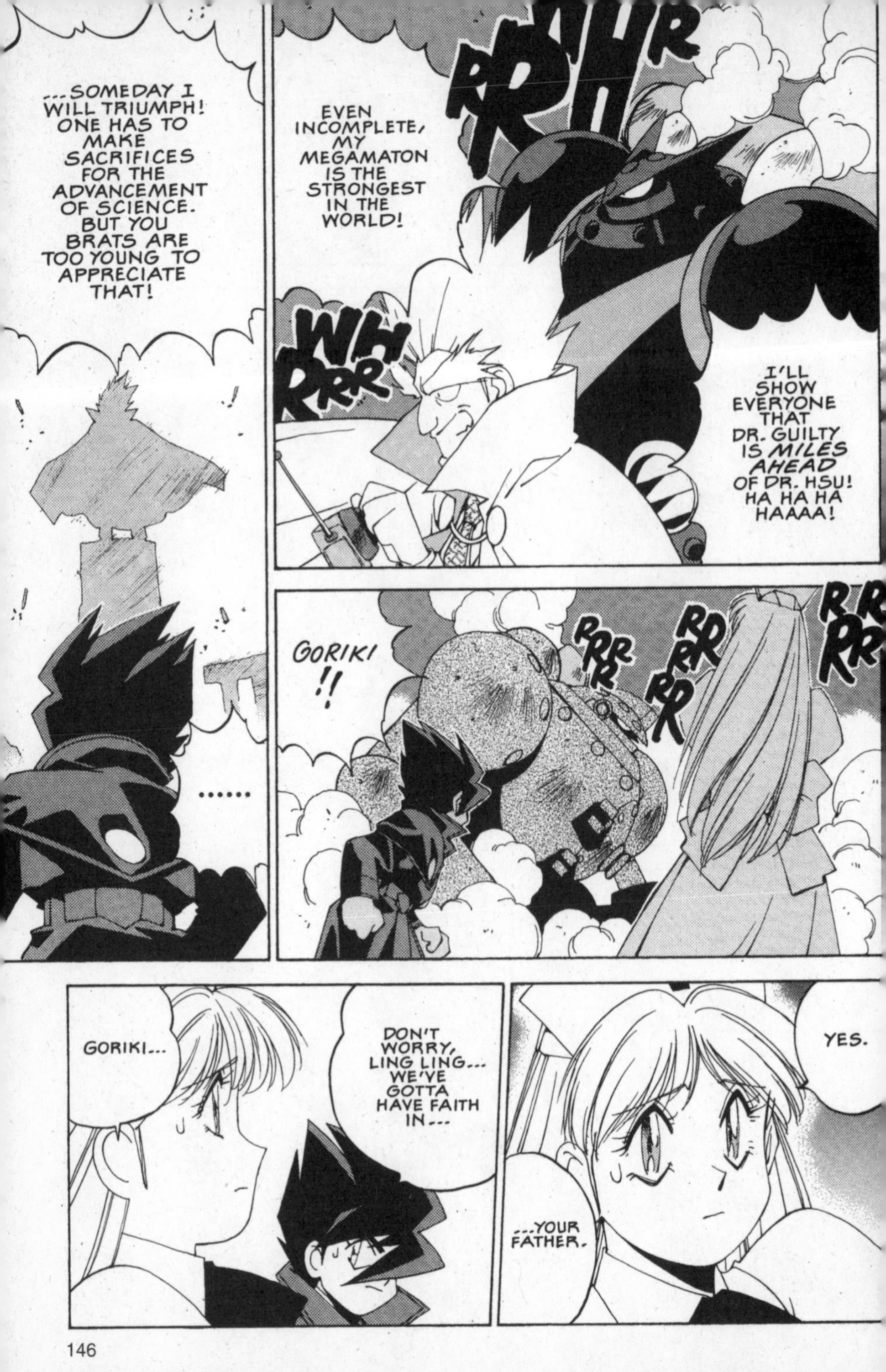

...SOMEDAY I WILL TRIUMPH! ONE HAS TO MAKE SACRIFICES FOR THE ADVANCEMENT OF SCIENCE. BUT YOU BRATS ARE TOO YOUNG TO APPRECIATE THAT!
......
EVEN INCOMPLETE, MY MEGAMATON IS THE STRONGEST IN THE WORLD!
RRHR
WHRRR
I'LL SHOW EVERYONE THAT DR. GUILTY IS MILES AHEAD OF DR. HSU! HA HA HA HAAAA!
GORIKI !!
RRRR
RRRRR
RRRR
GORIKI...
DON'T WORRY, LING LING... WE'VE GOTTA HAVE FAITH IN...
...YOUR FATHER.
YES.

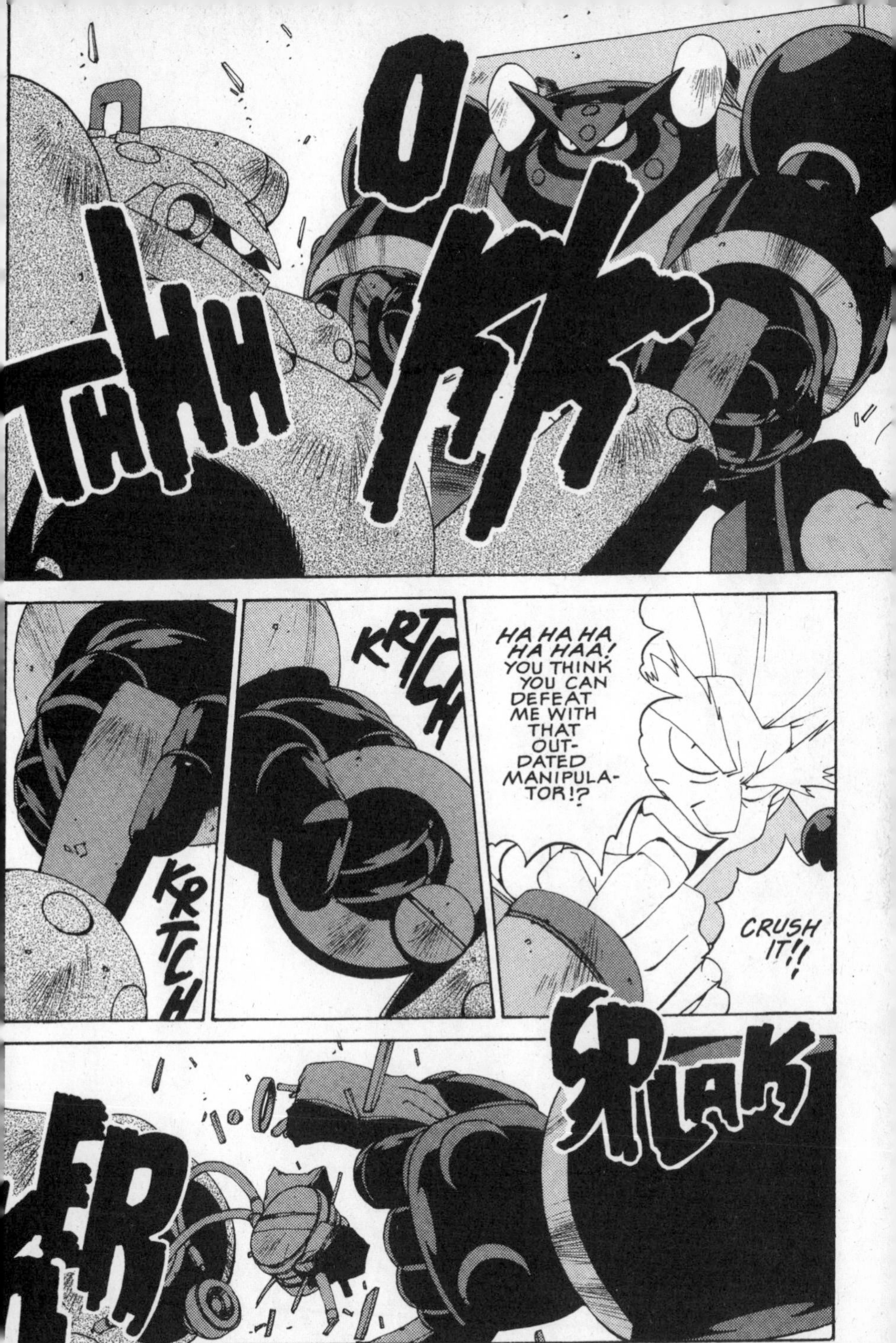
KRTCH
KRTCH
HA HA HA HA HAA! YOU THINK YOU CAN DEFEAT ME WITH THAT OUT-DATED MANIPULATOR!?
CRUSH IT!!

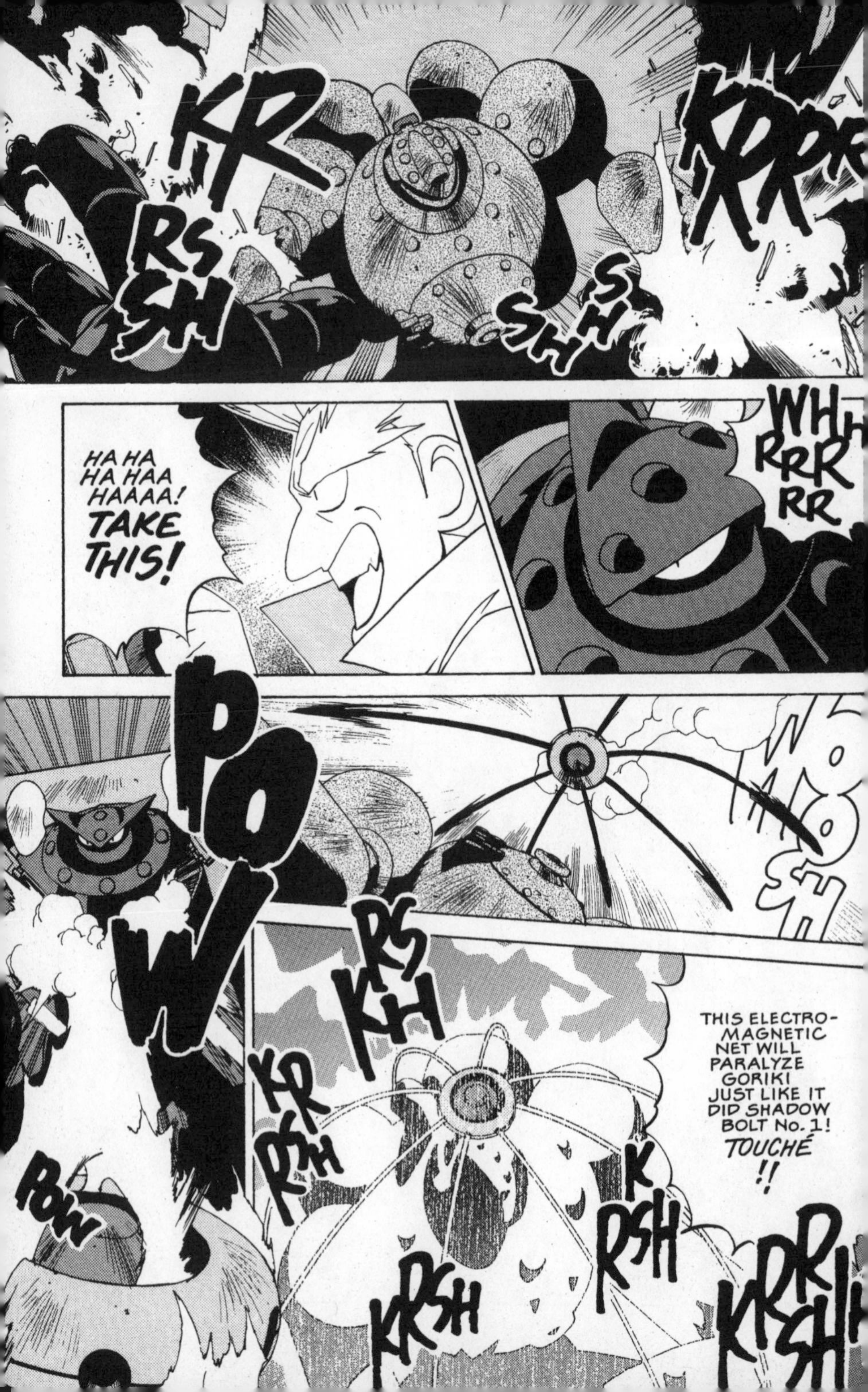
KR
RS SH
HA HA HA HAA HAAAA! TAKE THIS!
WHH RRR RR
POW
RS KRH
KR RSH
THIS ELECTRO-MAGNETIC NET WILL PARALYZE GORIKI JUST LIKE IT DID SHADOW BOLT No. 1! TOUCHÉ !!
POW
K RSH
KRSH
KRR KRSH

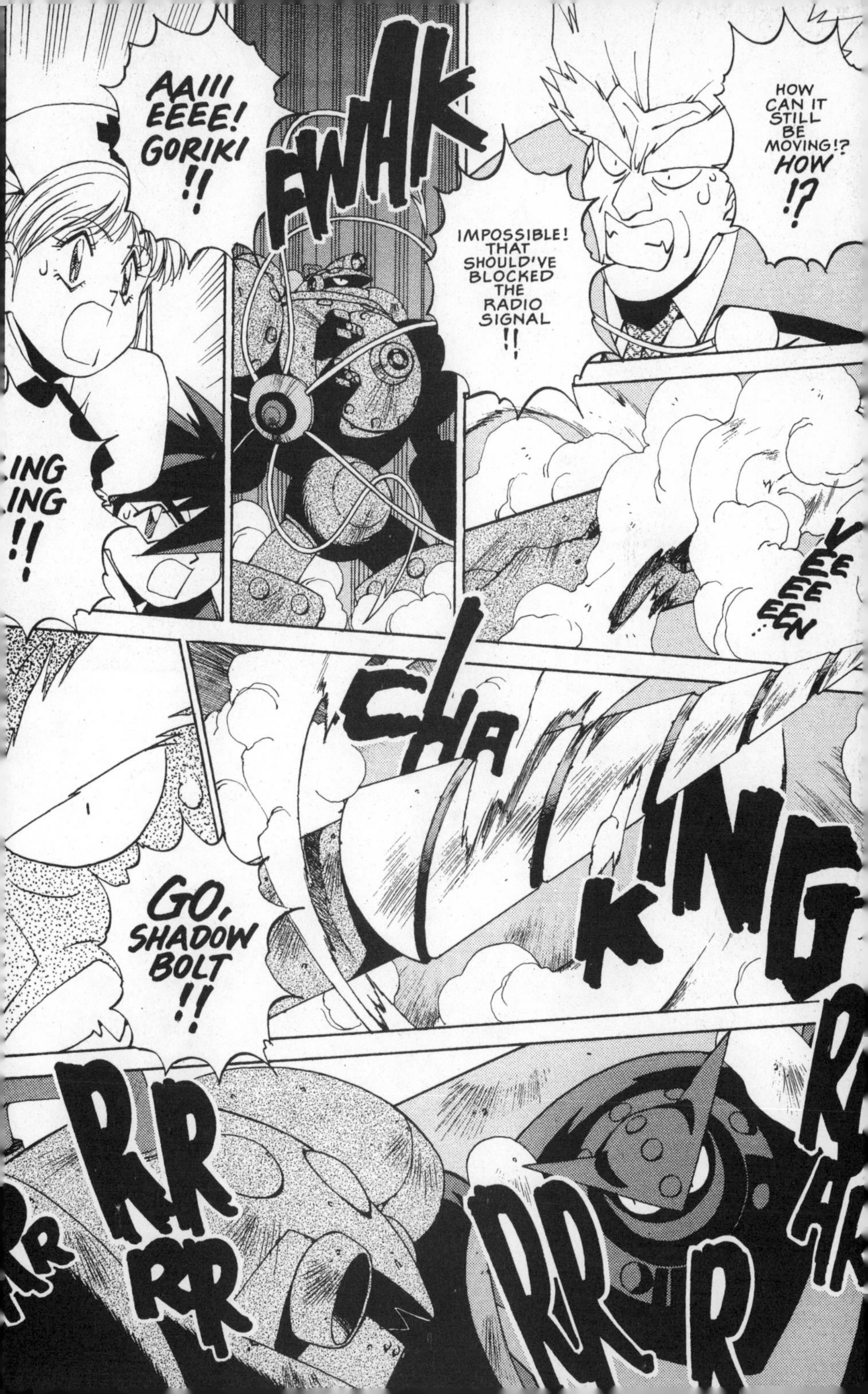
AAIII EEEE! GORIKI !!
ING ING !!
FWAK
IMPOSSIBLE! THAT SHOULD'VE BLOCKED THE RADIO SIGNAL !!
HOW CAN IT STILL BE MOVING!? HOW !?
VEEEEEEN...
GO, SHADOW BOLT !!
CHA KING
RRR RRR RRR
RRRRR
RRAR

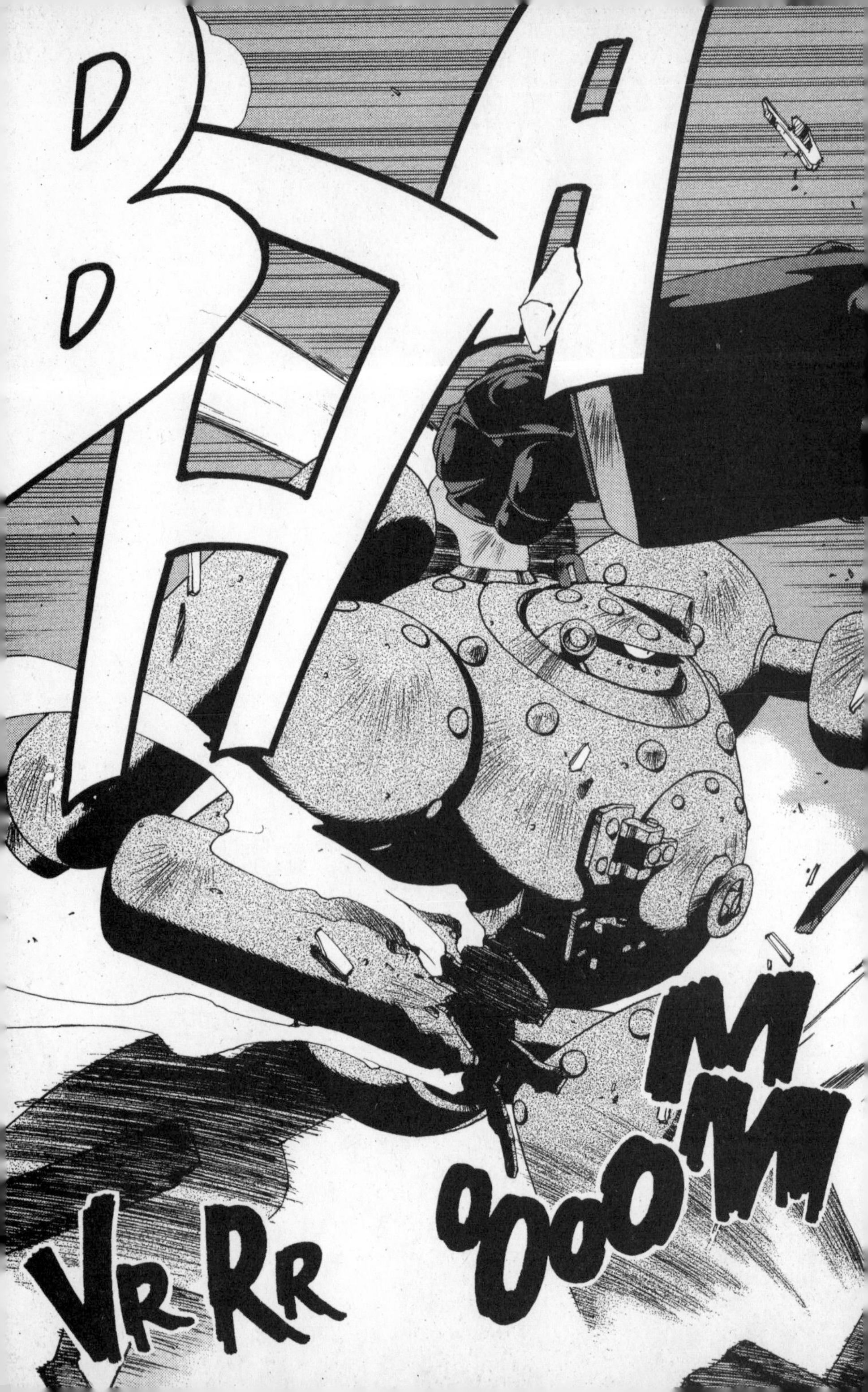
VRRR
OOOOMMM

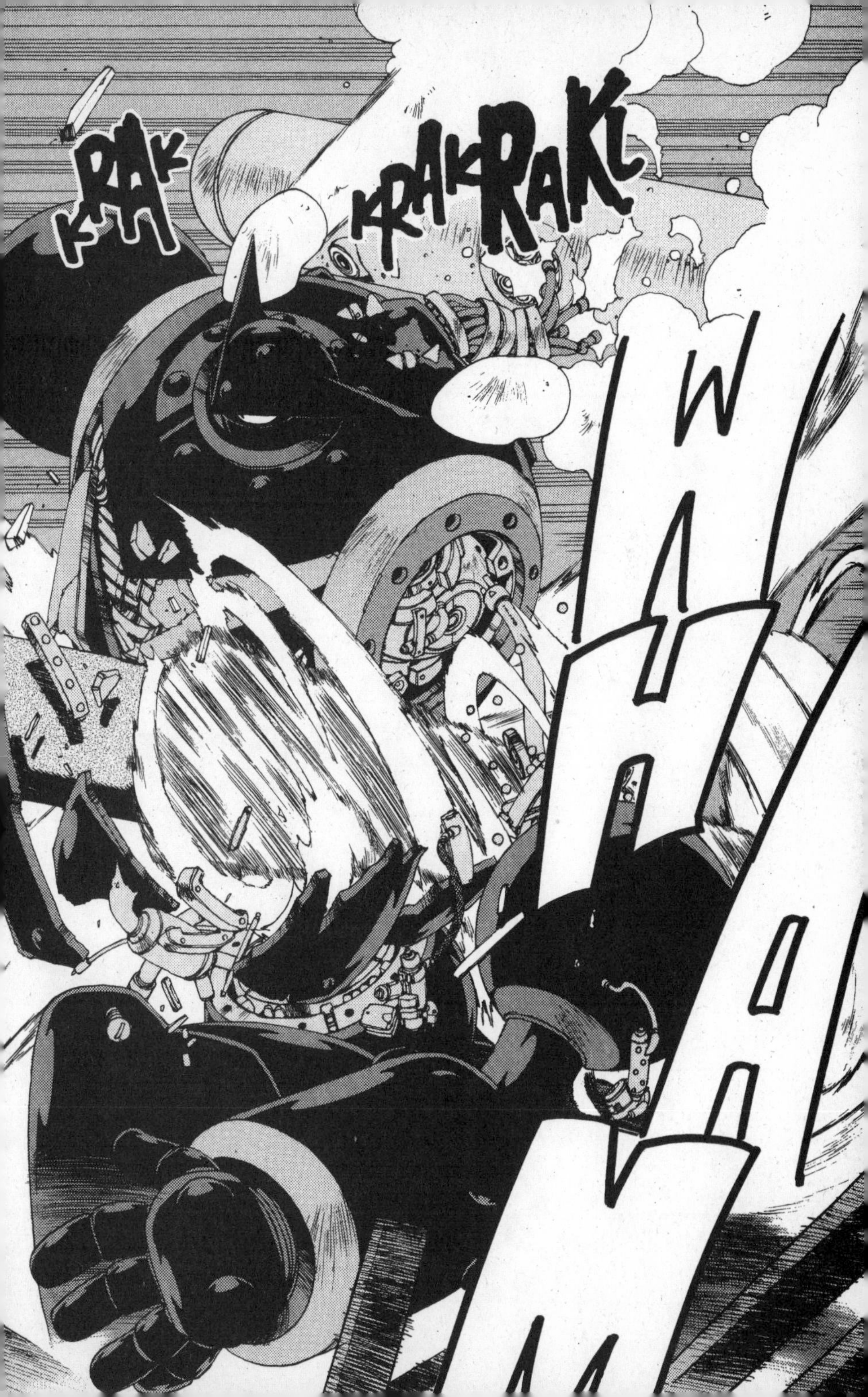
KRAK
KRAKRAKL
WAAAAAAH

INSPECTOR, DR. GUILTY HAS ESCAPED!!

AFTER HIM!

HE MIGHT STILL BE IN THE VICINITY!!

YES, SIR!

I'LL BE BACK, NARU-TAKI!!

YOU'LL PAY FOR THIS!

WAIT AND SEE!!

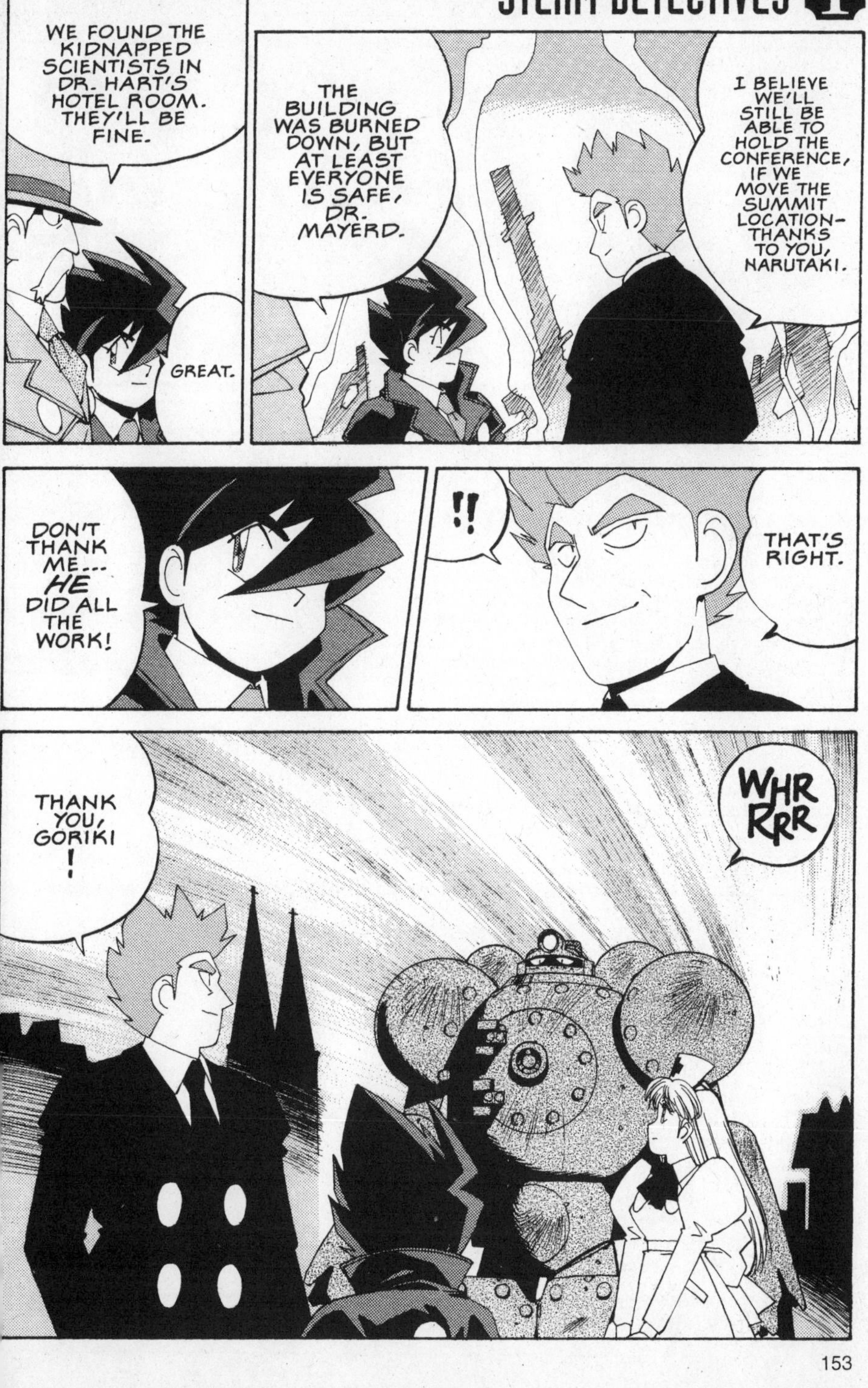
WE FOUND THE KIDNAPPED SCIENTISTS IN DR. HART'S HOTEL ROOM. THEY'LL BE FINE.
GREAT.
THE BUILDING WAS BURNED DOWN, BUT AT LEAST EVERYONE IS SAFE, DR. MAYERD.
I BELIEVE WE'LL STILL BE ABLE TO HOLD THE CONFERENCE, IF WE MOVE THE SUMMIT LOCATION- THANKS TO YOU, NARUTAKI.
DON'T THANK ME... HE DID ALL THE WORK!
!!
THAT'S RIGHT.
THANK YOU, GORIKI!
WHR RRR

STEAM DETECTIVES PRESS

MONSTER MEGAMATON APPEARS IN CAPITAL! ROBOT IDENTIFIED AS SHADOW BOLT NO.1!

The mysterious case of the kidnapped World Scientist Summit scientists has finally been solved. They were imprisoned by a megamaton robot. And who was the operator of this megamaton, "Shadow Bolt No.1"? A mad scientist who identified himself as "Dr. Guilty"! Megamaton Goriki of the Narutaki Detective Agency fought Dr. Guilty's megamaton to a standstill. Such a battle between two megamatons is virtually unheard of. It appears that Shadow Bolt No.1 was constructed specifically for combat. In anticipation of further crimes committed by such monster robots, the police department has called for reinforcements.

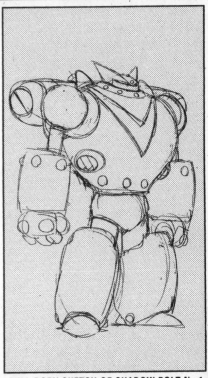

FULL BODY SKETCH OF SHADOW BOLT No.1

SHADOW BOLT No.1 USING ITS ARMS AS PROJECTILES (!?)

Through secret sources we managed to obtain a rough full-body sketch of Shadow Bolt No.1 (see diagram on right).

IRON STEAMMAN

Automatic Coal Burner

THE MACHINE THAT MADE COAL AN AUTOMATIC FUEL

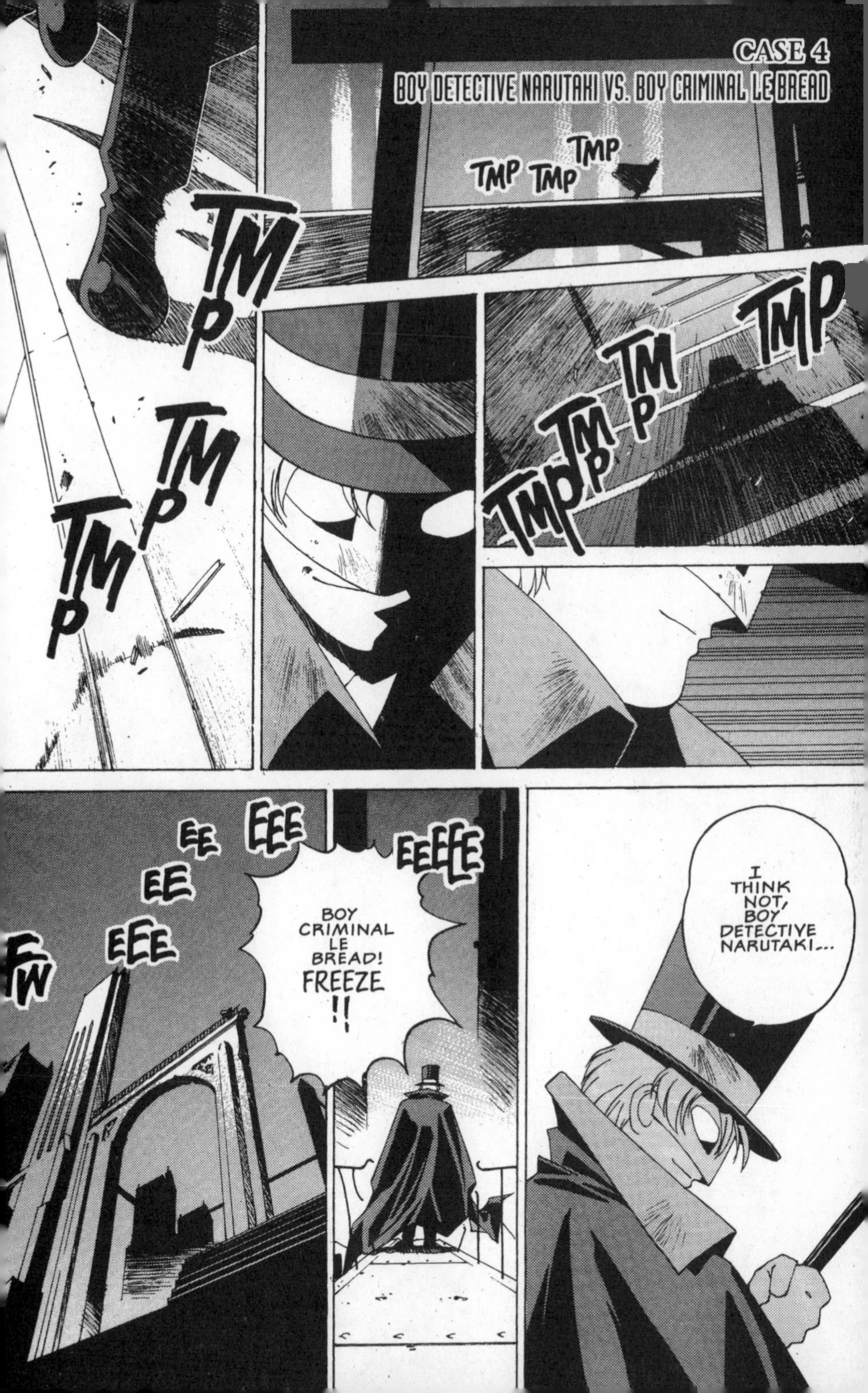

TMP
TMP
TMP
CASE 4
BOY DETECTIVE NARUTAKI VS. BOY CRIMINAL LE BREAD
TMP TMP TMP
TMP TMP TMP TMP
FW EEE EE EE EEE EEEEE
BOY CRIMINAL LE BREAD! FREEZE !!
I THINK NOT, BOY DETECTIVE NARUTAKI...

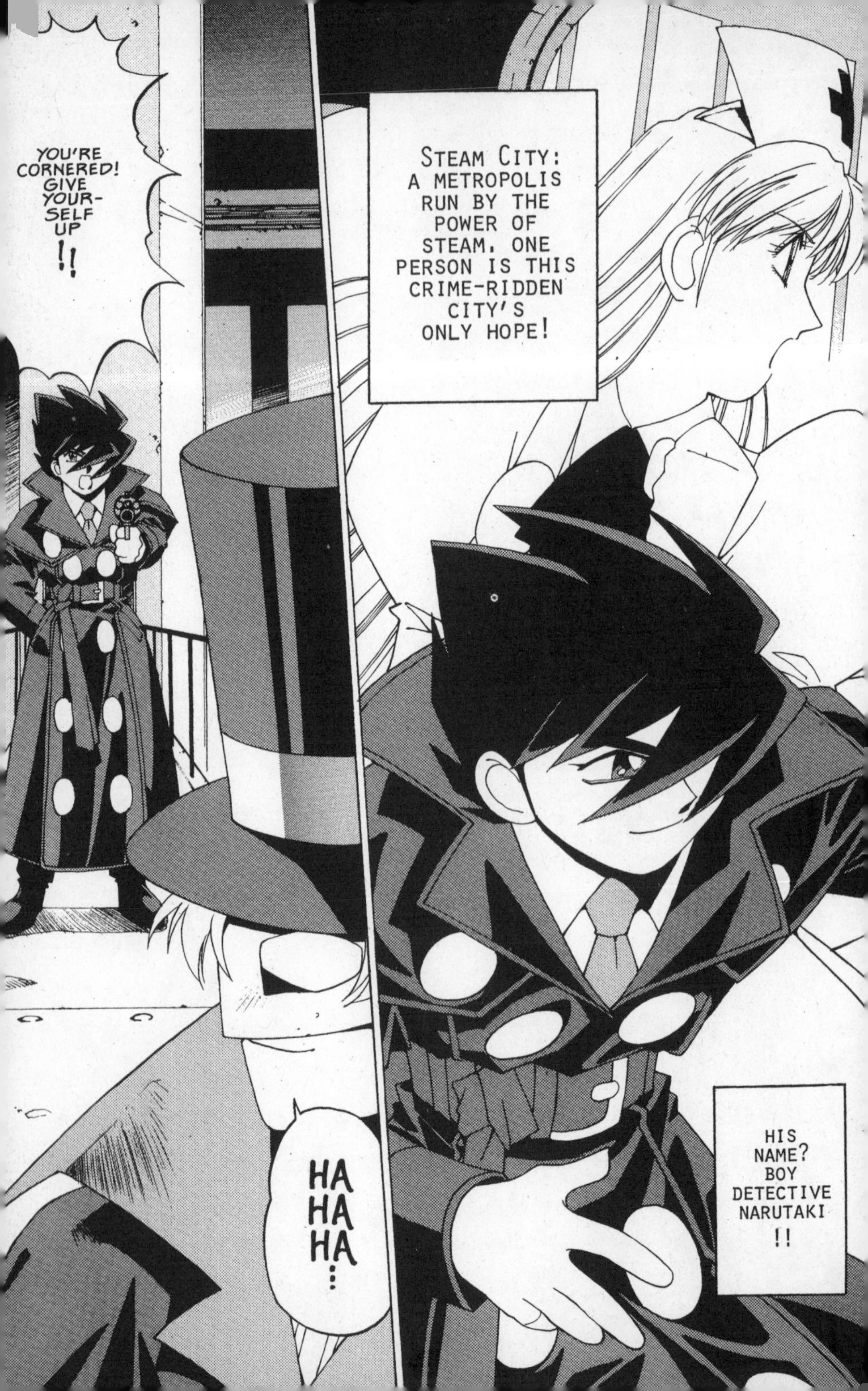
YOU'RE CORNERED! GIVE YOURSELF UP !!
HA HA HA...
STEAM CITY: A METROPOLIS RUN BY THE POWER OF STEAM. ONE PERSON IS THIS CRIME-RIDDEN CITY'S ONLY HOPE!
HIS NAME? BOY DETECTIVE NARUTAKI !!

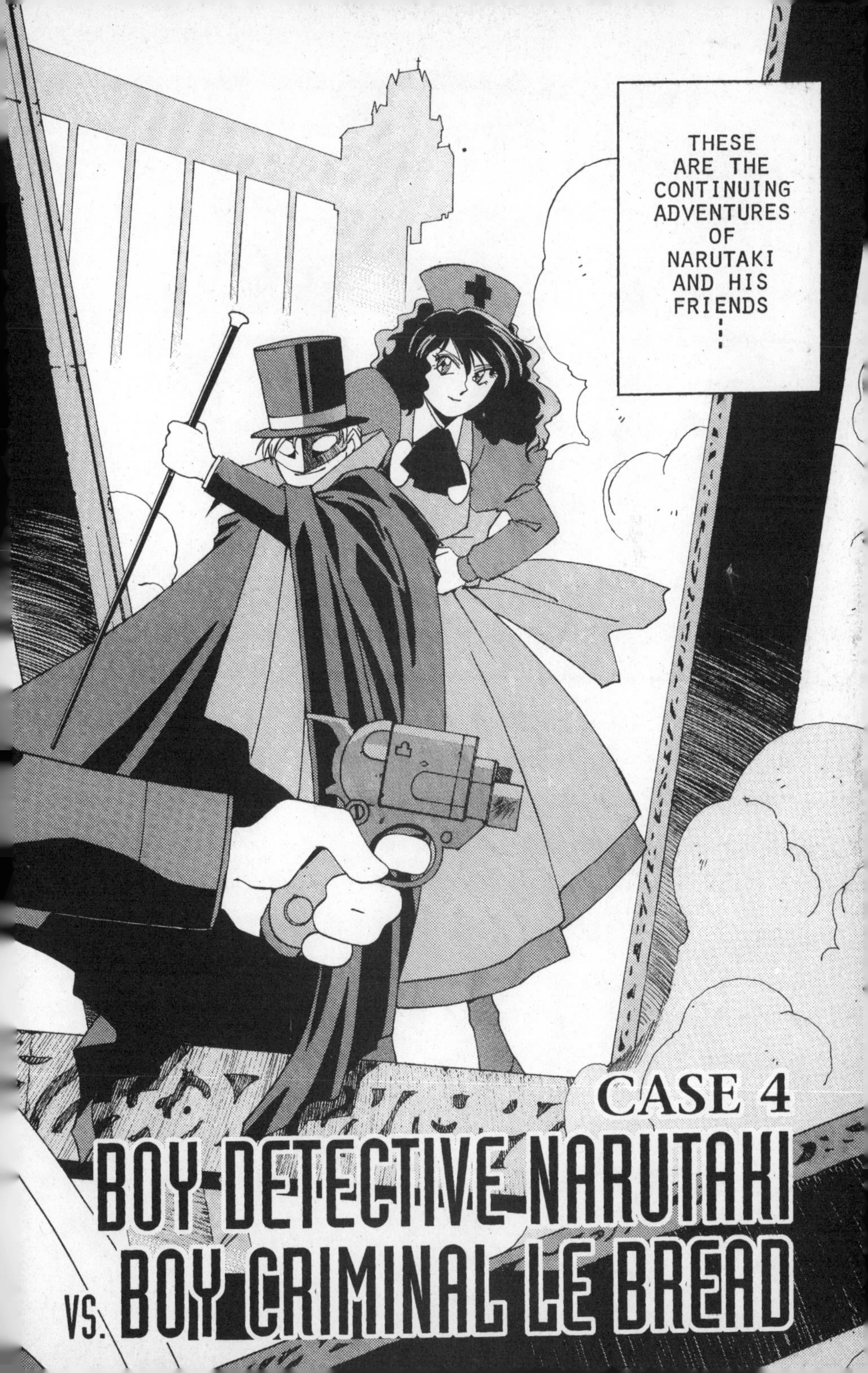
THESE ARE THE CONTINUING ADVENTURES OF NARUTAKI AND HIS FRIENDS …
CASE 4
BOY DETECTIVE NARUTAKI
VS. BOY CRIMINAL LE BREAD

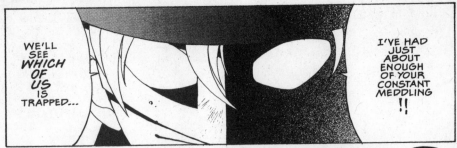

WE'LL SEE *WHICH* OF US IS TRAPPED...

I'VE HAD JUST ABOUT ENOUGH OF YOUR CONSTANT MEDDLING!!

WHAT THE--!?

!!

!?

FWEEEEEEE

ARRGH!

HA HAA HAA

PSSSSST

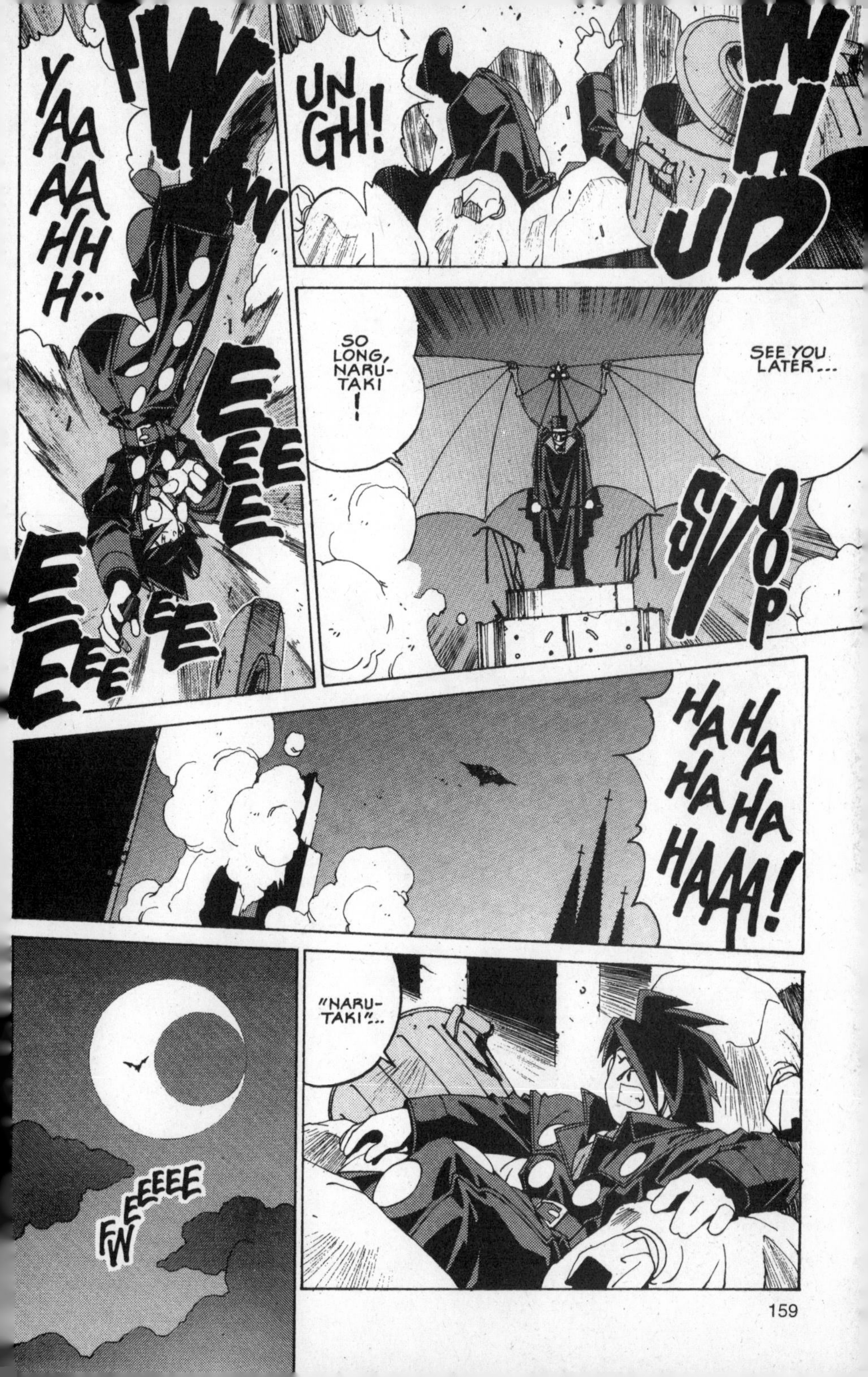

YAAAAHHHH..
FWW
EEEEEEEEEEE
UNGH!
WHUD
SO LONG, NARUTAKI!
SEE YOU LATER...
SWOOP
HAHAHAHAHAHAAAA!
FWEEEEE
"NARUTAKI"...

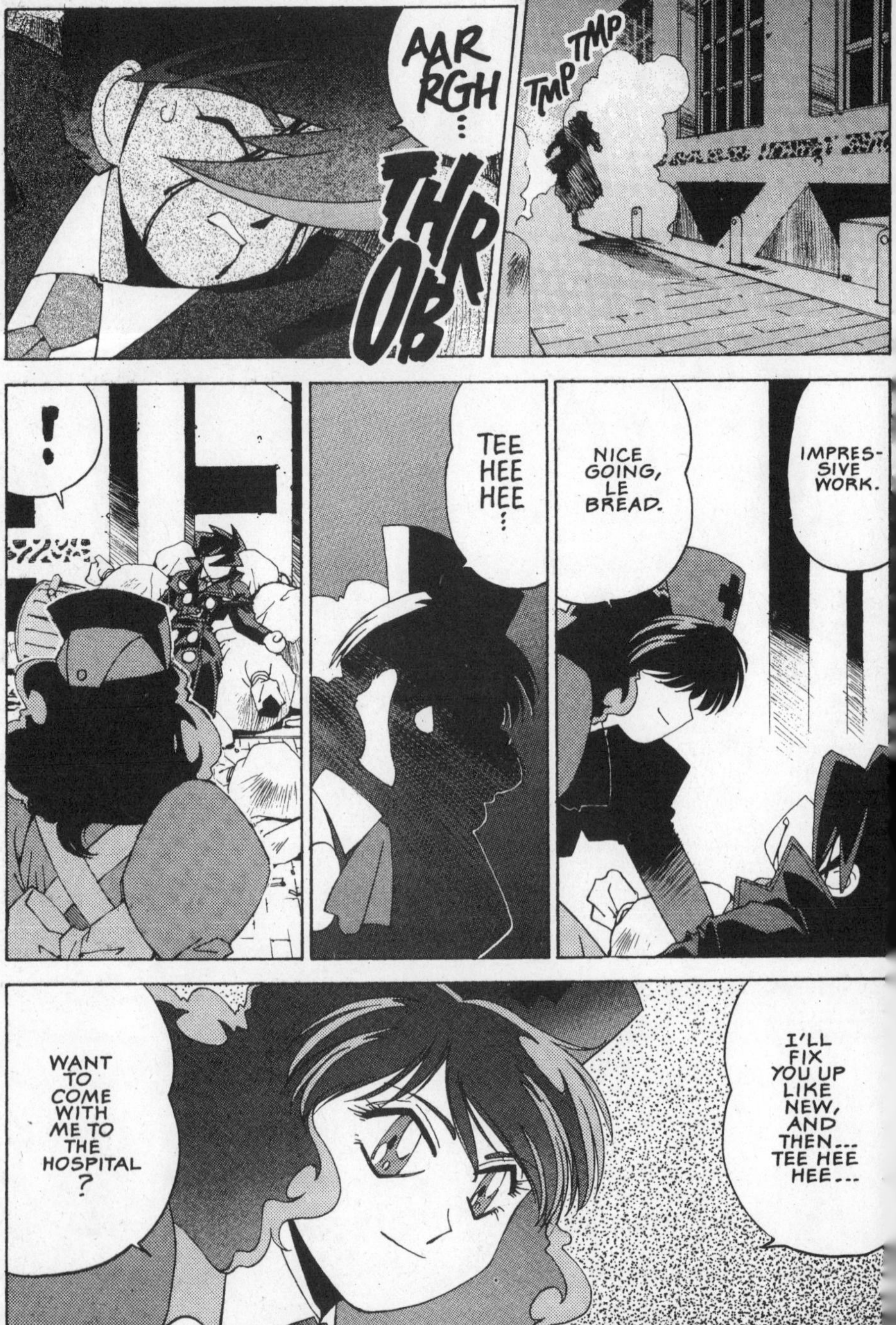
AARRGH...
THROB
TMP TMP TMP
!
TEE HEE HEE...
NICE GOING, LE BREAD.
IMPRESSIVE WORK.
WANT TO COME WITH ME TO THE HOSPITAL?
I'LL FIX YOU UP LIKE NEW, AND THEN... TEE HEE HEE...

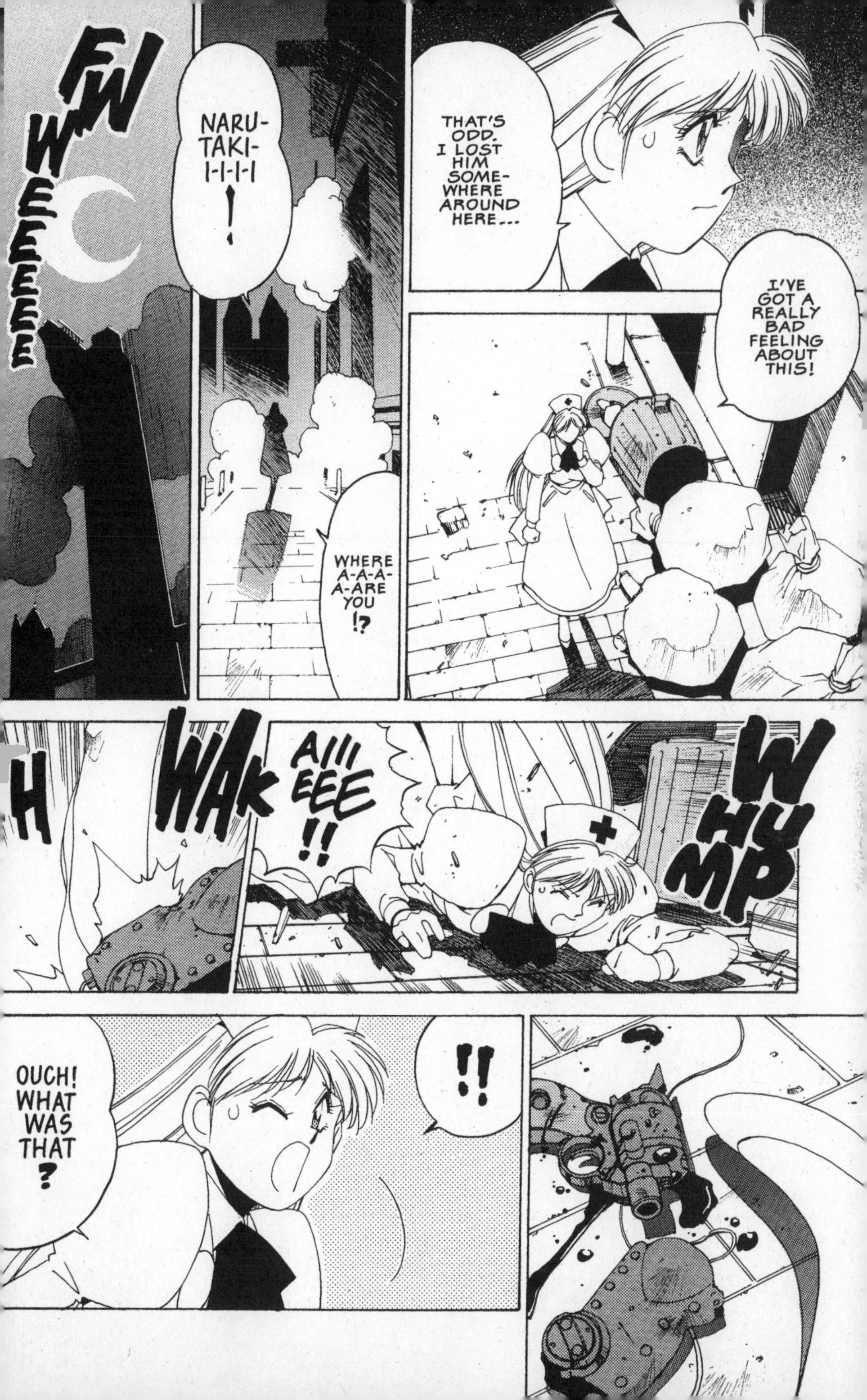
FWWEEEEEEE
NARU-TAKI-I-I-I-I !
WHERE A-A-A-A-ARE YOU !?
THAT'S ODD. I LOST HIM SOMEWHERE AROUND HERE...
I'VE GOT A REALLY BAD FEELING ABOUT THIS!
H
WAK
AIII EEE !!
WHUMP
OUCH! WHAT WAS THAT ?
!!

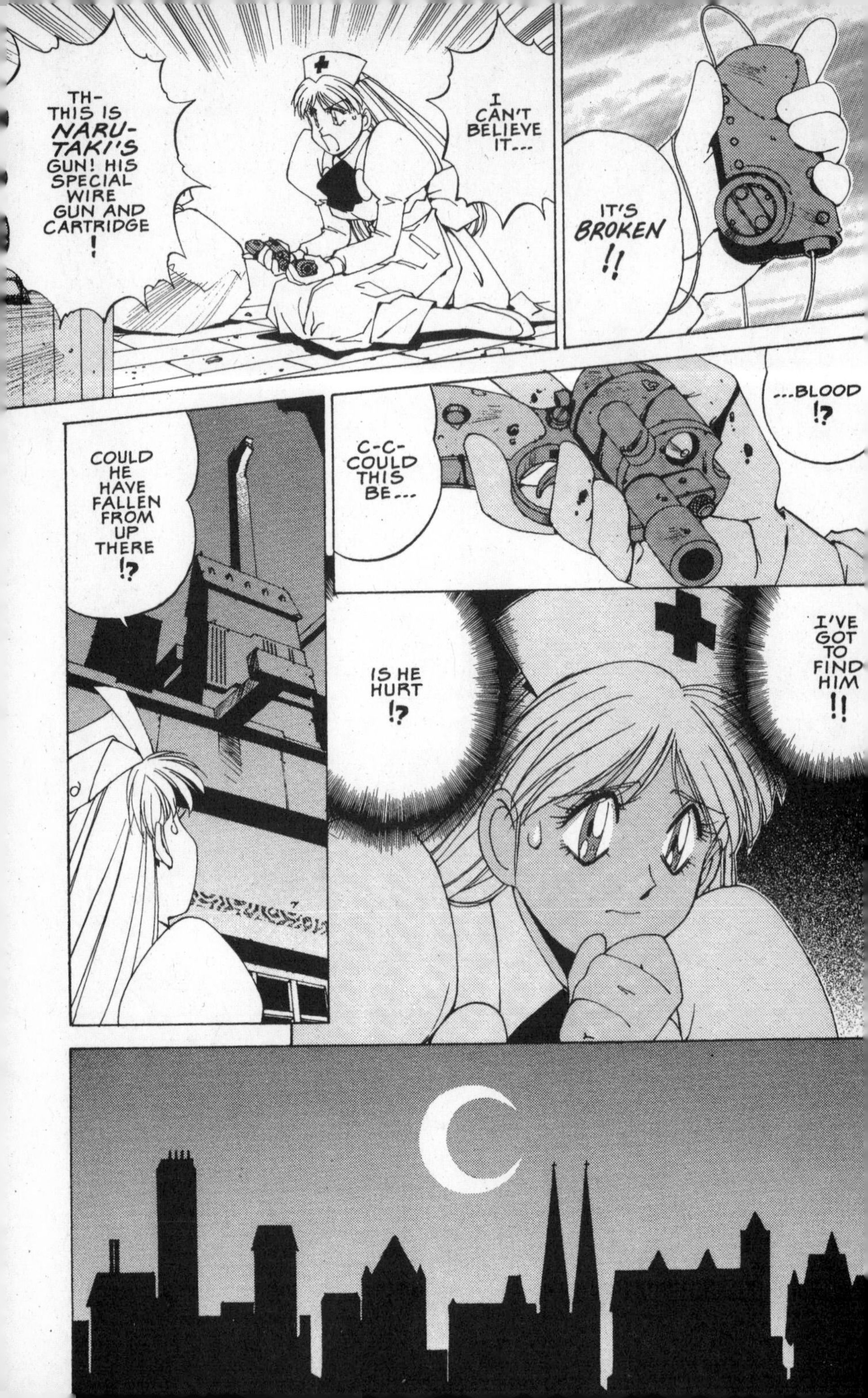
TH- THIS IS NARU-TAKI'S GUN! HIS SPECIAL WIRE GUN AND CARTRIDGE!
I CAN'T BELIEVE IT...
IT'S BROKEN!!
C-C-COULD THIS BE...
...BLOOD!?
COULD HE HAVE FALLEN FROM UP THERE!?
IS HE HURT!?
I'VE GOT TO FIND HIM!!

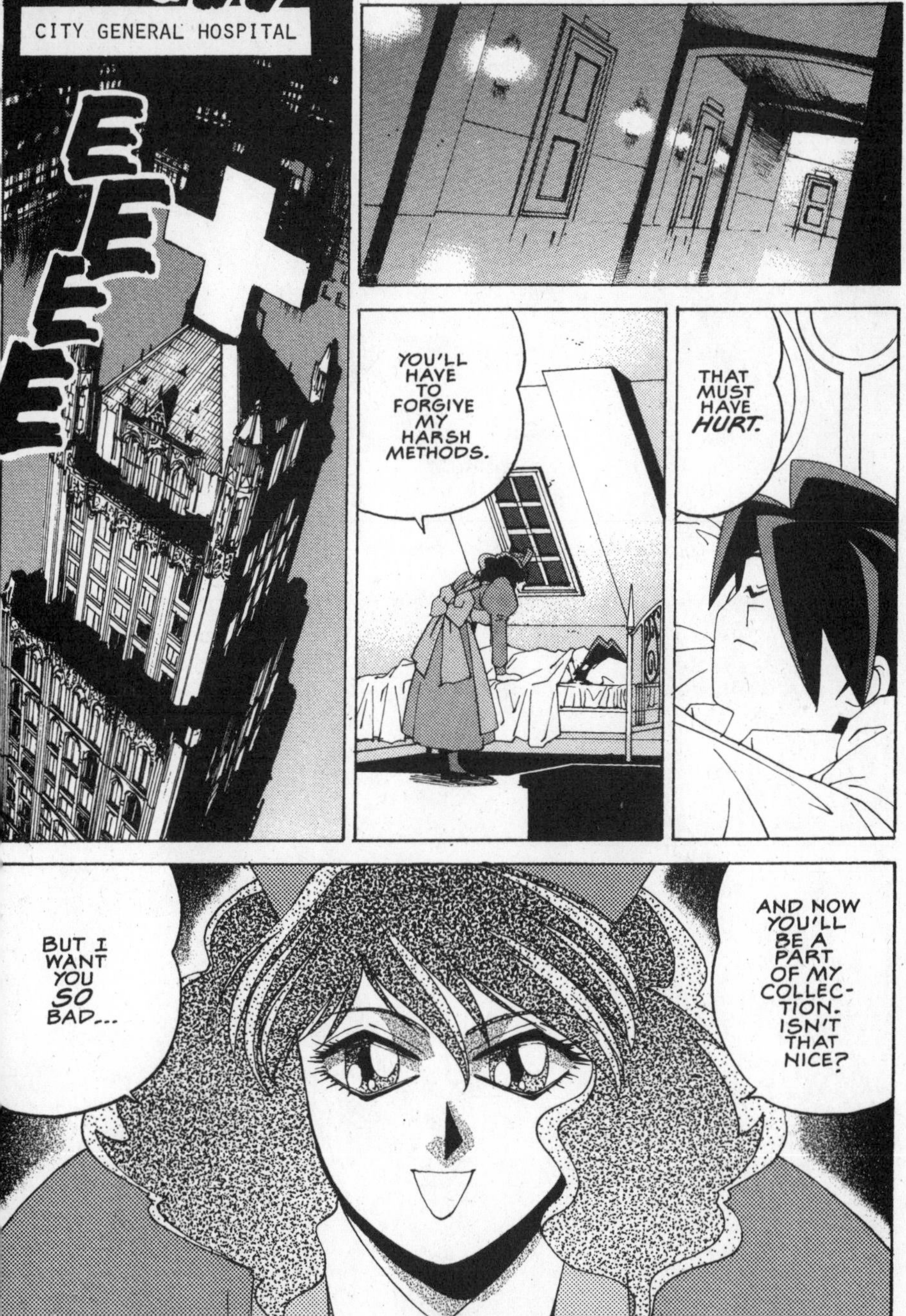
IFW
CITY GENERAL HOSPITAL
EEEEE
YOU'LL HAVE TO FORGIVE MY HARSH METHODS.
THAT MUST HAVE HURT.
BUT I WANT YOU SO BAD...
AND NOW YOU'LL BE A PART OF MY COLLECTION. ISN'T THAT NICE?

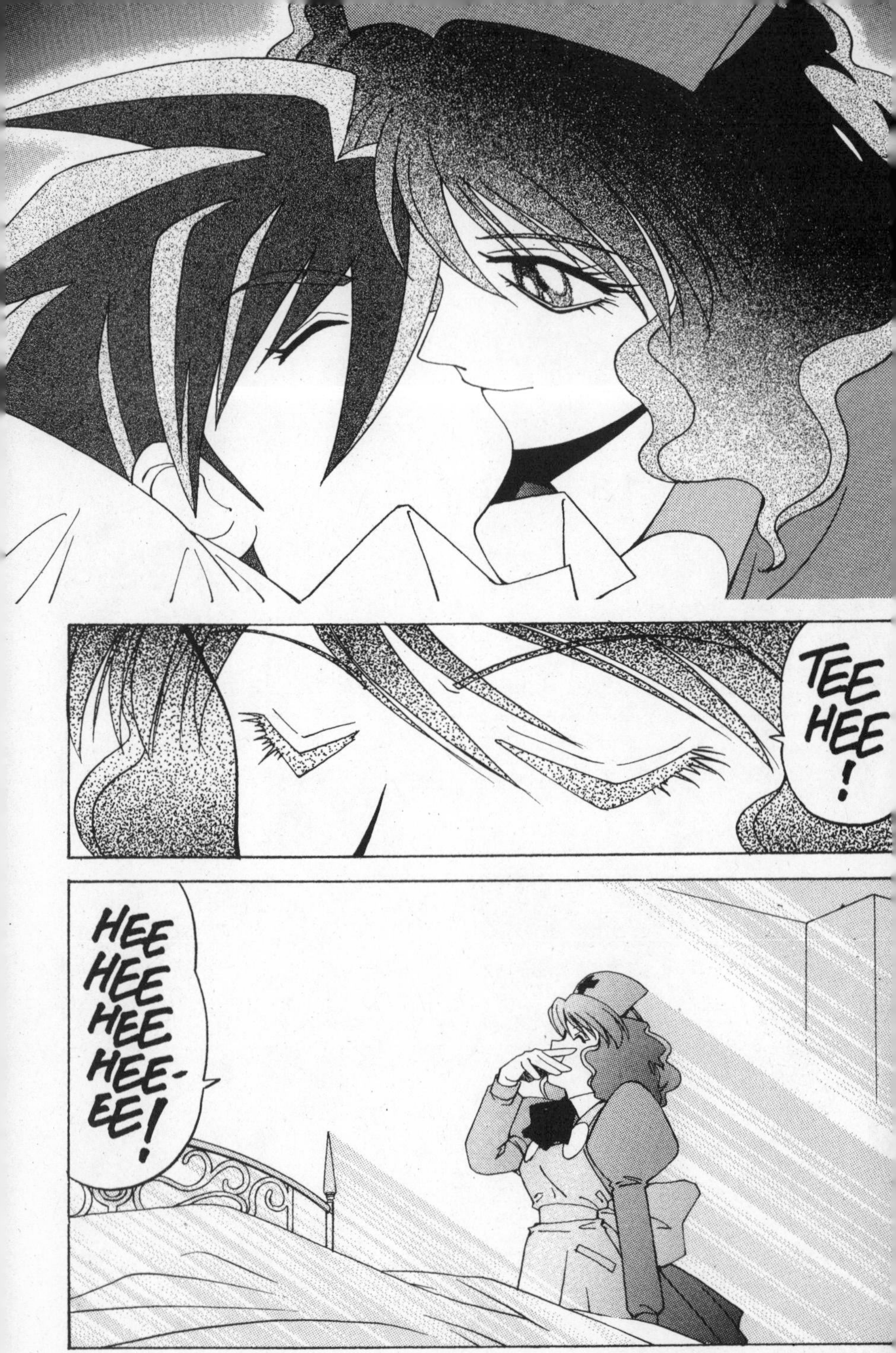
TEE HEE!
HEE HEE HEE HEE-EE!

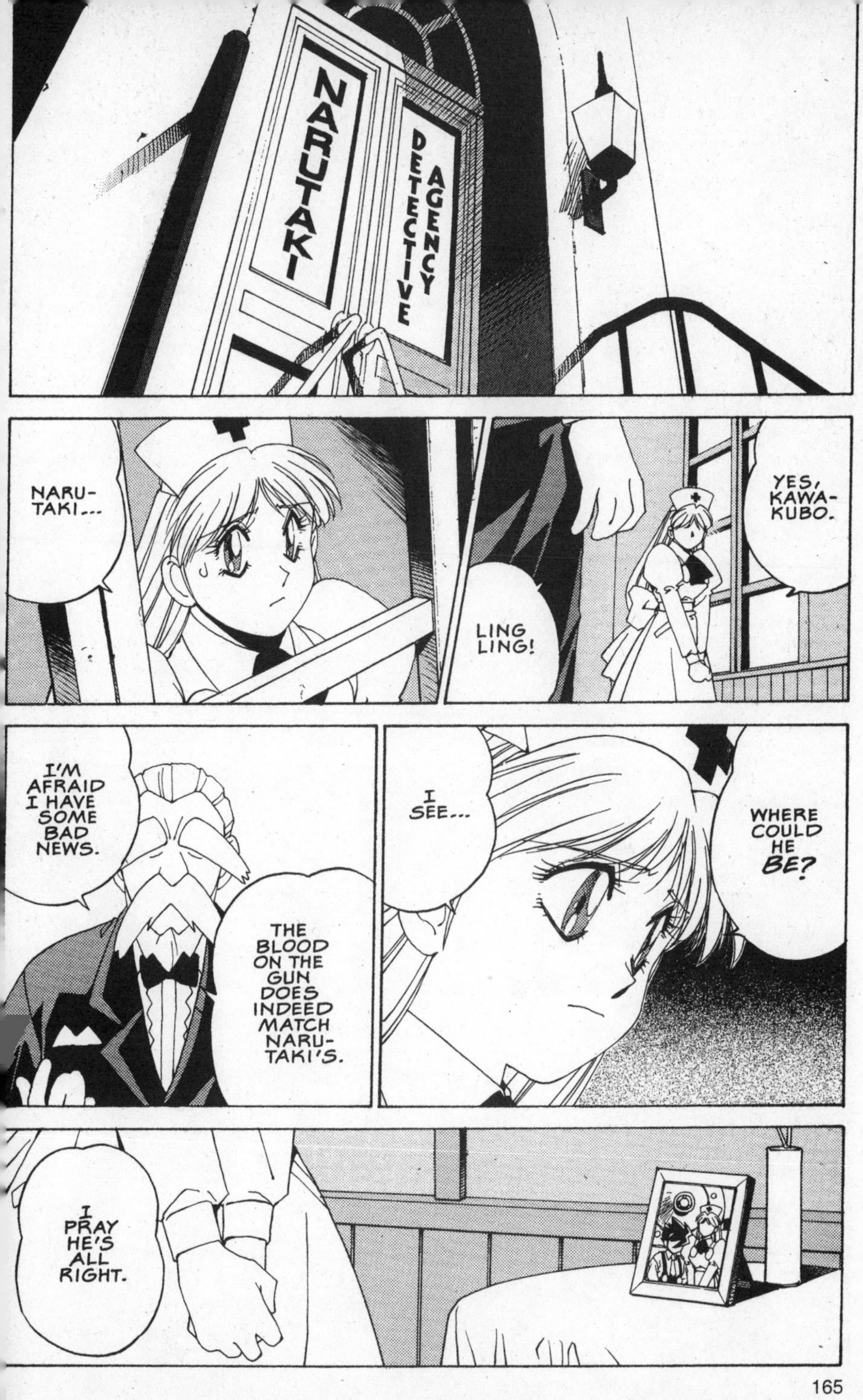
NARUTAKI DETECTIVE AGENCY
NARU-TAKI...
LING LING!
YES, KAWA-KUBO.
I'M AFRAID I HAVE SOME BAD NEWS.
THE BLOOD ON THE GUN DOES INDEED MATCH NARU-TAKI'S.
I SEE...
WHERE COULD HE *BE?*
I PRAY HE'S ALL RIGHT.

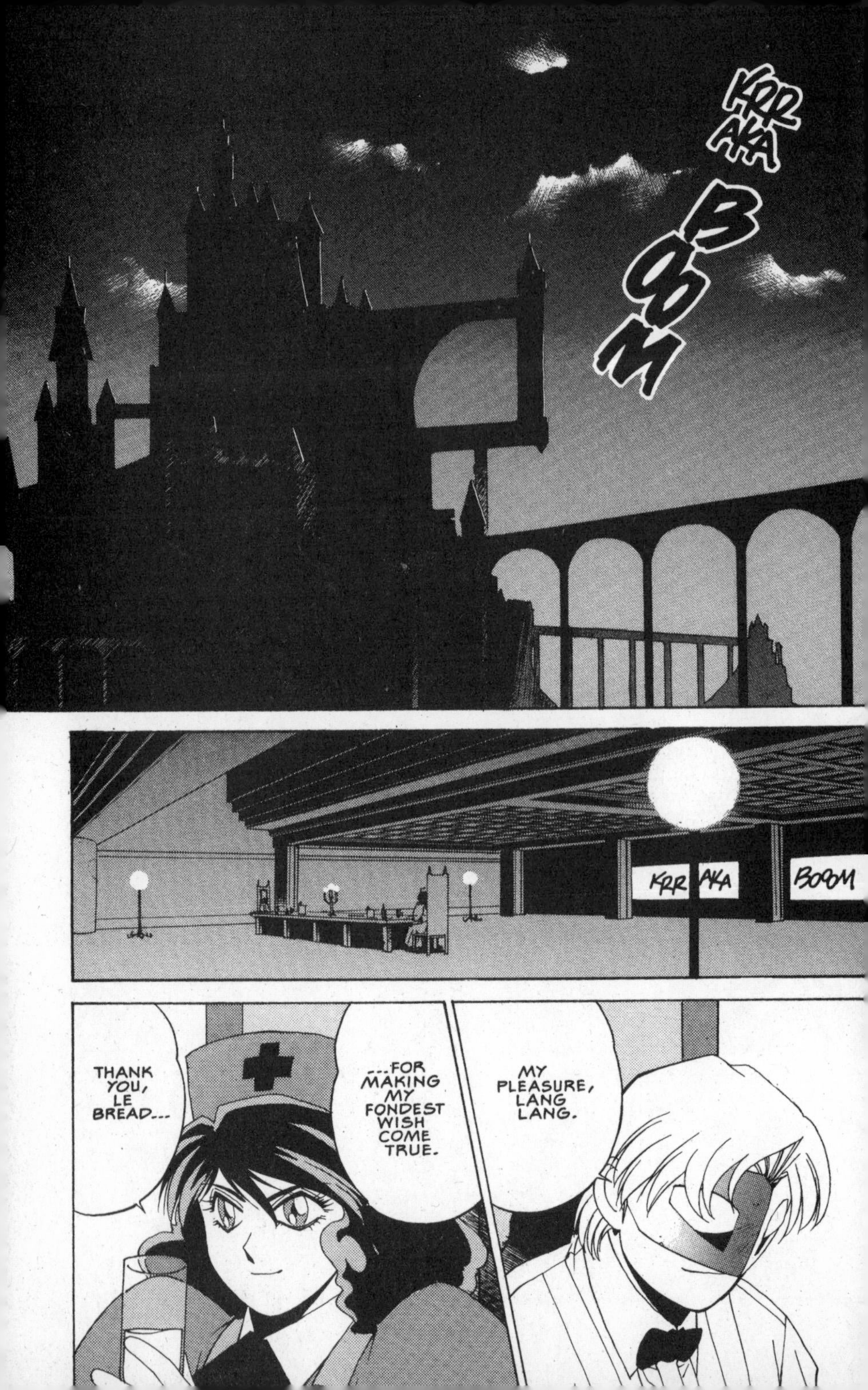
KRRAKA
BOOM
KRR AKA BOOM
THANK YOU, LE BREAD...
...FOR MAKING MY FONDEST WISH COME TRUE.
MY PLEASURE, LANG LANG.

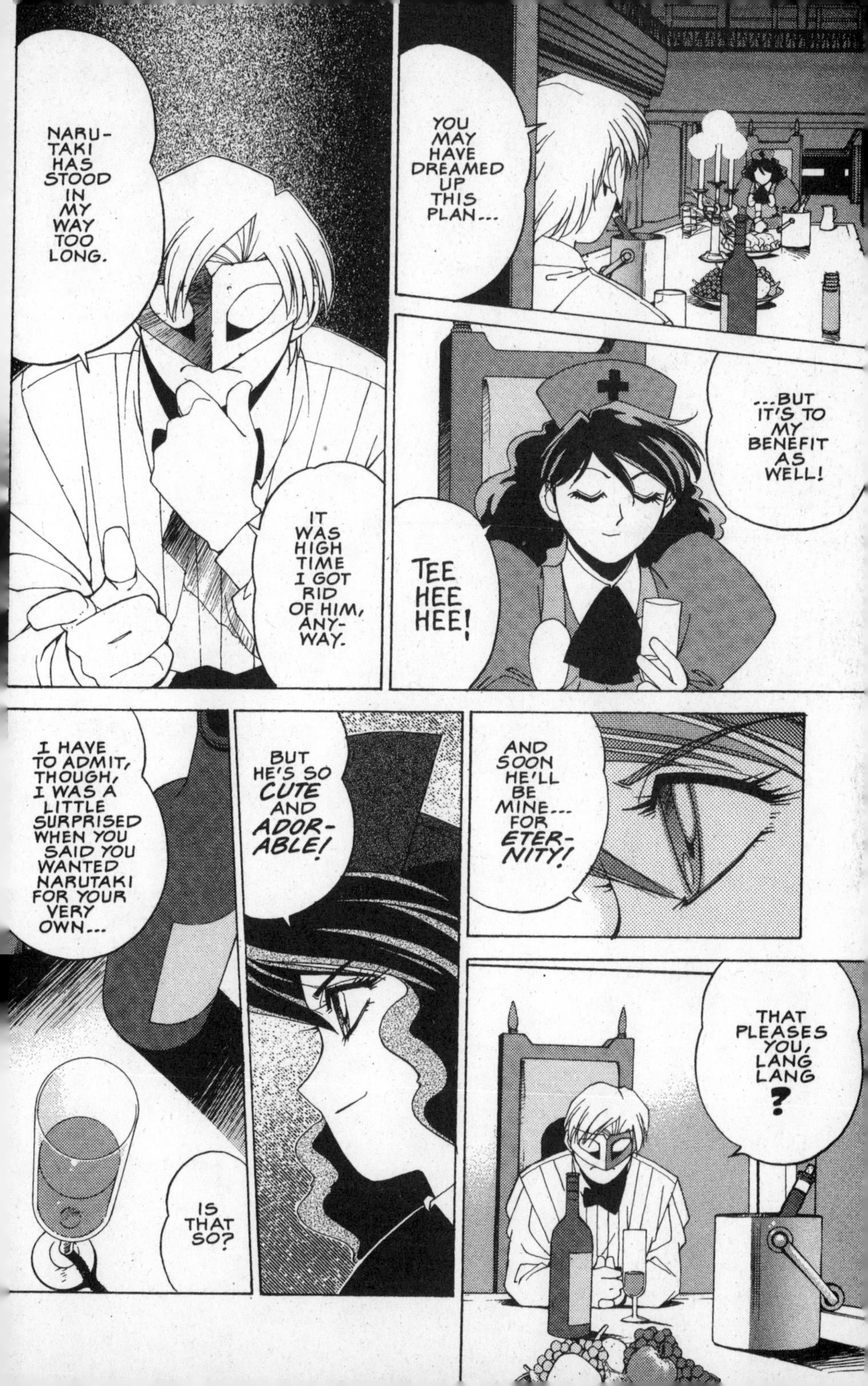
NARU-TAKI HAS STOOD IN MY WAY TOO LONG.
IT WAS HIGH TIME I GOT RID OF HIM, ANY-WAY.
YOU MAY HAVE DREAMED UP THIS PLAN...
...BUT IT'S TO MY BENEFIT AS WELL!
TEE HEE HEE!
I HAVE TO ADMIT, THOUGH, I WAS A LITTLE SURPRISED WHEN YOU SAID YOU WANTED NARUTAKI FOR YOUR VERY OWN...
IS THAT SO?
BUT HE'S SO CUTE AND ADOR-ABLE!
AND SOON HE'LL BE MINE... FOR ETER-NITY!
THAT PLEASES YOU, LANG LANG?

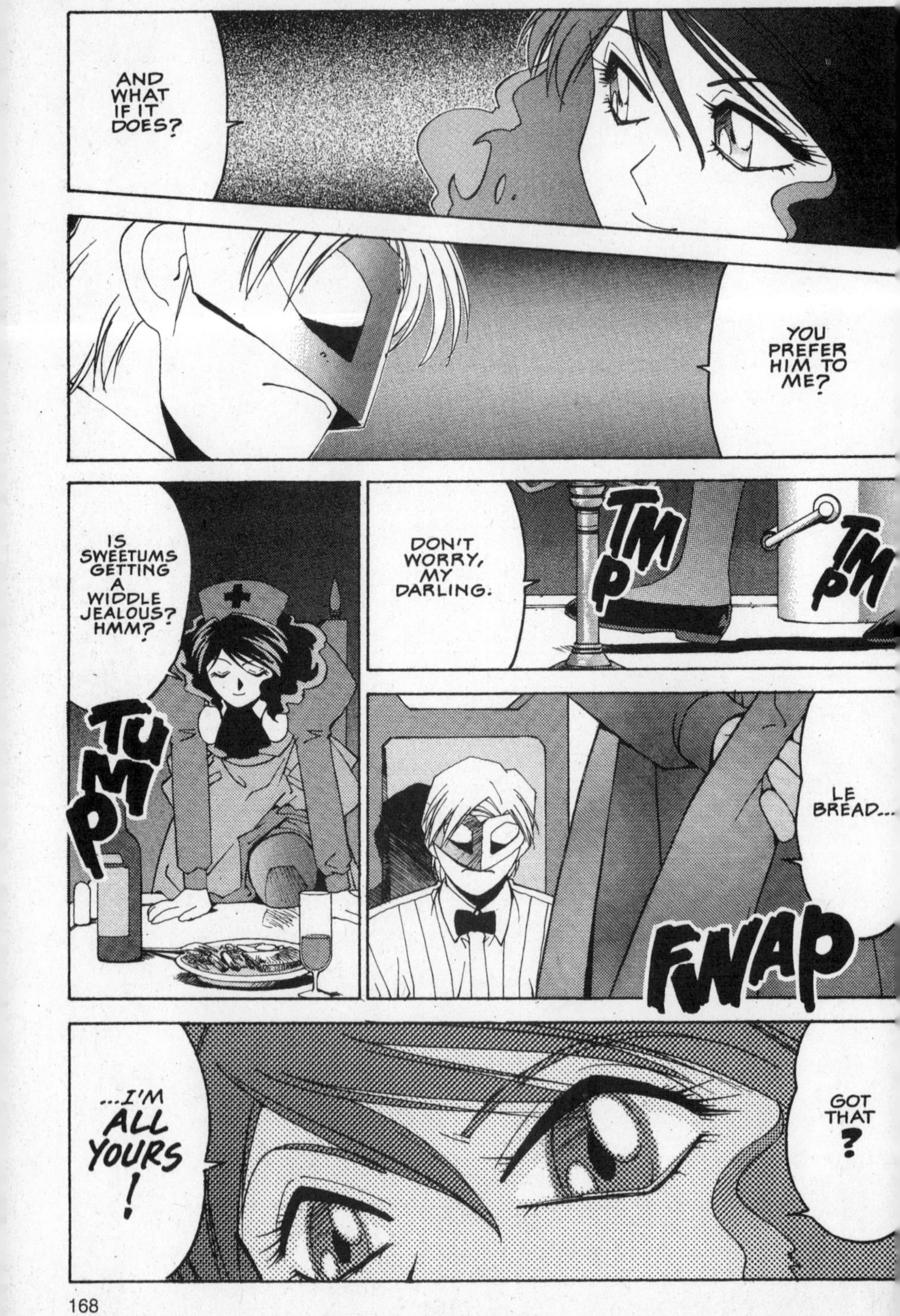
AND WHAT IF IT DOES?
YOU PREFER HIM TO ME?
IS SWEETUMS GETTING A WIDDLE JEALOUS? HMM?
TUMP
DON'T WORRY, MY DARLING.
TMP
TMP
LE BREAD...
FWAP
...I'M ALL YOURS!
GOT THAT?

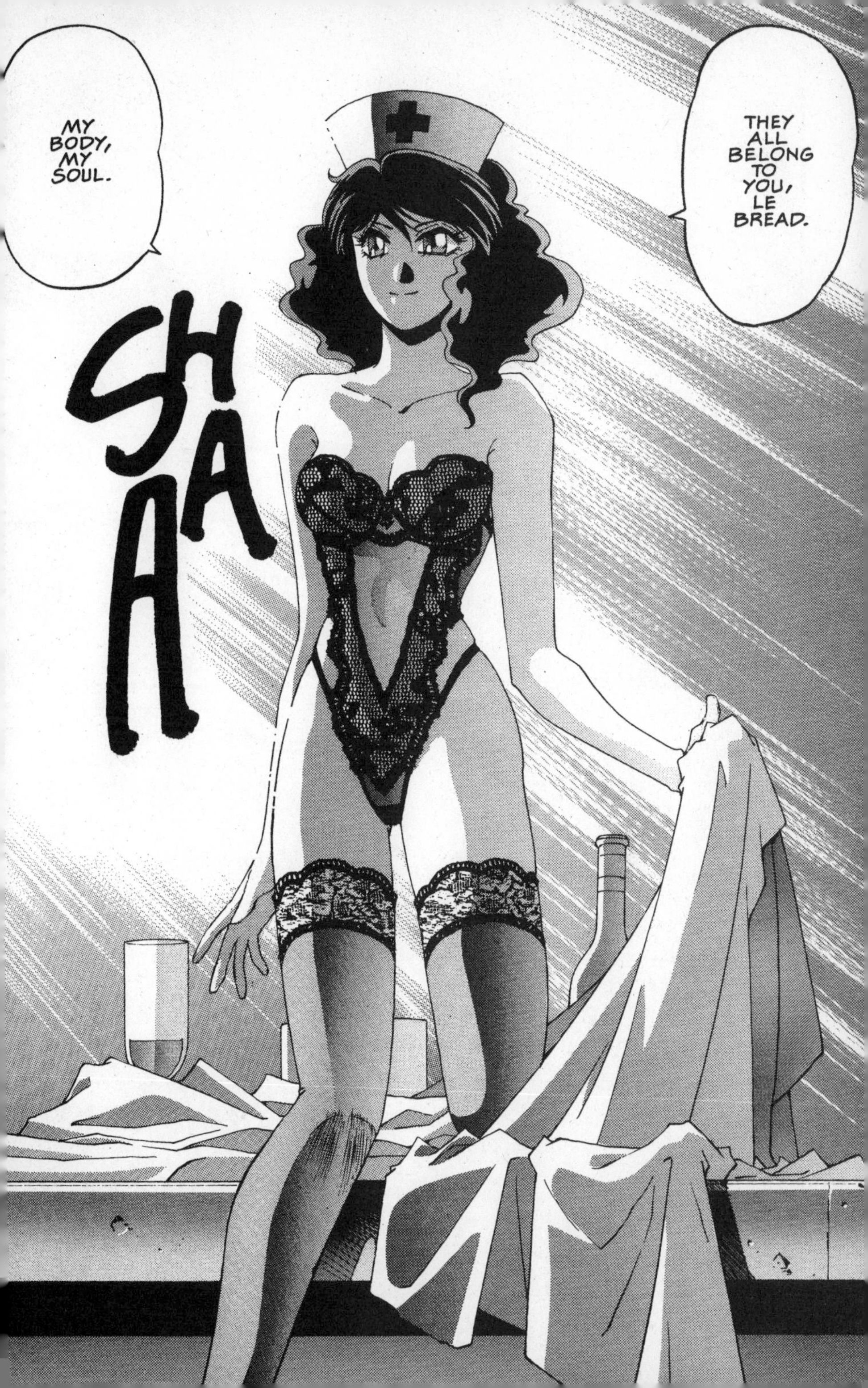
MY BODY, MY SOUL.
THEY ALL BELONG TO YOU, LE BREAD.
SHAAA

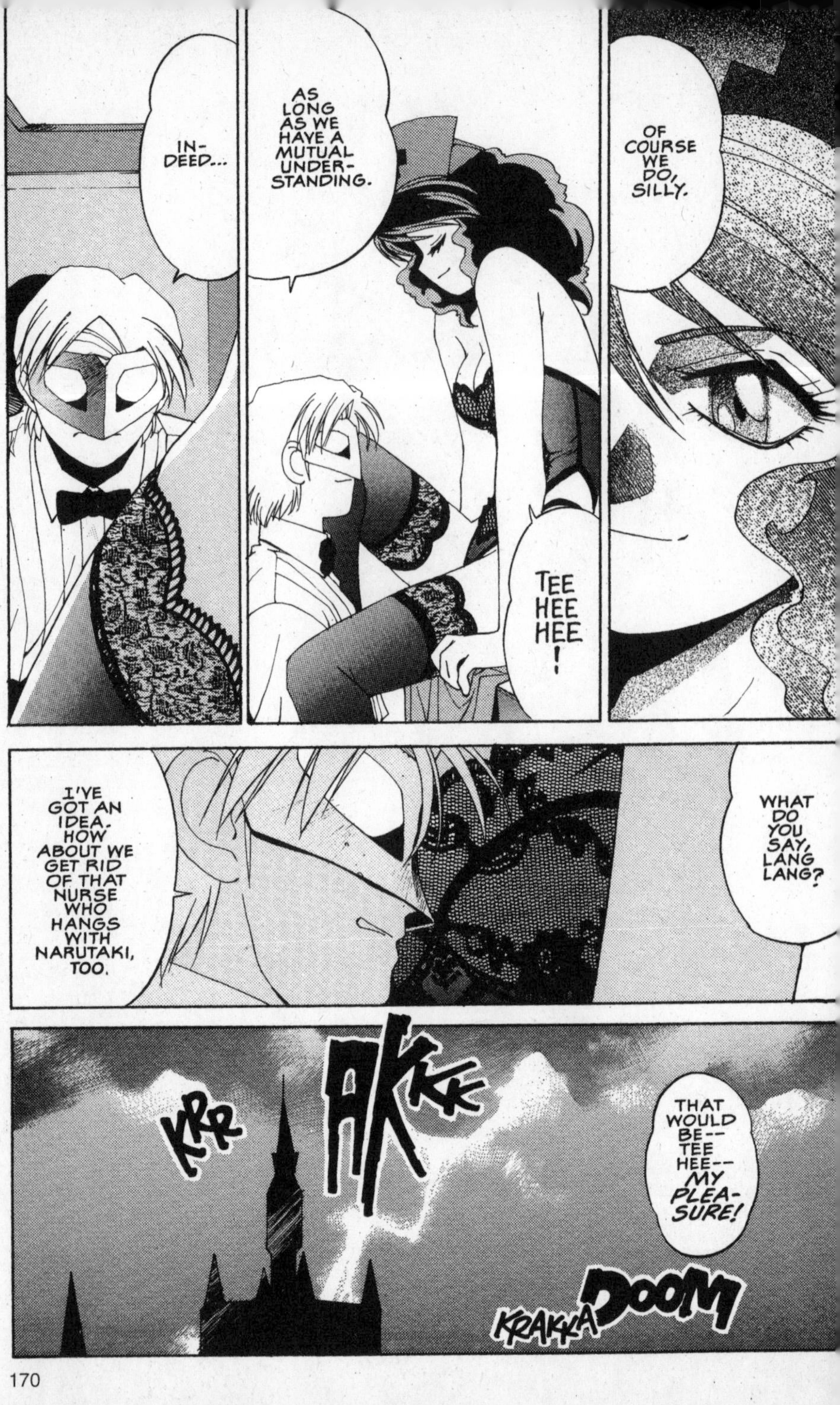
IN-DEED...
AS LONG AS WE HAVE A MUTUAL UNDER-STANDING.
OF COURSE WE DO, SILLY.
TEE HEE HEE!
I'VE GOT AN IDEA. HOW ABOUT WE GET RID OF THAT NURSE WHO HANGS WITH NARUTAKI, TOO.
WHAT DO YOU SAY, LANG LANG?
KRR AKKK
THAT WOULD BE--TEE HEE--*MY PLEA-SURE!*
KRAKKA DOOM

LING LING-- ARE YOU IN?

OH, HELLO, DETECTIVE ONIGAWARA.

YOU LOOK TERRIBLE, LING LING. HAVEN'T BEEN GETTING MUCH SLEEP, I BET.

I'M SO WORRIED ABOUT NARUTAKI.

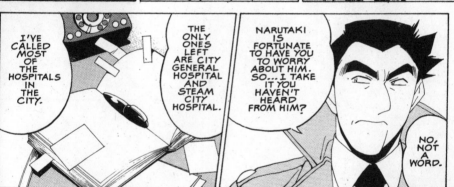

I'VE CALLED MOST OF THE HOSPITALS IN THE CITY.

THE ONLY ONES LEFT ARE CITY GENERAL HOSPITAL AND STEAM CITY HOSPITAL.

NARUTAKI IS FORTUNATE TO HAVE YOU TO WORRY ABOUT HIM. SO... I TAKE IT YOU HAVEN'T HEARD FROM HIM?

NO, NOT A WORD.

APPARENTLY, SOMEONE MATCHING NARUTAKI'S DESCRIPTION WAS BROUGHT INTO CITY GENERAL...

!

THEN I MUST GO THERE...

...IMMEDIATELY!!

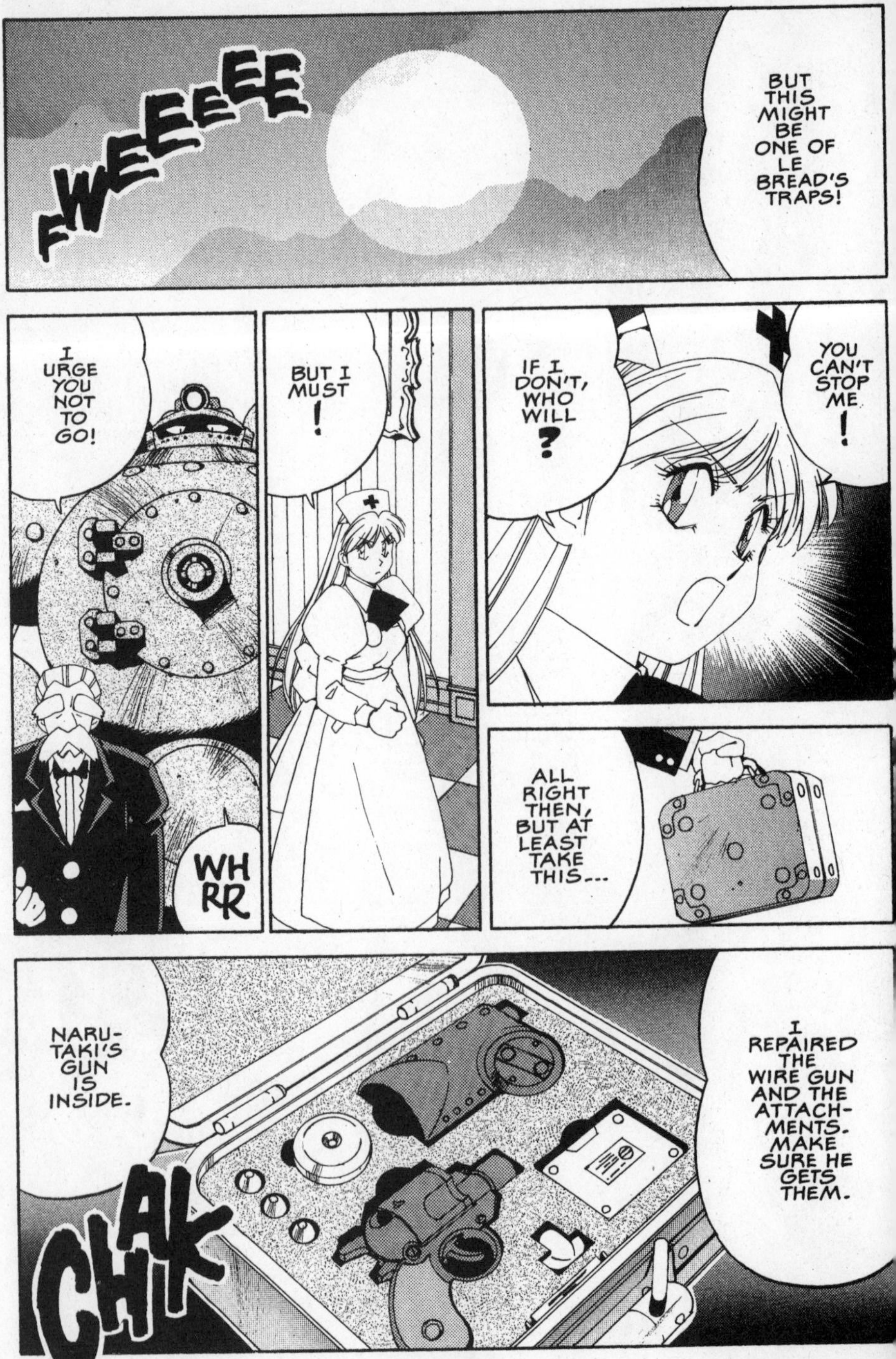
FWEEEEE
BUT THIS MIGHT BE ONE OF LE BREAD'S TRAPS!
I URGE YOU NOT TO GO!
WHRR
BUT I MUST!
IF I DON'T, WHO WILL?
YOU CAN'T STOP ME!
ALL RIGHT THEN, BUT AT LEAST TAKE THIS...
NARU-TAKI'S GUN IS INSIDE.
CHAK
I REPAIRED THE WIRE GUN AND THE ATTACH-MENTS. MAKE SURE HE GETS THEM.

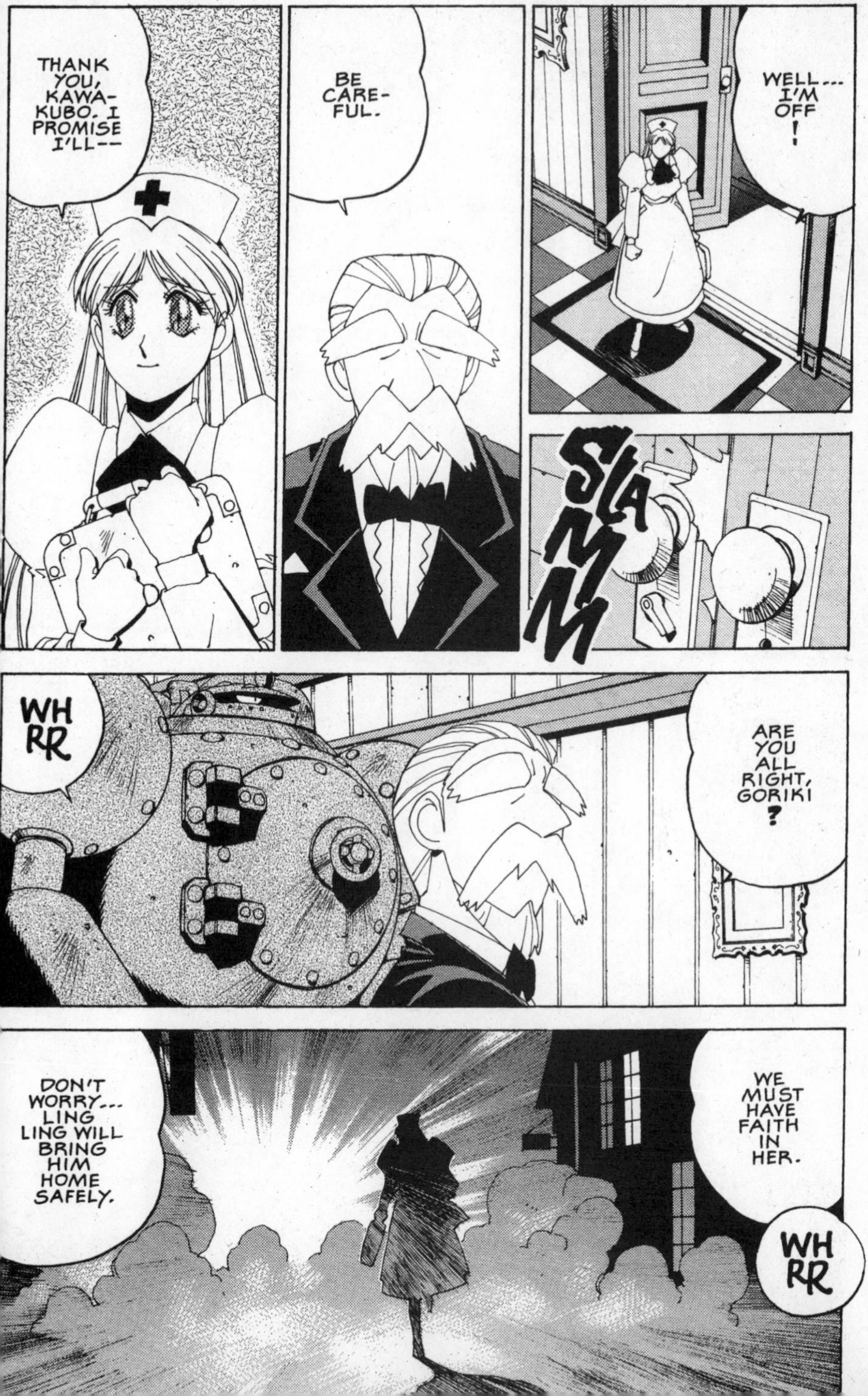
THANK YOU, KAWA-KUBO. I PROMISE I'LL--
BE CARE-FUL.
WELL... I'M OFF!
SLAMM
WHRR
ARE YOU ALL RIGHT, GORIKI?
DON'T WORRY... LING LING WILL BRING HIM HOME SAFELY.
WE MUST HAVE FAITH IN HER.
WHRR

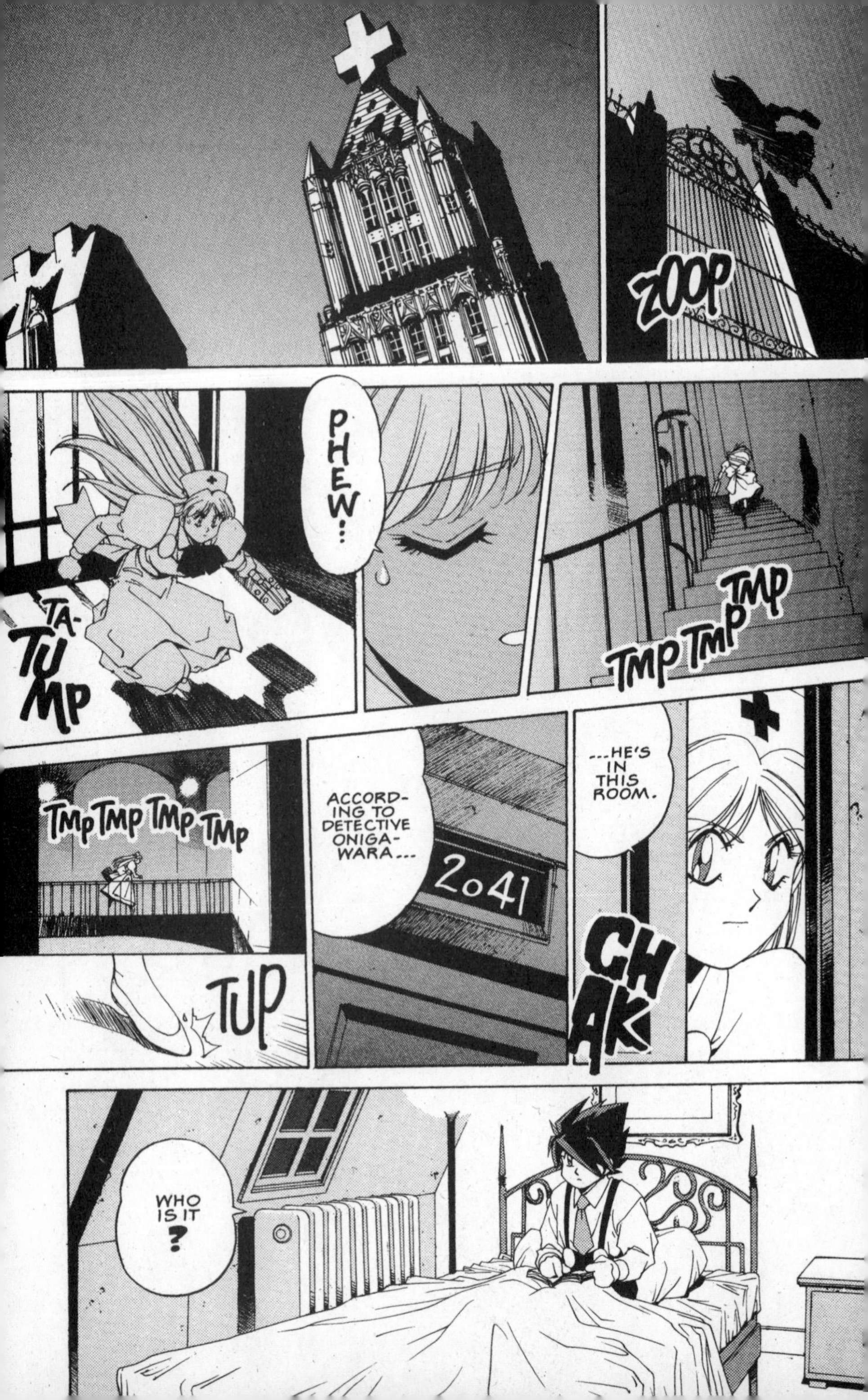
ZOOP
TA-TUMP
PHEW...
TMP TMP TMP
TMP TMP TMP TMP
TUP
ACCORDING TO DETECTIVE ONIGAWARA...
2041
...HE'S IN THIS ROOM.
CHAK
WHO IS IT ?

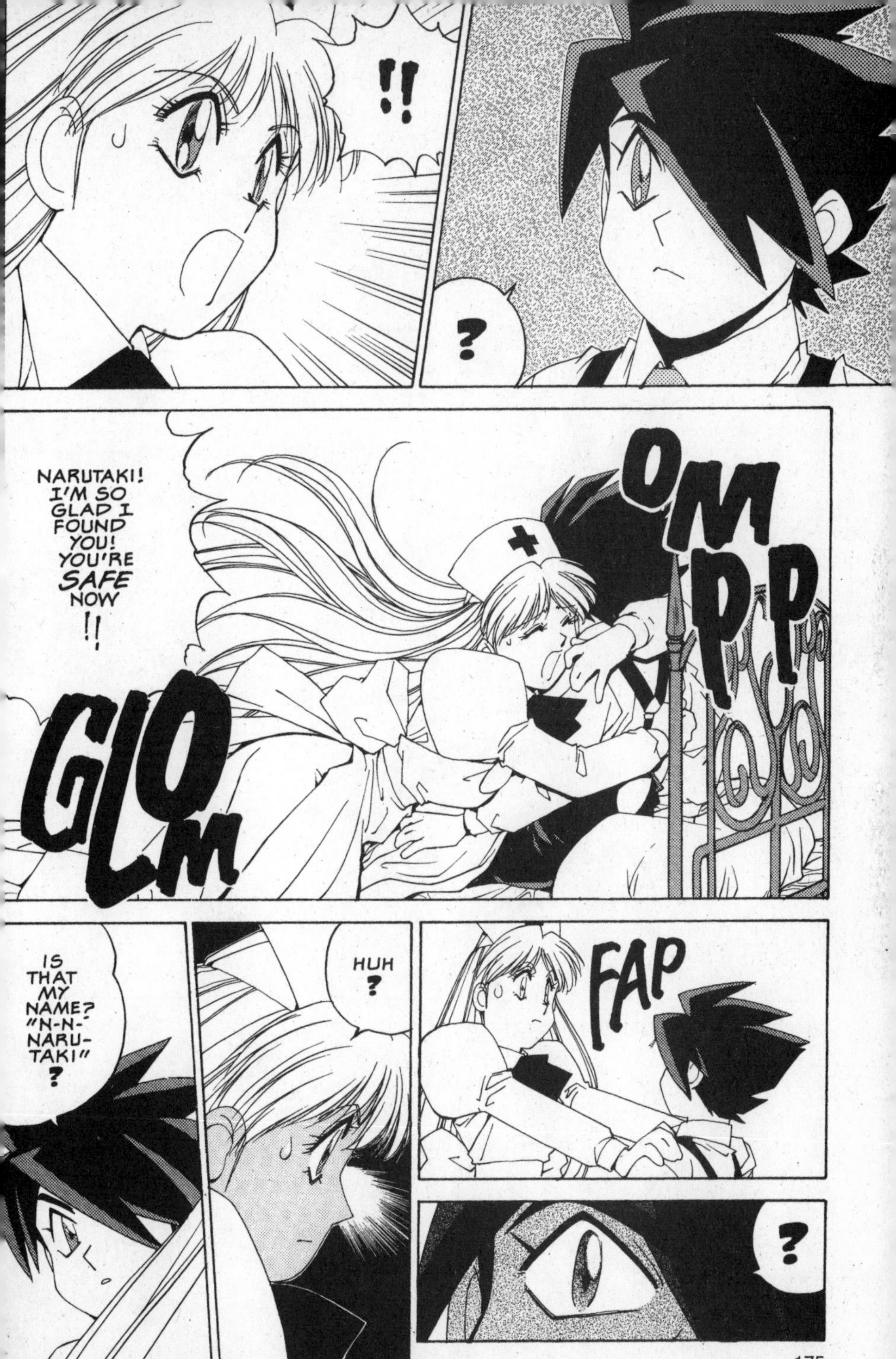
!!
?
NARUTAKI! I'M SO GLAD I FOUND YOU! YOU'RE SAFE NOW !!
OMPP
GLOM
IS THAT MY NAME? "N-N-NARUTAKI"?
HUH ?
FAP
?

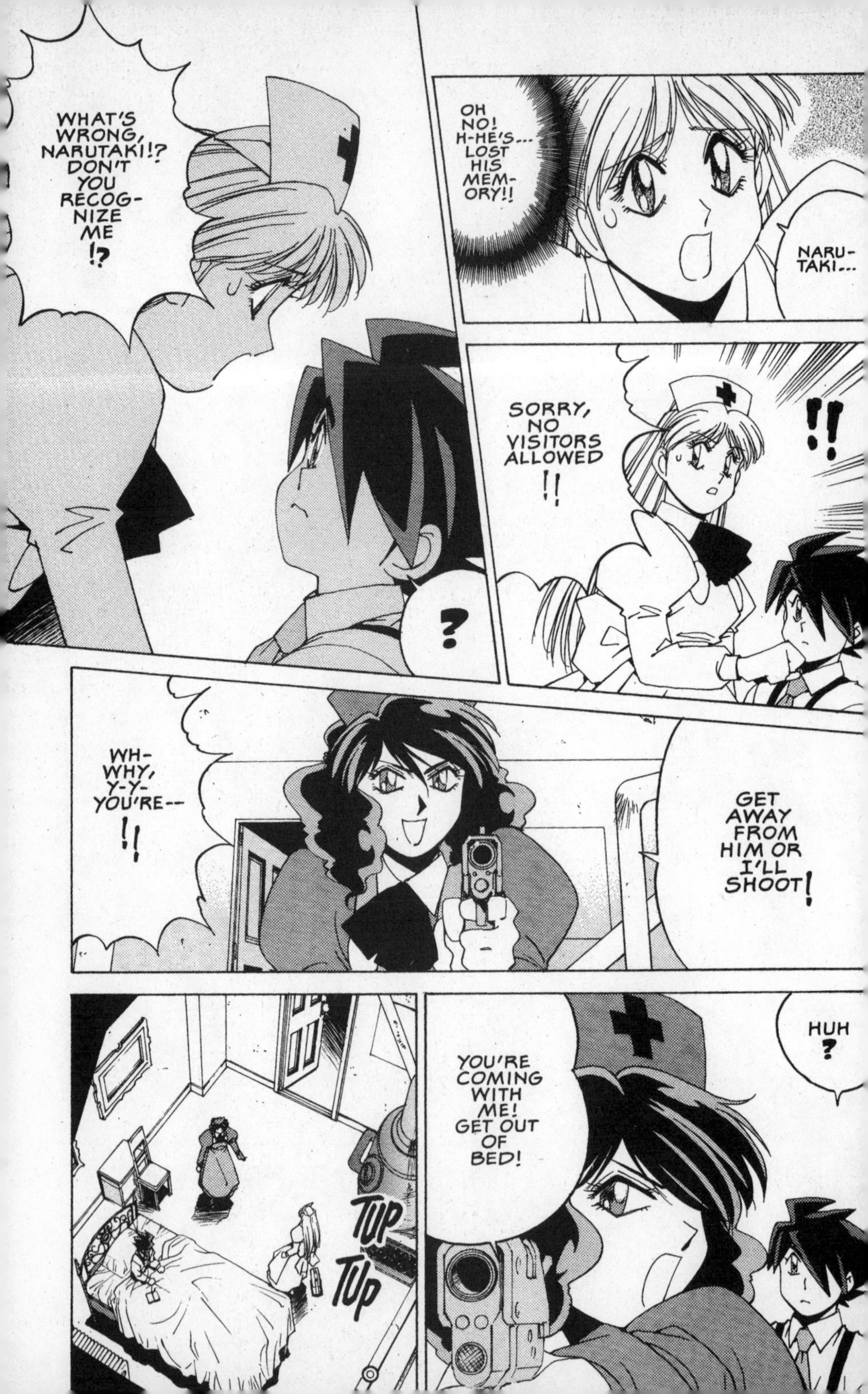

WHAT'S WRONG, NARUTAKI!? DON'T YOU RECOGNIZE ME !?
OH NO! H-HE'S... LOST HIS MEMORY!!
NARUTAKI...
?
SORRY, NO VISITORS ALLOWED !!
!!
WH-WHY, Y-Y-YOU'RE-- !!
GET AWAY FROM HIM OR I'LL SHOOT!
TUP TUP
YOU'RE COMING WITH ME! GET OUT OF BED!
HUH ?

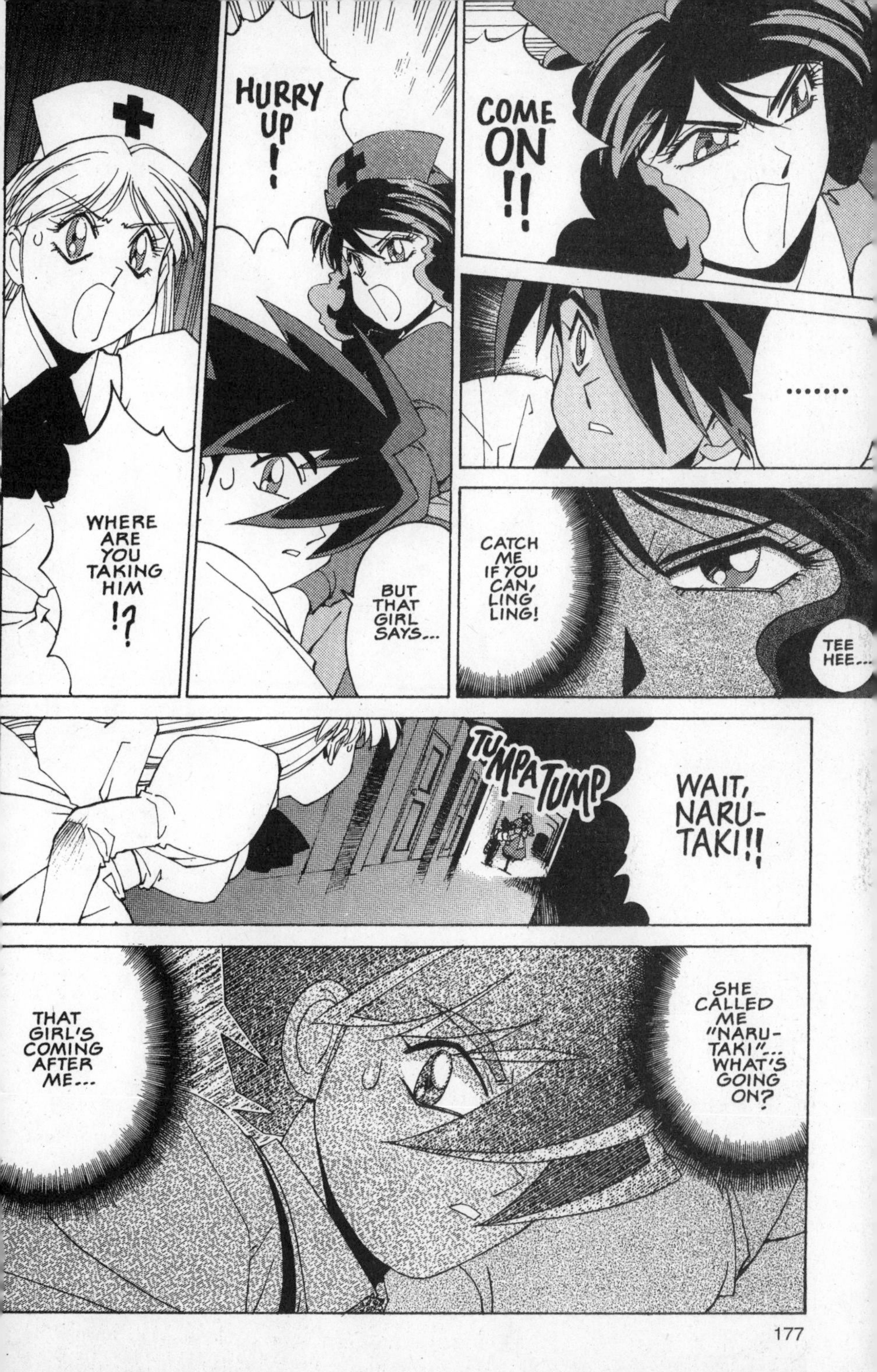
WHERE ARE YOU TAKING HIM !?
HURRY UP !
BUT THAT GIRL SAYS...
COME ON !!
....
CATCH ME IF YOU CAN, LING LING!
TEE HEE...
TUMPATUMP
WAIT, NARU-TAKI!!
THAT GIRL'S COMING AFTER ME...
SHE CALLED ME "NARU-TAKI"... WHAT'S GOING ON?

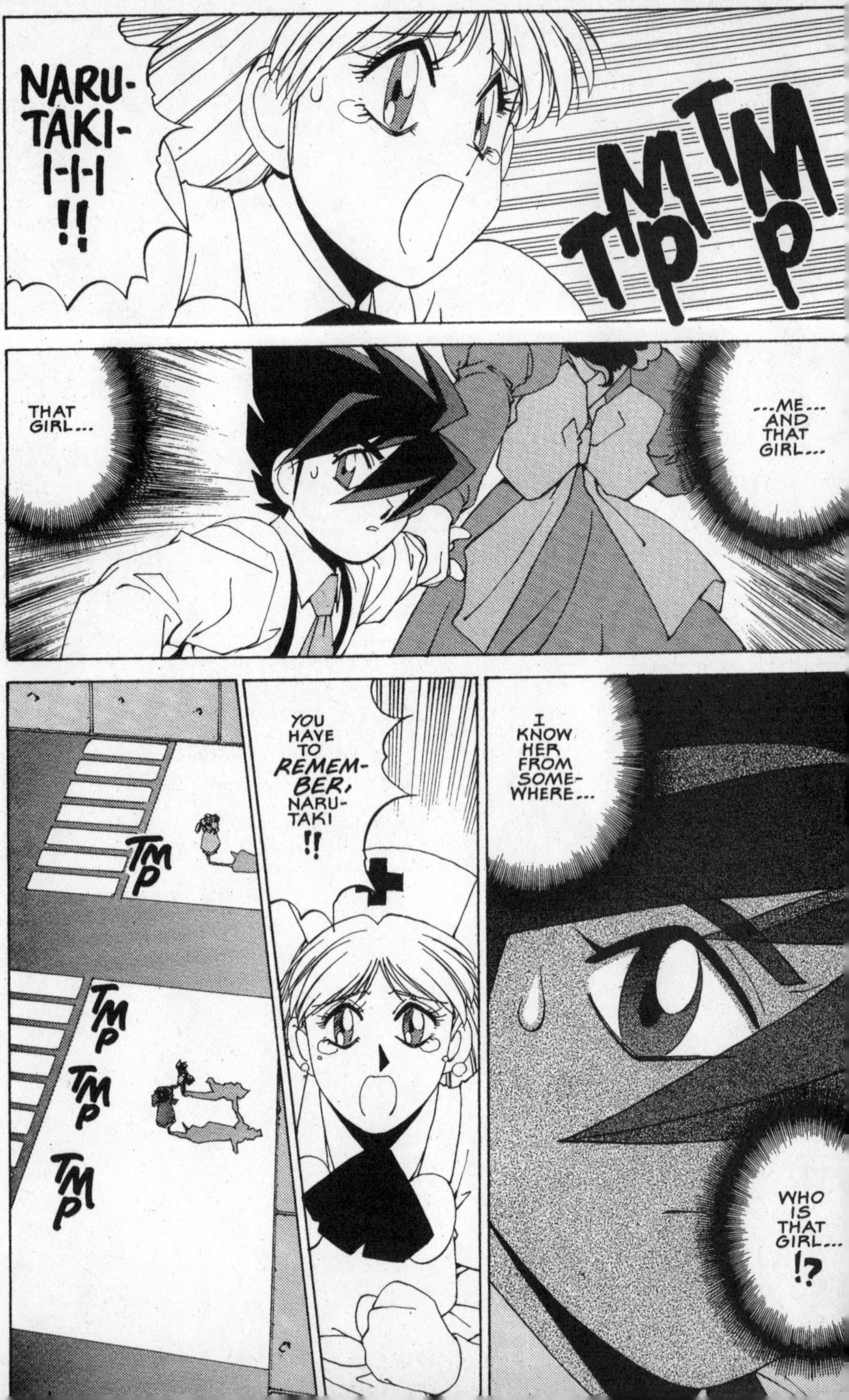
NARU-TAKI-I-I-I !!
TMP TMP
THAT GIRL...
...ME... AND THAT GIRL...
TMP
TMP TMP TMP
YOU HAVE TO REMEMBER, NARU-TAKI !!
I KNOW HER FROM SOMEWHERE...
WHO IS THAT GIRL... !?

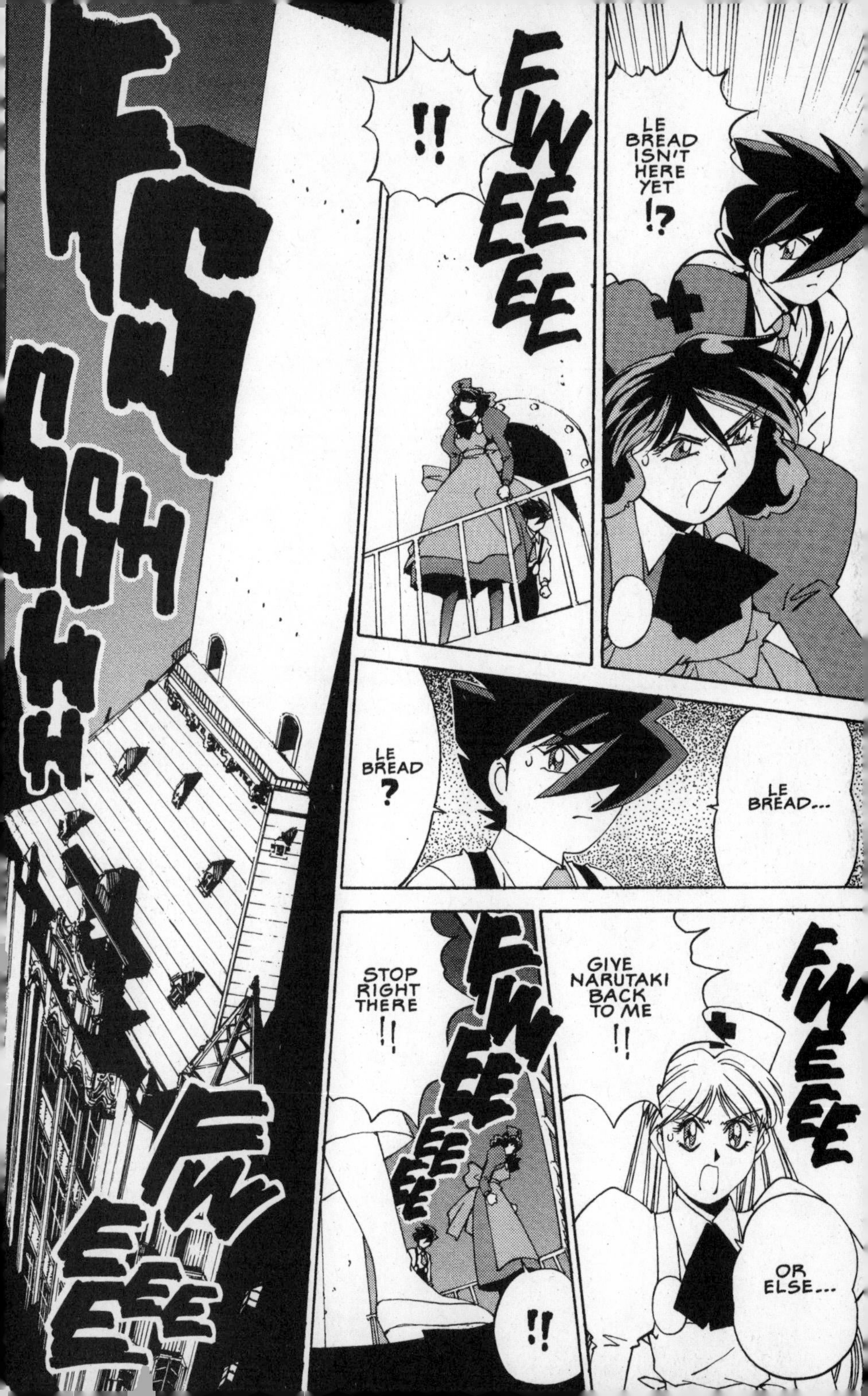
FWEEEEEE
!!
LE BREAD ISN'T HERE YET!?
LE BREAD?
LE BREAD...
STOP RIGHT THERE!!
FWEEEEEE
!!
GIVE NARUTAKI BACK TO ME!!
FWEEEE
OR ELSE...

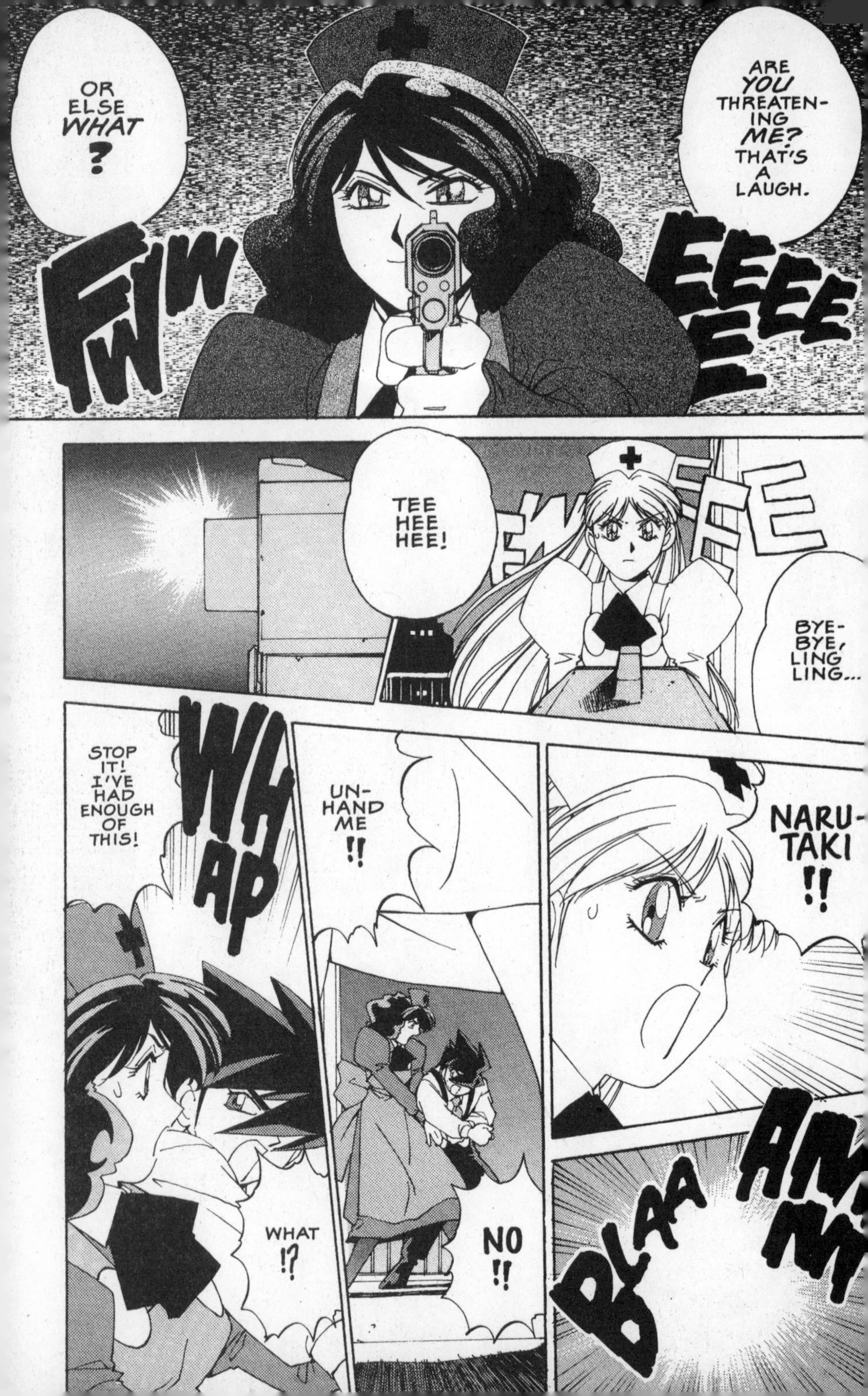
OR ELSE WHAT?
ARE YOU THREATENING ME? THAT'S A LAUGH.
TEE HEE HEE!
BYE-BYE, LING LING...
STOP IT! I'VE HAD ENOUGH OF THIS!
WHAP
WHAT!?
UN-HAND ME!!
NO!!
NARU-TAKI!!

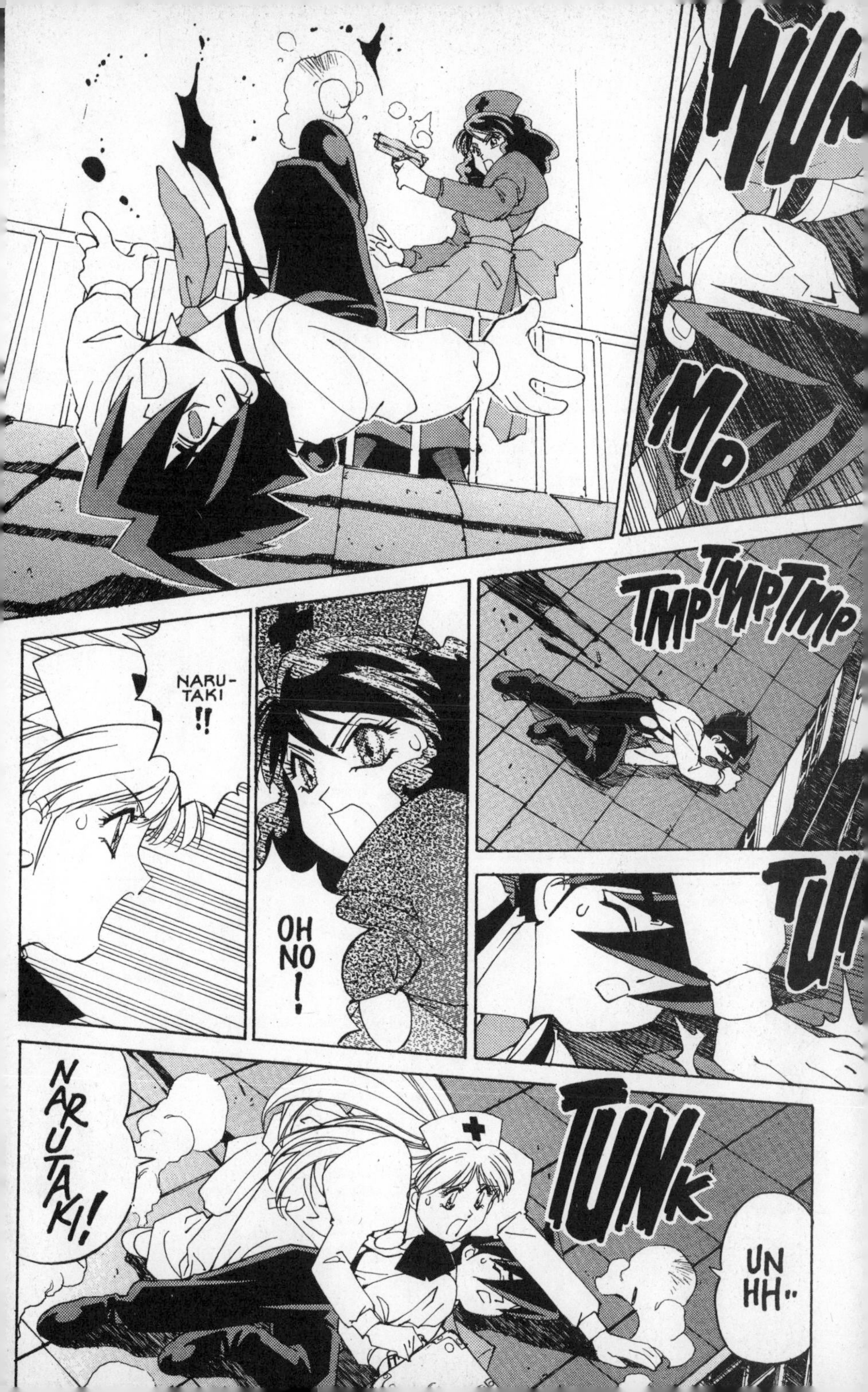
WUN
Mp
NARU-TAKI !!
OH NO !
TMP TMP TMP TMP
TUN
NARUTAKI!
TUNk
UN HH..

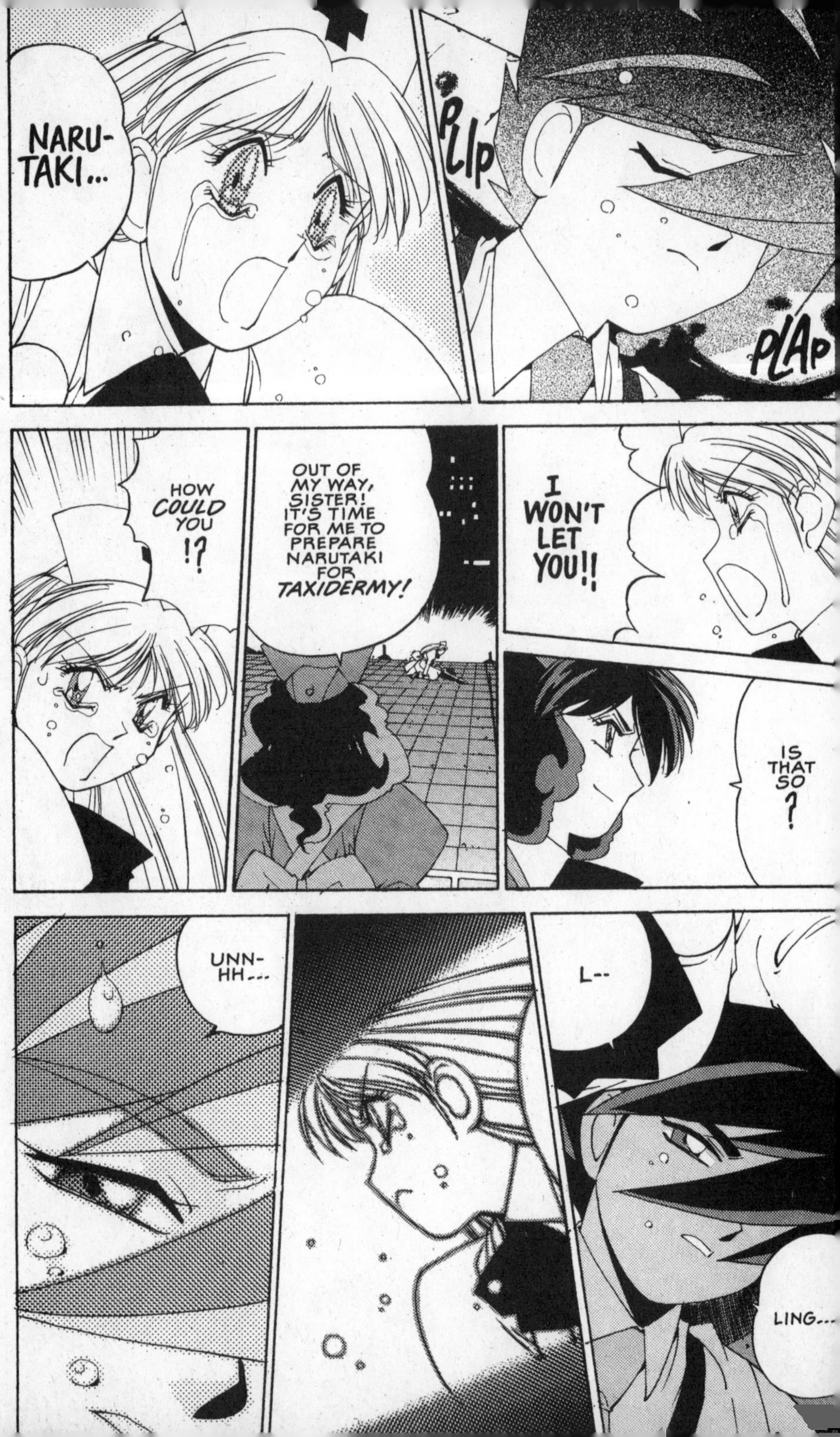
NARU-TAKI...
PLIP
PLAP
HOW COULD YOU !?
OUT OF MY WAY, SISTER! IT'S TIME FOR ME TO PREPARE NARUTAKI FOR TAXIDERMY!
I WON'T LET YOU!!
IS THAT SO ?
UNN-HH...
L--
LING...

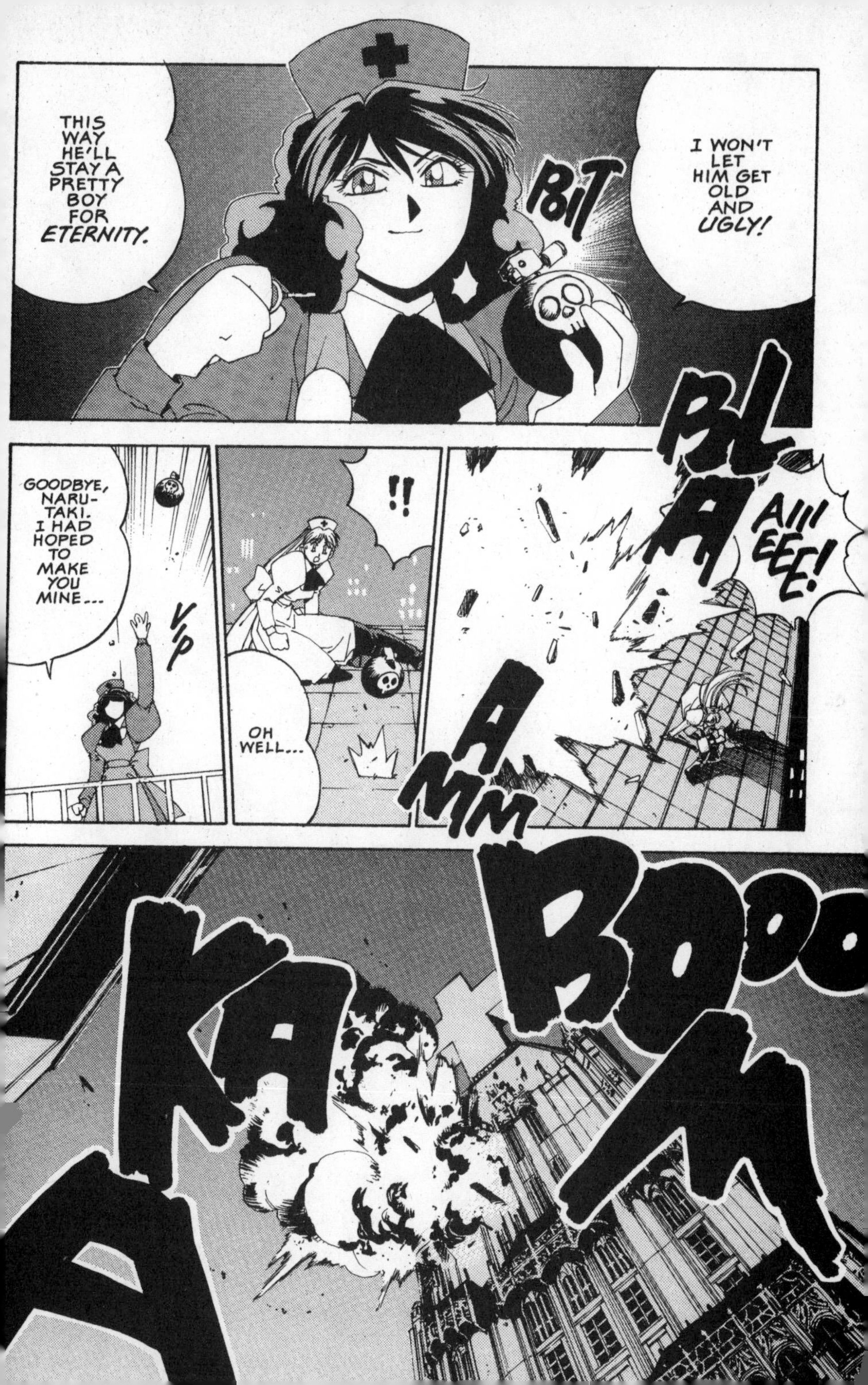
THIS WAY HE'LL STAY A PRETTY BOY FOR ETERNITY.
POIT
I WON'T LET HIM GET OLD AND UGLY!
GOODBYE, NARUTAKI. I HAD HOPED TO MAKE YOU MINE...
V/P
!!
OH WELL...
BLAAMM
AIII EEEE!
KABOOOM

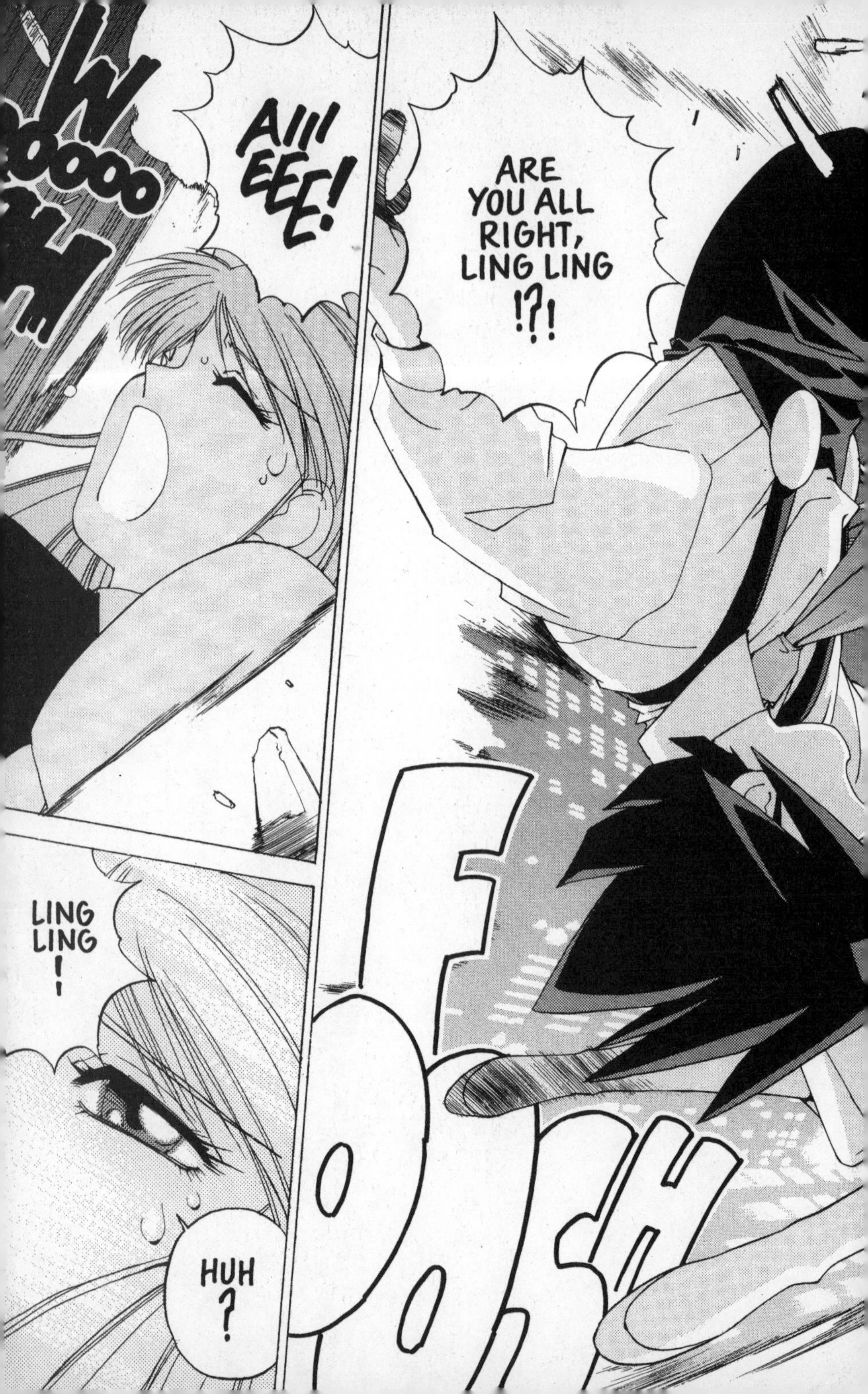
AIII EEEE!
LING LING!
HUH?
ARE YOU ALL RIGHT, LING LING !?!

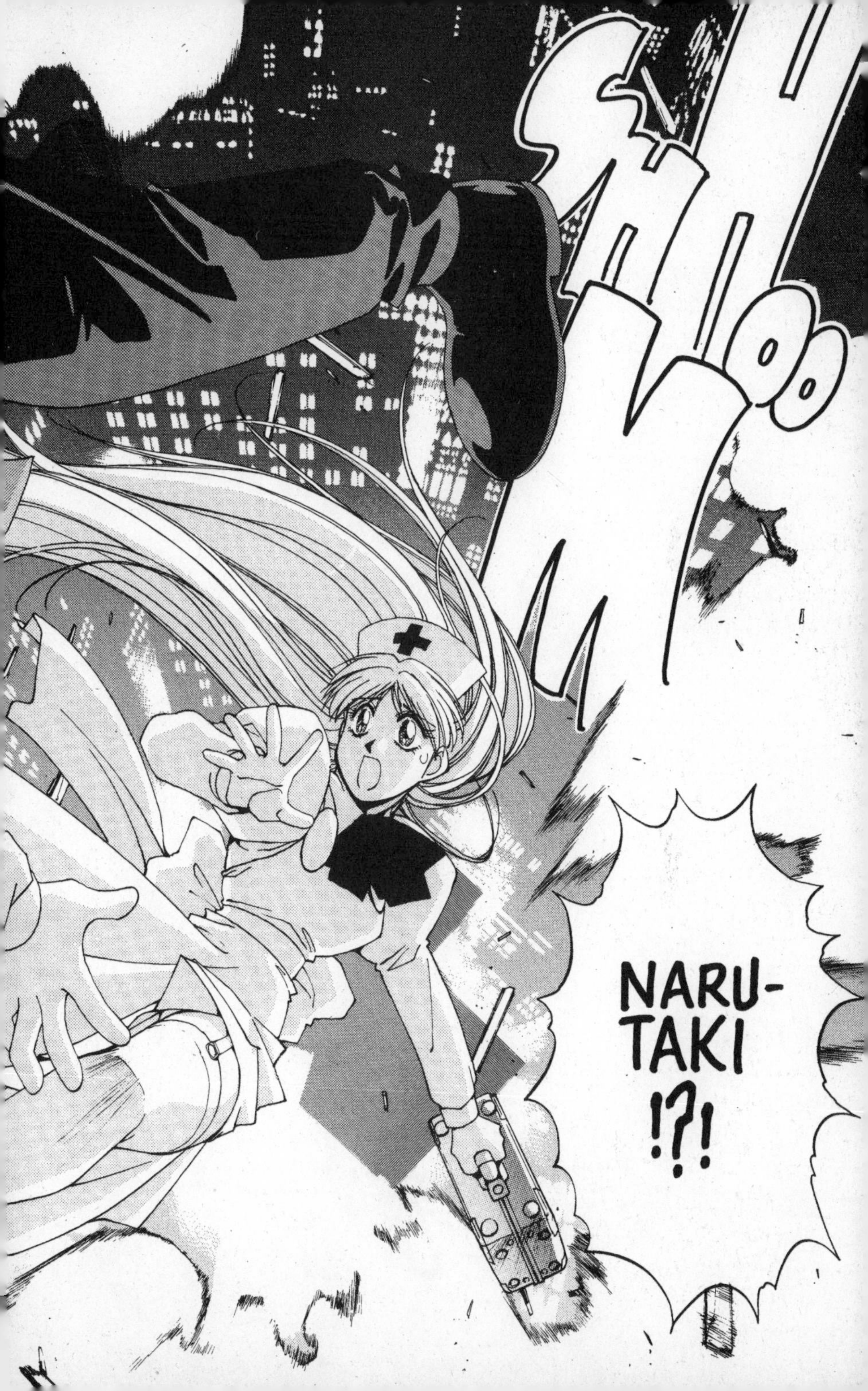
NARU-TAKI !?!

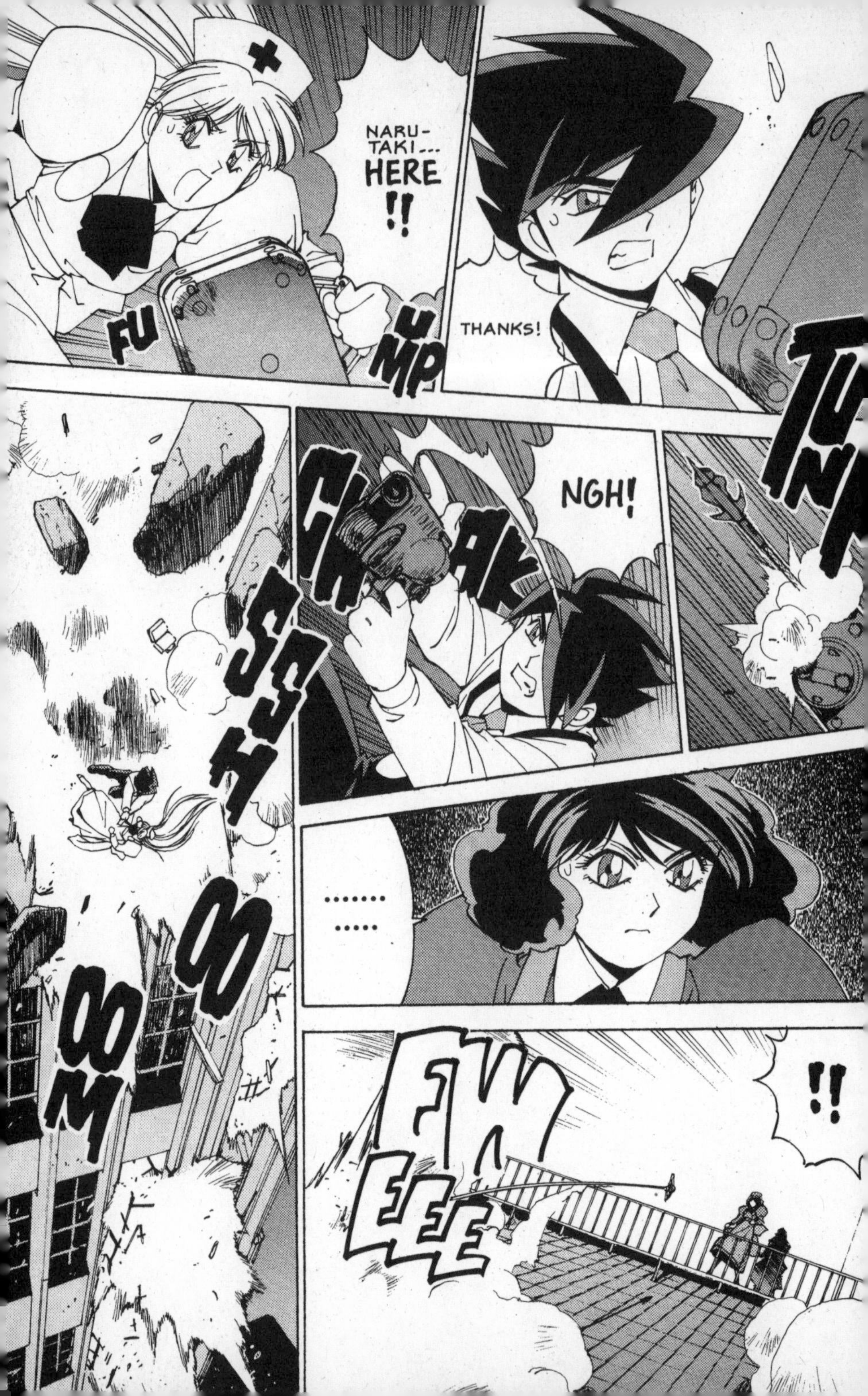
NARU-TAKI... HERE!!
FU
UMP
THANKS!
TU
NK
SSH
OO
OOM
CH
AK
NGH!
......
.....
FW
EEEE
!!

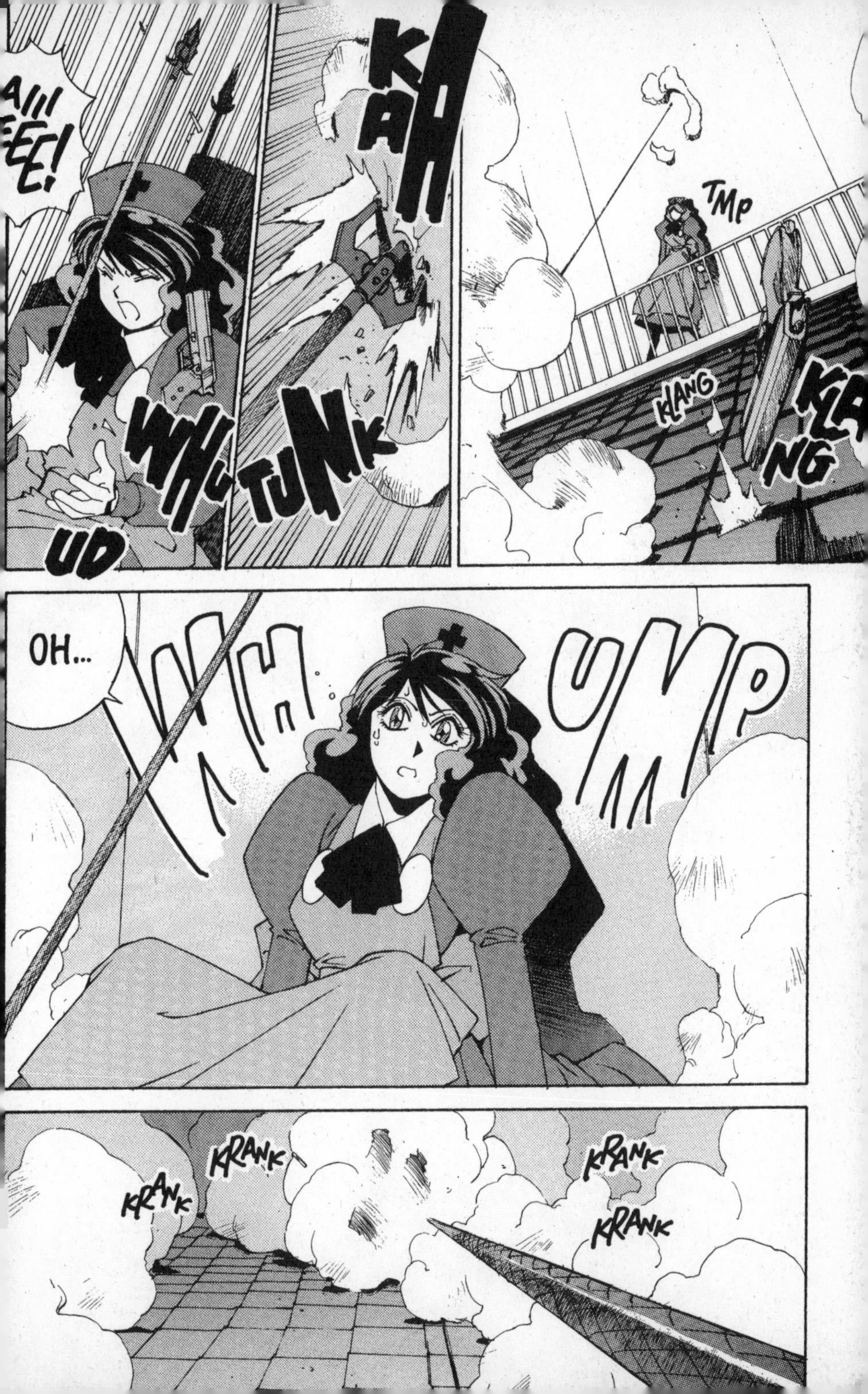
AIIII EEEE!
WHUD
TUNK
KAH
TMP
KLANG
KLANG
OH...
WHUMP
KRANK
KRANK
KRANK
KRANK

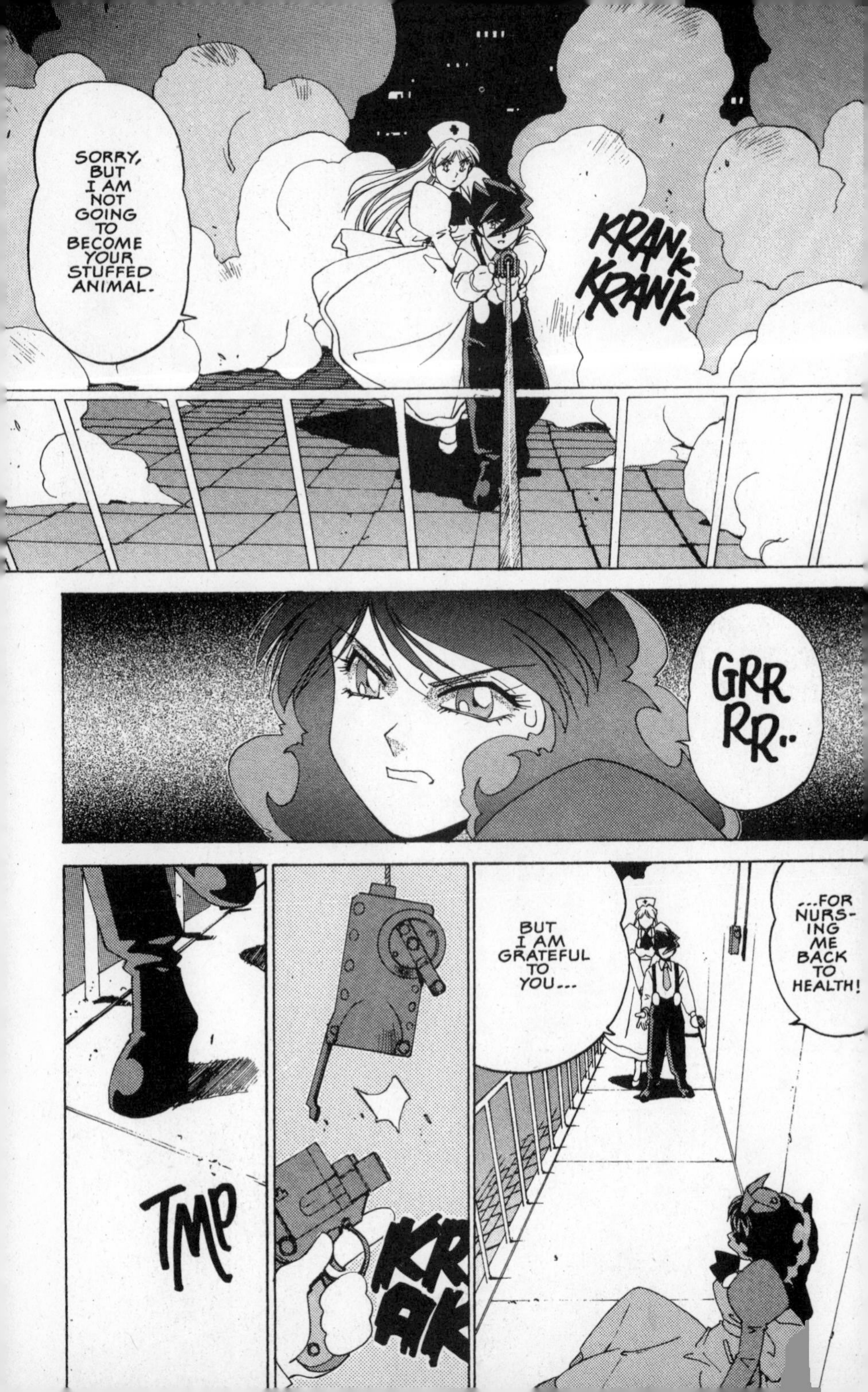
SORRY, BUT I AM NOT GOING TO BECOME YOUR STUFFED ANIMAL.
KRANK KRANK
GRRRR..
TMP
KRAK
BUT I AM GRATEFUL TO YOU...
...FOR NURSING ME BACK TO HEALTH!

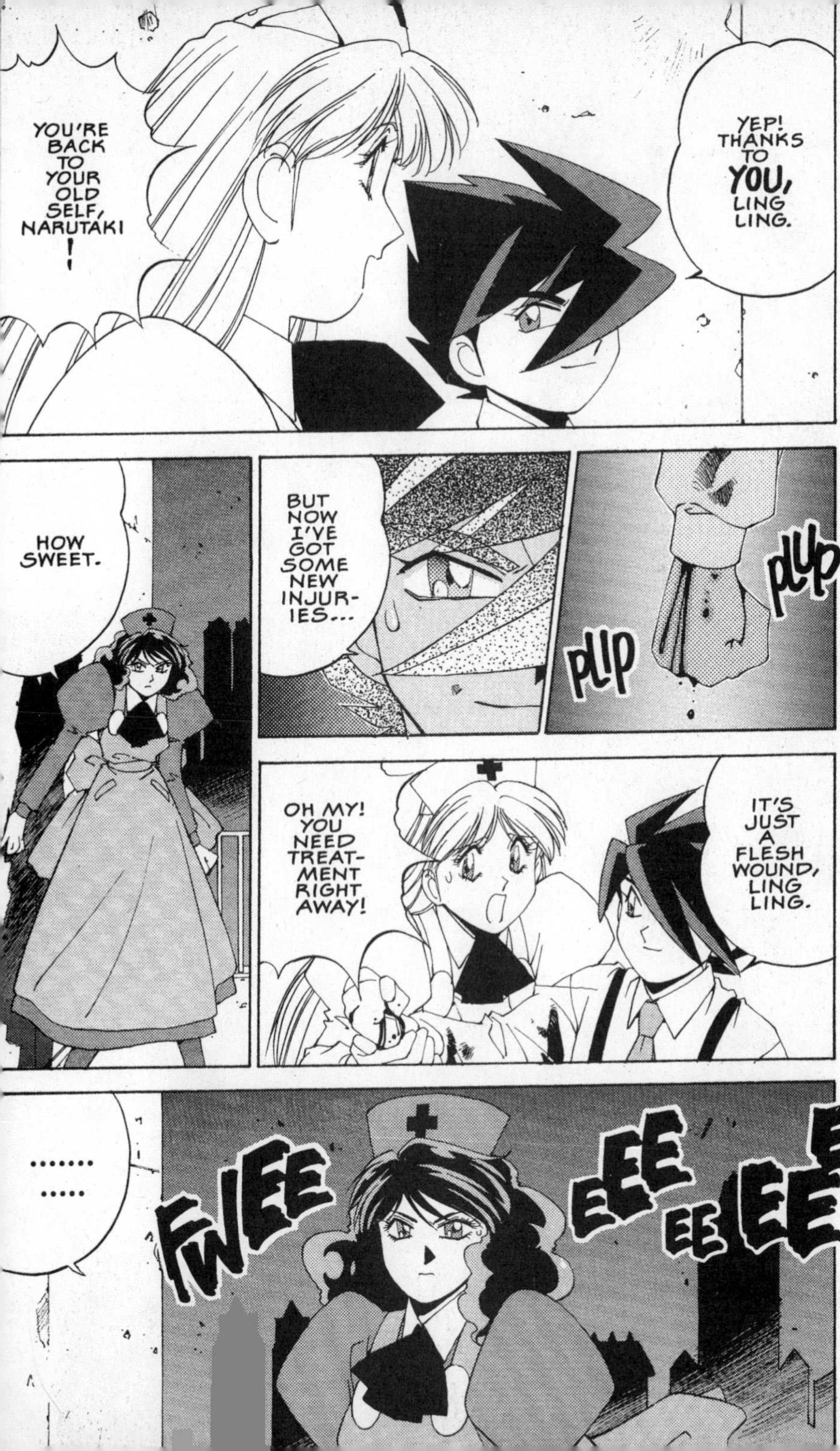
YOU'RE BACK TO YOUR OLD SELF, NARUTAKI!
YEP! THANKS TO YOU, LING LING.
HOW SWEET.
BUT NOW I'VE GOT SOME NEW INJURIES...
PLIP
PLIP
OH MY! YOU NEED TREATMENT RIGHT AWAY!
IT'S JUST A FLESH WOUND, LING LING.
....
FWEEEEEEEEEE

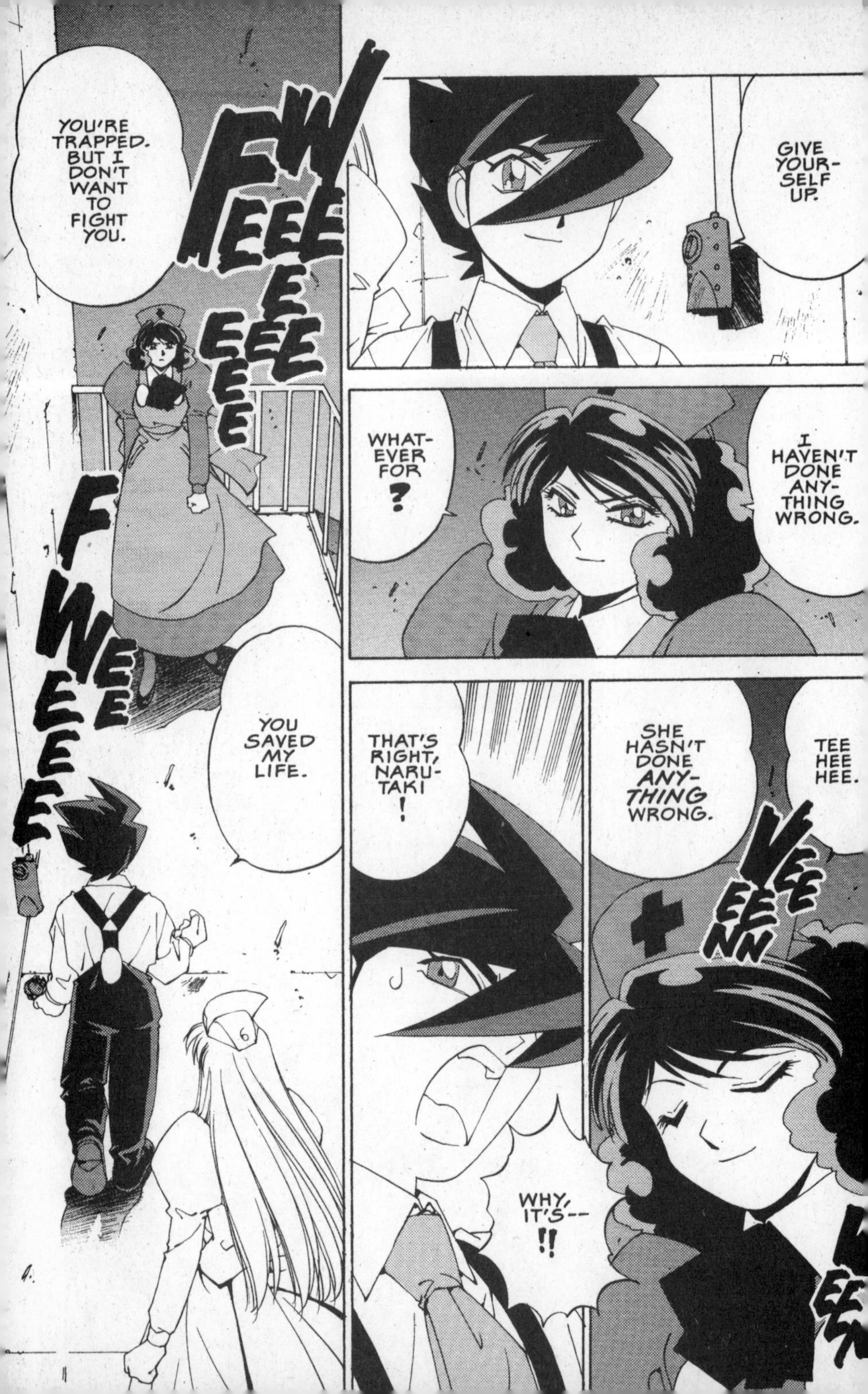

YOU'RE TRAPPED. BUT I DON'T WANT TO FIGHT YOU.
FWEEEEEEEEEE
FWEEEEEE
YOU SAVED MY LIFE.
GIVE YOURSELF UP.
WHATEVER FOR?
I HAVEN'T DONE ANYTHING WRONG.
THAT'S RIGHT, NARUTAKI!
WHY, IT'S--!!
SHE HASN'T DONE *ANYTHING* WRONG.
TEE HEE HEE.
VEEEENN

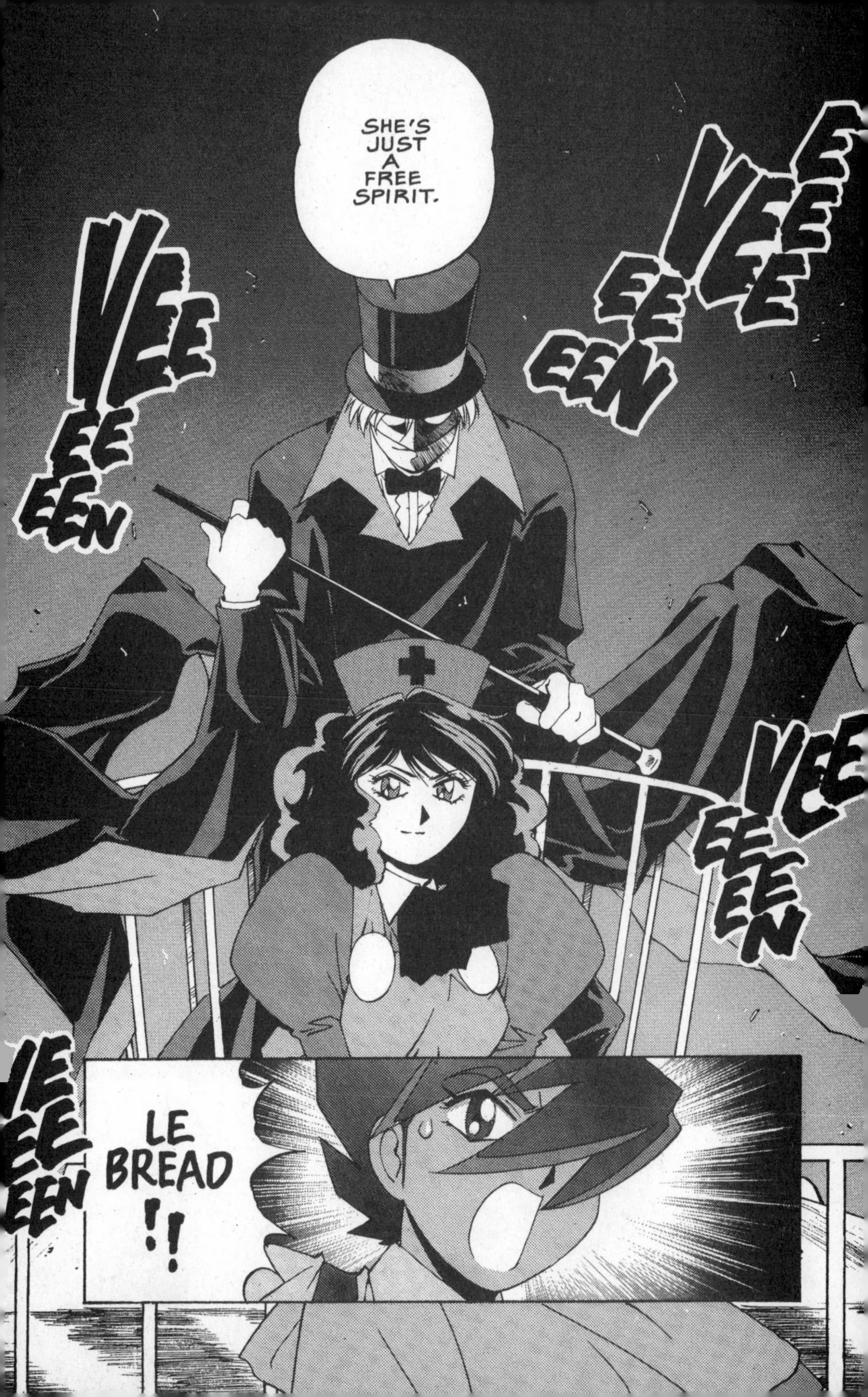
SHE'S JUST A FREE SPIRIT.
VEEEEEEEN
VEEEEEEEEEEN
VEEEEEEEEN
IEEEEEN
LE BREAD !!

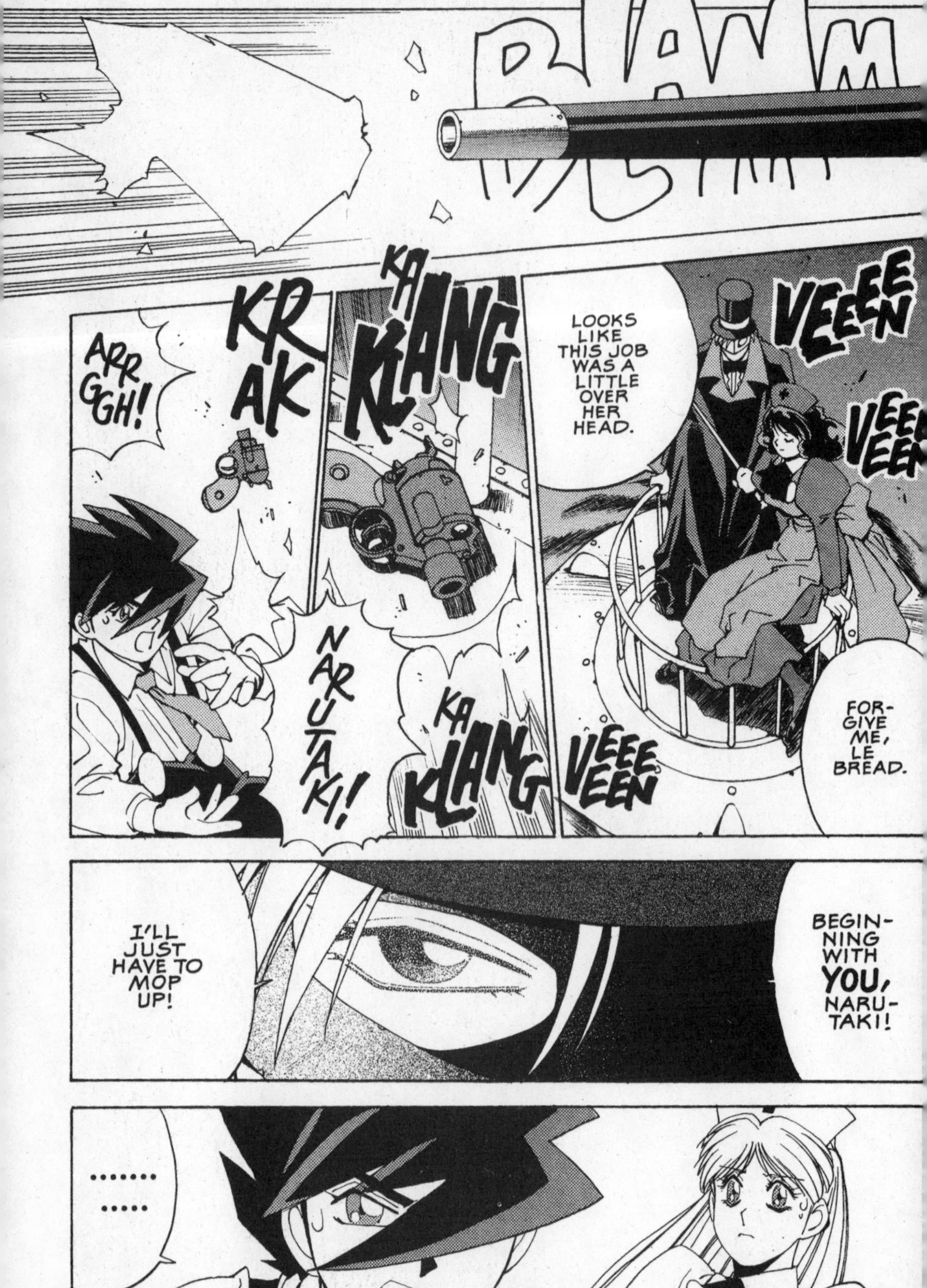
BLAMM
ARRGGH!
KRAK
KA KLANG
NARUTAKI!
KA KLANG
LOOKS LIKE THIS JOB WAS A LITTLE OVER HER HEAD.
VEEEEN
VEEEEN
VEEEEEN
FORGIVE ME, LE BREAD.
I'LL JUST HAVE TO MOP UP!
BEGINNING WITH YOU, NARUTAKI!
....
.....

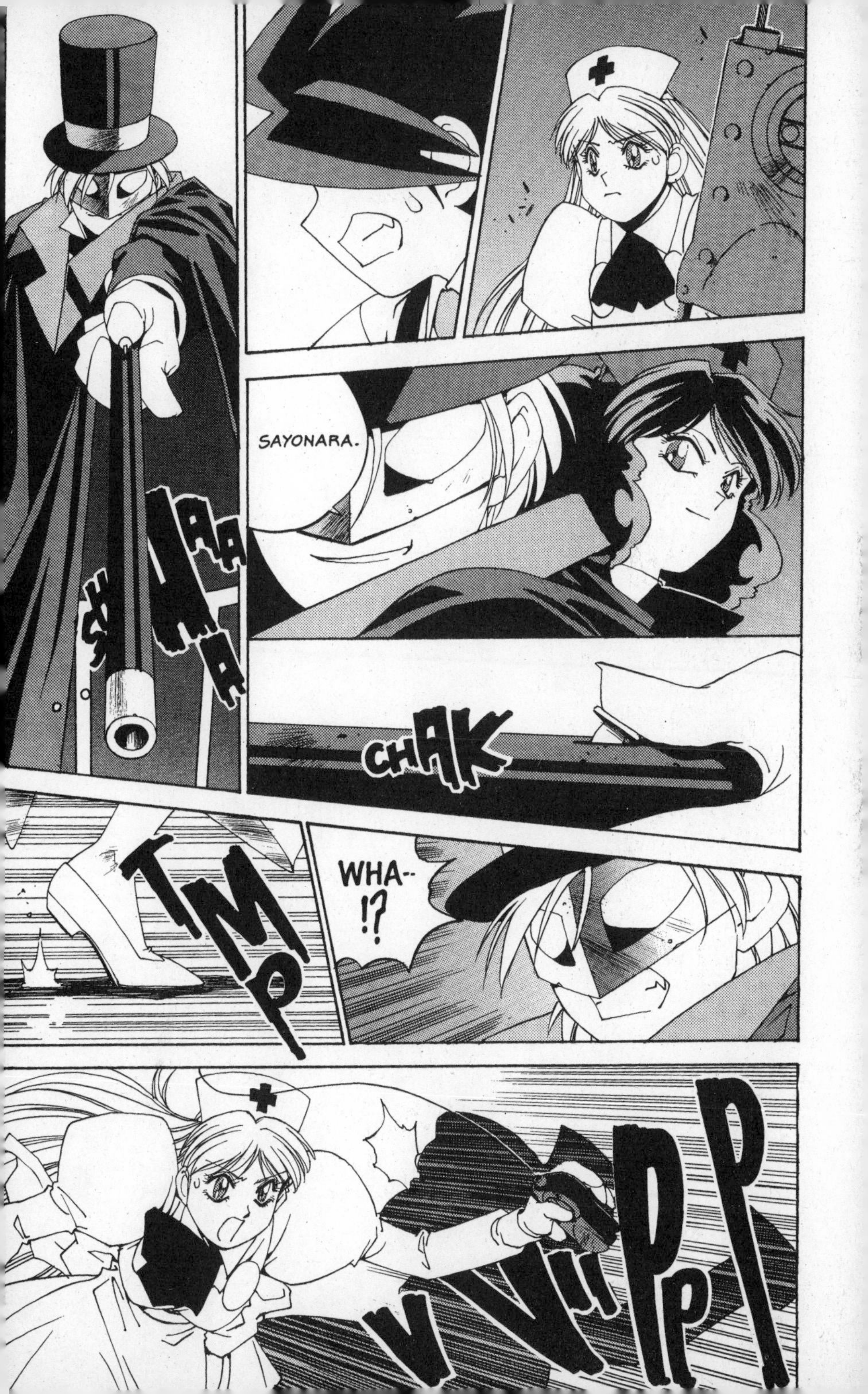
SAYONARA.
CHAK
TMP
WHA--
!?

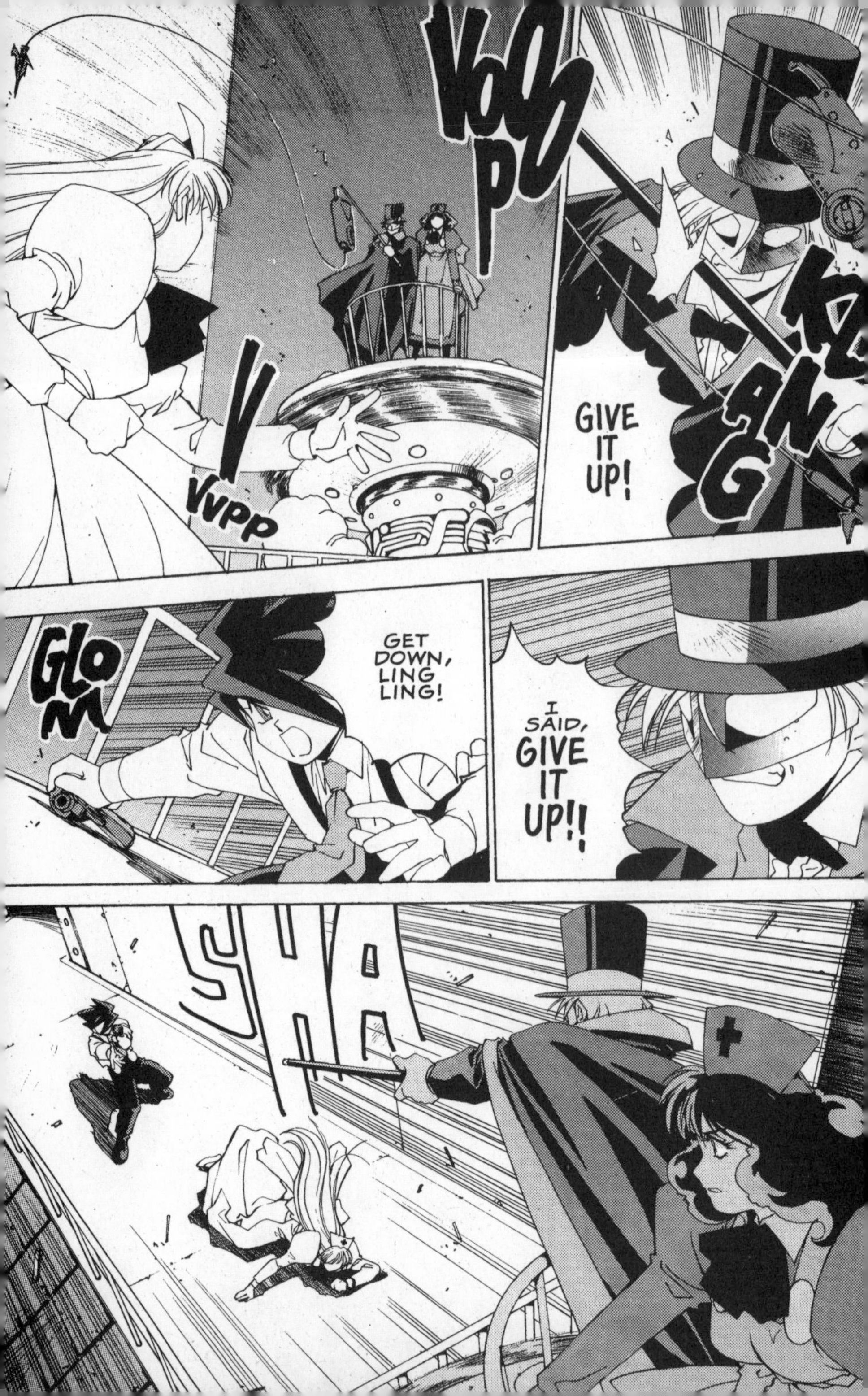
VVPP
GIVE IT UP!
GLOM
GET DOWN, LING LING!
I SAID, GIVE IT UP!!

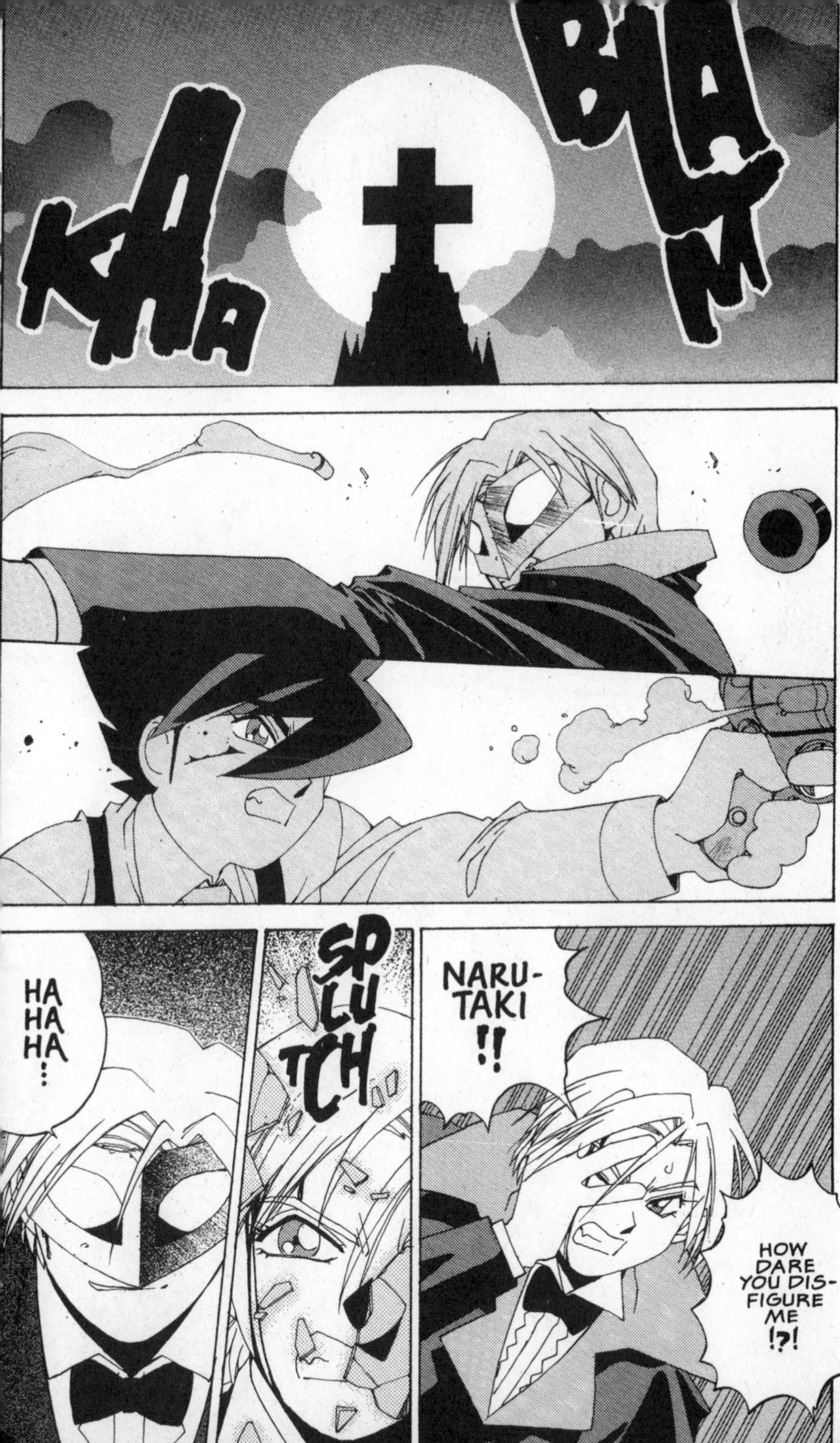
KAAA
BLAM
HA HA HA...
SPLUTCH
NARU-TAKI!!
HOW DARE YOU DIS-FIGURE ME!?!

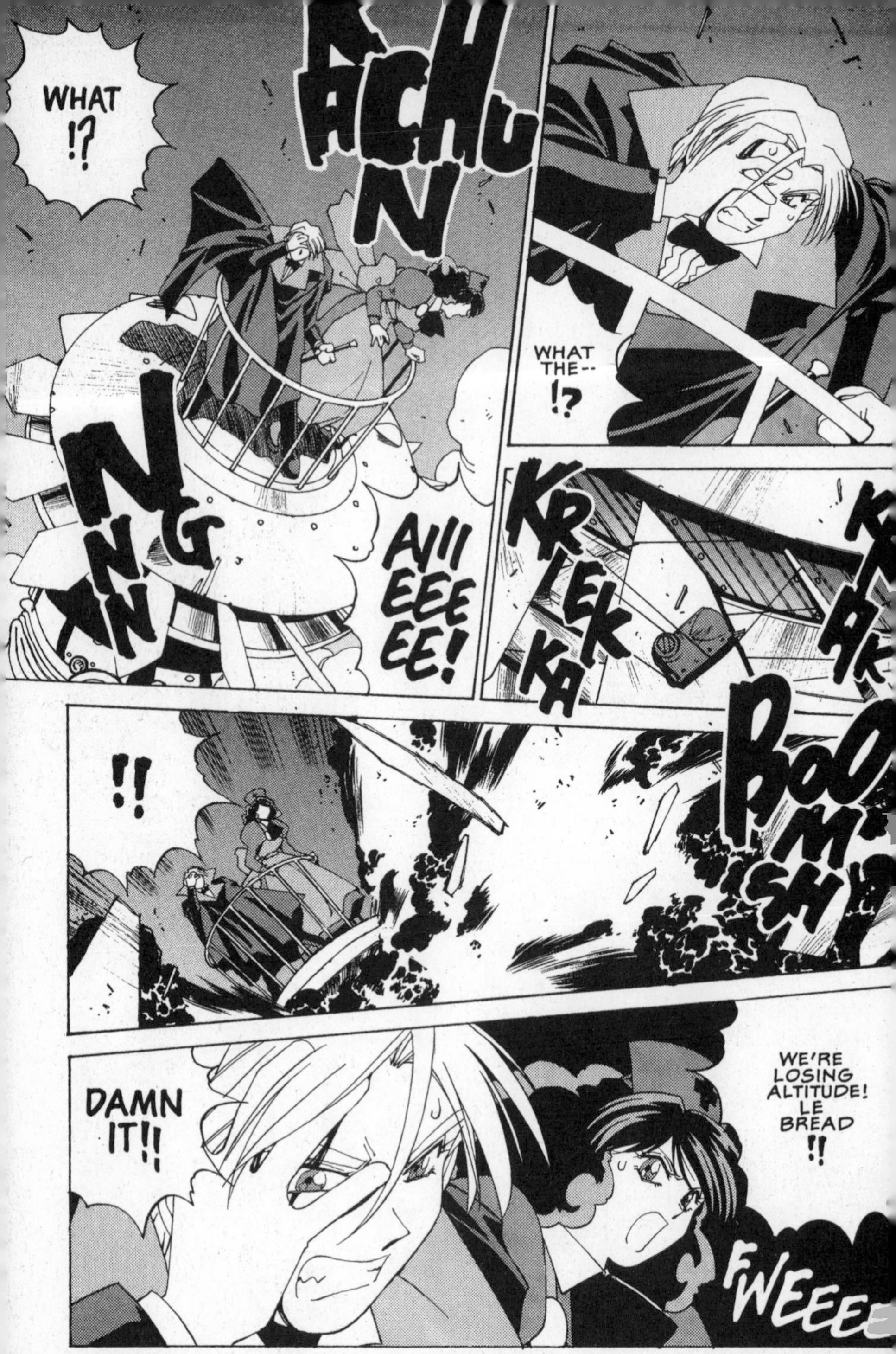
WHAT !?
ACHUN
AIII EEEEEE!
WHAT THE-- !?
KRIEKKA
!!
DAMN IT!!
WE'RE LOSING ALTITUDE! LE BREAD !!
FWEEEE

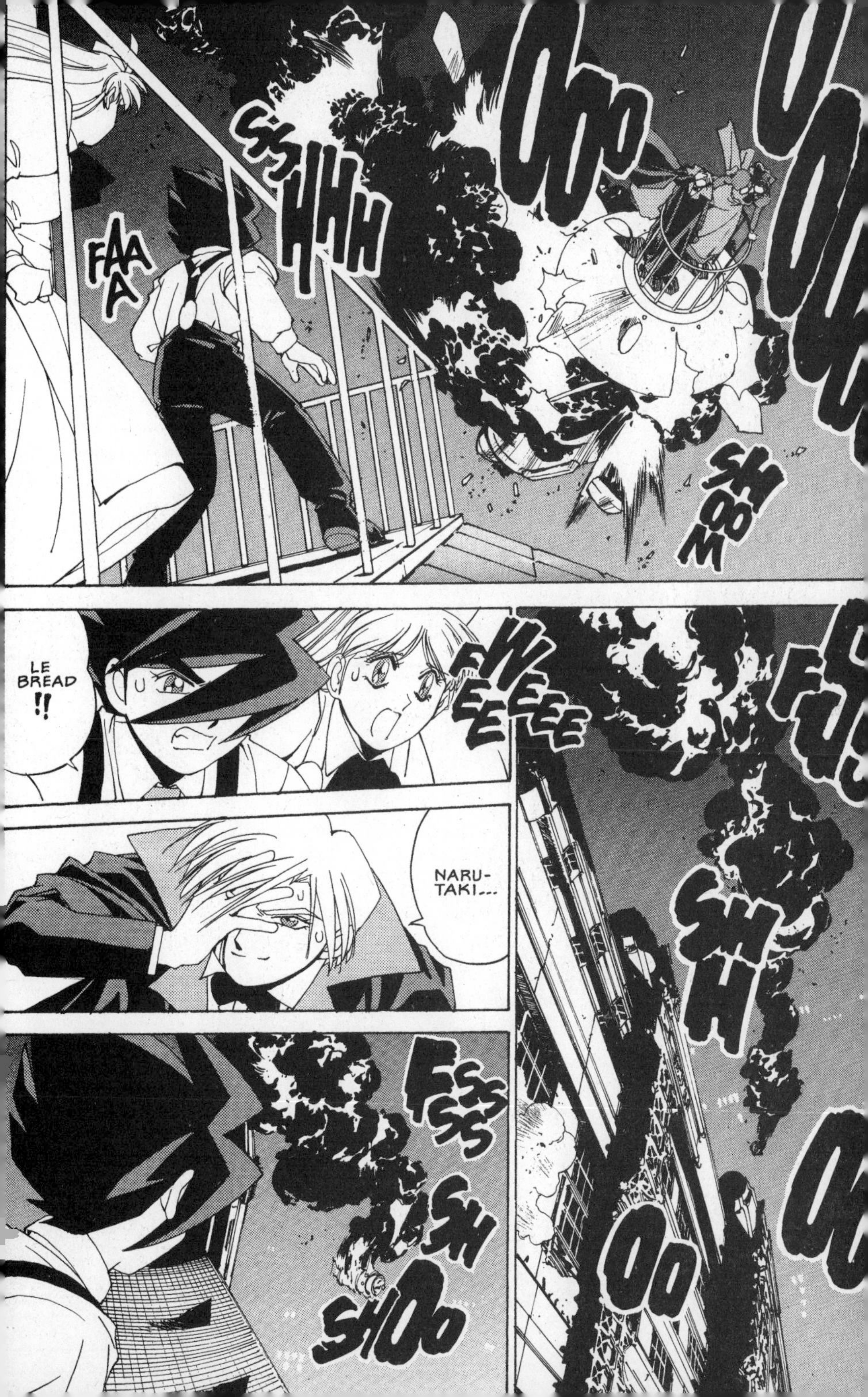

FAAA
SSHHHH
SHOOM
LE BREAD !!
FWEEEEE
NARU-TAKI...
SHH
FSSSSS
SH SHOO

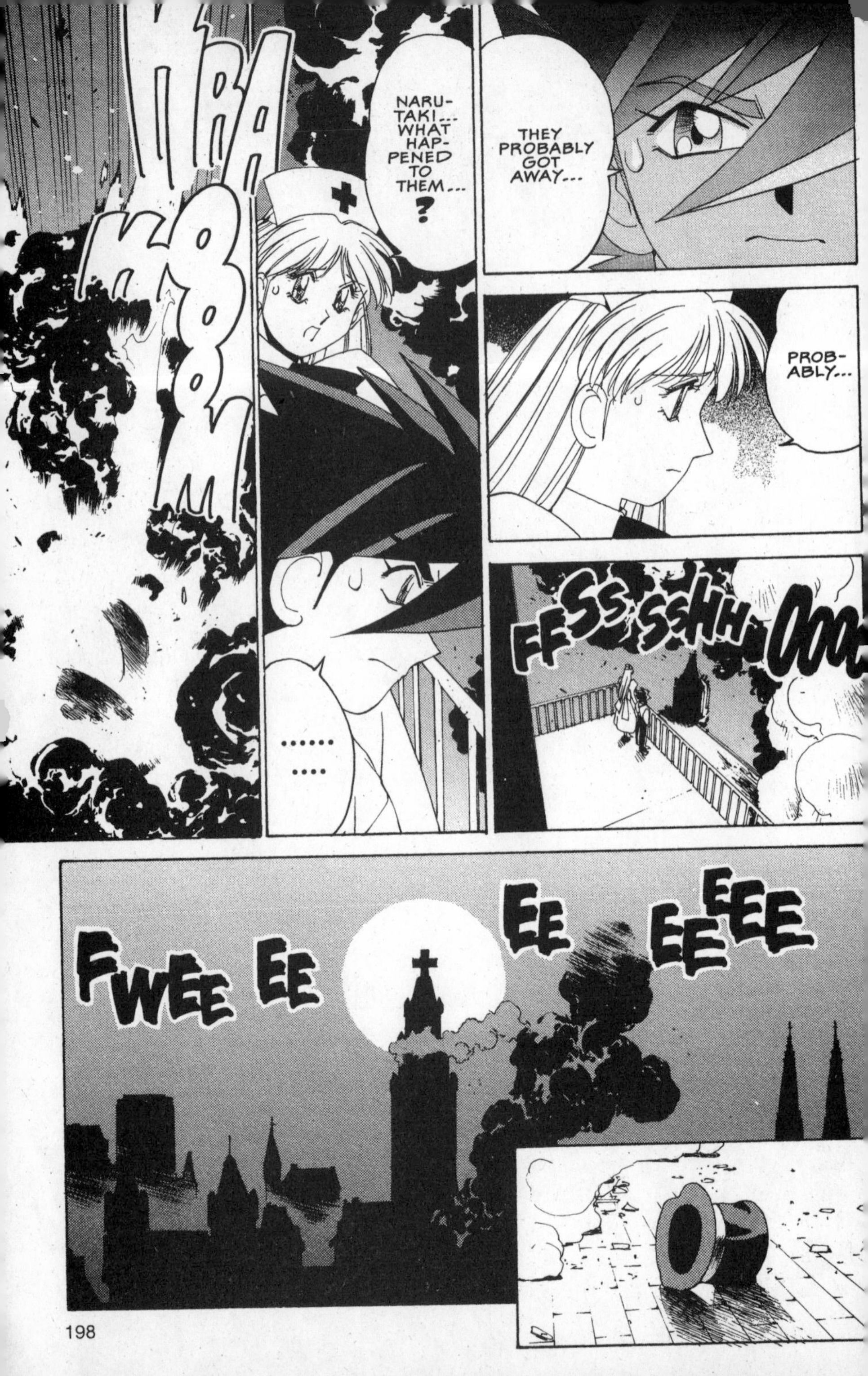

NARU-TAKI... WHAT HAP-PENED TO THEM...?
......
....
THEY PROBABLY GOT AWAY...
PROB-ABLY...
FFSSSSHHHOOOO
FWEE EE EE EEEEE

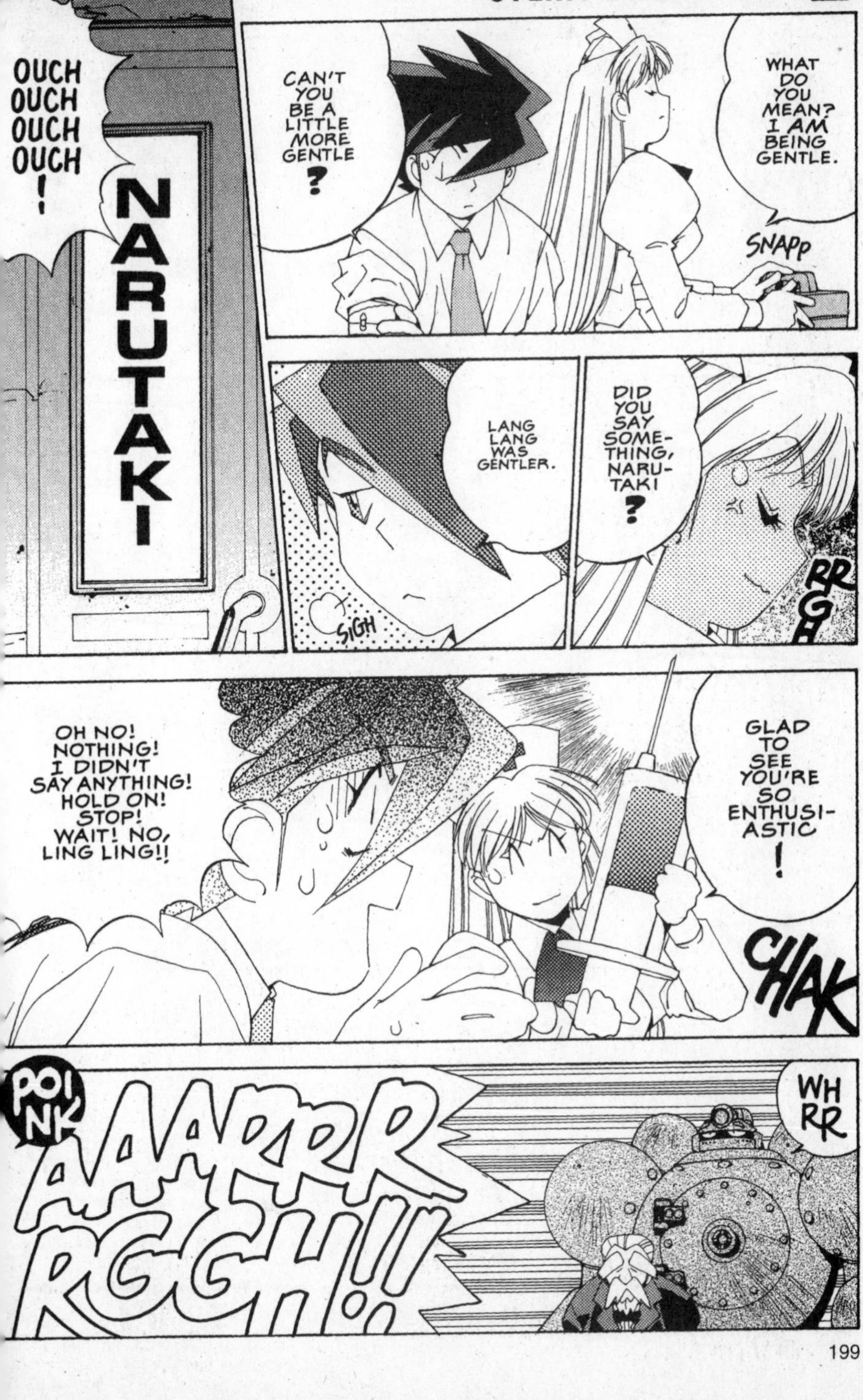
OUCH OUCH OUCH OUCH!
NARUTAKI
CAN'T YOU BE A LITTLE MORE GENTLE?
WHAT DO YOU MEAN? I AM BEING GENTLE.
SNAPP
LANG LANG WAS GENTLER.
SIGH
DID YOU SAY SOME-THING, NARU-TAKI?
RRGH
OH NO! NOTHING! I DIDN'T SAY ANYTHING! HOLD ON! STOP! WAIT! NO, LING LING!!
GLAD TO SEE YOU'RE SO ENTHUSI-ASTIC!
CHAK
POINK
AARRR RGGH!!
WHRR

STEAM DETECTIVES PRESS

Who is Lang Lang, the nurse in black? Is she the nurse cum secretary for the boy criminal Le Bread? More importantly, do Lang Lang and Ling Ling know each other from the past?

What transpired beween the two women? Why did they become nurses? Why does Lang Lang wear a black uniform?

The mysteries continue to multiply! The only thing we know for sure is that they both have nice figures. And that's certainly noteworthy!

Looks like we won't be able to take our eyes off the two beautiful nurses in the future! Next issue, we hope to provide you with a more in-depth report.

WHAT'S THE STORY BEHIND BEAUTIFUL NURSES LING LING AND LANG LANG?

Lang Lang

Ling Ling

24th ANNUAL CHIKI CHIKI STEAM MACHINE GRAND PRIX FINALS!

Empress of Steam

ROUND-THE-WORLD CRUISE
BY EMPRESS OF STEAM
FROM STEAM CITY...DEC. 1st

STEAM · PACIFIC

For Branch offices Travel Directory on page 10

We are finally approaching the long-awaited finals of the Chiki Chiki Steam Machine Grand Prix. The teams have all arrived in the capital with their steam-powered vehicles, and are anxiously awaiting the competition. Due to last year's major accident, we anticipate that strong precautions will be taken this year. In any case, we are all looking forward to the annual Capital Steam Race. Be there on the 6th!!

Volume 004 • Issued by Steam Press Co., Ltd.

End of STEAM DETECTIVES VOL.